Capitalism and Democracy in the 21st Century

Dennis C. Mueller · Uwe Cantner
Editors

Capitalism and Democracy in the 21st Century

Proceedings of the International
Joseph A. Schumpeter Society Conference,
Vienna 1998 "Capitalism and Socialism
in the 21st Century"

With 42 Figures
and 33 Tables

Springer-Verlag Berlin Heidelberg GmbH

Prof. Dr. Dennis C. Mueller
Universität Wien
Institut für Wirtschaftswissenschaften
Brünner Straße 72
1240 Wien
Austria

Prof. Dr. Uwe Cantner
Friedrich-Schiller-Universität Jena
Wirtschaftswissenschaftliche Fakultät
Lehrstuhl für VWL/Mikroökonomik
Carl-Zeiss-Platz 3
07743 Jena
Germany

First published in
"Evolutionary Economics", Vol. 10, No. 1–2 and 3, 2000.

ISBN 978-3-7908-2480-3

Library of Congress Cataloging-in-Publication Data
Die Deutsche Bibliothek – CIP-Einheitsaufnahme
Capitalism and Democracy in the 21st Century: Proceedings of the International Joseph A. Schumpeter Society Conference, Vienna 1998 "Capitalism and Socialism in the 21st Century"; with 33 Tables / Dennis C. Mueller; Uwe Cantner, ed.
ISBN 978-3-7908-2480-3 ISBN 978-3-662-11287-8 (eBook)
DOI 10.1007/978-3-662-11287-8

Originally published by Physica-Verlag Heidelberg New York in 2001

Cover design: Erich Kirchner, Heidelberg

SPIN 10784630 88/2202-5 4 3 2 1 0 – Printed on acid-free paper

Contents

The innovation process

The democratic process

Schumpeter and the history of ideas

Editorial

Uwe Cantner[1], **Dennis C. Mueller**[2]

[1] Wirtschaftswissenschaftliche Fakultät, Lehrstuhl für Volkswirtschaftslehre/Mikroökonomik, Friedrich-Schiller-Universität Jena, Carl-Zeiß-Str. 3, 07743 Jena, Germany
[2] Institut für Wirtschaftswissenschaften, Universität Wien, BWZ, Brünner Straße 72, A-1240 Wien, Austria

1 Introduction

In June 1998, the International Joseph A. Schumpeter Society held its biannual congress in Vienna. Approximately 140 papers were presented, and there were about 200 participants at the conference. The theme of the 1998 conference was *Capitalism and Democracy in the 21st Century.* This theme is an obvious take-off on the title of one of Schumpeter's most famous books. The intent in choosing this topic was to get at least some participants at the conference to take stock of where capitalist and democratic countries are at the close of the 20th century, and where they might be headed in the 21st century, just as Schumpeter did in *Capitalism, Socialism and Democracy* in the middle of the 20th century.

This volume contains a collection of papers all concerned either in a direct sense or in a wider perspective with the work of Joseph A. Schumpeter. Several important areas of research can be identified upon which Schumpeter's work had a lasting influenced. One obvious such area is Schumpeter's writing about the future of capitalism. Indeed, this area formed the underlying theme for the conference. A second major strand of Schumpeter's research concerns innovation and its consequences for economic development. A third area is concerned with the political process and the role of political leadership. The collection of essays in this volume is developed along these main lines, complemented by papers discussing the place of Schumpeter's work within the history of economic analysis. In the following sections we characterize each of the papers selected.

2 Capitalism and democracy in the 21st century

A first group of papers contains discussions and analyses rather closely related to the Schumpeter's *Capitalism, Socialism and Democracy,* first published in 1942. In this work Schumpeter put forward a number of interesting arguments and visions, which attracted a large number of scholars and initiated much further research. Most intriguingly in this work, Schumpeter explored the relationship between a capitalistic system and democracy, and questioned whether capitalism is viable in the long-run, given the attraction of socialism in democratic countries. This issue is taken up in papers by Peter Bernholz, Eyüp Özveren, and Dennis Mueller. All three draw the conclusion that capitalism and democracy are not complementary and do not have to necessarily coexist.

Peter Bernholz (*Democracy and Capitalism: Are they compatible in the long-run?*) emphasizes that over time democracy leads to the introduction of more and more regulations and increases the government share in GDP – either by higher taxes or by installing more regulative measures. These in turn weaken the capitalistic system. This evidences itself as lower efficiency, less investment, less innovation and thus lower growth rates. Several factors opposing this development are then discussed: (1) the crisis of government which then allows innovative politicians to succeed in finding majority support for reform policies; (2) the complementary effect of international comparison with countries having lower taxes, less regulation and higher growth rates. As Bernholz suggests, however, this does not guarantee that democracy will necessarily be restored once it is displaced, or that its failures can be avoided. Such crises of democratic capitalism may also contain the seeds for a quite different political system – as for example totalitarianism.

The relation between capitalism and democracy is also discussed by Eyüp Özveren (*Capitalism and democracy at a crossroads: the civilization dimension*). Referring to Schumpeter, Özveren argues that capitalism progresses following a process of creative destruction, where the creative component always dominates the destructive part. Thus, in economic terms capitalism is viable. This, however, implies that the economic infrastructure and the institutional set-up of the economy is constant. For Schumpeter, capitalistic development has a detrimental effect on those institutions. By uncreative destruction the institutional framework which makes capitalism viable is destroyed by capitalism itself, which guides the system into socialism. This relationship is questioned by Özveren. It is argued that capitalism and democracy do not necessarily coexist and that there are elements in both conceptions which are conductive for each other. Moreover, those constraints which one conception imposes on the other are discussed. In general the question is addressed, whether a fully working democracy is compatible with capitalistic development.

Dennis Mueller (*Capitalism, democracy and rational behaviour*) demonstrates how many of the paradoxes of rational actor models market and political behavior can be resolved by adopting a theory of preference formation based on behavioral psychology. Such an approach depicts individual behavior as adaptive and "backward looking." Mueller then shows that the viability of capitalism and of democracy heavily depends on the existence of farsighted actors which recognize that market actions today as well as voting today have both immediate and long run effects on an individual's welfare. For capitalism this materializes especially in activities such as saving, investment and innovation. For democracy this shows up in the often modest direct effects of elections on individual welfare coupled with the effects of individual actions in the political process on its the long-term viability.

Another theme that arises in Schumpeter's *Capitalism, Socialism and Democracy* concerns the pivotal role large firms play in advancing technological progress – an argument which runs directly counter to his reasoning in his *Theorie der wirtschaftlichen Entwicklung* (1912) (*Theory of Economic Development* (1934). In this much earlier work, the entrepreneur and thus the small firm are considered as the main forces driving technological progress and economic development. David Audretsch and Roy Thurik (*Capitalism and Democracy in the 21st Century: from the managed to the entrepreneurial economy*) present evidence related to this topic. They illustrate that capitalism, at least during the last quarter of the 20th century, does not show a tendency toward an ever greater dominance of giant firms. One rather observes a tendency for an increasing element of entrepreneurship in capitalist countries, although to differing degrees. This quite obviously is not in line with Schumpeter's vision of the future of capitalism. In particular David Audretsch and Roy Thurik investigate how in a number of OECD economies there has been observed a shift from the so-called managed economy – where large firms are the main carrier of technological know-how and driver of technological progress – towards an entrepreneurial economy – where small new firms are identified as being the technologically most advanced and dynamic. Among the large number of theoretical and empirical issues related to such a shift, Audretsch and Thurik are mainly interested in the observed employment effects. They argue that the traditional trade-off between wages and employment does not hold anymore. An empirical cross-section analysis for 23 OECD countries shows that those countries which succeeded in introducing a larger element of entrepreneurship before 1984 experienced a greater decrease in unemployment in the subsequent decade.

Douglas Mair and Anthony J. Laramie (*Capitalism and democracy in the 21st century: a Kaleckian interpretation of a Schumpeterian problem*) take up another issue in Schumpeter's work, the tax state. Schumpeter himself rejected all contemporary analytical frameworks dealing with the issue of taxation (i.e. the analyses of both Keynes and Marshall). Schumpeter assigned tax policy a role in influencing the business cycle. The authors suggest in this respect that a Kaleckian approach is suitable for investigating the influence of changes in the structure of taxation on the business cycle. On this basis Mair and Laramie develop a model able to show how taxation depending on the specific circumstances chosen may affect investment, innovation and the business-cycle. From the various results obtained, perhaps the most interesting concerns the effects of income inequality and the differential taxation of profits and wages. The more unequal incomes are, the less investment there tends to be. In an empirical test for the United Kingdom from 1980–1996 this relationship seems to hold, since the share of wages in income declined, while real investment activity within this period remained roughly constant. This finding leads the authors to follow Schumpeter and worry about the future of capitalism in a democratic society.

3 Capitalism and globalization

The second group of four papers also looks at the capitalistic process from a Schumpeterian perspective. Here, however, the focus is not on whether capitalism can survive or not, but rather on various attributes of the capitalist process as, for example, in a global economy.

William Kingston (*A spectre in haunting the world the spectre of globalisation*) again takes up Schumpeter's vision of the future of capitalism, but this time in the context of the process of globalization currently taking place. He discusses the viability of capitalism, described in terms of property rights and property rights systems, in a global economy. Kingston argues that the design of property rights may have a decisive influence on the degree of inequality between economies. The more inequality arises especially in international comparison, the more is this detrimental to the viability of capitalism. Kingston sees globalization as bringing about increasing inequality. He is not convinced that Schumpeter's vision about the future of capitalism has already been falsified, although he acknowledges that Schumpeter missed several crucial factors in his argument.

The paper by Maria Lucia Falcao Silva, Joaquim Pinto Andrade and Thomas S. Torrence (*Reflections on the perspectives of the global economy from the view of emerging economies*) is also concerned with international inequality, and here with respect to the position and ability of emerging economies to pursue a sovereign and independent monetary policy leading to macroeconomic stability. A fixed exchange-rate rule or a narrow-band arrangement can be an important source of instability, which a developing country can import. With domestic liquidity and credit highly dependent on foreign exchange reserves, an autonomous exchange rate policy becomes more and more difficult to maintain, because "periphery countries" continuously face unsteady capital inflows, and are highly vulnerable to both external shocks and speculative attacks. Since the center economies do not face these problems or are much better equipped to get rid of them, the authors finally question whether one has to accept these traps for emerging economies in a globalized world.

John Cantwell and Grazia Santangelo (*Capitalism, profits and innovation in the new techno-economic paradigm*) are interested in innovative activities organized on an international, i.e. global level. They investigate how multinational firms in a globalized world pursue technological progress. Based on the conception of localized and often tacit knowledge, they are interested whether and to what degree multinational firms diversify their innovative activities internationally. The empirical analysis shows (i) that the degree of diversification is rather different between sectors, (ii) that technologies developed abroad are normally not among the firms' core technologies, and (iii) that over time there is a tendency toward a convergence of technological diversification across large firms.

Majid Taghavi (*Debt, growth and inflation in large European economies: a vector auto-regression analysis*) investigates the effect of the governmental debt of European countries between 1970 and 1997 on their inflation, investment and to growth. Using the vector auto-regression technique, Taghavi analyses the possibility of manifold causal dependencies. After reducing these to a small number of cause-effect relations, he reports the effects on inflation, investment and growth that are to be expected from a 1% increase in debt in four EU core countries (France, Germany, Italy and UK) as well as for the EU area as a whole. Majid Taghavi finds that the increased debt clearly causes adverse effects on investment and in most cases on inflation in the long run. Debt increases impact on growth, however, are not unequivocal.

4 The innovation process

As is true of every International Schumpeter Society conference, several papers looked at the innovation process and research and development. This area of research is one where Schumpeter's influence shows up most vividly. The papers in this group have a special focus on innovation related industrial structures, on firms' R&D decisions, on industrial policy oriented towards innovative activities of firms, and on inter-firm cooperation in R&D.

This section starts with F.M. Scherer, Dietmar Harhoff and Jörg Kukies (*Uncertainty and the size distribution of rewards from innovation*) who approach an already traditional topic within industrial organization, the structural feature of a skewed size, profit etc. distribution of firms. They focus their analyses on the profit distribution of firms and herein they focus on innovative firms. An empirical analysis shows clearly that on the basis of several databases the skewed distribution always can be detected. In a second step the authors investigate what processes were responsible for such an outcome. Starting with a traditional Gibrat-process and extending this to a more sophisticated stochastic simulation model they are able to "produce" firm distributions which come reasonably close to those detected empirically.

The paper by Henry Grabowski and John Vernon (*The determinants of pharmaceutical research and development expenditures*) is concerned with the decision of a firm to invest in R&D – a research topic, which the two authors have addressed several times down through the years. Observing a rising trend in R&D intensity in the pharmaceutical sector over the years 1975 to 1997 – where this ratio had been constant in the years before 1975 – they search for an explanation. They find one in the important role played be cash flows in the financing of R&D in the pharmaceutical sector, and the increases in the returns to this investment that occurred at that time.

Gunnar Eliasson (*Industrial policy, competence blocs and the role of science in economic development*) is concerned with the role of public policy in fostering technological change with all its consequences for industrial competitiveness and economic growth. To identify the policy function Eliasson – relying on his impressive account of research in this area – introduces the concept of competence blocs, which are understood as a setting within which technological change and innovations are "produced" in an experimental and consciously or unconsciously collective way. The selection among different technological solutions and innovations is performed on several levels. The functioning of such competence blocs relies heavily on the competencies and the kind of actors and institutions involved. This is demonstrated by referring to five case studies. Eliasson proposes that not the outcomes of, but the procedures within competence blocs should be the major focus, i.e. the efficiency and the completeness of competence blocs.

Inter-firm cooperation in R&D and their potential anti-competitive effects are the interest of Nicholas Vonortas (*Multimarket contact and inter-firm cooperation in R&D*). Such cooperation is widely seen as a device to combine different technologies in a complementary way. Critics often argue that those cooperative agreements, which are rather pre-competitive in design, could easily be used to collude in the market. For research joint ventures between firms with multi-market and multi-project contact those arguments seem to be of even more relevance. Vonortas examines this problem using data on 575 research joint ventures – registered between 1985 and 1995. His data reveal a considerably high degree of multi-market and multi-project contacts among participants. To get an account of whether anti-competitive targets are followed three safeguards against anti-competitive behavior are investigated: (i) the number of foreign participants, (ii) the technological and market uncertainty, and (iii) the stability of research joint ventures over time with respect to the participating firms. It is shown these safeguards are all working which, however, does not ensure that anti-competitive collusion in the competitive stage is prevented.

5 The democratic process

A few papers of the Vienna conference focused on the democratic process of which only that of Michael Wohlgemuth (*Political entrepreneurship and bidding for political monopoly*) is included here. He discusses democracy, from the view point of a competition for political leadership, a conception introduced by Joseph A. Schumpeter. In a first part Wohlgemuth discusses this issue with the help of a model suggested by Harold Demsetz seeing elections rather similar to franchise bidding, where political stability and reliability is always reinforced by future competition in the next election. The second part of the paper is devoted to a thorough discussion about innovative policy makers and here Wohlgemuth presents a discussion in terms of the well-known Schumpeter-hypotheses – where it has been disputed whether small or large firms are more likely to further technological progress. He investigates first whether and under what conditions (small) new policy makers could make the election race, which leads to the result that – contrary to the case of small firms – small and new parties are highly unlikely to win an election. Looking at the innovative policy coming from established parties, Wohlgemuth argues that the strategies of the larger parties are much more likely to come to dominate. Interestingly, the factors which in the Demsetz-type model provide for political stability, here hinder innovative policy.

6 Schumpeter and the history of ideas

Another recurring theme at all International Schumpeter Society conferences is to look at the place of Joseph Schumpeter in the history of ideas, to contrast Schumpeter's approach and contributions to those of his contemporaries or followers. A fifth and final group of papers is concerned with this broad issue. A first approach to mention which is influenced by the work of Schumpeter is evolutionary economics; here Schumpeter is even considered as one of the fathers of that school of thought. The papers by Brian Loasby and by John Foster are devoted to this topic. The relation of Schumpeter's supply-side oriented analysis to the demand oriented approach by Hirschman is discussed by Peter Wynarczyk. A comparative view on the competitive process as discussed by Schumpeter and also by Steindl is found in the essay by Harry Bloch. The volume closes with an essay by Alexander Ebner relating Schumpeter's work to that of the German Historical School.

The first paper of this group, by Brian Loasby (*Market institutions and economic evolution*) deals with the market as an institution guiding economic development or evolution on the one hand, but on the other hand being also the outcome of an evolutionary process. Loasby's discussion nicely contributes to the understanding of markets in an evolutionary setting. Here the market is seen in a process perspective where producers and consumers can "test" products. For this purpose the market is seen as an institution, which governs the behavior of the market participants; furthermore, in this way it serves as a selection mechanism with respect to competing products and as a coordination mechanism with respect to the actors involved. In this respect markets are seen as an institution for reducing transaction costs. However the market, as an institution that provides a reasonably stable environment for transactions, can also be the subject of change. In this respect Loasby stresses market making in the sense that entrepreneurs in most cases have to create the market for their new product, they cannot rely on any existing market. By this action the institution of the market changes, with e-commerce being a most prominent example.

Also with relation to evolutionary economics John Foster (*Competitive selection, self-organisation and Joseph A. Schumpeter*) discusses the influence of evolutionary biology on evolutionary economics. He clearly works out the differences and commonalties between both ways of applying evolutionary mechanisms, and by this he hints at one of the major analytical problems of evolutionary economics in particular and the application of evolutionary concepts in the social sciences in general the generation of novelty. Foster argues that a simple causality from variety to selection is an inappropriate way of dealing with economic evolution. One rather has also to look in the other direction of causality with selection or competition driving or influencing the generation of novelty. This view then implies a shift in focus towards a conception of self-organization, where selection processes are only a part of the story. As Foster demonstrates this kind of approach comes rather close to Schumpeter's view of economic development.

The third paper in this group by Peter Wynarczyk (*Convergencies with Schumpeter: An essay Hirschman has yet to write*) relates the work of Schumpeter to that of A.O. Hischman. Both writers have attempted to explain the economic development of democratic, capitalistic societies. The starting points of their respective analyses are, however, quite different: Whereas Schumpeter relied on the supply side of the economy as the source of innovations and driving force behind economic growth and development, Hirschman has focused on the demand side. In Hirschman's work, economic growth arises as a result consumer-citizens striving after happiness.

In the fourth paper of this group, Harry Bloch (*Schumpeter and Steindl on the dynamics of competition*) compares Schumpeter's analysis of the competitive process with that of Joseph Steindl. In some ways the two authors shared a common ground, especially in so far as they saw competition not in the static way in which it is depicted in most of neoclassical economics, but as a dynamics process. Differences between Schumpeter and Steindl appear, however, in their analysis of the main drivers of progress, in their views of the role that the financing of innovative activity plays, and in their analysis of the main factors reducing the speed of progress. In the final section of the paper, Bloch relates these complementarities and differences to recent work of a neo-Schumpeterian nature, and lists the steps required to improve our understanding of the competitive process.

The collection of essays ends with an article by Alexander Ebner (*Schumpeter and the 'Schmollerprogramm': integrating theory and history in the analysis of economic development*). He relates Schumpeter's view of economic development and economic evolution to the German historical school. Referring to Gustav Schmoller on the one hand and the so-called "Young Historical School" which included Sombart, Spiethoven and Weber, Ebner investigates the relationship between the analytical insights of Schmoller and those of the historical school. Ebner then relates his discussion of the work of the historical school to Schumpeter's analysis, especially as it appeared in the *Theory of Economic Development* (1912/34). There Schumpeter explicitly and implicitly demands an all embracing approach that combines analytical, empirical and historical analyses.

7 Concluding remarks

This collection of papers presents only a sampling of those presented in Vienna. The goal is both to publish a set of articles that advances our knowledge in several important dimensions, and to give the reader a sense of both the breadth and depth of the ideas presented and discussed at an International Joseph A. Schumpeter Society Congress.

Uwe Cantner, Jena and Dennis C. Mueller, Wien,
August 2000

Democracy and capitalism: Are they compatible in the long-run?

Peter Bernholz

WWZ, Center for Economics and Business, Universität Basel, Postfach, CH-4003 Basel, Switzerland (e-mail: bernholzp@ubaclu.unibas.ch)

Abstract. Starting from a discussion of Schumpeter's analysis of the relationships of capitalism, socialism and democracy, it is shown that, in a complex society, democracy is only compatible with a decentralized market economy with safe property rights. But in time democracy shows a tendency to weaken the capitalist system by more and more regulations and an ever-increasing share of government (including the social security system) in GDP. This tendency is a consequence of political competition because of the development of interest groups and the presence of rationally uninformed voters. It leads to a weakening of efficiency, investment, innovation and thus to lower growth rates of GDP. But in time forces opposing this development arise. First, because of the negative consequences of growing government the welfare and regulatory state is bound to move into a crisis in the long run. Thus innovative politicians have a chance to win the support of a majority of voters for reform projects, who perceive finally the ever-increasing burden of higher taxes and regulations and realize that these burdens are not worth the benefits bestowed on them. In doing so, they may face, however, the competition of ideologies. Second, there are other states with lower taxes and less unnecessary regulations which show higher growth rates of GDP, and gain thus relative advantages in international political and military competition since they can command greater resources with the passage of time. To maintain their relative international power position, reforms are thus considered as necessary by rulers. This may be helped by pressure resulting from comparisons of the standards of living done by their citizens.

Paper presented at the 1998 World Conference of the International Joseph A. Schumpeter Society, Vienna, June 13–16, 1998.

Key words: Capitalism – Democracy – Growth of government – Welfare state – Regulations – Uninformed voters – International competition – Ideologies

JEL-classification: D78, L33, P16

1 Introduction: Schumpeter on capitalism, socialism and democracy

The life-work of Joseph Schumpeter is distinguished by two major accomplishments: his Theory of Economic Development and his Theory of Democracy. The latter is perhaps less well-known. Its analysis, however, of democracy as a competitive process, with the assumption that politicians and political parties are vying peacefully for government power and office, has influenced the later development of Public Choice Theory in this field, especially Anthony Downs' *An Economic Theory of Democracy* (1957). Given these two accomplishments it is not surprising that Schumpeter turned his attention to the relationship between the process of economic development and the political system, especially democracy. As a consequence, the change of political-economic systems was at the center of his interests in *Capitalism, Socialism and Democracy* (1943/1966), Here again, many of the problems occupying political economists, political scientists and sociologists up to this day, were already discussed by Schumpeter.

Schumpeter asked and tried to answer several questions. Can *capitalism* survive? His answer was "*no*", but in contrast to Marx he thought, that this was true not because of the failures but because of the successes of capitalism. It is because of them that capitalism will inevitably give way to socialism, probably in its form of a centrally planned economy. This prediction contrasts sharply with Hayek's warning in the *Road to Serfdom*, written at about the same time and looking at the same empirical evidence. Indeed, Hayek, Mises, Röpke, Eucken, Knight, Friedman and others founded the Mont Pelerin Society, obviously in the hope that the battle of ideas against socialism still could be won. Schumpeter derided these efforts in one of hist last addresses *The March into Socialism*, given to the American Economic Society in New York on December 30, 1949:

I believe that there is a mountain in Switzerland on which congresses of economists have been held which express disapproval of all or most of these things. But these anathemata have not even provoked attack (1966, p. 418).

A second question asked by Schumpeter was the following. Is democracy compatible with socialism, even with that of the planned economy version? And he answers as follows:

Between socialism as we defined it and democracy there is no necessary relation: the one can exist without the other. At the same time there is no incompatibility: in appropriate states of the social environment the socialist engine can be run on democratic principles (1966/1943, p. 284).

Given this answer, it is important to know what are the *appropriate states of the social environment*. Schumpeter makes it clear that in a socialist regime with a planned economy an

operating socialist democracy .... would be a perfectly hopeless task except in the case of a society that fulfills all the requirements of "maturity" listed in Part III (p. 301).

These requirements (for a functioning democracy) are:

1. *...the human material of politics – the people who man the party machines, the elected to serve in parliament, rise to cabinet office – should be of sufficiently high quality* (p. 290).
2. *...that the effective range of political decision should not be extended too far* (p. 291).
3. *...democratic government in modern industrial society must be able to command ... the services of a well-trained bureaucracy of good standing and tradition, endowed with a strong sense of duty and a no less strong* ***esprit de corps*** (p. 293).
4. *...Democratic Self-control. ... all the groups that count in a nation are willing to accept any legislative measure as long as it is on the statute book and all executive orders issued by legally competent authorities. But democratic self-control implies much more than this* (p. 294).
5. *...effective competition for leadership requires a large measure of tolerance for difference of opinion* (p. 295).

Schumpeter recognizes that perhaps the biggest problem with these conditions refers to point 2. How is it possible to contain the range of political decision in a planned economy? He believes that this should be possible with the help of a well-functioning bureaucracy (p. 302), but agrees that

...in socialist society these limitations will raise a much more serious problem [than in capitalist society]. *For socialist society lacks the automatic restrictions imposed upon the political sphere by the bourgeois scheme of things. Moreover, in socialist society it will no longer be possible to find comfort in the thought that the inefficiencies of political procedure are after all a guarantee of freedom. Lack of efficient management will spell lack of bread* (p. 299).

Finally he points out

...as a matter of practical necessity, socialist democracy may eventually turn out to be more of a sham than capitalist democracy ever was.
In any case, that democracy will not mean increased personal freedom (p. 302).

It is interesting for our proper subject that according to Schumpeter

...modern democracy is a product of the capitalist process.
Whether or not democracy is one of those products of capitalism which are to die out with it is of course another question. And still another is how well or ill capitalist society qualifies for the task of working the democratic method it evolved (p. 297).

We know already that Schumpeter answered the first question in the negative. The second question, however, leads us directly to the subject of this paper.

2 Conditions for a functioning democratic regime

Let us accept the five above conditions for a functioning democracy given by Schumpeter. Are these conditions sufficient? I believe not. Let me begin by quoting the sociologist Stanislav Andreski (1965):

Up till now representative government has flourished only where there was in existence a large class of economically independent persons, not necessarily independent in the sense of enjoying unearned incomes but in the sense of having no boss. Whenever democratic institutions were promulgated in countries where wealth was concentrated in the hands of the few, they existed only on paper. In districts dominated by one large estate, whose owner could deprive of their livelihood even the persons who were not in his employment, there could be no free elections. An industrialized country in which the means of production would be monopolized would provide a more complex and sophisticated equivalent of the large estate (p. 357 sq.).

In an economy in which all property is owned by the state and directed and controlled by the government, everybody is dependent on the ruling elite for his employment and his livelihood. Thus, to take action or even to vote against the wishes of the government, its functionaries and bureaucracy is only possible if tolerated by them. But why should the ruling elite agree to a limitation of its powers or to its tenure as government? Also, an independent press, radio and television are scarcely possible for the same reasons if even the means of production like printing presses and paper are owned by the state. An exception would only be possible during passing periods in which a balance of power between different groups within government takes place. Similar considerations would be true for a market economy in which a few giant firms controlled the labor market and were able to influence the decisions of government.

By contrast, look at a market economy with safe property rights, sufficient competition and rule of law. In such a system people have several possibilities to find employment and to earn their livelihood, even if they are employees. Moreover, there are quite a number of independent farmers, entrepreneurs, professional persons and wealthy people. All of them can engage in political activities whether these are frowned on by the governing politicians or not. Moreover, every individual or group able to command the necessary finances can found newspapers, radio and television stations (but until recently the latter was prohibited in some countries like Germany, Austria and Switzerland because of a state-ordered monopoly of public television) in competition with others. Thus different opinions and ideas diverging from those in political power can compete.

If, on the other hand, property rights are not safe and the rule of law does not protect persons and contracts, the government or other groups are able to punish people taking actions conflicting with or only not promoting their own goals. Property can be confiscated, taxes levied at discretion and contracts be broken or not be enforced.

We thus conclude in contrast to Schumpeter that in a modern complex society only a market economy with safe property rights, rule of law and competition can preserve the freedom and independence of a sufficient number of individuals necessary to maintain democracy. This conclusion seems to be supported by the empirical fact, that until now no planned economic regime has enjoyed democracy.

3 The erosion of a capitalist market economy as a consequence of unlimited democracy

Democracy is no precondition for a capitalist market economy, as can be seen by looking at the examples of Hong Kong, Chile under Pinochet and South Korea under Park. Moreover, democracy may endanger a free market economy in the long run and thus, if the deliberations of Section 2 are true, even threaten its own existence. This usually occurs in unlimited or scarcely limited total democracies.

Schumpeter obviously recognized this danger to a certain degree, here again establishing himself as one of the founders of Public Choice Theory. He doubted in his 1949 address, already mentioned above, that the capitalist engine would go on to work as before under what he called *laborist capitalism,* and which we would call the *welfare state:*

> *We need not accept the stagnationist thesis ... in order to be disturbed by the possibility that this thesis may come true* [that the capitalist engine would not go on to work] *after all if the private-enterprise system is* ***permanently*** *burdened and "regulated" beyond its powers of endurance. In this case, an outright socialist solution may impose itself even on the enemies of socialism as the lesser evil* (1966, p. 419).

Before turning to a discussion of the dangers posed by democracy to a functioning capitalistic system, let me define what I understand by a *total democracy.* I use this concept for a democratic regime which is not restricted in its jurisdiction by constitutional or other safeguards.

Now in such a democracy with unlimited potential domain, shifting majorities in parliament, i.e., small minorities of the population only inadequately controlled by rationally uninformed voters, can enforce their goals on the rest of the population. Since several parties compete for votes and need financial support to cover the expenses for their organizations and for election campaigns, one has to expect in time an ever-increasing sphere of government activities. Thus growing public expenditures, more and more regulations by government, tax loopholes and subsidies to special minority interests and pressure groups, flow from the incessant activity of legislative bodies (Fig. 1). Such developments can happen because the majority of voters is rationally uninformed about issues. This is true for issues in which decisions impinge only marginally on the situation of consumers or taxpayers, since they then have little reason to incur the costs of informing themselves, given the negligible effect of individual votes on election outcomes.

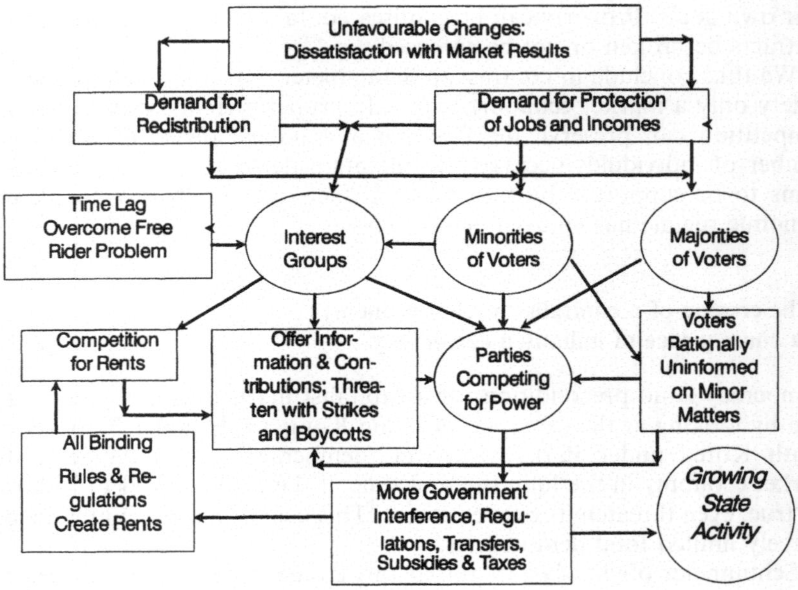

Fig. 1. Growth of government in market economies

Thus protection of certain industries against foreign competition, the fixing of agricultural prices above market clearing levels, subsidies to coal or steel industry and the toleration or even promotion of cartels can be observed, though a majority of voters is hurt by higher taxes and/or prices. On the other hand, whenever changes like rent increases for housing are perceived by a majority of voters, since the expenditures for rents amount to a substantial part of their budgets, the government will take action in favor of the majority e.g., by introducing rent controls (Downs, 1957; Bernholz, 1966).

If the above arguments are correct, why is it that government activities are not increased at once under the pressure of political competition to a Nash equilibrium level in which each party maximizes votes, if such an equilibrium exists? Why does it take decades for government activity to rise to ever higher levels? Several reasons have been given to explain this empirical fact. Olson (1965, 1982) points out that since it is difficult to form interest groups because they provide public goods to their members, it takes time to organize them (see also Bernholz, 1969). The more diverse the interests and the greater the number of potential members, the more difficult the task and the longer the time needed to organize an interest group. As a consequence, cartels can only be formed and influence on the political system be exerted by potential interest groups after they have found enough time to be organized.

Bernholz (1966) has pointed out a second reason for the gradual extension of government, namely changes of the industrial structure brought about again and again by economic development. These changes threaten old industries, their capital owners and managers as well as the jobs and the wage level of the people employed by them. This leads to voter dissatis-

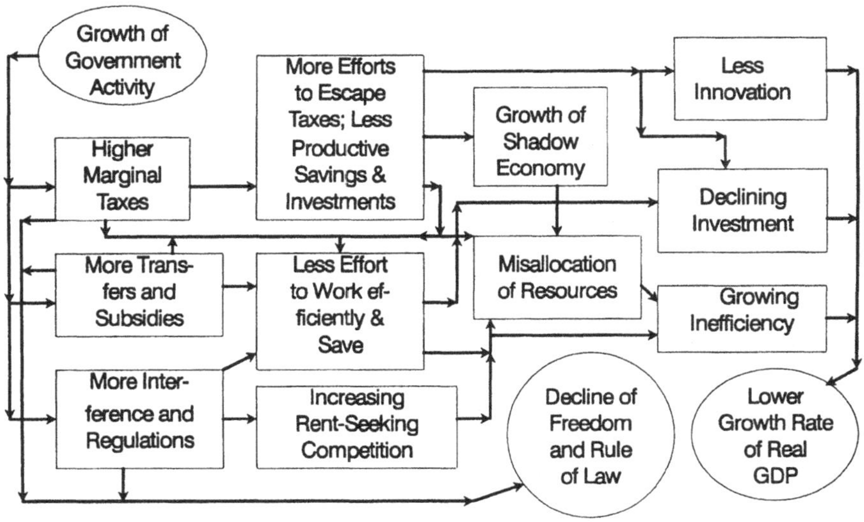

Fig. 2. Consequences of growing government activity in democratic market economies

faction and thus, under the pressure of political competition, to government intervention to maintain or to win the support of those voters and of their families who suffer from the changes in the industrial structure. A third reason sometimes mentioned in the literature is more or less closely related to the second: "The need to keep in check the forces which might produce unemployment is not the only root of the expansion of government control over industry and trade, because the sheer growth of complexity of economic structures requires more co-ordination, and the number of tasks which cannot be left to private initiative – such as prevention of soil erosion, traffic control, smoke abatement and so on – grows incessantly" (Andreski, 1965, p. 355). Finally, time is obviously needed to invent new governmental measures, to introduce and to pass new legislation, taxes and subsidies.

If our analysis is correct, state activity will be growing in time in democracies. A democratic system with competing parties reacts to the demands of different minorities and majorities of voters and of special interest groups which arise over time. As a consequence, the older and the less disturbed a democracy by wars, revolutions and other crises enforcing a restructuring of the political economic system, the higher the level of regulations, of subsidies, transfers and taxes one would expect at comparable levels of per capita incomes (Olson, 1982, 1983). But since excessive state activity also makes for less efficiency, savings, and innovation (Fig. 2) one would also expect negative consequences for real economic growth, as measured e.g. by the real growth rate of GDP per capita. This expectation seems to be supported by empirical evidence (Fig. 3 and 4) (Bernholz, 1986, 1990; Marlow, 1986; Peden and Bradley, 1989; Weede, 1986, 1990; Tanzi and Schuknecht, 1997).

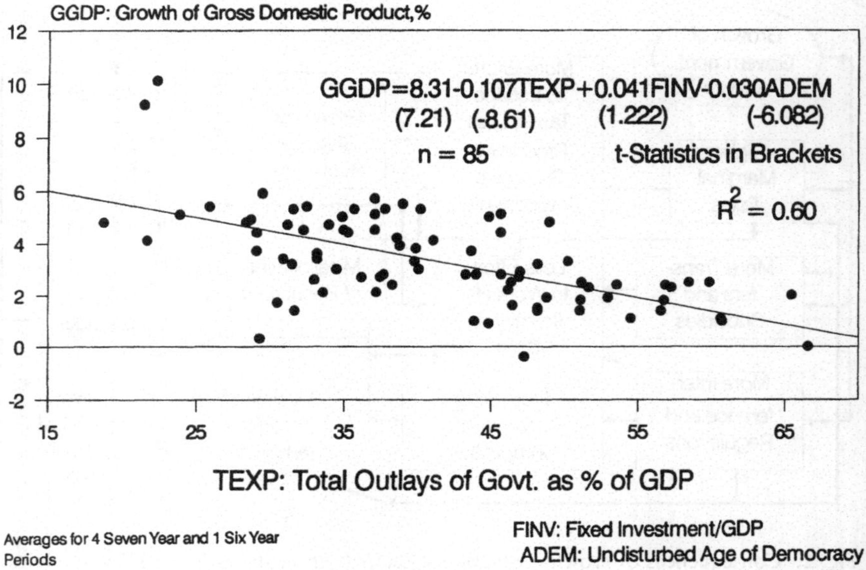

Fig. 3. Growth of real GDP 1960–93 for seventeen OECD countries

4 Are there forces maintaining democracy?

Our analysis has shown that Schumpeter's condition 2 for the existence of a democracy, namely the restriction of the domain of government, is eroded more and more in the long-run by tendencies inherent in this form of

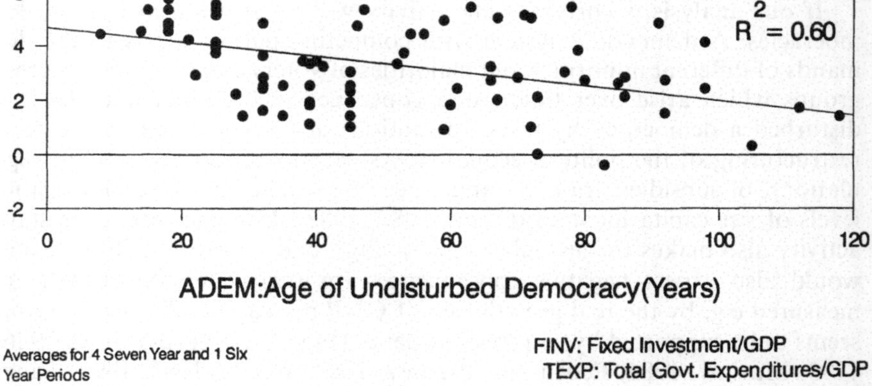

Fig. 4. Growth of real GDP 1960–93 for seventeen OECD countries

government. We may also doubt, whether the growth of bureaucracy implied by this development will not also violate in time his third and fourth conditions, i.e. the existence of an efficient and honest bureaucracy.

We have thus to ask ourselves, whether, given these tendencies, there exist counteracting forces which are strong enough to hold or even to reverse these tendencies. Tendencies which may be strengthened by dangers stemming from ideologies (see below) striving for supreme values that contradict democratic and free-market principles.

The problem we have stated has, of course, been recognized already for a long time. One proposal, the separation of legislative, executive, and juridical power has been proposed by Montesqieu and been further elaborated on in the Federalist Papers. Other proposals which have been institutionalized are federalism as a device to limit the domain of central government, or rules like the rule that no private property can be taken by the government without due compensation. Human rights in the constitution, freedom of speech etc. are also devices limiting the sphere of government. But these safeguards have only been able to retard the growth of government for several decades, but not permanently.

It is obvious, e.g. that a constitutional court must exist to ensure that parliament and executive do not overstep the boundaries imposed on them by the constitution. But how can the court itself be prevented from reinterpreting and thus slowly eroding the original content of the constitution. The US Supreme Court has often played a decisive role in extending the domain of the Federal Government, especially during the years of the New Deal. Neither the Supreme Court nor the German Bundesverfassungsgericht have been able or willing to maintain the domain of the states or Länder and thus to prevent the erosion of federalism. On the other hand, the Swiss decided in 1848 not to establish a constitutional court when they otherwise took over many ideas of the American into their own constitution. But, as a consequence, the constitutional limitations of the central government were in time eroded by political decisions changing or extending the constitution with the simple majority of voters and of cantons (Ständemehr). Even worse, the government even sometimes just broke the rules of the constitution, and was not hindered by parliament to do so.

We have thus to conclude, that even a democracy, in which government and parliament were heavily restricted constitutionally, will in time remove more and more of these restrictions and allow growing government and centralization. Constitutional and institutional safeguards may retard such a development even for several decades. But all of them will be eroded in time. The Hobbesian problem can perhaps be better and longer contained by devising new such institutions and rules, but it will probably never be solved.

This leaves us with a bleak outlook or rather with the question, whether there are other forces at work counteracting the tendencies just described. Indeed, we may also ask, how could free societies with rule of law and democracy arise at all, given the Hobbesian problem. Let us turn to answer this last question first.

Why should the ruling elite in an autocracy agree to strong and secure property rights, to minimal state intervention, to a strong limitation of taxes, and thus of its own powers to command and to take away goods at their own discretion? It seems that the 'New Economic Historians' have tried with a certain success to answer these questions (North and Thomas, 1973; North, 1981; Jones, 1981). They have stressed that 'European disunity has been our good luck'. Feudalism with its many power centers developed during the Middle Ages and a split opened up between religious and temporal powers. A strong rivalry arose among the many rulers to extend and preserve their powers by foreign policy and military endeavours. This forced them to become interested in the well-being and loyalty of their subjects and in economic development to secure a greater tax base and thus stronger armies. However, economic development itself depended on establishing adequate property rights, a reliable legal system, free markets and limited taxes. As a consequence, those states were successful in this fierce foreign policy and military competition in the long run who, by chance or by design, made the greatest progress in introducing such institutions. Thus competition among states forced on unwilling rulers a limitation of domestic powers. The development of competing legal systems, of the rule of law and of property rights was helped not only by interstate competition but also by the increasing separation of church and state, the preventing of a theocracy (Berman, 1983). Because of these developments limited government and a pluralistic society arose in Europe as a predemocratic achievement. First capitalism and later democracy were their progeny.

I have argued elsewhere (Bernholz, 1995) that international competition among states is a driving force even until today, motivating rulers like in Japan in the Meiji Era, or Gorbatchew and Deng during the 1970s and 1980s to limit their domestic powers with the purpose to strengthen their economies as a base of international power. Whether the reforms are adequate and thus successful is, of course, another question. But if this is a true consequence of international competition, then it follows that democracies in which government has grown too much, will also face the military and political competition of other capitalistic regimes, which are more efficient and innovative and show thus higher growth rates of GDP and lower rates of unemployment. Moreover, their population may become aware, especially with the spread of modern mass media and of tourism, of the better economic performance of these countries or of the better plight of people living there. As a result, dissatisfaction with the government may arise, and an emigration of capital and of the more talented and entrepreneurial strata of the population take place. It is thus obvious, that in time strong pressures on government arise which may lead to political reforms cutting government expenditures as a share of GDP and reducing overextended regulations.

We have argued above that there exists an inherent tendency in democracies for government to grow. The situation, however, is different in situations which are perceived by the population and (or?) politicians as crises. In such cases public-minded statesmen or advisors may have great influence, if their ideas succeed against competing simplifying ideologies. Examples are the success of the West German (ordo-) liberals after the catastrophe of the second world war (Peacock and Willgerodt, 1989); the reforms by Mrs. Thatcher in Britain after it had lagged more and more economically compared to other European countries and even been overtaken by Italy; or the drastic reforms first taken by the labour government in New Zealand after the extended welfare state based on a mainly agricultural economy had led the country into a deep unemployment, budget deficit and foreign exchange crisis. It follows, moreover, from the above argument, that also a weakening of the relative foreign policy and military position of (potential) Great Powers caused by a relatively bad economic performance as a consequence of an increasing share of government in GDP and of overregulation may be perceived as a crisis and lead to reforms in the direction of reestablishing limited government.

It is obvious that these relationships have yet to be studied much more deeply and that there are still many gaps in our knowledge today. How do we, e.g., define a crisis? How deep has it to be?

Finally, let us ask, whether we are able to explain such political turnarounds with the help of Public Choice Theory. We know that one of the strong forces driving the expansion of government are special interest groups who can be successful because of rationally uninformed voters. The latter do not perceive the burdens they have to carry because these burdens are spread over all of them and are discounted because they may turn up mainly in the future, like lower growth rates or ecological problems. The special interest groups, however, are well aware of the sizable benefits concentrated on them. But now, if more and more government interventions favoring interest groups occur, the burdens for ordinary voters increase and will finally be perceived by them. In such a situation each voter may benefit from one or more government interventions, but the total burden on him or her by all interventions together outweighs the benefits. Such a situation may be perceived as a crisis. But then it becomes profitable for politicians (especially of the opposition) to propose an election program which contains an implicit logrolling agreement: Namely, each participating group is prepared to forego its special benefits, if so many other groups do the same, that they form together a majority of voters. Recently a formal model addressing such relationships has been presented by Dur and Swank (1997).

5 The influence of ideologies on the political economic system during crises

Our analysis has perhaps finally led to a more optimistic view concerning the long-term survival of free market regimes with rule of law and democratic government. To sum up: We have first discussed the tendency of democracies with free markets and private property, towards more and more interventions and redistribution. This development leads in time to decreasing efficiency and freedom and reduces productive investment and innovative activity. Resources are misallocated and the growth rates of GDP fall. As a consequence, after some time the political-economic system moves into a crisis engendering widespread voter dissatisfaction. It seems that Sweden experienced such a situation in the 1980s. Such a crisis, however, provides chances of a turnaround because of international competition of other capitalist states and the fact, that the burdens of an ever-extending welfare and regulatory democracy will be perceived in time by the majority of voters.

Unfortunately, crises are not only a fertile ground for sound ideas allowing successful reforms, but also for the tempting promises of ideologies. We finally have to turn to this danger which threatens the return to a healthy market economy with limited government and democracy, we have finally to turn.

Let us first mention, that there exist other reasons for crises than those already mentioned above, namely wars, religious and ethnic strife, hyperinflations, depressions, etc. Obvious examples are the consequences of World War I, especially for the defeated countries with the harsh peace treaties of Versailles, St. Germain, Trianon and Neuilly. Further examples are the Great Depression, beginning in 1929 and the hyperinflations in Germany, Austria, Hungary and Poland in the 1920s, in China and Greece in the 1940s and during the last decades in Bolivia, Argentina, Brazil, Nicaragua, Peru, Zaire and several former member states of the Soviet Union.

Crises provide a fertile ground for reform plans proposing new political-economic regimes. They are thus also favorable for the success of ideologies claiming to have the right recipe for solving the perceived problems. The same is, as mentioned, true for the application of correct ideas like, e.g., those of the neo-liberals after World War II in Western Germany. In this case, men like Eucken, Böhm, Röpcke and Müller-Armack had already prepared their theoretical concepts concerning a new free market system during the Nazi regime and the war (Peacock and Willgerodt, 1989). Their ideas were available in 1948, when the German currency reform took place and were implemented by Ludwig Erhard, Müller-Armack and others. Thus a successful change from a degenerating planned economy to a free market regime took place.

Taken generally, different theories and ideologies compete during crises with their often widely diverging proposals for problem solutions. Here, by an ideology, let us understand a world view, a Weltanschauung, which tries to interpret major aspects of the world and their interrelationships. Usually such ideologies contain supreme values which have to be pursued to solve the problems of individuals and/or society. Ideologies thus respond to widespread human demands for spiritual goods, for the implied Weltanschauung offers safety and provides meaning in an otherwise incomprehensible world. As far as it is shared with others, it offers feelings of warmth and belonging, of safety in the womb of collectivity. Major religions, but also Communism and National-Socialism are examples of such ideologies.

It is not surprising that ideologies become most attractive to people disoriented and suffering during crises. This is especially true, if they seem to offer through their world view simple and appealing solutions to the problems perceived by the masses. It was only during the crisis of the Great Depression that both Nazis and Communists gained strong voter support in Germany (Frey and Weck, 1981), after they had widely lost it with the end of the German hyperinflation in November 1923. Lenin and his supporters also gained power in Russia in 1917 as a consequence of the defeats and suffering brought about by World War I. And it is also doubtful whether the communists under Mao's leadership would have defeated the

Kuomintang in 1948/49 without the dismal economic situation, hyperinflation and corruption in China.

It follows that ideological movements enjoy a good chance to grasp power during crises, provided they have a belief system perceived by the masses of the population as offering solutions to their problems. But if they succeed in democracies, it is highly probable that they will not only transform the economic but also the political system. For their supreme values are usually in conflict with at least a substantial part of democratic institutions. And these values have to be implemented either by constitution or law, and to shape many organizations of the state, since by the very definition of supreme values, they have to dominate all other goals. As a consequence an ideological movement may thus even turn the nation into a totalitarian state, if the supreme values of the creed demand it (Bernholz, 1995, 1997).

The supreme values of ideologies, moreover, often contain rules referring to the economic regime wanted. Christianity forbade usury and Islam does not allow interest, Nazism and Communism implied a more or less centrally planned economy, the latter, additionally, socialist or state property. Thus, as far as the supreme values of the respective ideology contain comprehensive rules referring to the organization of the economy, the success of an ideological movement to grasp power necessarily leads to a change of the economic regime. This is exactly what happened in Nazi-Germany, the Soviet Union, in Eastern Europe after World War II, in Communist China, Cuba, Vietnam and Cambodia.

But if such a transformation of a former market economy with private property takes place, what consequences would this have for a democratic system? Assume for a moment that the victorious ideology did not contain any supreme values contradicting the political system of a democracy. Even then, if our above proposition is true, the democratic regime would be eroded in time. For it states that a free market system is a precondition for democracy, and exactly this system would be transformed since the supreme values of the creed call for a different economic regime. Of course, in reality, the changes called for by the ideology may be so limited that the main characteristics of a market economy can be preserved. This shows that it may be a matter of the intensity and scope of the transformation whether the democratic system will be eroded or can be preserved. Anyhow, we conclude, that a crisis may – under the influence of ideologies – prevent a successful restoration of a degenerating democratic market regime and may even turn it for decades into a totalitarian or at least authoritarian regime. The demise of the Weimar Republic and of Argentina under the hands of Peron are telling examples.

References

Andreski S (1965) The uses of comparative sociology. University of California Press, Berkeley Los Angeles

Berman HJ (1983) Law and revolution. Harvard University Press, Cambridge, MA London

Bernholz P (1966) Economic policies in a democracy. Kyklos 19: 48–80

Bernholz P (1969) Einige Bemerkungen zur Theorie des Einflusses der Verbände auf die politische Willensbildung in der Demokratie. Kyklos 22: 267–278

Bernholz P (1986) Growth of government, economic growth and individual freedom. Journal of Institutional and Theoretical Economics (Zeitschrift für die Gesamte Staatswissenschaft) 142: 661–683

Bernholz P (1990) The completion of the internal market: opportunities and dangers seen from an institutional perspective. In: The macroeconomics of 1992. Papers from CEPS macroeconomic Policy Group. Centre for Economic Policy Studies, CEPS Paper No. 42, Brussels

Bernholz P (1991) The constitution of totalitarianism. Journal of Institutional and Theoretical Economics 147 (3): 425–440

Bernholz P (1995) Supreme values, tolerance and the constitution of liberty. In: Radnitzky G, Bouillon H (eds) Values and the social order, Vol 1, pp 235–250. Avebury Ashgate, Aldershot

Bernholz P (1997) Ideology, sects, state and totalitarianism: a general theory. Forum für osteuropäische Ideen- und Zeitgeschichte 1 (1): 51–84. Also in: Maier H, Schaefer M (eds) Totalitarismus und politische Religionen. Konzepte des Diktaturvergleichs, pp 271–298. Schoeningh, Paderborn München Wien Zürich

Downs A (1957) An economic theory of democracy. Harper and Row, New York

Dur RAJ, Swank OH (1997) An explanation of policy reversals. Why do voters vote for a smaller government if they voted for a large government in the past? Unpublished Manuscript, presented at the 1997 Silvaplana Public Choice Workshop, Pontresina

Frey B, Weck H (1981) Hat Arbeitslosigkeit den Aufstieg des Nationalsozialismus bewirkt? Jahrbuch fuer Nationaloekonomie und Statistik 196 (1): 1–31

Marlow ML (1986) Private sector shrinkage and the growth of industrialized economies. Public Choice 49 (2): 143–154

Jones EL (1981) The European Miracle. Cambridge University Press, Cambridge

North DC (1981) Structure and change in economic history. Norton, New York

North DC, Thomas RP (1973) The rise of the western world: a new economic history. Cambridge University Press, Cambridge

Olson M (1965) The logic of collective action. Harvard University Press, Cambridge, MA

Olson M (1982) The rise and decline of nations: economic growth, stagflation, and social rigidities. Yale University Press, New Haven

Olson M (1983) The political economy of comparative growth rates. In: Mueller D (ed) The political economy of growth, pp 7–52. Yale University Press, New Haven London

Peacock A, Willgerodt H (eds) (1989) German neo-liberals and the social market economy. Macmillan, London

Peden EA, Bradley MD (1989) Government size, productivity, and economic growth: the post-war experience. Public Choice 61: 229–245

Schumpeter JA (1966) Capitalism, socialism and democracy. Unwin University Books, 5th edn, 11th impression. London, George Allen & Unwin (1st edn 1943)

Weede E (1986) Catch-up, distributional coalitions and governments as determinants of economic growth or decline in industrialized societies. British Journal of Sociology 37: 194–220

Weede E (1990) Wirtschaft, Staat, Gesellschaft. Mohr, Tübingen

Tanzi V, Schuknecht L (1997) Reforming government: an overview of recent experience. European Journal of Political Economy 13 (3): 395–417

Capitalism and democracy in the 21st Century: from the managed to the entrepreneurial economy*

David B. Audretsch[1], A. Roy Thurik[2,3]

[1] Institute for Development Strategies, Indiana University, SPEA, Suite 201, Bloomington, IN 47405-2100, USA (e-mail: daudrets@indiana.edu)
[2] Tinbergen Institute, Erasmus University Rotterdam, Rotterdam, The Netherlands
[3] EIM Small Business Research and Consultancy, P.O. Box 7001, NL-2701 AA Zoetermeer, The Netherlands (e-mail: rth@eim.nl)

Abstract. This paper explains how and why the developed countries are undergoing a fundamental shift away from a managed economy and towards an entrepreneurial economy. This shift is shaping the development of western capitalism and has triggered a shift in government policies away from constraining the freedom of business to contract through regulation, public ownership and antitrust towards a new set of enabling policies which foster the creation and commercialization of new knowledge. The empirical evidence from a cross-section of countries over time suggests that those countries that have experienced a greater shift from the managed to the entrepreneurial economy have had lower levels of unemployment.

Key words: Entrepreneurship – Knowledge – Growth – Schumpeter – Unemployment

JEL-classification: O0

* This paper is the result of a series of visits by David Audretsch as a Visiting Research Fellow at the Tinbergen Institute and as a Research Fellow at EIM in 1997 and 1998. We are grateful to Sander Baljé, Martin Carree, Luuk Klomp, Jacqueline Snijders, Andre van Stel, Sander Wennekers and Wim Verhoeven for their comments and suggestions on earlier drafts of this paper. Earlier draft has been read in Brussels (European Commission, November 25, 1997) The Hague (Ministry of Economic Affairs, January 20, 1998).

Paper presented at the 1998 World Conference of the International Joseph A. Schumpeter Society, Vienna, June 13–16, 1998.

1 Introduction

Joseph Schumpeter oscillated in his view about the type of economic system that was most conducive to growth. In his 1911 treatise, Schumpeter argued that a more decentralized and turbulent industry structure where the process of creative destruction was triggered by vigorous entrepreneurial activity was the engine of economic growth. But by 1942 Schumpeter had modified his theory, arguing instead that a more centralized and stable industry structure was more conducive to growth. According to Schumpeter (1942, p. 132), under the managed economy there was little room for entrepreneurship because, "Innovation itself is being reduced to routine. Technological progress is increasingly becoming the business of teams of trained specialists who turn out what is required to make it work in predictable ways" (p. 132). Schumpeter (1942) reversed his earlier view by arguing that the integration of knowledge creation and appropriation bestowed an inherent innovative advantage upon giant corporations, "Since capitalist enterprise, by its very achievements, tends to automize progress, we conclude that it tends to make itself superfluous – to break to pieces under the pressure of its own success. The perfectly bureaucratic giant industrial unit not only outsets the small- or medium-sized firm and expropriates its owners, but in the end it also ousts the entrepreneur and expropriates the bourgeoisie as a class which in the process stands to lose not only its income but also, what is infinitely more important, its function." This later interpretation by Schumpeter anticipated the emergence of the managed economy of the post-war period.

The purpose of this paper is to explain how and why the developed countries are undergoing a fundamental shift away from a managed economy and towards an entrepreneurial economy. The managed economy of the post-war era performed marvellously for over three decades, providing the engine of jobs, growth, stability and security.[1] It is not a coincidence that the end of the Cold War ushered in a new economic era. The second section of this paper explains how the fall of the Berlin Wall helped triggered a wave of new participants in the global economy, spanning from Eastern and Central Europe to Southeast Asia. Combined with the communications revolution, this globalization led to the demise of the comparative advantage of Europe in many of the traditional industries, such as machine tools, metalworking, textiles and automobile production. The twin forces of globalization and the information revolution have made it difficult to maintain jobs in high-cost locations. This has created the rather gloomy perception of a policy dilemma that is being debated throughout Europe. The perceived tradeoff between wages and employment seems to demand that European countries choose between more jobs but at a cost of a lower standard of living, or higher wages, but at the sacrifice of fewer jobs. The third section of this paper argues that this perceived policy tradeoff between employment and wages is not at all inevitable. The comparative advantage of much of Europe is shifting towards knowledge-

[1] See Audretsch and Thurik (1997) and Wennekers and Thurik (1999).

based economic activity. Because economic activity based on new ideas and new ways of doing things cannot be easily transferred or emulated in low-cost locations, jobs lost due to corporate downsizing can be replaced with even better jobs.[2]

The fourth section explains how entrepreneurship is a fundamental characteristic of knowledge-based economic activity.[3] This is because the potential value of new ideas and knowledge are inherently uncertain. The existing firms will not pursue many new ideas because they have different agendas or simply do not recognize their potential value. If a new firm is not started to pursue such ideas they will simply remain untapped. Thus, the industrial structure of a knowledge-based entrepreneurial economy is very different from one based on the mass-production of relatively known products using established processes. It is a much more fluid and turbulent economy, where people are quick to move into situations where their ideas are valued. It is an economy where failure looses much of its pejorative connotation, because it is recognized that trial and error and experimentation are essential to innovation and the creation of new ideas.

In the fifth section of the paper we present an empirical analysis examining whether the rise in the number of entrepreneurs per labor force leads to lower levels of unemployment. We use data material of 23 OECD countries including EU-15, Japan and US for the period 1974 through 1994. We find that those countries that have introduced a greater element of entrepreneurship in the decade preceding 1984 have been rewarded with a greater decrease of unemployment in the subsequent decade. Section six is devoted to discussing some policy implications. In particular, a fundamental shift in the role of government towards business is taking place. The traditional stance of constraining the freedom of firms to contract, in the form of government regulations, public ownership and antitrust, is being replaced by a new set of enabling policies, where the emphasis is on the creation and commercialization of new knowledge.

2 The economic challenge of the 1990s

When the Berlin Wall fell in 1989 many people expected a dramatic reduction of the economic burden in both the West and the East that had been imposed by four decades of Cold War. Substantial unemployment and general economic stagnation did not disappear during the subsequent eight years. Unemployment and moderate growth are the twin economic problems confronting Europe. The number of unemployed in the European Union is twice as high as that in Japan and the U.S. together. Over 11

---

[2] Thurik (1996) and Carree and Thurik (1999) show that the benefits are directly related to the degree to which a country or industry has shifted economic activity away from large corporations and towards small firms. See also OECD (1996b).

[3] See Brock and Evans (1989), Loveman and Sengenberger (1991) and Carree (1997, chapter 2).

percent of the work force in the European Union was unemployed in 1996, ranging from about 3 percent in Luxembourg and about 4 percent in Austria and to 15 percent in Finland and over 20 percent in Spain.[4] Germany has experienced the highest rates of unemployment since World War II.

Perhaps most revealing, in countries like the Netherlands and the United Kingdom which have managed to reverse the upward trend in unemployment, job creation and quality of jobs have ranked among the most prominent subjects of political debate. Not only was employment creation the number one topic in the recent elections in France and Germany, but it was also the focus of debate during the 1996 American presidential election and 1997 national elections in the United Kingdom.

The policy debate throughout Europe and in other OECD countries about how to solve the chronic unemployment problem has revolved around a perceived tradeoff between higher wage levels but higher rates of unemployment on the one hand, or less unemployment but lower wages on the other. This debate has resulted in a caricature of the "Anglo-American" solution of more jobs through lower wages and the "European tradition" of higher wages, but at a cost of less employment. It certainly is true that the American and British economies have generated millions of new jobs, thereby reducing unemployment, and that at the same time, the mean real wage levels have risen the least. It is also true that these countries have experienced a considerable dismantling of social services provided by the government. This leaves policy makers with an apparent uncomfortable choice – either reduce wages and the social safety net to generate more employment, or else accept an upward spiral of unemployment in order to maintain the European standards concerning wages and the social safety net. The fifth annual report of the *European Observatory for SMEs* (p. 131) characterizes this tradeoff as, "The stagnation of employment since 1970 in the EU as opposed to the employment growth in the U.S. could, at least partially, be explained by the fact that real wages increased significantly in the EU while in the U.S. it only increased slightly."

This perceived policy trade-off between wages and unemployment is an illusion. The Dutch example shows that it is possible to achieve rising employment while maintaining an adequate social safety net. The key to breaking out of the perceived tradeoff between wages and jobs is to understand how the twin forces of globalization combined with the communications revolution has fundamentally shifted the comparative advantage of the leading European economies.

3 The emergence of the knowledge-based economy

The Cold War combined with internal political instability rendered potential investments in Eastern Europe and much of the developing world as risky and impractical. During the post-war era most trade and economic

[4] OECD (1997), standardized rates.

investment was generally confined to Europe and North America, and later a few of the Asian countries, principally Japan and the Asian Tigers. The comparative advantage was generally attained through large-scale production, which facilitated low-cost production through exploiting scale economies. Large-scale mass production was essential to gaining the comparative advantage. The relatively small domestic markets in most European countries seemed to pose a serious threat to European post-war competitiveness. However, they quickly developed two strategies to compensate for their small domestic markets. The first strategy was to internationalize by developing markets outside of the domestic market. The second was to rely on skilled labor and high levels of human capital to produce products that, although they might cost more, were of superior quality. Large transnational corporations thrived on this dual strategy basing the comparative advantage on large-scale production made possible by superior management and organization combined with high-skilled labor. By and large, the comparative advantage of Europe lies in large-scale production of moderate-technology products in traditional industries, such as machine tools, automobile parts, metalworking, chemicals and the food industry (Audretsch and Thurik, 1997).

This comparative advantage has been lost in the high-cost countries of Europe and North America in the last decade for two reasons. The first has to do with globalization, or the advent of competition from not just the emerging economies in Southeast Asia but also from the transforming economies of Central and Eastern Europe. The production costs, and in particular labor costs, are considerably lower in these countries. At the same time, the potential labor force of about 500 million in China and 350 million in India will put a pressure on any upward lift of the wage rate. While the uncertainties of the Cold War and internal political instabilities rendered transnational activities too risky during the first four post-war decades, this is less the case today.

The second factor triggering the loss of the traditional comparative advantage in Europe has been the communications revolution. The new communications technologies have triggered a virtual spatial revolution in terms of the geography of production.[5] The (marginal) cost of transforming information across geographic space has been rendered to virtually nothing. Confronted with lower cost competition in foreign locations, producers in the high-cost countries have three options apart from doing nothing and losing global market share: (1) reduce wages and other production costs sufficiently to compete with the low-cost foreign producers, (2) substitute equipment and technology for labor to increase productivity, and (3) shift production out of the high-cost location and into the low-cost location.

Many of the European and American firms that have successfully restructured resorted to the last two alternatives. Substituting capital and

---

[5] According to *The Economist*, "The death of distance as a determinant of the cost of communications will probably be the single most important economic force shaping society in the first half of the next century." "The Death of Distance," *The Economist*, 30 September, 1995.

technology for labor, along with shifting production to lower-cost locations has resulted in waves of *Corporate Downsizing* throughout Europe and North America. At the same time, it has generally preserved the viability of many of the large corporations. As record levels of both European and American stock indexes indicate, the companies have not generally suffered.

Corporate downsizing triggered by the shifting comparative advantage as a result of globalization has not been restricted to just a few countries such as Sweden and Germany. Rather, the response to globalization has led large corporations to downsize throughout the OECD countries.[6] For example, between 1979 and 1995 more than 43 million jobs were lost in the United States as a result of corporate downsizing.[7] This includes 24.8 million blue-collar jobs and 18.7 million white-collar jobs. Similarly, the 500 largest U.S. manufacturing corporations cut 4.7 million jobs between 1980 and 1993, or one quarter of their work force.[8] Perhaps most disconcerting, the rate of corporate downsizing has apparently increased over time in the United States, even as the unemployment rate has fallen. During most of the 1980s, about one in 25 workers lost a job. In the 1990s this has risen to one in 20 workers.

This wave of corporate downsizing has triggered cries of betrayal and lack of social conscience on the part of the large corporations.[9] But it is a mistake to blame the corporations for this wave of downsizing that has triggered massive job losses and rising unemployment in so many countries. These corporations are simply trying to survive in an economy of global competitors who have access to lower cost inputs.

There is, however, an alternative. It does not require sacrificing wages to create new jobs, nor does it require fewer jobs to maintain wage levels and the social safety net. This alternative involves shifting economic activity out of the traditional industries where the high-cost countries of Europe and North America have lost the comparative advantage and into those industries where the comparative advantage is compatible with both high wages and high levels of employment – knowledge based economic activity.

The emergence of high-technology regions, such as Silicon Valley in California, Research Triangle in North Carolina, and Cambridge in the United Kingdom may seem surprising and even paradoxical in a world increasingly dominated by e-mail, fax machines, and cyberspace, which should have rendered the importance of geographic proximity to be irrelevant. The resolution of this paradox lies in *a crucial distinction between knowledge and information*. Information consists of facts, such as the price

---

6 "Big is Back," *The Economist*, 22 June, 1995 and "The Year Downsizing Grew Up," *The Economist*, 21 December 1996.

7 "The Downsizing of America," *New York Times*, 3 March, 1996, p. 1.

8 See Audretsch (1995).

9 As the German newspaper *Die Zeit* (2 February, 1996, p. 1) pointed out in a front page article, "When Profits Lead to Ruin – More Profits and More Unemployment: Where is the Social Responsibility of the Firms?" the German public has responded to the recent waves of corporate downsizing with accusations that corporate Germany is no longer fulfilling its share of the social contract.

of gold in Tokyo, or the weather in New York, and can be costlessly transmitted around the globe. By contrast, knowledge consists of ideas that are subjective, uncertain and difficult to explicitly write down. Many of these ideas arise as a result of face-to-face contact and interchange. Many of the most creative ideas have been the result of chance meetings at a social event or an industry function.

Economic activity based on ideas and new knowledge cannot be easily copied by competitors located outside of the source and cannot be easily transferred to lower-cost countries by multinational corporations (Audretsch and Feldmnan, 1996; Audretsch and Stephan, 1996). While the processes and organizational methods required to produce automobiles can be transferred from Stuttgart to, say, Hungary, it is not so easy to transfer innovative work in biotechnology around the globe.[10] Economic activity based on new ideas, such as fashion in Milan, culinary arts in Paris, and movies in Hollywood have remained geographically concentrated. Higher wages can be maintained for economic activity that is based on new ideas. The emerging source of comparative advantage for Europe is economic activity based on creativity and new ideas.[11]

The global demand for products in emerging knowledge-based industries is high and growing rapidly; yet the number of workers who can contribute to producing and commercializing new knowledge is limited to just a few areas in the world. Economic activity based on skills that can be found throughout large parts of the world is doomed to generate lower wage rates as a result of global competition. By contrast, economic activity based on new knowledge will generate higher wages and greater employment opportunities reflecting the exploding demand for new and improved products and services.

There are many indicators reflecting the shift in the comparative advantage of the high-wage countries towards an increased importance knowledge-based economic activity. For example, Kortum and Lerner (1997, p. 1) point to "the unprecedented recent jump in patenting in the United States," as evidenced by the rise in applications for U.S. patents by American inventors since 1985, which exceeds the increase in any other decade in this century. Throughout this century, patent applications fluctuated within a band of between 40,000–80,000 per year. By contrast, in 1995 there were over 120,000 patent applications. Similarly, Berman, Bound and Machin (1997) have shown that the demand for less skilled workers has decreased dramatically throughout the OECD, while at the same time the demand for skilled workers has exploded. See also OECD (1996a) where a discrimination is made between forms of knowledge.

Why has it proven so difficult to shift economic activity out of the traditional industries where the products are now fairly standardized and

---

[10] As *Fortune* points out, "Business is a social activity, and you have to be where important work is taking place." "The Best Cities for Knowledge Workers," *Fortune*, 15 November, 1993, pp. 44–57.

[11] For a compelling statement of the importance of knowledge to the competitiveness of Europe, see the statement by Martin Bangemann in Dumort and Dryden (1997).

where production can be easily transferred out of high-cost locations?[12] The great established companies of Europe and North America have what is called their core competence in traditional products. They have limited capacity for shifting their activity out of these traditional industries and into new industries.

Part of this inability to shift into new knowledge-based industries is that large corporations excelled in an economy where it was more or less known what was to be produced and how to produce it. The large corporations excelled at bringing together the essential inputs of machinery, workers, and natural resources to generate manufactured products. Knowledge is a qualitatively different input in the production process than machinery or workers who serve as cogs in an assembly line (Audretsch and Thurik, 1997). While a consensus can arise about the contribution of a worker in an assembly line process, no such consensus exists for new ideas which workers have. New ideas are inherently uncertain. What one worker thinks is a good idea may be disputed by colleagues and bosses. Therefore, the ability of people to move into new situations to create and try out new ideas rejected elsewhere is fundamental in a knowledge-based economy. Sometimes such new opportunities to try out new ideas can be found within existing firms. But often people with new ideas find that, because of the fundamental uncertainty, starting a new firm is the only way in which the idea can be pursued and commercialized. What might be termed, as the entrepreneurial society is conducive to innovative activity because it encourages people to create new ideas and to actively commercialize those ideas.

4 The entrepreneurial society

An economy whose comparative advantage is new knowledge requires a very different industrial structure as well as economic values. People who can create new ideas and implement them become highly valued. New products and new firms generate large increases in employment where the global demand is virtually untapped but the supply of workers able to produce such innovative products is limited. Of course, the degree of uncertainty inherent in new knowledge dictates that many of the new ideas, and therefore new firms, will not, in fact, prove to be viable or successful. Those firms and workers must abandon such attempts and move on. Thus, the knowledge-based economy is in motion and is characterized by a high degree of people starting new firms to pursue, explore or implement new ideas. Those new firms that prove to be viable grow rapidly and expand employment. Those based on an idea that is not viable stagnate and may

---

[12] What *Der Spiegel* concludes for Germany is equally valid for much of Europe, "Global structural change has had an impact that only a short time ago would have been unimaginable. Many of the products, such as automobiles, machinery, chemicals and steel are no longer competitive in global markets. And in the industries of the future, like biotechnology and electronics, the German companies are barely participating." *Der Spiegel*, number 5, 1994, 82–83.

ultimately exit. What appears to be a turbulent and wasteful economy is actually the process by which new ideas are generated and explored, ultimately creating new high-paying jobs to replace those lost due to downsizing.

The American industrial landscape has been transformed in a relatively short period of time from a static and rigid economy dominated by corporate dinosaurs such as IBM, U.S. Steel, and RCA to an economy in full motion where new firms are generating not just most of the new jobs, but also the new industries. In the 1950s and 1960s it took two decades for one-third of the 500 largest corporations in America to be replaced. In the 1970s it took the entire decade to replace one-third of the 500 largest corporations. By contrast, in the 1980s, it took just five years.[13] Perhaps even more impressive than the handful of new enterprises that grow to penetrate the elite club of corporate giants are the armies of startups that come into existence each year – and typically disappear into oblivion within a few years. In the 1990s there are around 1.3 million new companies started each year in the United States.[14] The knowledge-economy is characterized by a high degree of turbulence. It is an economy in motion, with a massive number of new firms entering each year, but only a subset surviving for any length of time, and an even smaller subset, such as Microsoft and Intel, that ultimately become the new corporate giants.

Some of this turbulence is attributable to new firms started in desperation to avoid (the threat of) unemployment resulting from corporate downsizing. The decision to become self-employed is often a response to impending unemployment and does not have a high likelihood of success (Storey, 1991). But on balance, this motion shifts the economy out of the old traditional sectors, where neither employment maintenance nor high wages are compatible with the comparative advantage, and into new industries based on new knowledge. In the 1950s and 1960s the most important industries in the United States were steel and automobiles, along with other heavy manufacturing industries. In the present decade information technology has emerged as the largest U.S. industry. Information technology, which includes computing and communications, has grown by 57 percent during the 1990s, to $866 billion.[15] In 1996 4.3 million workers were employed in information technology, at a mean wage level of 73 percent higher than that in the private sector.

Large corporations have been downsizing employment in order to maintain competitiveness. By contrast, it has been new firms in new industries that have created jobs.[16] For example, small firms between 1976

[13] Audretsch (1995). For evidence documenting the increase in job mobility across a broad spectrum of countries see Davis, Haltiwanger, and Schuh (1996a, b) and Broersma and Gautier (1997).

[14] Cited from the *United States State of Small Business*, 1997.

[15] United States Commerce, Cybernation: The Importance of the High-Technology Industry to the American Economy," Washington: U.S. Government Printing Office, 1997.

[16] The literature on job generation and firm size can be found in Davis, Haltiwanger and Schuh (1996a, b) and Carree and Klomp (1996).

and 1986 created 1.3 million new jobs in U.S. manufacturing, while the number of large manufacturing jobs actually decreased by 100,000.[17] Subsequently, between 1987 and 1992, small companies (with fewer than 500 employees) created 5.8 million new jobs in the United States. Over that same period, large companies recorded a net loss of 2.3 million jobs. Between 1980 and 1993 the 500 largest U.S. manufacturing corporations, or the Fortune 500, cut 4.7 million jobs, or one quarter of their work force. Most recently, between 1990 and 1995, firms with fewer than twenty employees experienced a 17.68 percent increase in employment, while firms with at least 500 employees experienced an increase in employment of 4.79 percent (Acs and Armington, 1998). This difference in job generation was even more pronounced in manufacturing, where employment grew by 21.25 percent in firms with fewer than 20 employees and decreased by 8.47 percent in firms with at least 500 employees.[18] The contribution of small and new firms to job generation has not escaped the attention of policy makers in the United States[19] or Europe (*European Observatory*, 1997).

The propensity for new and small firms to create the bulk of jobs is not restricted to the United States. Konings (1995) found that for the United Kingdom there is a negative relationship between job creation and plant size and a positive relationship between gross job destruction and plant size. This means that small firms are creating the bulk of new jobs in the United Kingdom (Hughes, 1993). Robson and Gallagher (1994) show that about one-third of all new employment in the United Kingdom between 1971 and 1981 was in firms with fewer than twenty employees. In the 1980s nearly one-half of all jobs were created in such small and new firms. Between 1987 and 1991 large firms in the United Kingdom were net job shedders. Small firms contributed most new employment. Hughes (1993) provides evidence suggesting that this was in part due to downsizing of the largest firms in the economy, and in part due to an actual expansion of economic activity contributed by small firms. Baldwin and Picot (1995) have found virtually identical results for Canada.[20]

A study undertaken by the EIM (Bais, Bangma and Verhoeven, 1997) found that there were 768,000 jobs lost in the Netherlands between 1990 and 1994.[21] The reason that unemployment did not drastically increase during this decade is that these job losses were more than offset by the

[17] Audretsch (1995).

[18] These job creation statistics are from the Longitudinal Establishment and Enterprise (LEEM) file of the Bureau of the Census, Department of Commerce and are calculated using the base year method. This is explained in more detail in Acs and Armington (1998).

[19] Susan Dentzer in *U.S. News and World Report* (16 August, 1993) reports that "What do Bill Clinton, George Bush and Bob Dole have in common? All have uttered one of the most enduring homilies in American political discourse: That small businesses create most of the nation's jobs."

[20] Most studies cited her deal with the manufacturing sector. Klomp and Thurik (1998) deal with very small Dutch hospitality and retail firms. They find that small firms do not outperform their larger counterparts with respect to net job creation.

[21] Taken from Table 38 (p. 84) and Figure 5 (p. 86) of Bais, Bangma and Verhoeven

creation of 973,000 new jobs, of which 44 percent came from existing establishments and 56 percent from new establishments. At the same time, new firms were responsible for only 15 percent of the job losses. Thus, new firms in the Netherlands have largely provided the net job growth of 205,000 new jobs.

As a study by Wagner (1995) shows, Germany is apparently one of the only developed industrialized countries where net job creation is not systematically and negatively related to firm size. Wagner finds that while gross job creation and destruction rates tend to decline with firm size in Germany, net job creation rates and firm size are not systematically related. However, with the exception of Germany, these two stylized facts appear to be remarkably robust – small firms have created most of the new jobs in Europe and North America.

One concern about the job creation contributed by small and new firms is that they are associated with lower wages. Some critics hold the shift towards increased entrepreneurial activity as responsible for the increased gap in incomes. The discussion above suggests that entrepreneurship can be a response to impending unemployment as well as to perceived opportunities to pursue innovative ideas. The first type of entrepreneurship tends to generate marginal firms with a low likelihood of survival and lower wages, while the second type of entrepreneurship creates new opportunities and higher wages. The standard of living generated by entrepreneurial activity will generally reflect the education and training of the individuals involved. Untrained, uneducated workers with low skill workers may be able to start new firms, but rarely the kind of firm generating stable jobs and higher wages. Virtually every western country has experienced a widening gap in the income distribution during the last decade (Houseman, 1995). But it is important to remember that entrepreneurship is not the cause of this increased gap in the income distribution. Rather, it reflects the response of individuals to the twin forces underlying the shifting comparative advantage in high-wage countries – globalization and technology.[22] The real policy issue therefore is not whether a society will become more entrepreneurial, but rather which of the two types of entrepreneurship will prevail. The policy challenge will be how to provide access to knowledge and skills for all workers, and an environment enabling them to fully utilize those abilities.

Examples of both types of entrepreneurship, even within the same country, abound. For example, by shifting economic activity to new industries, generated largely by entrepreneurial activity, Silicon Valley in California has managed to break out of the apparent tradeoff between wages and jobs presented in mature industries. The Silicon Valley mean income is 50 percent higher than that for the rest of the country. The higher standard of living has not come at the price of a reduction in employment. Employment has increased by 15,000 jobs, or 15 percent between 1992 and

[22] Clearly, the lowering of the level of taxes and that of social security benefits also plays a role.

1996 in Silicon Valley.[23] In the entrepreneurial economy there is no tradeoff between high wages and employment growth. It is possible to have both, at least in those sectors where economic activity is based on new knowledge. By contrast, self-employment in the rural areas of New England and Appalachia, which are based largely on handwork and crafts, as well as many small firms in the rural South, which are based on traditional mature industries such as textiles, have been able to maintain employment only at the cost of falling real wages.

There is a large body of consistent empirical evidence linking the size of a firm to wages. This is important because the main vehicle for entrepre5neurship is the new and small firm. Virtually every study covering a broad spectrum of time periods and OECD countries has found a positive relationship between firm size and wages.[24] However, the apparent trade-off between wages and firm size is the result of static, cross-section studies taken at a single point in time. A different picture emerges when a dynamic analysis is introduced. This dynamic analysis suggests that people start firms to pursue new but uncertain ideas. The only way they can discover if these new ideas are viable is thorough the trial-and-error experience provided by the market (Jovanovic, 1982). They subsequently learn, or discover, through experience, whether or not the idea is viable. If it is viable, the firm will survive and grow. If it is not viable, the firm stagnates and ultimately exits. An important line of research, spanning a broad spectrum of time periods and countries, supports this dynamic view of industries (Geroski, 1995). In addition, there is systematic evidence that negative relationships exist between firm age and growth, and firm size and growth, as well as positive relationships between firm size and the likelihood of survival, and firm age and the likelihood of survival (Geroski, 1995). This evidence supports the dynamic view of industries where people start firms to experiment with new ideas. Many of these new experiments fail, but some succeed, resulting in low survival rates but high growth rates of the successful new startups.

A different line of research, based on longitudinal data sets, shows that the wages and productivity of new firms increase as the firm ages (Baily, Bartelsman and Haltiwanger, 1996). Taken together, these two lines of research imply that, as new firms mature, some of the small low wage firms of today become the high wage firms of tomorrow. Similarly, some of the small low productivity firms of today become the high productivity firms of tomorrow (Baily, Bartelsman and Haltiwanger, 1996). Through growth new firms generate not just greater employment but also higher wages. The growth of new firms ensures that the greater employment does not come at a cost of lower wages but rather the opposite – higher wages.

The cross-section tradeoff between firm size and wages emerged for two reasons. First, the composition of small firms includes many enterprises that will ultimately fail. Stagnant small enterprises with no growth prospects

[23] "The Valley of Money's Delights," *The Economist*, 29 March 1997, special section, p. 1.

[24] The most cited study is that of Brown, Hamilton and Medoff (1990). See also Oosterbeek and Van Praag (1995).

typically provide low wages. Their inclusion pulls down the mean wage of small firms. Second, the higher growth rates of surviving small firms result in subsequent higher rates of productivity and wages.

5 Empirical results

As we have seen above there are many consequences of the shift from a managed economy to the entrepreneurial one. The most important question is whether, at the end of the day, the entrepreneurial economy leads to less unemployment than the managed one. We present some calculations as to whether a rise in the number of entrepreneurs, i.e., self-employed per labor force, leads to lower levels of unemployment. We use data material of 23 OECD countries including the fifteen countries of the EU-15, Iceland, Norway, Switzerland, Canada, Australia, New Zealand, Japan and US for the period 1974 through 1994. We estimate the following equation:

$$U_{94} - U_{84} = \alpha + \beta(E_{84} - E_{74}) + \gamma(U_{84} - U_{74}) \ ,$$

where U_t is the standardized number of unemployed per labor force in year t and where E_t is the number of entrepreneurs per labor force in year t. Unemployment data are from OECD (*Historical Statistics 1960–1990* and *1960–1993* and *Main Economic Indicators*), standardized is according to the *13th Conference of Labor Statistics* and entrepreneurs is from the *OECD Labor Force Statistics 1974–94* and the *Eurostat Labor Force Survey* and worked upon by EIM (1997). Long ten-year intervals are applied because a change in the number of entrepreneurs is assumed to have an influence only after a considerable period. Startup firms do not contribute to bringing down unemployment. Usually they are very small and a large number of them do not survive for more than five years. The surviving successful ones generate employment in a later phase. Our equation also includes lagged unemployment growth in order to correct for the autocorrelation of unemployment growth over time. Moreover, the change in the level of unemployment will probably affect the propensity of people to start firms. This "refuge" principle occurs most notably in periods of downturns in the business cycle. If the change in the number of unemployed is high (low) the lagged change in this number may also be high (low) due to autocorrelation. If $U_{84} - U_{74}$ is left out of the regression equation, coefficient β might become positive because of this cyclical effect. This has nothing to do with the structural effect of the rate of entrepreneurship shift influencing unemployment growth we are looking for.[25] That is why lagged unemployment growth is used in the regression equation and γ can be interpreted as the 'mean' degree of autocorrelation of unemployment growth in the 23 OECD countries.

Weighting with the number of entrepreneurs (in thousands) straightforward OLS regression yields a value of −.008 (−2.2) of α, a value of −.76 (−2.8) of β and a value of .26 (3.2) of γ. The t-statistics are between pa-

[25] See Granger (1969).

rentheses. Our main conclusion is that growth in the number of entrepreneurs leads to reduction in the rate of unemployment. Also, there appears to be a moderate autocorrelation of the rate of unemployment, since γ is in excess of zero. The negative value of the intercept is a representation of the general decline in the rate of unemployment in the period 1984 through 1994 in the 23 countries. This decline is greater if the rate of entrepreneurship increased in the preceding decade and it is moderated if unemployment increased in the preceding decade.

The other coefficients are not affected if either β or γ is set equal to zero. This implies that the "chicken and egg" effect of the "refugee" principle would not have distorted our results.

An important qualification to our results is that the data of the number of entrepreneurs across different countries are always difficult to compare since practically every country uses specific definitions. Also, they include a number of estimates. Lastly, there are many determinants of unemployment not taken into account in our analysis, which are not covered by the inclusion of effect of autocorrelation. Follow-up studies are required for corroboration of our results.[26] Still, the effect of the growth rate of entrepreneurship is found to have a negative effect on the growth rate of unemployment in the period 1994 through 1974 for 23 OECD countries. We have to conclude that, based on the findings of this exercise, there is at least some evidence suggesting that entrepreneurship contributes to the creation of new jobs and the reduction in unemployment.[27]

6 Policy implications

When the comparative advantage of a nation is based upon existing products targeting specific industries and even firms for support or promotion can be effective. Targeting specific firms in selected industries was clearly a successful policy for Japan in the post-war period and helped the Japanese achieve the comparative advantage in industries such as automobiles and electronics. Targeting outputs has also had a long tradition in Europe. As a response to *The American Challenge* in the form of "the dynamism, organization, innovation, and boldness that characterize the giant American corporations," Servan-Schreiber (1968, p. 153) prescribed an industrial policy that would undertake "the creation of large industrial units which are able both in size and management to compete with the American giants."

[26] Carree and Thurik (1999) provide an analysis showing the consequence of lagging behind in the restructuring process from large to smaller firms in manufacturing. Using a sample of 14 manufacturing industries in 13 European countries they find that, on average, the employment share of large firms in 1990 has a negative effect on growth of output in the subsequent four-year period.

[27] Complementary evidence, though not dealing with unemployment, is provided by Schmitz (1989). Schmitz presents a theoretical endogenous growth model which relates entrepreneurial activity and economic growth. He shows that an increase of the proportion of entrepreneurs in the working force leads to an increase in long-run economic growth.

Because giant corporations were thought to be needed to amass the requisite R&D resources for innovation, Servan-Schreiber (1968, p. 159) argued that "The first problem of an industrial policy for Europe consists in choosing 50 to 100 firms which, once they are large enough, would be the most likely to become world leaders of modern technology in their fields." This industrial policy prescription of targeting outputs and outcomes is echoed in the 1988 Cecchini Report to the Commission of the European Union, where the anticipated gains from European integration are measured in terms of reduced costs achieved through increases in scale economies.

How appropriate is an industrial policy of targeting outputs and outcomes in the knowledge-based economy? One has to wonder what would have happened to the United States computer and semiconductor industries had IBM been selected as a national interest around 1980 and promoted through favorable treatment as well as protected from threats like Apple Computer, Microsoft, and Intel. Would the United States have been able to shift so much economic activity and new jobs into the emerging software and semiconductor industries? While the proclamation, "What is good for General Motors is good for America" may have been sensible three decades ago, it no longer holds in the entrepreneurial knowledge-based economy.

The entrepreneurial economy is based less on the traditional inputs of natural resources, labor and capital, and more on the input of knowledge and ideas. It is no longer certain what products should be produced, how they should be produced, and by whom (Audretsch and Thurik, 1997). This increased degree of uncertainty increases the difficulty of selecting the correct outcomes and increases the likelihood that the wrong firm and industry will be targeted. Rather, the appropriate industrial policy in what Paul Krugman (1994) terms as The Age of Uncertainty is to target inputs, and in particular those inputs involved in the creation and commercialization of knowledge. Such policies involve basic and applied research at universities and research institutes, investments in the general level of education as well as advanced technical specialties, and the training and upgrading of the skill levels of workers. The entrepreneurial economy calls for polices that create an environment, or what the Germans call the *Rahmenbedingungen*, facilitating the creation and commercialization of knowledge.

When the comparative advantage is based on large corporations exploiting scale economies in production and R&D, the major public policy emphasis is constraining the market power of large corporation. On the one hand, the large corporation is essential for efficient production. But on the other hand, such a large concentration of economic assets poses a threat not just to the market process but even to democracy.[28] The resulting social partnership in virtually every developed country has involved unions, government and the large corporations. At the heart of this social partnership was constraining the power of large corporations.

In the knowledge-based entrepreneurial economy the relevant policy question shifts away from "How can governments constrain firms from

[28] Usually, this is referred to as the "anti trust dilemma".

abusing their market power?" to "How can governments create an environment fostering the success and viability of firms?" The major issues in the entrepreneurial economy have shifted away from concerns about excess profits and abuses of market dominance to international competitiveness, growth and employment.

As the waves of small start-ups in knowledge-based industries demonstrate, the link between success and market power has been broken. The appropriate response for government policies is to shift away from constraining policies to policies of enabling and stimulation. Policies that channel finance to potential entrepreneurs who would like to try out new ideas are essential. The deficiency of venture capital and informal capital has impeded the restructuring of economic activities out of the traditional industries where Europe has a competitive disadvantage and into new knowledge-based industries that are compatible with both high employment and high wages. In 1994 only about five percent of European venture capital was allocated towards start-up companies. In the United States about 70 percent of venture capital is invested in high-technology startups, while only about 30 percent of venture capital in the Netherlands is devoted towards high-tech.[29] As a result, equity investment in small firms in new industries is slow to develop in Europe. Bright men and women with good ideas have a hard time finding start-up finance.[30]

Other policies include de-emphasizing penalties associated with new-firm failures, an increased flexibility of the labor force and increased access to research and development results undertaken at universities and national research institutes. The downsizing of the federal agencies charged with the regulation of business in the United States and Great Britain has been interpreted by many economists as the eclipse of government intervention. But to interpret deregulation and privatization as the end of industrial policy ignores an important shift in the locus and target of government industrial policy (Van Bergijk and Haffner, 1996). The last decade has seen the emergence of a set of enabling policy initiatives that fall outside of the jurisdiction of the traditional regulatory agencies. Sternberg (1996) shows how the success of a number of different high-technology clusters spanning a number of developed countries is the direct result of enabling policies.[31] This support has generally provided diversified technology development involving a mix of activities encompassing a broad spectrum of industrial

[29] Statistics provided by Sander Balje of the Netherlands Ministry of Economic Affairs.

[30] According to Helmuth Guembel, who is the research director of the Gartner Group in Munich, "Put Bill Gates in Europe and it just wouldn't have worked out." "German Innovation: No Bubbling Brook," *The Economist*, 10 September, 1994, pp.75–76.

[31] For example, the Advanced Research Program in Texas has provided support for basic research and the strengthening of the university infrastructure, which played a central role in developing a high-tech cluster around Austin (Feller, 1997). The Thomas Edison Centers in Ohio, the Advanced Technology Centers in New Jersey, and the Centers for Advanced Technology at Case Western Reserve University, Rutgers University and the University of Rochester have supported generic, precompetitive research.

collaborators spanning technology-intensive multinational corporations and new-firm startups.

References

Acs ZJ, Armington C (1998) Longitudinal establishment and enterprise microdata (LEEM) documentation. Center for Economic Studies, Bureau of the Census, Washington

Audretsch DB (1995) Innovation and industry evolution. MIT Press, Cambridge

Audretsch DB, Thurik AR (1997) Sources of growth: the entrepreneurial versus the managed economy. Tinbergen Institute discussion paper TI 97-109/3, Erasmus University Rotterdam

Audretsch DB, Feldman MP (1996) Knowledge spillovers and the geography of innovation. American Economic Review 86(3): 630–640

Audretsch DB, Stephan PE (1996) Company-scientist links: the case of biotechnology. The American Economic Review 86(3): 631–640

Baily MN, Bartelsman EJ, Haltiwanger J (1996) Downsizing and productivity growth: myth or reality? Small Business Economics 8(4): 159–178

Bais J, Bangma KL, Verhoeven WHJ (1997) Het belang van bedrijfstypen voor de werkgelegenheidsontwikkeling. EIM, Zoetermeer

Baldwin J, Picot G (1995) Employment generation by small producers in the Canadian manufacturing sector. Small Business Economics 7(4): 317–331

Berman E, Bound J, Machin S (1997) Implications of skill-biased technological change: international evidence. Working paper 6166, National Bureau of Economic Research (NBER)

Brock WA, Evans DS (1989) Small business economics. Small Business Economics 1(1): 7–20

Broersma L, Gautier P (1997) Job creation and job destruction by small firms: an empirical investigation for the Dutch manufacturing sector. Small Business Economics 9(3): 211–224

Brown C, Hamilton J, Medoff J (1990) Employers large and small. Harvard University Press, Cambridge

Carree MA (1997) Market dynamics, evolution and smallness. Ph.D. series, Tinbergen Institute Research Series, Erasmus University Rotterdam

Carree M, Thurik AR (1999) Industrial structure and economic growth. In: Audretsch DB, Thurik AR (eds) Innovation, industry evolution and economic performance. Cambridge University Press, Cambridge (forthcoming)

Carree M, Klomp L (1996) Small business and job creation: a comment. Small Business Economics 8(4): 317–322

Davis SJ, Haltiwanger J, Schuh S (1996a) Job creation and destruction in U.S. manufacturing. MIT Press, Cambridge

Davis SJ, Haltiwanger J, Schuh S (1996b) Small business and job creation: dissecting the myth and reassessing the facts. Small Business Economics 8(4): 259–278

Dumort A, Dryden J (eds) (1997) The economics of the information society. The Commission of the European Community, Brussels

EIM (1997) Het belang van bedrijfstypen voor de werkgelgenheidsontwikkeling. EIM, Zoetermeer

European Observatory for SMEs: Fifth Annual Report (1997) EIM, Zoetermeer

Feller I (1997) Federal and state government roles in science and technology. Economic Development Quarterly 11(4): 283–296

Geroski PA (1995) What do we know about entry? International Journal of Industrial Organization 13: 421–440

Granger CWJ (1969) Investigating causal relations by econometric models and cross-spectral methods. Econometrica 37: 424–438

Houseman SN (1995) Job growth and the quality of jobs in the U.S. economy. Working paper 95-39, Upjohn Institute

Hughes A (1993) Industrial concentration and small firms in the United Kingdom: the 1980s in historical perspective. In: Acs Z, Audretsch DB (eds) Small firms and entrepreneurship: an east-west perspective, pp 15–37. Cambridge University Press, Cambridge

Jovanovic B (1982) Selection and evolution of industry. Econometrica 50(2): 649–670

Klomp L, Thurik AR (1998) Job flows in traditional services. In: Acs Z, Carlsson B, Karlson C (eds) Entrepreneurship, small and medium-sized enterprises and the macro economy. Cambridge University Press, Cambridge (forthcoming)

Koedijk K, Kremers JJM (1996) Market opening, regulation and growth in Europe. Economic Policy: a European Forum, pp 443–460

Konings J (1995) Gross job flows and the evolution of size in U.K. establishments. Small Business Economics 7(3): 213–220

Kortum S, Lerner J (1997) Stronger protection or technological revolution: what is behind the recent surge in patenting? Working paper 6204, National Bureau of Economic Research (NBER), Cambridge

Krugman P (1994) The age of uncertainty. MIT Press, Cambridge

Loveman G, Sengenberger W (1991) The re-emergence of small-scale production: an international perspective. Small Business Economics 3(1): 1–38

OECD (1996a) The knowledge based economy. OECD, Paris

OECD (1996b) SMEs: Employment, innovation and growth. OECD, Paris

OECD (1997) Employment outlook. OECD, Paris

Oosterbeek H, van Praag M (1995) Firm-size wage differentials in the Netherlands. Small Business Economics 7(3): 173–182

Robson GB, Gallagher CC (1994) Change in the size distribution of UK firms. Small Business Economics 6(4): 299–312

Schumpeter JA (1911) Theorie der wirtschaftlichen Entwicklung. Eine Untersuchung über Unternehmergewinn, Kapital, Kredit, Zins und den Konjunkturzyklus. Duncker und Humblot, Berlin

Schumpeter JA (1942) Capitalism, socialism and democracy. Harper and Row, New York

Servan-Schreiber J-J (1968) The American challenge. Hamish Hamilton, London

Schmitz JA (1989) Imitation, entrepreneurship, and long-run growth. Journal of Political Economy 97: 721–739

Sternberg R (1996) Technology policies and the growth of regions. Small Business Economics 8(2): 75–86

Storey DJ (1991) The birth of new firms: does unemployment matter? A review of the evidence. Small Business Economics 3(3): 167–179

Thurik AR (1996) Small firms, entrepreneurship and economic growth. In: Acs Z, Carlsson B, Thurik AR (eds) Small business in the modern economy, pp 126–152. Basil Blackwell Publishers, Oxford

United States Commerce (1997) Cybernation: The importance of the high-technology industry to the American economy. U.S. Government Printing Office, Washington

Van Bergeijk PAG, Haffner RCG (1997) Privatization, deregulation, and the macroeconomy: measurement, modelling, and policy. Edward Elgar, Cheltenham

Wagner J (1995) Firm size and job creation in Germany. Small Business Economics 7(6): 469–474

Wennekers S, Thurik R (1999) Linking entrepreneurship and economic growth. Small Business Economics (forthcoming)

Capitalism and democracy in the 21st century: a Kaleckian interpretation of a Schumpeterian problem

Douglas Mair[1], Anthony J. Laramie[2]

[1] School of Management, Heriot-Watt University, Riccarton, Edinburgh, EH 14 4AT, UK (e-mail: d.mair@hw.ac.uk)
[2] Merrimack College, Merrimack, MA 01845, USA

Abstract. The paper reinterprets Schumpeter's views on the dynamic effects of taxation, as originally expressed in *Crisis of the Tax State*, from a Kaleckian perspective. In light of Schumpeter's rejection of Keynesian and Marshallian approaches to taxation, the paper argues that a recently developed Kaleckian approach provides an appropriate basis from which to analyse the effects on the business cycle of balanced changes in the structure of taxation. It is shown that, under certain shifting assumptions, increases in the taxation of wages or profits will stimulate investment and attenuate the amplitude of the business cycle. Ultimately, the shifting of taxes reduces to a conflict over income shares. The changing distribution of income in the United Kingdom in recent years suggests that investment is likely to remain sluggish unless there is a significant reversal of income shares. This may give rise to increasing economic and political tensions into the 21st century.

Key words: Schumpeter – Kalecki – Business cycles – Dynamic tax effects – Income distribution

JEL-classification: H22, H30

1 Introduction

In the closing years of World War II, three of the great economists of the 20th century set out their visions of post-war society. The most apocalyptic was Hayek (1944) in *Road to Serfdom* who saw the extended collectivism

---

Paper presented at the 1998 World Conference of the International Joseph A. Schumpeter Society, Vienna, June 13–16, 1998.

towards which the free nations were moving as incompatible with democracy. The social planning of that time, based on what he considered to be fallacious economic ideas, would, he thought, eventually destroy all political and economic freedoms and return society to a state of mediaeval serfdom. Schumpeter (1943) in *Capitalism, Socialism and Democracy*, also presaged the demise of capitalism, its essential driving force being strangled under the weight of increasing bureaucracy, although he was more optimistic than Hayek about the viability of socialism. And Kalecki (1943) was of the opinion that even if governments had the means of achieving full employment, the class interests of business would prevent it from happening. Of the three, it is arguably Hayek who has had the greatest influence.

Our purpose in this paper, however, is to look forward into the 21st century rather than back over the 20th. We do so by bringing together ideas from Schumpeter and Kalecki on the role of taxation and fiscal policy. Both men had at early stages of their careers arrived at quite profound insights on taxation, Schumpeter (1918) in *Crisis of the Tax State* and Kalecki (1937) in *A Theory of Commodity, Income and Capital Taxation*. Neither man, however, developed his insights beyond an initial stage. But, by extending and integrating them, we arrive at conclusions we think may have important implications for the future of capitalism, at least in the United Kingdom.

2 Exorcising Keynes

Before we proceed to the main argument of the paper, there is a spectre that must be exorcised and that is Keynes. Macroeconomic policy is considered to comprise either monetary policy or fiscal policy or some rather uneasy combination of the two. Macroeconomic fiscal policy is conceived exclusively in Keynesian terms. This is, in our opinion, what we term a synedochic[1] fallacy.

We have shown (Laramie, 1991; Laramie and Mair, 1996, 1997) that it is possible to develop a macroeconomic theory of taxation which derives from Kalecki's (1937) *aperçu* that the publication of *The General Theory* (Keynes, 1936) required a whole new approach to the study of taxation. While Kalecki himself never developed his theory beyond a simple short-period closed economy model, his insight is, we think, of profound significance, although it has never been recognised as such by the overwhelming majority of the profession, not even by post Keynesians. By integrating Kalecki's theories of taxation, income determination, income distribution, investment and business cycle, we have developed a macroeconomic theory of taxation that is *non-Keynesian* in a number of important respects.

Important non-Keynesian aspects of Kaleckian theory include explicit dynamics, a distinction between investment orders and investment outlays and, most significantly, income distribution. As we shall see later in the paper, tax-induced changes in the distribution of income and the reactions thereby generated are extremely important. Keynes implicitly espoused the marginal productivity theory of income distribution, failing to appreciate that it is a theory which holds, if at all, only at full employment (Rothschild,

1961). Kalecki developed his own rather controversial 'degree of monopoly' theory of income distribution, a consequence of which is that, contrary to Keynesian theory, real wages are determined in the product market and not in the labour market.

In terms of tax theory, the two major features of our Kaleckian formulation which distinguish it from orthodox neoclassical theory are: (i) its micro- and macroeconomic elements are properly integrated, unlike orthodox theory, (Kriesler, 1996; Musgrave, 1997); and (ii) it is dynamic, unlike orthodox theory (Stern, 1992; Laramie and Mair, 1998).

Schumpeter's rejection of Keynesian economics is well known (Schumpeter, 1954, pp. 1143–1144). Schumpeter emphasised not only the importance but also the difficulty of developing dynamic theory. It was not enough to add dynamic qualifications to static theory and this is why Schumpeter rejected Keynes. The Keynesian system, according to Schumpeter, was macrostatic and Keynes's assumptions of unchanging amounts of industrial equipment and methods of production precluded technological change – 'the essence of the capitalist process' – thereby excluding the salient features of capitalist reality. This was anathema to Schumpeter.

3 Framework for Schumpeter's tax theory

In order to evaluate Schumpeter's ideas on fiscal policy, it is necessary to establish a theoretical framework within which to operate. Schumpeter rejected the prevailing paradigms but did not develop himself a coherent alternative. The Keynesian paradigm he rejected as macrostatic. He also rejected Marshallian partial equilibrium analysis as irrelevant to an understanding of the dynamic consequences of taxation (Schumpeter, 1939, p. 47 and pp. 710–712). Thus, he left a discussion of the role of fiscal policy in influencing the amplitude and structure of the business cycle as one of the self-confessed 'glaring lacunae' in *Business Cycles*. This lacuna can be filled, we think, by interpreting Schumpeter in a non-Keynesian, non-Marshallian (i.e. Kaleckian) framework. We do not presume to speculate whether or not Schumpeter would have welcomed this association with Kalecki.

Is it possible to interpret Schumpeter willy-nilly within the framework of a dynamic Kaleckian macroeconomic theory of taxation? We feel there are a sufficient number of basic similarities between Schumpeter's and Kalecki's views of economics for this to be considered seriously. Each belonged to the early 20th century Continental tradition of business cycle theoreticians; each had a vision of capitalism as dominated by large monopolistic firms; each had a vision of the importance of dynamics and the irrelevance of static equilibrium; each was sceptical of the relevance of neoclassical microeconomic theorising.

More specifically, the effect of the correction by Gomulka, Ostaszewski and Davies (hereafter GOD) of Kalecki's growth theory has been to render Kalecki's theory essentially Schumpeterian (GOD, 1990, p. 526). Essentially, in his growth theory, Kalecki had concentrated on conditions of 'cautious' capitalism when, either investors react slowly to changes in profitability or the rate of innovation is low and/or the response of investors to innovation is weak. He did not develop his theory sufficiently to say anything specific about the properties of the rate of innovation-induced investment. However, by generalizing Kalecki's growth theory to encompass situations of 'rash' capitalism, GOD have provided a mathematical formulation of what they call Kalecki's Growth Proposition that 'technological innovation is good for employment'. It is this, they argue, that brings Kalecki and Schumpeter close together.

In *Crisis of the Tax State*, Schumpeter expressed serious concerns about the dynamic effects of taxation. However, because of the lack of a properly developed analytical framework, he never fully worked these out. *Crisis of the Tax State* is generally interpreted as an essay in fiscal sociology (Musgrave, 1992). But it also contains the essential elements of Schumpeter's views on the dynamic effects of taxation. The two passages from *Crisis of the Tax State* in which Schumpeter set out his concerns read:

".....Entrepreneurial profit proper ... arises in the capitalist economy whenever a new method of production, a new commercial combination or a new form of organisation is introduced... As it arises continuously so it disappears continuously through the effect of competition which, baited by profit, follows up immediately on the entrepreneur. *If this process were taxed away, that element of the economic process would be lacking which at present is by far the most important individual motive towards economic progress. Even if taxation merely reduced this profit, industrial development would progress considerably more slowly....*" (Schumpeter, 1918, p. 22, emphasis added).

and

".....the tax [on interest and wages] cannot penetrate too deeply into the tax object. Since we are here considering taxation of all forms of capital yield and wages, we need not worry about a shift of capital and labour into alternative uses. And since we are dealing here with a problem common to all tax states, with a problem of the system and not of a particular tax state, we shall disregard also the tendency of labour and capital to migrate to countries of lower taxation........ But even so there are still two reactions which occur with capital and labour. *Insofar as they result in higher interest and wages which entrepreneurs have to pay, taxes counteract the expansion of production which would have occurred without them. Insofar, however, as these taxes are a charge on the income of the capitalists or the workers, they may even result in more saving and more work than without them.* But such cases are rare exceptions for capital and significant only for labour only if the working day was relatively short prior to the imposition of the tax. *In all other cases, capital formation is paralysed and may even turn into capital consumption through lack of amortization and repairs*" (Schumpeter, 1918, p. 23, emphasis added).

In these two passages, Schumpeter is expressing his concern over what might be called the 'dynamic' excess burden of taxes on entrepreneurial profits, interest and wages. However, he also recognised that quite different effects would follow if the taxes were shifted. As we shall see, it is the social and economic significance of tax shifting that gives rise to our concerns for the future of capitalism in the 21st century, at least in the United Kingdom.

4 Kaleckian tax theory

We now demonstrate how, in a Kaleckian model, taxation can effect the amplitude of the business cycle (Laramie and Mair, 1996). Kalecki focused on private sector fixed capital investment as the source of cyclical fluctuations. We simplify and generalise Kalecki's (1971/1968) theory of the business cycle while losing none of its essential ingredients. Our principal refinements are (i) to introduce government purchases and taxation into Kalecki's analysis; and (ii) to drop the autonomous element of capitalists' consumption from the analysis and replace it with a variant of Weintraub's (1979, 1981) consumption coefficient as developed by Laramie (1991).

Kalecki (1971/1968, p. 171) considered three determinants of new investment decisions: (i) entrepreneurial savings, E; (ii) the prerequisites for the reinvestment of these savings; and (iii) an innovation factor. Whether entrepreneurial savings are reinvested depends on the relationship between the actual level of investment, I, and investment that yields the standard (or 'normal') rate of profits, $I(\pi)$. The extent to which the difference $I - I(\pi)$ has an impact on investment decisions depends on r, 'the intensity of the reaction of entrepreneurs' (Kalecki, 1971/1968, pp. 172). To this is added innovations-induced investment decisions which he represented (Kalecki, 1971/1968, p. 173) as B(t), 'a semi-autonomous function, changing slowly over time'.

Kalecki's equation for investment decisions, D, is:

$$D = E + r(I(\pi) - I) + B(t) \qquad (1)$$

He expressed the rate of investment that generates the standard rate of profits as:

$$I(\pi) = [n\Delta P + \omega(Y - P)]/\pi; \qquad (2)$$

where n is the proportion of new 'real' profits generated by $I(\pi)$; ΔP are the new 'real' profits; $\omega(Y - P)$ measures the loss in profits to existing equipment as a consequence of the gain in productivity/profitability from investment in new equipment and is assumed to be proportional to the difference between national income, Y, and aggregate profits, P; π is the rate of profit on new equipment.

To introduce taxation into Kalecki's theory, we rewrite Eq. (2) by expressing national income as a function of profits in the following way. We follow Kalecki by arguing that businesses set markups over prime costs to cover overhead costs and attain profits. In aggregate, profits are largely determined by capitalists' spending decisions, independently of pricing decisions. Pricing decisions, as reflected in business markups, help to determine wages' share of national income. Given injections of capitalist spending and the resulting level of profits, the *level* of national income is determined by the wage bill that is generated by wages' *share* of national income. Taxation is introduced by recognising that total taxes are a function of both the pre-tax wage bill and of profits.

We write national income as:

$$Y = P(1 - t_w)/(1 - t_\pi)(1 - t_w - \alpha); \qquad (3)$$

where t_w is the tax rate on wages; t_π is the tax rate on profits; and α is the wage share. Equation (3) is important because it shows that in a Kaleckian framework, the tax system influences the relationship between profits and national income (i) directly, through taxation of wages and profits; and (ii) indirectly, through the level of profits and the wage share. Laramie (1991) modified Kalecki's expression of the wage share by accounting for taxes on wages. A tax on wages reduces the after-tax wage share by a factor equal to t_w, the rate of tax on wages.

Thus, the after-tax share of wages can be written as:

$$\alpha = (1 - t_w)[(k - 1)(1 + j) + 1]; \tag{4}$$

where k is the markup; and j is the ratio of material costs to the pre-tax wage bill.

By substituting Eq. (3) into Eq. (2), $I(\pi)$ can be written as:

$$I(\pi) = [n\Delta P + \delta P]/\pi; \tag{2$'$}$$

where

$$\delta = \omega[\alpha + t\pi(1 - t_w - \alpha)]/(1 - t_\pi)(1 - t_w - \alpha);$$

δ is the rate of depreciation in the sense that it represents the rate at which profits are lost to existing capital equipment as the result of technical progress.

Following Kalecki by translating investment decisions in time period t into investment expenditures in $t + \tau$, so that $D_t = I_{t+\tau}$, Eq. (1) is rewritten as:

$$I_{t+\tau} = \lambda P_t + r(\{[n\Delta P_t + \delta P_t]/\delta\} - I_t) + B(t); \tag{1$'$}$$

where λ is the fraction of total after-tax profits which is saved by entrepreneurs.

The Kaleckian investment function specified in Eq. (1′) provides the basis from which to examine the impact of the tax system on the business cycle, assuming a balanced budget constraint. The impact of taxation is through two channels (i) δ; and (ii) the level of profits. We concentrate on how taxation affects δ and thus investment and the business cycle as this is the essentially 'Schumpeterian' part of our story.

The impact of taxation on δ is by affecting the real tax bill associated with old equipment. Technical progress, through new investment, results in productivity gains to new equipment which, *ceteris paribus*, result in lower prices. This increases the real costs and lowers the real profits associated with existing equipment. The decline in real profits to existing equipment accelerates its obsolescence. Thus, an *increase* in the rate of tax on profits will *increase* δ, given the rate of technical progress. An increase in taxation may also have a positive effect on the level of profits through the operation of a balanced budget multiplier effect.

5 Kalecki and rational expectations

These results are, of course, counter-intuitive. Keynes, in his capacity as editor of the *Economic Journal*, recognised this difficulty for Kalecki.

During correspondence between them prior to the publication of Kalecki's paper *A Theory of Commodity, Income and Capital Taxation* in the *Economic Journal* in 1937, Keynes wrote:

"If the capitalists assume that their income subject to tax will remain the same, the effect of the tax will surely be to reduce their spending. *It is only if they have read your article and are convinced by it* that their profit will rise by the amount of the tax that they will maintain their spending as before" (Moggridge, 1983, p. 791, emphasis added).

Keynes's comment may be seen as an anticipation of Muth's (1961) well-known statement that expectations, since they are predictions of future events, *are essentially predictions of the relevant theory*. Kalecki, however, rejected any rational expectations interpretation of his paper and replied to Keynes:

"Much more difficult is the question of my assumption about the behaviour of the capitalists immediately following the introduction of the tax. *I do not think they must necessarily read my article in order not to curtail at once their expenditure on consumption and investment. ... I think however that capitalists' consumption is rather insensitive to expectation: and that it is only the actual fall of their income which can compel them – and this is often only with a time lag – to reduce their standard of living*" (Moggridge, 1983, p. 793, emphasis added).

In a Kaleckian tax model, even if capitalists have formed the theoretically *incorrect* expectation that their incomes will fall after the introduction of a tax, they cannot immediately reduce their investment because it is the result of previous investment decisions which require a certain time period for completion. If, as a Kaleckian model predicts, capitalists' expectation of a fall in income is *not* confirmed, then they will make no adjustment to their expenditure. The *rational* decision for capitalists to make is the one based on their *actual* experience of any change in taxation. Kalecki's expectations hypothesis may be interpreted as rational, in a Muthian sense, but rational in a nonergodic world, as opposed to rational in the ergodic world of mainstream economics.

6 Kaleckian tax theory and the business cycle

With this in mind, we now consider how changes in either t_w or t_π affect π for two cases: (i) with no tax shifting; and (ii) with tax shifting. We define tax shifting by reference to changes in the markup, k. In the no tax shifting case, k is constant with respect to changes in t_w and t_π; in the tax shifting case, we assume an inverse relationship between k and changes in t_w, and a positive relationship between k and changes in t_π (Laramie and Mair, 1996, pp. 455–456).

With no tax shifting:

(i) an increase in t_w simultaneously increases the surplus (i.e. aggregate profits plus tax receipts) and reduces the basic Kaleckian income multiplier, $1/(1 - \alpha)$, causing Y and δ to remain *constant*:

(ii) an increase in t_π causes the surplus to expand but leaves the basic income multiplier constant, thereby increasing Y relative to P and *increasing* δ.

With tax shifting:

(i) an increase in t_w dampens the change in the basic income multiplier. Thus, the impact on national income of the increase in the surplus is less than fully offset by the reduction in the basic income multiplier and, therefore, an increase in t_w *increases* δ:

(ii) an increase in t_π results in a fall in the basic income multiplier which dampens the increase in Y and *dampens* the increase in δ.

Having demonstrated that a change in δ affects the level of new investment, we now show taxation will affect the level of investment and the structure of the business cycle (Laramie and Mair, 1996, pp. 457–459). We derive the following expression for the business cycle:

$$I_{t+\tau} - y_{t+\tau} = (q' - r)(I_t - y_t) + s'[(1 - \alpha)\Delta(I_t - y_t)]; \tag{5}$$

where y = the trend value of I, $q' = [[\lambda(1 - \alpha) + (r/\pi)\delta]/(1 - a\alpha)]$; $s' = (r/\pi)n/(1 - a\alpha)$, a = Weintraub's consumption coefficient[2].

As we are focusing our discussion in this paper on the impact of taxation on the business cycle, we assume that the trend level of investment is zero[3]. Therefore, $y_{t+\tau}$ drops out of equation (5). The impact of taxation on future investment is channelled through q', s' and α (the wage share). As can be seen from Eq. (5), δ enters via q'.

The impact of taxation on the business cycle in a Kaleckian model can be shown to depend on three things: (i) the cyclical variation in investment; (ii) the change in the cyclical variation in investment; and (iii) three parameter shift effects (a) a depreciation effect, (b) a distribution effect and (c) a tax shifting effect. Thus, the effects of taxation on the business cycle depend critically on knowing (i) the stage of the cycle at which the economy happens to be; (ii) the long-run trend of investment; (iii) the direction of tax policy; and (iv) the process and degree of tax shifting. The extent of tax shifting, which operates through changes in business mark-ups, is absolutely critical in determining the impact of taxation on the business cycle.

With no tax shifting:

(i) a change in t_w *has no effect on* δ and operates on investment and the structure of the business cycle through a distribution effect: an increase (decrease) in t_w dampens (heightens) the amplitude of the business cycle.

(ii) a change in t_π *increases* δ but has no distribution effect: an increase (decrease) in t_π heightens (dampens) the amplitude of the business cycle.

With tax shifting:

(iii) a change in t_w *increases* δ and the level of profits: an increase (decrease) in t_w heightens (dampens) the amplitude of the business cycle relative to the no tax shifting case.

(iv) a change in t_π *reduces* δ and the level of profits: an increase (decrease) in t_π dampens (heightens) the amplitude of the business cycle relative to the no tax shifting case.

Thus, tax shifting has a fundamental effect. In our opinion, two important sets of implications follow from this analysis. The first is that taxation and fiscal policy can modify the very nature of capitalism; and the second is that the incidence and effects of changes in the structure of taxation can have a major impact on the structure of the business cycle.

7 Schumpeterian implications of Kaleckian tax theory

What 'Schumpeterian' implications may be drawn from these conclusions? The conventional Keynesian macroeconomic role for fiscal policy is stabilisation, i.e., the use of changes in taxation and/or government spending to smooth out cyclical fluctuations in aggregate activity. But as we have already stated, in this paper we are eschewing any Keynesian influence. We expressly assume throughout a balanced budget stance. Government budget surpluses or deficits, therefore, play no part in the stabilisation process.

In the 'Schumpeter-Kalecki' world of this paper, (de)stabilisation is achieved by altering the structure of taxation as between taxation of wages and taxation of profits. The effects operate through the channels we have identified above. In a 'non-Keynesian' world, it is appropriate to ask what is the macroeconomic objective of fiscal policy. A 'Schumpeterian' fiscal objective, presumably, would be to reinforce the 'perennial gale of creative destruction' by stimulating investment and attenuating rather than dampening the amplitude of the business cycle. This could be achieved in either of the scenarios (ii) or (iii) we identify above.

A (non-shifted) increase in t_π will operate through δ and have the effect of reducing the after tax real profits of existing equipment, thereby accelerating its replacement by new lower cost technologically superior equipment. A (shifted) increase in t_w which will increase δ, again adversely affecting the real after-tax profits of existing equipment, and heightening the amplitude of the business cycle. The faster the rate of innovations-induced investment, the more rapid the deterioration in the profitability of existing equipment. So, contrary to using tax increases to *stabilise* the economy, a 'Schumpeter-Kalecki' approach could use tax increases to *de-stabilise* the economy.

Would this be a problem for Schumpeter? In *Business Cycles* (Schumpeter, 1939, pp. 711–712) he saw the principal fiscal problem of the time not with the revenues required by the modern state but rather that these revenues must be raised:

"...by heavy taxes framed not only with a view to minimum disturbance but, regardless of disturbance, in some cases even with a view to maximising it".

The most important effect of these 'heavy taxes' was on the sum total of private savings and investment:

"...as far as this goes, therefore, our opinion on how such taxes will affect 'progress' and 'industrial efficiency' depends on where we stand in the controversy about the importance and modus operandi of private saving".

Schumpeter gave no indication in *Business Cycles* where he himself stood on the savings controversy. In a Kaleckian world, capitalists' investment and consumption decisions determine profits. Because Kalecki assumed that workers do not save, savings out of profits influence the availability of finance. Savings are then forced to adjust to the level of investment. As we show above, there can be circumstances under which 'heavy taxes' will promote 'progress' and 'industrial efficiency'. It seems to us that this is a role for taxation and fiscal policy that Schumpeter would have endorsed.

Our analysis identifies two 'Schumpeterian' scenarios under which changes in the structure of taxation will stimulate investment through the Kaleckian depreciation effect and attenuate the amplitude of the business cycle. The first is a (non-shifted) increase in the profits tax, t_π. In the United States in the 1980s, major changes were introduced in the tax treatment of business fixed investment with a view to stimulating investment. An extensive neoclassical research programme has sought to establish the effect on investment of changes in investment tax incentives but has found evidence of little impact, either on investment or on its share of GDP. None of this literature, however, considered the incidence effects of taxation on investment. Using a Kaleckian model of tax incidence of the kind discussed in this paper, Laramie et al. (Laramie, Mair, Miller and Stratopoulos, 1997) find that in the United States over the period 1983–1993 the effects of changes in *average wages tax rates* on gross private non-residential fixed investment swamped those of changes in *average profits tax rates*. This result confirms the conclusion that when considering the effectiveness of tax incidence, the economic incidence of taxation must be explicitly considered.

This apparent ineffectiveness of investment tax incentives in the United States points to the significance of changes in the wages tax, t_w, in influencing investment. The US study of Laramie et al. indicates that changes in t_w have a much more direct effect on investment than changes in t_π. If that is so, then there are two circumstances in which a change in t_w will have a positive effect on investment and heighten the amplitude of the business cycle. The first is the 'Schumpeterian' scenario identified in (iii) above in which a (shifted) *increase* in t_w will achieve this effect through an *increase* in δ. The second is the 'non-Schumpeterian' scenario identified in (i) above where a (non-shifted) change in t_w has *no effect* on δ and operates instead on investment and the structure of the business cycle through changes in income distribution. In this scenario, a *reduction* in t_w will heighten the amplitude of the business cycle.

If we focus on the 'Schumpeterian' scenario (iii), for this to have the desired effect requires wage earners to be able to recover fully any increase in t_w. In other words, the markup, k, will have to fall by an amount sufficient to restore wage earners to their (pre-wage tax increase) level of real wages.

In Kaleckian theory, k reflects the 'degree of monopoly' and the wage share, α, is expressed as $1/k$[4]. Following Reynolds (1983, 1996), we use the

Table 1. Income shares, propensity to consume and investment in the UK, 1980–1996

Year	Ratio of profit:wage income	Propensity to consume out of wage income	Wage share	Manufacturing investment at 1990 prices (£ million)
1980	0.356	0.438	0.685	12,307
1981	0.369	0.445	0.684	9,985
1982	0.387	0.459	0.667	9,518
1983	0.402	0.475	0.650	9,413
1984	0.424	0.466	0.646	10,975
1985	0.423	0.473	0.639	12,170
1986	0.430	0.507	0.647	12,097
1987	0.435	0.561	0.638	12,641
1988	0.453	0.613	0.639	13,846
1989	0.457	0.596	0.645	14,984
1990	0.450	0.575	0.659	14,227
1991	0.445	0.567	0.669	12,803
1992	0.466	0.548	0.661	11,828
1993	0.466	0.597	0.642	11,230
1994	0.462	0.649	0.629	11,997
1995	0.505	0.640	0.627	13,181
1996	0.510	0.645	0.623	12,442

Sources: Laramie, Mair and Toporowski (op.cit), *Economic Trends 1997*, The Stationery Office

term 'degree of monopoly' to refer to those institutional and environmental influences which affect firms' pricing decisions. Kalecki (1954) listed a number of factors as causes of changes in the 'degree of monopoly', including industry concentration, expenditures on advertising and sales promotion and the bargaining power of trade unions. Observing a rise in markups, Kalecki argued that trade unions would seek to negotiate an increase in wages and their ability to do so would act as a constraint on the size of k. Therefore, the extent to which scenario (iii) will operate depends on what happens to markups and, consequently, to the distribution of income. Only with fully restored real wages will scenario (iii) achieve its 'Schumpeterian' objective. Bottom line, the attainment of a t_w-induced stimulus to investment via δ reduces to a conflict over income shares. Only if the wage share is rising will a rise in t_w lead to an increase in investment and an attenuation of the business cycle.

Laramie, Mair and Toporowski (forthcoming) show that in the United Kingdom since the mid-1970s there has been a substantial increase in the ratio of non-employment income: employment income. Defining these crudely as 'profits' (non-employment income) and 'wages' (employment income), the UK evidence shows a substantial fall in the share of 'wages' since 1980. This fall in the wage share is the obverse of changes in aggregate k (GDP/wages). From a level of around 1.45 in 1980, aggregate k has risen to around 1.6 in the mid-1990s. From a 'Schumpeter-Kalecki' perspective this decline in the wage share does not augur well for investment and so it transpires. In 1990 prices, fixed capital investment in manufacturing industry in the UK is virtually the same in 1996 as it was in 1980. Data supporting these conclusions are given in Table 1.

8 Conclusion

In the United Kingdom, as we approach the millennium, economic policy may be described as 'new monetarism' (Arestis and Sawyer, 1998). 'Old monetarism' was characterised by a belief that inflation was caused by an excessive growth of the money supply, that the private sector was essentially stable and tended to operate at the 'natural rate of unemployment' and that Say's Law operated. 'New monetarism' adds 'rational expectations', rapid market clearing, a belief that financial markets know best and a conclusion that full employment will be the norm. This 'new monetarism' shares a belief in NAIRU with new Keynesianism. Fiscal policy is downgraded and plays second fiddle to monetary policy.

The rules for the conduct of fiscal policy into the 21st century have been set out in the Code for Fiscal Stability (HM Treasury, 1998). These have been established in order to ensure that future British governments will always set policy in ways which promote economic stability. The Code for Fiscal Stability enshrines the two cardinal rules which will henceforth determine fiscal policy:

- the golden rule: over the economic cycle the government will borrow only to invest and not to fund current expenditure; and
- public debt as a proportion of national income will be held over the cycle at a stable and prudent level.

The intention of these rules is to establish a sound long-term basis for fiscal policy. Their application over the cycle, it is claimed, will enable the automatic stabilisers to operate and contribute to fiscal stability. Even for the limited macroeconomic role that fiscal policy will play into the 21st century, the British government regards it as axiomatic that that role should be stabilisation.

Nothing, of course, could be further from the 'Schumpeter-Kalecki' scenario we have outlined in this paper and raises in our minds serious concerns about the future economic prospects for the UK economy. The issue that concerns us most is income distribution. There is clear evidence, from a number of studies, of a significant shift in income distribution in the United Kingdom over the past twenty years or so towards the higher income groups. Leaving equity considerations to one side, what concern us are the macroeconomic implications of this change in the functional distribution of income. The 'Schumpeter-Kalecki' analysis we have presented above suggests that a declining share of wages in national income will result in a slackening of investment. The wage share in the United Kingdom has fallen by nearly 10 per cent since 1980 as a consequence of a rising degree of monopoly. The increasing economic and social power of capitalists, as mirrored in the rising k (the obverse of the falling wage share) has enabled them to increase the profit (non-employment income) share of national income. This has been accompanied by a rising propensity to consume out of that profit income. Income, which might have been expected to finance investment, is being increasingly used to finance consumption (Laramie, Mair and Toporowski, forthcoming) (see Table 1).

We are concerned that the United Kingdom, even under a Labour government, may find itself increasingly locked into a downward economic spiral as a consequence of a redistribution of income away from income from employment. There is the prospect in the United Kingdom of an ever-decreasing wage share resulting in ever-declining investment which the government, as a consequence of its commitment to neo-Keynesian fiscal philosophy, is powerless to reverse because it has effectively denied itself the fiscal instruments with which to address the problem. Schumpeter was right to be worried about the future of capitalism in a democratic society.

Notes

1. 'Synedoche' is the figure of speech that puts the part for the whole. We are grateful to Dr. T. Torrance for reminding us of the meaning of synedoche.
2. The model requires that the consumption coefficient be greater than one. It has lain within the range 1.2–1.5 in the UK over the period 1972–1995 (Laramie, Mair and Toporowski, forthcoming).
3. We have also considered the effects of taxation when the trend level of investment is non-zero. The theoretical and mathematical exposition would greatly extend this paper (Laramie and Mair, 1998).
4. Bearing in mind that $\omega = 1/k$, assuming $j = 0$.

References

Arestis P, Sawyer M (1998) The macroeconomics of New Labour. Mimeo, University of Leeds

Gomulka S, Ostaszewski A, Davies R (1990) The innovation rate and Kalecki's theory of the trend, business cycle and unemployment. Economica 57: 525–540

Hayek FA (1944) The road to serfdom. University of Chicago Press, Chicago

Treasury HM (1998) Code for fiscal stability

Kalecki M (1937) A theory of commodity, income and capital taxation. Economic Journal 47: 444–450

Kalecki M (1943) Political aspects of full employment. Political Quarterly 14: 322–331

Kalecki M (1954) Theory of economic dynamics. Allen and Unwin, London

Kalecki M (1968) Trend and business cycle. Reprinted in: Kalecki M (1971) Selected essays in the dynamics of the capitalist economy. Cambridge University Press, Cambridge

Keynes JM (1936) The general theory of employment, interest and money. Macmillan, London

Kriesler PM (1996) Microfoundations: a Kaleckian perspective. In: King JE (ed) An alternative macroeconomic theory: the Kaleckian model and post-keynesian economics. Kluwer, Boston

Laramie AJ (1991) Taxation and Kalecki's distribution factors. Journal of Post Keynesian Economics 4: 583–594

Laramie AJ, Mair D (1996) Taxation and Kalecki's theory of the business cycle. Cambridge Journal of Economics 20: 451–464

Laramie AJ, Mair D (1997) A Kaleckian theory of taxation. International Papers in Political Economy 4: 1–43
Laramie AJ, Mair D (1998) The micro-macro dichotomy of public finance: a Kaleckian solution to the problem of growth and taxation. Mimeo, Heriot-Watt University
Laramie AJ, Mair D, Toporowski J (1999) Weintraub's consumption coefficient: some economic implications and evidence for the UK. Cambridge Journal of Economics (forthcoming)
Laramie AJ, Mair D, Miller AG, Stratopoulos T (1997) The impact of taxation on gross private non-residential fixed investment in a Kaleckian model. Journal of Post Keynesian Economics 19: 243–256
Moggridge D (1983) The collected writings of John Maynard Keynes, Vol XII. Economic articles and correspondence. Macmillan, London
Musgrave RA (1992) Schumpeter's crisis of the tax state: an essay in fiscal sociology. Journal of Evolutionary Economics 2: 89–114
Musgrave RA (1997) Micro and macro aspects of fiscal policy. In: Blejer MI, Ter-Minassian T (eds) Macroeconomic dimensions of public finance. Routledge, London
Muth JF (1961) Rational expectations and the theory of price movements. Econometrica 29: 315–335
Reynolds PJ (1983) Kalecki's degree of monopoly. Journal of Post Keynesian Economics 5: 493–503
Reynolds PJ (1996) Kalecki's theory of prices and distribution. In King JE (ed) An alternative macroeconomic theory: the Kaleckian model and post-keynesian economics. Kluwer, Boston
Rothschild KW (1961) Some recent contributions to a macroeconomic theory of income distribution. Scottish Journal of Political Economy 2: 173–199
Schumpeter JA (1918) Crisis of the tax state. Leuschner and Lubensky, Graz Leipzig
Schumpeter JA (1943) Capitalism, socialism and democracy. Unwin University Books, London
Schumpeter JA (1939) Business cycles, Vols I and II. McGraw-Hill, New York
Schumpeter JA (1954) History of economic analysis. Allen and Unwin, London
Stern N (1992) From the static to the dynamic: some problems in the theory of taxation. Journal of Public Economics 47: 273–297
Weintraub S (1979) Generalising Kalecki and simplifying macroeconomics. Journal of Post Keynesian Economics 1: 101–106
Weintraub S (1981) An eclectic theory of income shares. Journal of Post Keynesian Economics 4: 10–24

Capitalism and democracy at a crossroads: the civilizational dimension

Eyüp Özveren*

Department of Economics, Middle East Technical University,
06531 Ankara, Turkey (e-mail: ozveren@metu.edu.tr)

"I had my own tale to tell."
– Joseph A. Schumpeter (1939), *Business Cycles.*

"A prejudiced man may yet be speaking the truth."
– Joseph A. Schumpeter (1942), *Capitalism, Socialism and Democracy.*

Abstract. This paper evaluates Schumpeter's grand vision as reflected in his *Capitalism, Socialism and Democracy*, and elaborates it in conjunction with the so-called "globalization" trends characteristic of the wake of the twenty-first century. In addition to the evolutionary nature of his methodology, the institutionalist dimension of Schumpeter's definitions are brought to light. A case is made for a fundamental process of "uncreative destruction" as far as the institutional setup of the economy is concerned. The contention of this paper is that there is ample support in Schumpeterian analysis for a counterpoint to the liberal thesis that envisages the worldwide spread of individualism, market economies, and democratic forms of government.

Key words: Schumpeterian analysis – Capitalism – Democracy – Institutions – Globalization

JEL-classification: B25, B31, P16, P17

1 Introduction

Writing only during the first half of the twentieth century, J.A. Schumpeter nevertheless developed one of the most profound grand visions of this

---

Paper presented at the 1998 World Conference of the International Joseph A. Schumpeter Society, Vienna, June 13–16, 1998.

* I would like to thank Prof. Dennis C. Mueller of the University of Vienna and Prof. Oktar Türel of the Middle East Technical University, for their comments and suggestions on the earlier drafts of this paper. I assume full responsibility for its remaining vulnerabilities.

century. His work displayed a strong sense of the long-term tendencies at work. He believed that capitalism was fast approaching its final moment, and democracy could at best be partially salvaged by bringing it down to earth and justifying it as it actually existed. Understandably, it was not the best of times to be optimistic about the future. Not only had the Russian Revolution led to the emergence of an "alternative" camp outside of the orbit of capitalism, but shortly after the Great Depression that had shaken the world economic system, the world was led to a most destructive war, where fascism eliminated democracy from continental Europe. Hence, the historical setting within which the basic orientation of *Capitalism, Socialism, and Democracy* was shaped was indeed conducive to speculation about the main tenets of the system in question, but was indeed discouraging to the preservation of an optimistic outlook. So, while at a first glance, time seems to have proven him wrong, we should not lose sight of the historical context which helps explain part of the pessimism. Looking back now, however, despite routinized innovation and heavy taxation which Schumpeter despised, far from having collapsed, capitalism has been reinvigorated and may yet enter perhaps its most rapid phase of growth (Easterlin, 1996). As for politics, there are more pluralistic democracies around than ever before and their numbers may yet increase. In spite of this, we need to turn back to Schumpeter to understand why this is so (Heertje, 1981). His way of thinking still has much to offer for developing an accurate vision of the twenty-first century. To be able to do that, however, we should proceed very cautiously. First, we should avoid picking up and isolating from their context certain fragments of Schumpeter's work that tend to link with our own interests, as many contemporary references to Schumpeter do. Secondly, before passing an unfair verdict on Schumpeter's work, we ought to become conscious of the time-span of his predictions and his carefully stated reservations. It is quite clear that in his *Capitalism, Socialism and Democracy*, Schumpeter attempted a foray into the "calculable future" (Schumpeter, 1942, p. 131) to forecast whether capitalism would survive over the next forty to fifty years (Schumpeter, 1942, pp. 110, 113, 115). Finally, when dealing with the long-term transformation of the structural underpinnings of capitalism, Schumpeter emphasized that "a century is a 'short run'" for such mental exercises (Schumpeter, 1942, p. 163).

2 Definitions of capitalism and democracy

Schumpeter had an original definition of capitalism which differed substantially from other definitions that were commonplace in his time. Fully aware of this fact, he sought to spell out his definition in his *Business Cycles*:

"capitalism is that form of private property economy, in which innovations are carried out by means of borrowed money, which in general, though not by logical necessity, implies credit creation. A society, the economic life of which is characterized by private property and controlled by private initiative, is according to this definition not necessarily capitalist, even if there are, for instance, privately owned factories, salaried workers, and free exchange of goods and services, either in kind or through the medium of money." (Schumpeter, 1939, vol. I, p. 223)

Schumpeter argued that, without credit creation, most of the economic and cultural attributes normally associated with a capitalist society would remain wanting. He went on to emphasize that this was essentially an "institutional" definition of capitalism (Schumpeter, 1939, vol. I, p. 224), with the proviso that his analysis concentrated on the process that helped explain the creation and destruction of such institutions usually treated as data.

As for democracy, for Schumpeter it was, before anything else, a "method", that is, a way of doing things. It was that "institutional arrangement" for coming to terms with the practical problem of the political organization of a complex modern society (Schumpeter, 1942, p. 250, 269). Schumpeter's definition is as follows:

"the democratic method is that institutional arrangement for arriving at political decisions in which individuals acquire the power to decide by means of a competitive struggle for the people's vote." (Schumpeter, 1942, p. 269)

Schumpeter's definition of democracy is formulated in terms of its formal attributes with an emphasis on their functional relevance. It should be noted, to his credit, that he deliberately avoided addressing the substantive aspect of democracy in his definitional quest. As such, he came up with a non-idealistic, down-to-earth conception of democracy that was not value-loaded as is the case with many substantivist definitions.

Schumpeter's definitions of both capitalism and democracy shared a common feature, the emphasis he placed on the institutional dimension. It should be recalled that Schumpeter had a full grasp of the importance of institutional analysis without necessarily restricting himself exclusively to its horizon, and he outperformed many self-proclaimed institutionalists of his time by their very own standards (Gordon, 1963, pp. 141–146). In this context, Schumpeter's work begs for a novel reinterpretation within the context of a broader institutionalist research program that would include the legacy of other scholars of stature such as Karl Polanyi who did not call themselves institutionalists in the narrow sense. In his *Business Cycles*, Schumpeter counterpoised a "capitalist sector" and a "precapitalist world":

"It must also be granted that the smaller the capitalist sector embedded in an otherwise precapitalist world. . ." (Schumpeter, vol. I, 1939, pp. 224–225)

Clearly, for Schumpeter, the precapitalist world was something more than the precapitalist economy. What was at issue was the embeddedness of a nascent economic phenomenon within the broader context of an all-embracing "world", a conception surprisingly parallel to what Polanyi described as the embeddedness of the economy in an all-inclusive precapitalist "society" (Polanyi, 1944)[1].

---

[1] It should be noted here that Schumpeter made repeated analytical use of the concept of "embeddedness" – a concept so dear to contemporary Polanyi-esque scholarship – some years before the *Great Transformation* appeared, and in a manner reminiscent of Polanyi.

3 The economy as a metaphor for the political realm

It is well known that Schumpeter concentrated his work basically in two areas. First, the study of the economy as a dynamic capitalist process motivated by an entrepreneurial quest for profits and a strong sense of rivalry as competition in the classical sense. Second, the study of the political realm with a focus on democracy. The originality of Schumpeter's work in this second realm waits to date for full acknowledgement. In sharp contrast to the idealistic conceptions of democracy borrowed from the eighteenth-century philosophical tradition, as noted above, Schumpeter sought actively to develop a realistic working-definition of democracy on grounds first prepared by Max Weber (Held, 1987, pp. 165–170). To do this, however, he turned back to the metaphor of the economy. He deployed the idea of competition as rivalry and transplanted it into the realm of politics, where he interpreted the quest of political parties for representation of the populace as one of competition. The "competitive struggle for power and office" (Schumpeter, 1942, p. 282) was an effective means to fulfil the quest for producing "efficient government" (Schumpeter, 1942, p. 272) in a modern, complex society. Furthermore, leaders were to the political function what his entrepreneurs were to the all important entrepreneurial function. Just as the entrepreneurs brought about new combinations, or applied economically inventions that may have been neglected for quite some time, political leaders articulated and shaped group-wise volitions (Schumpeter, 1942, p. 270).

If the leadership played an active part in orchestrating the political realm, the question remains as to the role of individual choice. After all, contemporary theories of the competitive democratic process take the individual as a rational choice-maker for their point of departure, just as do contemporary neoclassical economic theories of choice. Schumpeter, however, dissented from this tradition:

"For mankind is not free to choose. This is not only because the mass of people are not in a position to compare alternatives rationally and always accept what they are being told. There is a much deeper reason for it. Things economic and social move by their own momentum and the ensuing situations compel individuals and groups to behave in certain ways whatever they may wish to do – not indeed by destroying their freedom of choice but by shaping the choosing mentalities and by narrowing the list of possibilities from which to choose." (Schumpeter, 1942, pp. 129–30)

Schumpeter, who had formulated a rather unusual monopolistic yet competitive notion of the capitalist process, in a similar vein insisted on emphasizing the limits to individual choice within the realm of politics. In compliance with his view of leadership and party politics, he argued that the role of the electorate was rather passive and consisted of delegating the right to rule on its behalf for a given period of time to the leaders before it withdrew to its own sphere of immediate interests. On that basis, Schumpeter reached a rather strong and controversial conclusion: "Voters do not decide issues." (Schumpeter, 1942, p. 282)

The somewhat Weberian yet fresh air Schumpeter brought to the theory of democracy remains to be fully acknowledged. Schumpeter transcended the narrow horizons of political analysis by way of a transdisciplinary venture. He superimposed the images of the democratic and economic processes only to arrive at a novel conclusion at a time when they were consciously kept apart under the spell of the classic nineteenth-century liberal illusion. Schumpeter's economistic reading of the political realm was a deliberate exercise in the transgression of disciplinary boundaries, that is, the structures of knowledge by means of which academic specialization is instituted.

4 The case for creative destruction

Discussing all kinds of economistic arguments that seemed to single out various elements which he summed up under the rubric of Vanishing Investment Opportunity, Schumpeter concluded that capitalism as a purely economic logical construct was free from a tendency towards self-destruction. This meant that one could not argue that the capitalist engine would eventually fail for good because it could not run any longer. By reaching this conclusion, Schumpeter broke his ties with various kinds of classical arguments, underconsumptionist or otherwise.

Schumpeter inaugurated his own version of evolutionary economics, more Marxian than Darwinian, in the sense that the emphasis was put on broader laws of social change and not on the biological metaphors of selection and adaptation (Hodgson, 1996, pp. 139, 150). Schumpeter argued that

"stationary capitalism is impossible, is, in fact, a contradiction in terms. For the central figure on the capitalist stage, the entrepreneur, is concerned not with the *administration* of existing industrial plant and equipment but with the incessant *creation* of new plant and equipment, embodying new technologies that revolutionize existing industrial structures." (Schumpeter, 1946, p. 193)

Having thus defined the capitalist process as essentially evolutionary (Schumpeter, 1942, p. 82), Schumpeter matched it with the business cycle. By doing so, Schumpeter identified a patterned behavior of cyclical ups and downs coinciding with the entrepreneurial introduction of innovations and their gradual assimilation by way of which entrepreneurial profits were undermined and the benefits of new technology passed over to the consumers in the form of reduced prices. Hence the economy alternated between phases in which there were first positive profits due to monopolistic advantages and then zero profits and competition among the many equals, a phenomenon that approximated the perfect-competition case (Schumpeter, 1983). What counted as competition for Schumpeter was not mere price-competition as text-books envisaged,

"but the competition from the new commodity, the new technology, the new source of supply, the new type of organization (the largest-scale unit of control for instance) – competition which commands a decisive cost or quality advantage and which strikes not at the margins of the profits and the outputs of the existing firms but at their foundations and their very lives." (Schumpeter, 1942, p. 84)

Far from being led towards a final collapse, as long as the entrepreneurial function remained effective, capitalism was revitalized periodically by way of innovations that brought with them temporary monopolistic profits:

"that incessantly revolutionizes the economic structure *from within*, incessantly destroying the old one, incessantly creating a new one." (Schumpeter, 1942, p. 83)

According to Schumpeter, this phenomenon reflected the inherently self-reinvigorating characteristic of capitalism which he labeled "creative destruction". Creative destruction is essentially repetitive and connotes a positive meaning in Schumpeterian terminology. In the final analysis, the overall balance sheet is in favor of the creativity aspect in spite of its destructive side. It implies the very dynamism and success of capitalism rather than its failure to deliver its promises.

5 Capitalism's uncreative destruction

Had Schumpeter not been influenced by a rich blend of theoretical and methodological approaches, he may not have ventured beyond the disciplinary territory of economics to emphasize the "interrelationship of economic and noneconomic areas" (Shionoya, 1996, pp. 305–306). Having made the above case for the success of capitalism in purely economic terms, Schumpeter went on to argue that it would nevertheless fail to survive into the future because of the inevitable non-economic consequences that were bound to undermine it (Schumpeter, 1942, p. 61). Capitalism was thus fast becoming the very victim of its own economic success by destroying its institutional framework essential for upholding it.

Capitalism, in Schumpeter's view, benefited parasitically from the pre-capitalistic crust that it inherited and which it had, in the course of time, undermined. Those remnants of the past which the liberal discourse abhorred as "fetters" yet to be broken, were actually protective "shelters" the very abolition of which would leave the economic process in a vacuum (Schumpeter, 1942, p. 135). The economic success of the bourgeoisie allied with the prolonged control of the aristocracy as a political ruling-class reflected an efficient "symbiosis" (Schumpeter, 1942, p. 136). In other words, the bourgeoisie nurtured by the capitalist process was successful in pursuing its own economic interests, so long as it could entrust the running of the state to the ruling-class of the old order. Schumpeter placed a strong emphasis on the difference attributable to the existence of the elements of the old order:

"A purely capitalist society – consisting of nothing but entrepreneurs, capitalists, and proletarian workmen – would work in ways completely different from those we observe historically, *if indeed it could exist at all*." (Schumpeter, 1943, p. 172).

In other words, these elements constituted a matter of life or death for historical capitalism.

For Schumpeter, the capitalist process was like a liquid that cannot take shape without a container:

"In breaking down the pre-capitalist framework of society, capitalism thus broke not only barriers that impeded its progress but also flying buttresses that prevented its collapse. That process, impressive in its relentless necessity, was not merely a matter of removing institutional deadwood, but of removing partners of the capitalist stratum, symbiosis with whom was an essential element of the capitalist schema." (Schumpeter, 1942, p. 139)

According to Schumpeter, therefore, there was no simple one-to-one correspondence between what the Marxists would call "superstructure" and "infrastructure":

"customary modes of political thought and feeling in a given age can never be mere "reflexes" of, or counterparts to, the production situation of that age. Because of the persistence of such habits, they will always, to a considerable degree, be dominated by the production context of past ages." (Schumpeter, 1951, pp. 7–8)

Obviously, it took longer for the institutions to change than it did for the dynamic economic realm. For Schumpeter, economic infrastructure determined the institutional superstructure with a lag. In other words, the economy at a given period was embedded in the "infrastructural" institutional setup inherited from the previous period and created the institutions that remained subordinate in its own institutional superstructure, but would probably become dominant as the embedding framework for the economy of the next period. Put differently, capitalism is embedded in the precapitalist crust, yet creates a new set of institutions conducive to socialism which will probably embed a socialist economy in the next epoch of human history. In the survival of old clothing for capitalist substance, Schumpeter identified the illustration of "the ancient truth that the dead always rule the living" (Schumpeter, 1951, p. 130). In contradistinction to many institutionalists who would share his view concerning the lag, however, Schumpeter went further to argue that this was beneficial; it was, in fact, a *sine qua non* for a capitalist economy. Thus we see the switch of institutions from the superstructure to the infrastructure in the above discussion.

In addition to destroying the protective framework that held it intact, without being able to replace it from within, the capitalist process also undermined the institutional arrangements such as private property rights and free contracting that were vital to the functioning of a capitalist economy. The large scale elimination of small-proprietorship, the genesis of intricate mechanisms of partnership through stock-holding, and the abolition of a free-contracting labor market all attest to this process by way of which the indispensable and authentic institutional framework of the capitalist process are undermined (Schumpeter, 1942, p. 141). Precisely because capitalism as a dynamic process was a shaky ground on which institutions could not last long, capitalism constantly created and destroyed, only to create in new forms again, the kinds of institutional arrangements vital for its survival. If anything, various forms of property rights such as intellectual property rights have actually come into existence with the era of capitalism. While Schumpeter somewhat underestimated this creativity, the very phenomenon of high-turnover itself could help undermine a solid public confidence in the phenomenon of simple private property.

Capitalism had reinforced the overall drive towards rationality and the spread of a critical frame of mind. After undermining the moral authority of many historic institutions, this mentality was bound to turn against its own in the hands of a hostile intelligentsia influential over the bureaucracy (Schumpeter, 1942, pp. 143, 155). Whatever we may think of the merits of this civilization propelled by a confident belief in rationality and critical thinking, its weakness for self-defense should not escape our attention. Of all the major social systems in history, capitalism remains alone in being too weak to cultivate a civilization that would eventually escape its own destruction.

In the background of the above gloomy picture of institutional breakdown, for Schumpeter the family remained as the last bastion of resistance against the tide that would eventually kill capitalism. The family provided the minimal institutional arrangement for the survival of bourgeois values. It continued to condition the individual so that he could continue to function in a social environment increasingly hostile to capitalism:

"When we look more closely at their [economists] idea of the self-interest of entrepreneurs and capitalists we cannot fail to discover that the results it was supposed to produce are really not at all what one would expect from the rational self-interest of the detached individual or the childless couple who no longer look at the world through the windows of a family home. Consciously or unconsciously they analyzed the behavior of the man whose views and motives are shaped by such a home and who means to work and to save primarily for wife *and children*. As soon as these fade out from the moral vision of the businessman, we have a different kind of *homo oeconomicus* before us who cares for different things and acts in different ways" (Schumpeter, 1942, p. 160).

Schumpeter's discussion of the central role of the family refers us conveniently back to the role of institutional limitations on individual choice. Schumpeter envisaged intermediary levels of analysis which occupied a place between the atomistic individuals on the one side, and large structures such as that of capitalism on the other. Within those intermediary levels, institutions interacted with individuals. The process held responsible for the eventual collapse of capitalism was the historical destruction of those very intermediary levels.

Schumpeter's argument boils down to the conclusion that capitalism as a primarily economic phenomenon failed to develop a distinct political culture of its own that would serve to reproduce it. Schumpeter made this argument in the 1940's. Indeed, it was possible to see the First World War era as the last instance of *ancien regimes*, and the process unfolding towards the Second World War as a protracted crisis with no conceivable way out. However, some fifty years have lapsed since then, and the capitalist system's performance over this period casts doubt on Schumpeter's interpretation of the relationship of the non-economic crust to the economic substance. One plausible conclusion would be that Schumpeter exaggerated the role of the remnants of the past and underestimated the ability of capitalism to influence politics. There is indeed some truth in this statement. However, it is the contention here that a second plausible conclusion does more justice to the originality of Schumpeter's work. A narrow definition of capitalism as found in the works of Weber and Schumpeter would preclude noneconomic concepts such as the capitalist state, and choose to work instead with the idea of state in a capitalist society, thereby acknowledging that the state pre-existed capitalism and was shaped by it. This approach would mean that capitalism would occupy only a part, and not the whole, of the social arena as broadly defined.

The constituent elements outside of the immediate realm of capitalism can therefore acquire a dynamic and life-cycle of their own, and develop from being mere remnants into active agents fulfilling new functions in the system. It would be worth remembering that Schumpeter saw a difference between capitalism and the fiscalist state which nevertheless co-existed with reciprocal interaction (Schumpeter, 1991). It may well be that the Keynesian welfare state that emerged in the post World War II period, of which Schumpeter was a vociferous opponent, while assuming an economically interventionist role, became also an axis of organization for all kinds of social elements outside the immediate domain of capitalism, thereby recreating a crust that could help contain capitalism for the decades to come. The original recruits of this process were indeed critics of capitalism as well as the cadres of technocrats and bureaucrats inherited from the old order. Yet they have been cast into a new form in the course of this process and brought into a working relation with capitalism within the context of which they could become the seeds of a new middle class. While having fettered capitalism in some ways, this process may nevertheless simultaneously have helped preserve it despite its own inherent tendency, albeit in an artificial way. Attributing the existence of such a process exclusively to the success of capitalism would, however, be a grave error. The *raison d'être* of Keynesian policies was to compensate for the failure of the market and thereby to salvage capitalism.

6 The civilizational setup of institutional arrangements

If, contrary to what Schumpeter feared yet predicted, an ongoing reinvigoration of the capitalist economy occurs, this would imply a further destruction of the civilizational supporting structure of capitalism, unless Schumpeter wrongly underrated the ability of capitalism to build up its own institutional cocoon from within. It should be mentioned here that implicit in Schumpeter is a conception that capitalism was more successful in creating the institutional arrangements essential to its working from within than in designing its own specific outer framework. Furthermore, Schumpeter had a vision of the historical process where, chronologically, first the outer protective setup and then the inner arrangements essential to a capitalist economy would be eliminated. Underlying this vision was a belief that the institution-creating capacity of capitalism, despite being low, was better suited to the second task than to the first. Time has proven him right. For example, the prolific contemporary property rights literature attests to the creativity of capitalism in this respect. Within the level of the protecting setup, however, Schumpeter believed old structures were being irreversibly replaced by new structures that did not quite measure up to the standards set by their predecessors. Hence ideologies such as socialism, proper to an industrial society, were emerging in place of imperialist inclinations of a war-oriented aristocracy. As the economic foundations of an aristocracy were irreversibly undermined, such ideological leftovers, however conducive and adaptable to capitalism, were on an inevitable decline, but with a lag. Time has proven Schumpeter wrong in this respect. It seems that the new creations of capitalism, such as socialist aspirations, are far more vulnerable to the inherent dynamism of the capitalist process than the haunting leftovers of the past. As far as the chronology is concerned, new macro structures are disappearing before more new ones can come into existence, and in the meantime old structures are rapidly resurfacing. The resurgence of nationalism and ethnic strife within once-communist Eastern Europe and the Soviet Union is a case in point. In this context, Schumpeterian optimism concerning the inherent peacefulness of capitalism and the survival of imperialism only as a leftover (Schumpeter, 1951, pp. 84–85) needs to be recast in a new light. Imperialism may yet display a frightful resurgence in the twenty-first century.

7 In search of the missing links

Two aspects remain conspicuously absent in Schumpeter's otherwise grand vision. First, while Schumpeter was among the first to have noticed the development-oriented nature of the capitalist process (Love, 1996, pp. 6, 230), he did not appreciate the global division of labor and/or the consequences of uneven development on a world scale. Second, again, while Schumpeter was among the few to explore long waves in capitalism, he did not link his discussion of democracy with this phenomenon. Both addenda have important consequences for the assessment of the twenty-first century from a Schumpeterian perspective that might yet be at odds with some of Schumpeter's own conclusions.

Irrespective of whether one believes that development and underdevelopment are two sides of the same coin, the mere fact that different countries enter onto the path of economic development at different times creates the potential for asymmetric statuses and unequal relations among them. This discrepancy in the global configuration of power has been a lasting phenomenon of the twentieth century and is likely to continue into the twenty-first in the form of a North-South division. This factor creates differential opportunities and constraints for the prospects of democracy in the North as well as in the South. In the course of the twenty-first century, one may expect to find a further economic dividend for democracy in the North, whereas the aggravating problems of developmental bottlenecks amidst an increasing urban population pressure will impose further limitations on the likelihood of democracy in the South. Furthermore, self-defensive measures on part of the North to protect itself as an island of wealth and civilization amidst a rising tide of potential immigrants as well as cultural enclaves of foreign workers may turn it into a fortress where the exercise of democratic rights may become more difficult under a rapidly spreading state-of-siege mentality.

The increasing proliferation of civilizational conflict scenarios (Fukuyama, 1992, p. 234; Huntington, 1993) and the rapid spread of various kinds of culturally-based identity politics attest to this trend. Problems of cultural politics and identity conflicts impact upon the existing forms of democracy and may contribute to the further degeneration of the supporting structures. Hence the prospects of the realization of democracy in the twenty-first century must be linked to the very shifts in the matrix of forces that made the odd couple of capitalism and democracy in the North possible in the first place.

The link between long waves of capitalist development and the proliferation of the democratic mode of governance also has important implications. The encouraging signs in the recent past for the spread of democracy from Southern Europe to Latin America and then to Eastern Europe may stimulate us to evaluate the past trend as one of cumulative worldwide democratization (Di Palma, 1990). However, there is good reason to approach this ground with great caution. Along with the secular trend, strong cyclical movements have been present, and democratization has proceeded in successive waves and reverse waves (Huntington, 1991, p. 16). Furthermore, it is not so much the transition to democracy that counts but rather the stability of the new democracy. The best test for democratic stability is provided by world-wide economic crises. Within the existing sample of democracies, very few (two examples being the United Kingdom and the United States) have successfully withstood the test of the Great Depression and international warfare. Even within Europe, not to mention Japan in the Far East, many democracies have yet to demonstrate their long run stability.

We are thus thrown back to the question of whether democracy is civilization-specific. It is no mere accident that the viable examples we have encountered in history all belong to the European civilization and its offshoots. This civilizational specificity would also imply that the analysis of democracy within a particular nation-state can be rather misleading, as a civilization would involve multiple nation-states with back and forth influences among them (Eley, 1995, p. 110). Assessing all of the evidence, it would be fair to conclude that modern representative democracy is more civilization-specific than capitalism. Even if capitalism has also emerged within the conducive parameters of the European civilization, it has tended to become all-inclusive by way of its inner logic. Having once emerged, it has successfully spread across the globe by way of universalization. The same cannot be said to a similar extent of democracy. It has entailed no logical necessity for proliferation. Furthermore, it has met conscious resistance on its way to diffusion not only in places such as Africa, the Arab Middle East, and China, but also in Singapore (Fukuyama, 1992).

8 Capitalism, market and democracy

The fact that both capitalism and democracy first emerged in the West has wrongly led many to think that they necessarily went together. In the wake of the twenty-first century, it may be worthwhile to re-conceptualize the old Weberian problematic of civilizational specificity (Weber, 1958, 1978). The relationship of democracy to capitalism and/or the market has been much debated since the time of Schumpeter. Schumpeter himself hinted that capitalism had proven itself conducive to democracy without discussing the matter in further detail: "whatever democracy there was, outside of peasant communities, developed historically in the wake of both modern and ancient capitalism." (Schumpeter, 1942, p. 126). Because capitalism in the West coincided historically with the emancipation of markets from mercantilist overregulation, some have gone further than Schumpeter and wrongly attributed a causality that runs from capitalism to democracy. While competitive markets with large numbers of buyers and sellers contribute to the consolidation of democracy, there is nothing in capitalism *per se* that directly reinforces democracy. The definition of competition is of critical import to this issue. Whereas the textbook neoclassical definition of competition emphasizes the number of buyers and sellers as the measure of the competitiveness of a given market situation, Classical economists such as Richard Cantillon and Adam Smith, the Austrian economists, and finally Schumpeter himself – as we have seen above in an earlier discussion of creative destruction – singled out a dynamic notion of competition focusing on competition as rivalry. Economically speaking, this definition is far more appropriate. Sociologically speaking, however, whether a market situation approximates perfect competition with many buyers and sellers makes a great difference as far as the diffusion of power in a more democratic way is concerned. Schumpeter was not unaware of this phenomenon:

"Even if the giant concerns were all managed so perfectly as to call forth applause from the angels in heaven, the political consequences of concentration would still be what they are. The political structure of a nation is profoundly affected by the elimination of a host of small and medium-sized firms the owner-managers of which, together with their dependents, henchmen and connections, count quantitatively at the polls" (Schumpeter, 1942, p. 141).

In this context, the kind of analytical distinction that the French historian Fernand Braudel maintained between the market and capitalism is of immense importance (Braudel, 1982, 1985). Furthermore, it overlaps with Schumpeter's insistence that capitalism is intrinsically competitive yet monopolistic, without losing track of the inherent gains of the market metaphor. It was markets specifically, and not capitalism in general, that helped *consolidate* democratic governance, wherever capitalism came into being.

It should be emphasized that we have so far only discussed the plausible effects of capitalism and markets on the stabilization of democracy. The question remains as to whether capitalism and competitive markets could alone *generate* democracy. In other words, where we have discovered a strong correlation – between competitive markets and democracy but not between capitalism and democracy – can we also identify a strong causality? I think not. European history demonstrates that the *origins* of democracy had to do, not with the formation of self-regulating markets or capitalism, but with the crucial link between taxation and representation. As such, the *origin* of democracy is a truly political economic process, in which political representation was traded for primarily the economic revenue quest of the modern state. In this sense, representative democracy is inextricably linked to the accountability of the modern state for its public finance. Schumpeter's conception of the tax state and the capitalist economy as two pillars of the modern political economic system deserves further consideration in this context (Schumpeter, 1991; Backhaus, 1994, p. 78). In the course of time, nineteenth-century representative democracy took its exemplary shape in Britain. It should be added that the idea of democracy with popular suffrage was a novel phenomenon – hence a break with ancient democracy – which was designed to redress property-ownership imbalances by way of giving a corrective weight to numbers of citizens irrespectively of wealth. Therefore, the numbers were supposed to counterbalance the otherwise inegalitarian distribution of property as sanctioned under liberal principles. One further reason representative democracy has drastically failed in places like former British Africa may have to do with the fact that the property structure that was supposed to accompany popular suffrage was missing.

9 One scenario or more?

Two important conclusions follow from the above discussion. First, replicating this process within a new set of countries is extremely difficult. Hence, to come into being and to survive, new democracies must be largely the result of conscious emulation and external stimulus – all the more reason to be pessimistic about their prospects. Second, the likely undermining of representative democracy by emerging technologies conducive to the direct exercise of choice-making under the rubric of accountability can lead the system to a deadlock. New computer facilities with wide network accessibility can turn voters into continuous choice-makers. Rather than investing political prerogative in their elected representatives and withdrawing to their own sphere of life as characterized by Schumpeter, they may choose to remain in the political arena and take up the task of making decisions all the time. It will not take long before we see that the kind of hypocrisy involved in the representational democracy was actually rather favorable to capitalism, as it left the ruling-class with room to maneuver. Public polls time and again demonstrate how the voters rather paradoxically prefer better social services on the one hand, and lower taxes on the other. Such contradictory objectives can lead the political process into a prolonged stalemate with no foreseeable way out. This would mean that insistence on a democratic process can have devastating consequences for the viability of capitalism. As such, perhaps the most deadly weapon in the hands of the critics of capitalism is democracy. It is plausible that core countries will experience this kind of a terminal crisis at a time when much of the periphery will not yet have experienced democracy. Furthermore, the crisis would also be terminal for direct democracy.

The above stalemate could help legitimize for good the brokerage of a political class. On the other hand, the political class will increasingly prove itself an obstacle on the way to the realization of a direct democracy because of its vested interest in the rent-producing process of a representative political scheme. It should be emphasized that not direct democracy but its technical conditions of existence are around the corner. However, this process will suffice to increase the pressures for the exercise of direct democracy, thereby making visible the real obstacles along the way.

The prospective increase in voter involvement in the political process in the traditional strongholds of democracy has to be posed against the background of an eroding protective framework. The disintegration of the leftovers from the precapitalistic crust is finally liberating individuals from all constraints – including the family – on their exercise of free choice. In a way, for the first time we may be fast approaching the ideally universal liberal society composed of free choice-making individuals. On the other hand, the liberation of the individuals from these seeming constraints leaves them in a vacuum with an explosive number of options ahead. As new work in institutional economics and game theory indicates, social constraints are mechanisms that shape individual preferences and expectations and help them process the information that continuously bombards them. When approached from this perspective, past constraints are like traffic signs that give a meaning to the entire process, precisely because they helped routinize much of human behavior so that the select number of choices became more important and rationally manageable.

In the course of the next century, while we may have more individualized behavior than ever before, and while the actual number of choices yet to be made may exponentially increase, their meaning may vanish from the horizon, leaving us all in the environs of a truly postmodern asymptote. The increasing quest for intermediary level identities such as gender, ethnicity, environment, and community is under way as a spontaneous reaction to extreme individualization. What is needed is to bring back the kinds of supporting structures that can shape individual decision making. It is no coincidence that, however utopian they may be, and however marginal a position they may occupy within the realm of politics, such quests constitute a fringe domain where potential for the re-substantiation of a highly formalized democracy exists. This may be desirable for mankind as a whole, but not necessarily good for the survival of capitalism.

Having noted a plausible constraint democracy imposes upon the prospects of capitalism, we should, in turn, list a number of constraints capitalism imposes on the future likelihood of democracy. First, had it not been for the phenomenon of capitalist creative destruction that combined technological change with the entrepreneurial function, the technological frontier would not have shifted by way of successive breakthroughs to make possible the return of direct democracy. Second, the balance between capitalism and the market tends to shift in favor of capitalism, stifling the participation of many in market processes. Third, the North-South polarization of capitalism on a world scale reduces the chances of democracies fulfilling their promise in the South, while it may yet cultivate a further state-of-siege mentality in the North. Last but not least, while capitalism was not necessarily conducive to the spread of democracy, according to a Schumpeterian distinction, the capitalist class was in one sense democratic. Unlike its predecessors, the capitalist class welcomed to its ranks new members on a periodic basis by way of meritocratic achievement; the entrepreneurial function secured constant upward mobility from all walks of life into its ranks (Schumpeter, 1951). Precisely because any factor owner could potentially become an entrepreneur in a Walrasian-Schumpeterian framework, Schumpeter elaborated this mechanism further to identify in it a sociological means for the periodic replenishment of the capitalist class. Now, if the Schumpeterian prediction that the entrepreneurial function is on a path of irreversible decline is true, this would further mean that the capitalist class will inevitably lose its recruitment mechanism, close its ranks and become an undemocratic caste in the core countries, whereas recruitment by way of entrepreneurship will continue for quite some time in the less developed countries. As the several constraints on democracy and the one restraining capitalism accumulate strength, capitalism and democracy fast approach a crossroads.

One tends to forget that democracies have come and gone even in the privileged domain of European civilization. There is good reason to think that the scenario of a worldwide capitalism matched with democracy is at the best possible, but not very probable. Encouraged by the recent democratic wave, however, some tend to think that democracy has demonstrated its absolute superiority over its rivals over a period of several hundred years, thereby heralding an end of history (Fukuyama, 1992). First of all, two qualifications need to be made. A natural selection process disguises the fact that, while democracy has remained a constant element of the choice set, its alternatives have changed in the course of time. As such, new alternatives may yet emerge. What is at issue is not a natural selection process with a pre-given set of outcomes. Second, the alleged superiority of democracy is not absolute, but relative to the given set of possibilities, which may not have included the best possibility in the first instance.

In light of the above, one can further argue that the long-term has witnessed a pendular motion between democracy and a non-democratic alternative, where this last has assumed successively different characterizations. The success of democracy has largely been due not to its own accomplishments, but to the failure of its authoritarian alternatives. Two reasons can be given for the failure of anti-democratic alternatives. First, they had been tried in the relatively less developed countries further crippled by geostrategic factors: neither the nineteenth-century Imperial Germany was a Great Britain, nor the Nazi Germany or the Soviet Union were a United States as far as economic strength and geostrategic layout were concerned. Second, the technical apparatus needed for the mastery of a full planning of the entire economic and social realm was not in place. Comparing the long-lasting communist experience with the fascist experience of the inter-war period, and fascism with the less distinguishable versions of nineteenth-century paternalistic regimes, one can see that, time and again, the authoritarian alternative has succeeded in bouncing back with greater weight. The authoritarian regimes of the twentieth century were far more penetrating and effectively institutionalized than the absolutist monarchies or despotic regimes of the past, which relied on arbitrary and forceful but not necessarily effective mechanisms for the control of civil society. Therefore, the above secular trend requires a closer investigation.

In coming to terms with the above problem, the Austrian socialist calculation debate is of crucial significance. The Austrians demonstrated the failure of central-planning to simulate the market as essentially a dynamic discovery process. There were two sides to this argument. First, no central planning agency could assemble and process the vast amount of information involved, an argument that was put forward before the first computer was designed, and has therefore been discredited. Second, even if a central planning agency could succeed in this formidable task, this process would lead to the supposedly equilibrium values *without* the dynamic discovery process that is vital for economic change (Lavoie, 1985). Schumpeter moved a step further and acknowledged the feasibility of socialism, as its solid foundations were increasingly laid by economic development and concomitant social change. While doing this, he admitted that the first technical obstacle could, in principle, be surmounted. To put it differently, communist authoritarianisms of the twentieth century were courageous attempts to solve a monstrous problem with limited equipment. Hence, when approached from the other side of history, twentieth-century communism may yet prove to be a rather pale and primitive prefiguration of what is yet to come. With the specter of technocratic authoritarianism haunting the future, we may be far from the Schumpeterian optimistic scenario wherein capitalism would wither away and democracy would remain the mode of governing for complex modern societies. The possibility of an organized capitalism with its global asymmetries and concomitant tensions coupled with a less than self-fulfilling individualism, may lead the way to the withering away of democracy instead, and the resurgence of technocratic forms of authoritarianism in the future.

One factor that has immense importance for the situation we find ourselves in has been the discrepancy between the domain of politics, namely the nation-state, and the domain of the economy, which has tended to spread beyond the reach of the nation-state. Hence, European civilization is characterized by the coexistence of an ever-expanding economic space that successfully evolves beyond the reach of any singular political unit. Both capitalism and the self-regulating market owe their existence and vitality to their capacity to avoid falling under the jurisdiction of a singular structure of governance. As there exists a geographical limit to global expansion, once the entire world becomes the domain of capitalism, global institutional arrangements for regulation should increasingly come to dominate the economic space in a one-to-one relationship. Hence, the prospects for authoritarian governance will be drastically enhanced once the discrepancy between the formation of economic and political spaces in favor of the economic ones is eliminated. For the first time in modern history, we may witness authoritarian rule emerging in the most economically advanced zones of the world rather than in the contestants of the hegemon. We may fast approach the limit where we would have global technocratic authoritarianism, a product of capitalist technological evolution, coupled with an unlimited individualism whereby the individual may become virtually paralyzed. To put it differently, a seemingly liberal vision, "one world, one people, but a people where all are individuals" may not necessarily be the best utopia for the next century.

References

Backhaus JG (1994) The concept of the tax state in modern public finance analysis. In: Shionoya Y, Perlman M (eds) Schumpeter in the history of ideas, pp 65–94. The University of Michigan Press, Ann Arbor
Braudel F (1982) Civilization and capitalism, 15th–18th century, Vol II. The wheels of commerce. Harper & Row, New York
Braudel F (1985) La dynamique du capitalisme. Flammarion, Paris
Di Palma G (1990) To craft democracies: An essay on democratic transitions. University of California Press, Berkeley
Easterlin RA (1996) Growth triumphant: The twenty-first century in historical perspective. University of Michigan Press, Ann Arbor
Eley G (1995) The social construction of democracy in Germany, 1871–1933. In: Andrews GR, Chapman H (eds) The social construction of democracy, 1870–1990, pp 90–117. New York University Press, New York
Fukuyama F (1992) The end of history and the last man. The Free Press, New York
Gordon RA (1963) Institutional elements in contemporary economics. In: Dorfman J, Ayres CE, Chamberlain NW, Kuznets S, Gordon RA (eds) Institutional economics: Veblen, commons, and Mitchell reconsidered, pp 123–147. University of California Press, Berkeley
Heertje A (ed) (1981) Schumpeter's vision: Capitalism, socialism and democracy after 40 years. Praeger, New York
Held D (1987) Models of democracy. Polity Press, Cambridge
Hodgson GM (1996) Economics and evolution: bringing life back into economics. The University of Michigan Press, Ann Arbor
Huntington SP (1993) Clash of civilizations? Foreign Affairs 72(3): 22–49
Huntington SP (1991) The third wave: Democratization in the late twentieth century. The University of Oklahoma Press, Norman, Oklahama
Lavoie D (1985) Rivalry and central planning: The socialist calculation debate reconsidered. Cambridge University Press, Cambridge
Love JL (1996) Crafting the third world: theorizing underdevelopment in Rumania and Brazil. Stanford University Press, Stanford
Polanyi K (1944) The great transformation. Beacon Press, Boston
Schumpeter JA (1939) Business cycles: A theoretical, historical, and statistical analysis of the capitalist process. McGraw-Hill, New York
Schumpeter JA (1946) Capitalism. Reprinted in: Clemence RW (ed) Essays of J.A. Schumpeter, pp 184–205. Addison-Wesley, Cambridge, MA
Schumpeter JA (1943) Capitalism in the postwar period. Reprinted in: Clemence RW (ed) Essays of J.A. Schumpeter, pp 113–126. Addison-Wesley, Cambridge, MA
Schumpeter JA (1942) Capitalism, socialism and democracy. Harper Torchbooks, New York
Schumpeter JA (1991) [1918] The crisis of the tax state. In: Swedberg R (ed) The economics and sociology of capitalism, pp 99–140. Princeton University Press, Princeton
Schumpeter JA (1951) Imperialism and social classes (edited by Sweezy PM). Kelly, New York
Schumpeter JA (1983) [1934] The theory of economic development. Transaction Publishers, New Brunswick
Shionoya Y (1996) The sociology of science and Schumpeter's ideology. In: Moss LS (ed) Joseph A. Schumpeter, historian of economics, pp 279–316. Routledge, London
Weber M (1978) Economy and society. University of California Press, Berkeley
Weber M (1958) The protestant ethic and the spirit of capitalism. Scribner, New York

Capitalism, democracy and rational individual behavior*

Dennis C. Mueller

Institut für Wirtschaftswissenschaften, Universität Wien,
Brünner Straße 72, A-1210 Wien, Austria

The collapse of communism in Eastern Europe and the Soviet Union beginning in 1989 to many observers seemed to signal the triumph of the capitalistic and democratic institutions of the West over the socialist and totalitarian institutions that had been the hallmark of communism.

In the nearly ten years that have elapsed since "the great transition" was launched, neither the West's capitalist nor its democratic institutions have been fully and successfully transplanted in the former communist countries. Nor have the benefits these countries have received from the transplants lived up to their, or most Westerners', expectations.

Given the magnitude of the transition process, and the depths to which the communist countries had fallen, the lack of "instant success" in transition is perhaps, with the help of hindsight, not so surprising. Nevertheless, the fact that the opening up of markets has not led to more visible improvements in living standards in the former communist countries must be judged as a contradiction of sorts to the predictions of standard neoclassical economics. Why have individuals in the former communist countries not responded more aggressively to the incentives for profits and self-gain that the opening up of markets has produced? Why has the unleashing of market forces not led to greater and more consistent improvements in welfare?

There are, of course, many possible answers to these questions, and no single answer is likely to come close to being correct. But a part of the answer may certainly be that the expectation that the opening up of markets would work wonders was unrealistic, as unrealistic as the assumptions

---

Paper presented at the 1998 World Conference of the International Joseph A. Schumpeter Society, Vienna, June 13–16, 1998.

*This paper has received financial support from the Hochschuljubiläumsstiftung of the City of Vienna.

regarding individual behavior that underlie the neoclassical models of competitive markets that engender such expectations.

The key behavioral assumption of neoclassical economics is, of course, that all individuals are rational egoists. This behavioral assumption is perhaps the most conspicuous methodological difference between economics and its sister social sciences.[1] It lies at both the *positive* and the *normative* hearts of the discipline. It is used by economists to explain *how* the competitive process allocates resources, and *why* this allocation is socially optimal. It has also been employed by practitioners of public choice to explain the behavior of political actors, and to proclaim the inherent irrationality of the democratic process.

Both the rationality and the egoistic components of the rational egoism assumption have been heavily criticized. These criticisms call into question both the positive and the normative predictions of economics regarding the workings of the market, and at least the predictive side of public choice. These criticisms may also help to explain the faltering start of capitalism and democracy in the aftermath of communism.

In this essay I do not belabor the criticisms of the rational egoism postulate that have been made. Instead, I accept many of them as valid, and offer an alternative "behavioralist" assumption about human behavior in its place. In certain contexts this behavioralist assumption leads to similar predictions as the rational egoism postulate, and thus can reinforce both the positive and normative claims of neoclassical economics. In other contexts it undermines these claims. With respect to political behavior, however, the implications are almost uniformly negative. Positing more realistic individual behavior undermines some of the positive analysis of public choice without necessarily overturning its pessimistic normative implications.

Having explored the implications of the more realistic behavioral assumption offered in this paper, I return to the question of the future of capitalism and democracy in both the former communistic countries, and in other countries that have yet to embrace one or both of these sets of institutions. I shall argue that the potential for capitalism and democracy to take hold does indeed depend on a limited degree of rational egoism on the part of the individuals living in these countries.

I The formation of habits and economic behavior

Rational agent models in their purest forms assume that individuals are forward looking optimizers correctly calculating which strategy promises the highest payoffs in each situation. When making a decision, each actor contemplates only the *future* payoffs from each possible action. Past payoffs are relevant only to the extent that they help the forward-looking rational agent to accurately predict the future. One implication is that in a one-shot prisoners' dilemma, each rational player chooses the noncooperative strategy with probability one.

---

[1] This statement is, however, less true today than say 25 years ago.

In the typical one-shot prisoners' dilemma experiment, however, the participants routinely violate this most basic prediction of rational actor models. For example, in public goods experiments participants normally voluntarily contribute in the neighborhood of 50 percent of the jointly optimal amount, when a contribution near zero would be individually optimal.[2] Such seemingly irrational actions can be readily explained with models of man that are *backward* looking, and that view human behavior as *adaptive*. Individuals are generally rewarded in every day life for cooperating in prisoners' dilemma situations, and when someone correctly perceives that she is in such a situation her response conforms to those that have been previously rewarded.

Consistent with this behavioralist psychology interpretation, we find that participants in PD-experiments are quickly conditioned to defect by the half-hearted cooperation of the other players. After a few repetitions of the game, the noncooperative Nash equilibrium predicted by rational choice does emerge. Only following *many* repetitions do the cooperative outcomes described in the supergame literature begin to be observed, if at all.[3] All of these experimental results are much more consistent with a theory of adaptive behavior than with rational choice theory. Indeed, the celebrated tit-for-tat strategy that most reliably generates the cooperative supergame outcome is nothing more than a formula for conditioning the other player to cooperate by rewarding past cooperation and punishing defections.

Anyone who has trained a dog to sit and roll over has successfully applied the principles of behavioral psychology, as has every parent. By applying the principles of operant conditioning parents develop good, and sometimes not so good, habits in their children. As children grow older, people outside of the home and the institutional environment play an ever increasing role in rewarding and punishing their actions.

Behavioral psychology's account of human action is fully consistent with the *egoistic* portion of the rational egoism postulate. Human behavior, as that of all other animals, is hedonistic. Humans respond unconsciously and almost unwillingly to various stimuli, and the recollections of past rewards and punishments that they arouse.

Despite the significant differences in assumptions about human behavior that underlie behavioral psychology and neoclassical economics, they can lead to similar predictions for *experienced* agents. A behavioral psychology account of the law of demand would run as follows. Each week the consumer spends a $100 on groceries at the supermarket. In those weeks when the consumer chooses items marked "on sale," he finds that his basket contains more items. Looking for and buying items on sale or with newly reduced prices is reinforced. The experienced (well-conditioned) shopper behaves *as if* he were consciously maximizing a utility function subject to a budget constraint. Psychologists have been able to confirm the law of

---

[2] The seminal contributions are by Marwell and Ames (1979, 1980, 1981). For a short summary of the major findings, see Hoffman (1997, pp. 415–419).

[3] See Isaac, McCue, and Plott (1985), and again Hoffman (1997, pp. 415–419).

demand and other predictions of economics in the laboratory (Staddon, 1983). The thirsty rat, like his human cousin, has a negative sloped demand schedule for water.

Thus, because of the egoistic dimension that behavioral psychology and rational actor models share, both lead to much the same predictions with respect to the repeat actions of individuals in an unchanging environment. Behavioral psychology has the advantage over rational actor models of also being consistent with the seemingly "irrational" behavior of individuals in unusual situations, as for example the failure of people who have not been flood victims to purchase insurance against floods even when it is offered at less than its actuarial value (Kunreuther et al., 1978). In the absence of past rewards and punishments, all actions are essentially random events and there is no reason to expect them to conform to a rational actor model.

If one is willing to substitute the sort of hedonism assumed by the behavioral psychologist for the economist's utilitarianism, then behavioral psychology's description of human behavior can also be used in a *normative* defense of competitive markets. The market process conditions search on the part of consumers and innovation and efficiency on the part of firms. Consumers are rewarded with greater consumer's surplus for each dollar spent, firms with greater profits. In an unchanging environment market competition tends to maximize the rewards to consumers.

II Collective conditioning mechanisms

Every society contains institutions that reward behavior that benefits the community, and punishes socially harmful behavior. Customs and taboos play this role in primitive societies, state enforced laws in advanced societies. All religions have commandments forbidding various types of anti-social behavior. All religions have their "golden rules" that prescribe cooperative behavior in prisoners' dilemma situations.

The existence of these sorts of institutions can be explained in either behavioralist or Darwinian terms. A random act of punishing theft reduces the frequency of theft and thereby benefits all members of the community. Over time the collective habit of punishing theft evolves. Tribes which happen to develop taboos against incest produce healthier and more intelligent members, and win out in the evolutionary struggle against tribes which condone incest.

III "Irrational behavior"

Habits develop as a result of a rather crude causal association in a person's mind or subconscious. An event following an action is interpreted as being caused by it. Correlation often does not imply causality, as we all know, and thus individuals often mistakenly infer causality. Out of such mistakes arise habits that are afunctional or even dysfunctional. The football player accidently dons different colored socks on a day when he scores three goals, and consciously begins to wear nonmatching socks on days when there is a game.

For actions that are often repeated, the failure of the chance sequencing of events to reoccur generally leads to a reduction in frequency. But for some actions, reinforcement may occur often enough to maintain a habit once formed. Events loosely match those predicted by the day's horoscope with enough frequency that the individual continues to check the morning newspaper to see what the stars have in store for her today.

The importance of chance sequencing can also account for the variety of "collective habits" that we observe across cultures, and their differing mores and traditions. The tribe has unusually good luck hunting on a day when a pair of bald eagles is spotted, and it begins to pray to the eagle. Good luck by a full moon leads to prayers to the moon.

All religions reinforce habits of compliance with rewards and punishments. Most supplement immediate rewards and punishments with promises of much greater ones in the hereafter. Not being verifiable, these constitute a particularly effective way to sustain modes of behavior that would otherwise disappear.

Thus, the behavior of most individuals is a mixture of "good" habits that lead directly to improvements in the welfare of the individual; actions with no substantive consequences that are sustained by chance reinforcement in the past, and a certain number of dysfunctional "bad" habits that arose in the same way. The same sort of triumvirate of social institutions – functional, afunctional and dysfunctional – can be identified.

It should be stressed that dysfunctional behavior need not be restricted to primitive societies or to those of low IQ. Thomas Kuhn's (1970) discussion of scientific paradigms fits behavioral psychology well. The young scholar follows the structures of the reigning paradigm and is rewarded by the accolades of her peers. By middle age, the scientific habits of this paradigm are so thoroughly conditioned that she can adopt no other, even though her research under the old paradigm produces many falsified predictions, and is now frequently criticized by the young. Old scientists, like old dogs, cannot learn new methodological tricks. It is the young who must be conditioned to adopt the new paradigm.

IV Political behavior

One of the most famous and venerable results in the public choice literature is the Hotelling-Downs prediction that two parties competing over a single dimensional issue space converge on the same, central position. This prediction is not born out in the course of a single election, but does seem to emerge over time. Candidates perceived to be far to the left or right of the median of the ideological spectrum, as Barry Goldwater and George McGovern were, suffer humiliating defeats. Tony Blair brought the Labour Party back into power by abandoning the most extreme of its traditional ideological positions, and Bill Clinton – dubbed "Republican Lite" by his opponent in the last election – has survived in the face of a Republican Renaissance by occupying the center of the American ideological spectrum.

The tendency for extremist candidates to lose to centralist candidates, and thus the dominance of middle-of-the-road politicians in two-party systems can be interpreted in either Darwinian or Skinnerian terms. Those candidates who take positions far from the center and stick to them, tend not to survive in a two-party system. Those candidates who experiment with different positions find that movement toward the center is rewarded with increases in votes, movements away from the center are punished with fewer votes. Under either interpretation, one expects the Downsian prediction of candidates locating near the center to emerge. Candidates are not the only people whose behavior is conditioned by election outcomes, however.

When the sportsfan's attendance at a game is rewarded by the home team's victory, the probability that the fan attends another game increases. Winning teams have higher attendance figures than losing teams. A party or candidate's victory in an election rewards its supporters, while punishing the actions of the loser's backers.[4] In a two-party electoral system, some 40 percent or more of the electorate is disappointed by the election's outcome. In contrast, under proportional representation virtually all competing parties win some seats, and thus all party supporters are rewarded by at least the partial victory of their party. One predicts greater voter turnouts in PR-systems, and that is what one observes (Powell, 1982).

Of course, the voter's only reward or punishment from an election is not the victory or defeat of her party. The policy outcomes that flow from the election results should also affect the voter's behavior. Here, however, the link between action and reward or punishment is attenuated. First of all, the consequences of the election enfold over several years, which tends to break the subconscious causal chain. Second, the government's policies are likely to contain some elements that improve the voter's welfare and some that do not. Third, the voter may not recognize that a given change in her welfare was in fact a consequence of the election. Thus, both the act of voting and the choice of candidate or party are likely to be weakly rewarded or punished in a democratic system. For this reason, a large proportion of the rewards and punishments a voter experiences through participation in the democratic process come through the reactions of her peers rather than from the outcomes of the election itself.

This behavioralist interpretation of voting matches well what we know about voters. Those individuals who do vote, do so not because they expect their vote to be decisive and the victory of their preferred candidate to have a significant impact on their future welfare, as the rational choice literature postulates, but out of a sense of civic duty.[5] Good citizens are conditioned to do a lot of seemingly irrational things like contributing to charities, not littering, and queueing at bus stops. The rewards for these actions are typically the approbation of one's neighbors. With time these rewards become *internalized*, the voter's reward for voting is simply avoiding the guilty conscience she would have, if she did not vote.

---

[4] Brennan and Buchanan (1984) draw an analogy between voting and cheering for a sports team.

[5] The literature on voting is vast. For surveys, see Mueller (1989, Ch.17), and Aldrich (1997).

The choices voters make at the polls also conform to the predictions of behavioral psychology. The best account of voter choices is provided by the theory of *retrospective* voting.[6] When making a party choice the voter looks *backward* at her past choices, and the past performance of the party in office. Most empirical studies of voter behavior also find that voters have short memories. It is only the recent performance of a party that influences voter choices.[7]

Thus, the picture of the voter which emerges from the empirical literature is quite different from that underlying rational choice theories. Individuals are creatures of habit when they vote, as when they work and play. They vote for the same party in the present election as in the last one, unless that decision is perceived to have been unrewarded or punished. Unlike in market transactions, however, the rewards and punishments that follow voting are neither immediate nor often clearly linked to the act of voting. Thus, rational or irrational political beliefs and behavior – like beliefs in the prognostic powers of constellations of stars – are likely to persist even in individuals whose everyday behavior in the market place conforms well to that predicted by rational actor models.

Despite the potential for irrational political behavior, one can imagine a democratic system evolving in which citizens actively participate, punish governments which provide bad policies and reward those providing good ones. Parties are conditioned to provide good policies and the political participation of individual citizens is rewarded by these policies. The strength of the country's democratic institutions increases over time, as the good performance of governments and the responsible actions of citizens reinforce one another.

One can also readily imagine less happy democratic scenarios, however. The bad luck or bad policies of a government produce unhappiness in a large fraction of the population. Politicians and parties step forward with a variety of proposals to improve the situation. Having no experience with any of the parties, voters are ill-equipped to choose from among the options offered to them. They punish the existing government and replace it with a new one. Should they fail to elect a government that can significantly improve matters, it too is likely to be replaced. If fundamental reforms are required to improve outcomes, and a lag exists between implementing any reforms and their beneficial effects, no government may be able to survive long enough to correct matters. The country shifts from one government to another, sometimes returning a previous party to power without ever hitting upon a party or a set of policies that voters judge to have benefitted them. Citizens perceive meagre benefits from democracy, and do not defend it when it comes under attack from a demagogic politician or general.

Such attacks on democracy cannot succeed, of course, without the support of some elements of the population. Such support is made possible, even for the most ruthless dictator with the most improbable ideology, by the irrationality inherent in politics. Having been punished by the present

[6] See Fiorina (1981, 1997) and Hibbs (1987).

[7] See Paldam (1997, p. 346).

government, citizens are willing to try a new one. Should this one fail too, its failure may not be linked to its improbable ideology or the actions of its leaders. With time the memory of a government's failures fades and is displaced by experience with the most recent government. Thus, failed parties with improbable ideologies survive to govern again.

V The dilemma of democracy

Philosophers have been well aware of dilemmas arising out of social interaction and have propounded one logical argument after another to convince themselves, and indirectly we nonphilosophers, of the wisdom and morality of behaving cooperatively. An Immanuel Kant can readily recognize that mankind's only real choice is between a world in which everyone cooperates and one in which no one does, and from this observation conclude that it is in every rational individual's self-interest to cooperate. Few people seem to follow this chain of reasoning, however. While under the Kantian logic, cooperation is rational in *all* prisoners' dilemma situations, we tend to observe it only where individuals have been conditioned to cooperate. Cooperation is strongest in the family, followed by groups with ethnic, religious or similar cultural ties. Large cities have always had a reputation for greater crime than their surrounding countrysides, as one anticipates given the changing identities and greater numbers of participants in the many prisoners' dilemmas that are enacted in a large city each day. Crime is no where more rampant today than in the teaming megapolises of the developing world, filled with their recent migrants from the countryside. When informal rewards and punishment do not suffice to induce cooperative behavior, society resorts to the state to mete out punishment. Here, as in many other areas, the United States has become the world leader with its ever escalating penalties for crime, and its ever expanding number of overcrowded prisons.

These developments have disturbing implications for the performance of democratic institutions, as individual participation in the democratic process is itself a sort of prisoners' dilemma. Joseph Schumpeter (1950, pp. 250–264) was perhaps the first to emphasize the irrationality of active and informed participation in the democratic process, and Anthony Downs's (1957) expression "rational ignorance" has joined "free rider" and a handful of other terms coined by economists in the layman's vocabulary. Despite the blatant irrationality of the act of voting, apparent to all economists, millions of citizens – and even a few economists – have persistently participated in the democratic process. Behavioral psychology can again come to the rescue and account for this anomaly. In the small New England or Swiss village, townspeople gather at the polling place on election day. Each citizen knows the other, and the absence of any one of them is readily observed. Where direct democracy is still practiced in Switzerland, the day on which the townspeople meet to exercise their rights as citizens is a local holiday in which citizens don their traditional customs and socialize with their neighbors.

But the small towns of New England and Switzerland, like small towns in all other industrialized parts of the world, have seen their young people move to the cities, and many who now live in them commute to the cities. Ties to community have weakened, and consequently the habit-reinforcing effects of peer group pressure have also weakened. Citizen participation in the democratic process is declining in every mature democracy in the world.

The social response to noncooperative behavior of other forms is to pass laws, impose penalties and hire police, that is to invoke the power of the state. But behind the *democratic* state is the *demos*. The essence of democracy is that the citizens rule. But if the citizens choose independently not to rule, the citizens collectively are not going to be able to compel them to do so, or at least not very easily. One can, of course, fine or bribe people to vote, and some countries do this. But one cannot fine people who choose to remain uninformed. Rational ignorance remains a challenge to democracy even if voter participation can be somehow compelled and sustained. Indeed, it becomes more of a problem, since the additional participation induced by compulsory voting is of the least well-informed members of the community. Their participation seems more likely to worsen the outcomes from democracy than to improve them.

VI The viability of market and democratic institutions

A. Market institutions

The rewards from trade are apparent to every pair of children when they first exchange a piece of candy for a piece of gum. Each exchange rewards both buyer and seller and reinforces their loyalty to the exchange process. Thus, the opening up of markets to unrestricted exchange as occurred in Eastern Europe and the Soviet Union following 1989 and 1991 could and has won quick converts to the merits of markets.

The benefits from spot market transactions are immediate and apparent, and thus this form of behavior is readily learned. The benefits from saving and investment are less immediate. The pain of reduced consumption is immediate, but the reward of additional consumption comes later and is more uncertain. Thus, both individuals and governments find it more difficult to acquire the habit of saving than that of spending. It is similarly difficult to establish institutions that encourage saving, investing, innovating and risktaking. Although the former Communist countries have by and large become *free market* economies, in the sense that much exchange taking place is at market determined prices, they have not succeeded nearly so well in becoming *capitalist* countries with institutions that secure property rights, enforce long-run contracts and encourage investment, innovation and risktaking.

This failure has resulted in the former Communist countries experiencing less investment and growth than they otherwise could have, of course. But it has had another perhaps even more unfortunate consequence. Market competition creates winners and losers. Many regard this aspect of a market/capitalist system as its most unfortunate characteristic. When the profits of the winners are obtained from innovations and investment, however, they can be defended by pointing to the new products, jobs, and overall increase in social welfare that accompanied them. Bill Gates' immense wealth can be tolerated, if not celebrated, by all, because it has come from the spectacular growth of a company whose success is due to a continual stream of product improvements.

Many of the nouveau riche in the post-communist countries, however, have earned their fortunes through arbitraging differences in spot market prices in the West and East, or by acquiring existing assets owned by the state at bargain prices. Although arbitrage can enhance social welfare, arbitragers do not create assets, jobs and wealth, and thus their conspicuously displayed riches are more difficult to defend.

If asked to explain the collapse of Communism, most Western economists would probably begin by talking about the virtues of markets, invisible hands, and the like. Most would, and this would certainly be true of members of the Schumpeter Society, go on, however, to discuss the failure of Communism to generate the product and process innovations that a dynamically competitive capitalist economy produces. Communism's singular failure was not its pricing and allocation of *existing products*, but its failure to develop new ones.[8] The post-Communist countries have also failed, relative to their potential, by not adopting institutions that facilitate the capital investment and innovation of a dynamically competitive capitalist economy. Introducing such institutions would require, however, the kind of forward looking, farsighted behavior on the part of citizens and politicians that our rational actor models typically assume exists, and psychological experiments seldom confirm.

B. Democratic institutions

When Communism collapsed, both those living in the Communist countries and those in the West expected these countries to adopt both the capitalist and the democratic institutions of the West. These institutions were conceptually conjoined. Capitalism and democracy in tandem would increase economic and social welfare. In no former Communist country has this prediction been realized to the degree that many thought would occur.

Our behavioralist discussion of human action helps us to understand why this has been so. Democracy, unlike market exchange, yields few immediate benefits. A free press allows the citizen to learn more about her government and those in it, but what she learns does not always make her happy. The right to vote allows her to express her preferences for public policies, but majoritarian democracy ensures that nearly half of the population fails to have its preferences satisfied. Where market exchange produces only winners, democratic action inevitably produces winners and losers. The benefits from democracy are both less immediate and less apparent. The frustrated citizen/voter can well wonder whether another party, or another set of institutions might not yield better outcomes. The

---

[8] Murrell (1990).

demagogue's promises of immediate prosperity can easily captivate someone who perceives little gain from democracy's outcomes. Democratic institutions, like the basic institutions of capitalism, can increase the welfare of society only over the long run. For this to happen, forward looking, farsighted behavior on the part of citizens and politicians is again required.

VII The future of capitalism and democracy

Behavioral psychology gives a good description of how humans learn, and can account for many of their actions, particularly at the early stages of their development. But as humans pass from childhood into adulthood, many seem to "breakout" of their conditioned behavior patterns. Many begin to question why it is that they should behave in this way or that. Many begin to think and act in at least some areas, as our rational actor models predict.

The same process seems to take place occasionally at the societal level. The behavior of members of a primitive society, heavily constrained by customs, traditions and superstitions, seems to conform to what one would expect from behavioral psychology. The same might be said of the rather static, slowly evolving societies of the Dark and Middle Ages. But during the first half of the present millennium Western Society, like many a bright adolescent, began to break out of its intellectual constraints. The advances in science, mathematics and philosophy that the European Renaissance unleashed suggest that the human mind possesses the capacity to engage in rational thought at the highest levels.

Probably no single sentence in all of philosophy is better known than Descartes' "I think therefore I am." In placing the individual and his thought process at the center of the search for a proof of God's existence, Descartes embraced the revolutionary idea that evidence of God's existence was not to be found in declarations of the Church, or the King, nor by consulting a holy book or a holy man, but in the reasoning process of the individual contemplating God's existence before his fireplace in the solitude of his study. If a thinking man could construct an argument for God's existence that convinced himself, then God existed. No higher authority was needed than the rational logic of an individual's own mind.

Descartes helped to advance the transformation in Western thought that began in the Renaissance and culminated in the Enlightenment, a transformation that saw the individual move to center stage in social and philosophical analysis, and which placed increasing faith in the individual's powers of reason. Democracy was also rediscovered during Europe's intellectual reawakening in Renaissance Italy. It was the thinking of the Enlightenment, however, with its optimistic faith in human reasoning that provided democracy its intellectual raison d'être. The optimism of the Enlightenment is reflected in Adam Smith's *Wealth of Nations* (1776), with its faith in the invisible hand of market competition, and in the U.S. Declaration of Independence with its faith in man's capacity for self-government.

The thinking of the Enlightenment can also be discerned in the U.S. Constitution. In putting this thinking into practice, however, the Founding Fathers exhibited considerable concern about democracy's potential excesses, and accordingly considerable caution. The popularly elected House of Representatives was to be held in check by both the Senate and the President, neither of whom was to be popularly elected. Considerable caution was also apparent in the original constitutions of the individual states, which often set the term of office of a governor at one year. Perhaps, no aspect of the early phases of American democracy reveals the Founders' ambivalence over democracy's potential better than the requirements each state placed on participation in the democratic process, requirements that limited participation to a tiny fraction of the population.

Writing almost a century after the signing of the Declaration of Independence, John Stuart Mill (1861, p. 114) would also express deep concern about the potential of democratic government.

The natural tendency of representative government, as of modern civilization, is toward collective mediocrity; and this tendency is increased by all reductions and extensions of the franchise, their effect being to place the principal power in the hands of classes more and more below the highest level of instruction in the community.

John Stuart Mill was arguably the greatest mind of the 19th century, and one of its most liberal thinkers. The quoted lines come from a treatise in which Mill proclaimed the newly invented proportional representation system to be "one of the greatest improvements yet made in the theory and practice of government." Mill believed, based "on principles of equal justice," that "every minority in the whole nation [was] entitled to a representative" (Mill, 1861, p. 111). Yet he also believed that the demands placed upon the citizen by a system of self-government were so great that participation in such a system had to be limited to those of "the highest level of instruction in the community."

Anyone today who even suggests that the privilege of voting be limited to those who can read and write, or to those possessing a modicum of knowledge about the institutions of government, is immediately labeled an arch conservative – or much worse. Yet we have seen that the rationale underlying democracy rests on the premise that the individual participant possesses a certain capacity to reason, a capacity to recognize the cooperative nature of the democratic game, and to perceive the long run benefits from playing this game cooperatively, despite being rewarded only intermittently and indirectly for such behavior. The history of democratic government, most of which has been written over the last 200 years, gives ample evidence of the fragility of democracy. This history offers no grounds for assuming that democratic government can thrive or even merely survive regardless of the cultural environment in which it is planted, or the inputs it receives from the citizens.

In a few places it has survived. Switzerland, the United Kingdom, and the United States have all enjoyed long, uninterrupted histories of democratic rule with only occasional threats to their democratic institutions as during the Civil War in the United States and World War II in the United

Kingdom. All of the Western Europe countries seem likely to continue being democracies into the indefinite future. Even if citizen participation in the democratic process continues to wane in the West, a total collapse of democracy does not seem imminent.

The notion that humans possess the intelligence and self-restraint to govern themselves democratically is distinctly of Western origin. It is among the ancient Greeks that concepts like individualism and humanism first appear, and perhaps no society has ever proclaimed and trusted man's capacity to reason more than the Greeks. That the Greeks would invent democracy seems almost natural in this respect. Yet even among their most formidable thinkers, like Plato, grave doubts were expressed about the *average* citizen's capabilities, and thus about the desirability of democratic government.

Democracy is Western in origin, and where it exists today, it is almost exclusively a Western transplant. It has its firmest roots where Western influence is the strongest. All of the democracies of the New World have Western origins. In Asia's oldest democracies, India, Japan, and the Philippines, a departing Western occupier either provided the model for the country's democratic institutions, or dictated their form. Africa's strongest democracy is arguably South Africa, its most Western country. Democracy has taken tenuous hold in only a few countries in the Middle East – Israel, Turkey, Egypt perhaps – and these too are the most Western-oriented of the Middle Eastern countries. No country has adopted democratic institutions that are not modeled on those of the West. Until only very recently, the origin of every democratic country's institutions could be traced directly back to Europe.

Samuel Hunington (1996) has recently emphasized how unique Western culture is among the world's civilizations with respect to the emphasis it places on individualism, humanism, rational behavior, and the like. Hunington goes so far as to predict a sometimes violent "*clash*" between Western civilization and its many rivals. Even if the differences between the West and the rest are not so great as to lead to major, armed confrontations, they are great enough to suggest that democracy may not take firm root in many non-Western countries, and may indeed never be tried in some.

Strong tribal alliances lead naturally to the kind of redistributive coalitions and winner-take-all approach to politics that so often produces violence and the overthrow of democracy. Tribal traditions can engender habits of obedience to leadership that make dictatorship seem like the natural form of government.

When tribal and ethnic loyalties do not stand in the way of democracy, religion often can. The only notable difference between the Northern Irish is that some are Catholic others Protestant, yet this difference has sufficed to make normal civil and democratic society impossible. Past conditioning has generated strong patterns of hatred, which are reinforced by occasional new acts of violence. Although Catholics and Protestants in Northern Ireland have been locked into a series of prisoners' dilemma supergames, they have continued to play the noncooperative strategies. It is difficult to reconcile day-to-day events in Northern Ireland over the 20th century with the postulate of rational, self-interested individual behavior.

The same can be said for Israel. Only an extreme optimist could envisage Jews and Moslems in Israel meeting to write a constitution that would advance their common interests, in the way that scholars in constitutional political economy assume that rational actors write constitutions.[9]

Where Descartes began his celebrated demonstration of God's existence with the words "I think," the Apostles' Creed begins with the words "I believe." In religion belief substitutes for thought, and most organized religions demand an unquestioning obedience to God. Religion can foster authoritarian modes of behavior that are easily transferred to a political leader, particularly when he dons the robes of the state's religion, or claims the support of the church for his rule. Why consult the citizens regarding which actions the state should undertake, when there are those in the society who can consult with and speak for God? The rise of fundamentalist religious movements in many parts of the world bodes ill for the future of democracy in these areas – and that is true also for the United States. One often hears Americans complain about the dearth in quality of the candidates for public office today in comparison with previous eras. Yet, if that quintessential man of the Enlightenment, Thomas Jefferson, where alive today, his agnosticism alone, not to mention his other liberal and radical views, would preclude his being elected President. Is it the quality of the candidates or the quality of the electorate that has declined in America compared with previous eras?

The claim is sometimes made – by political leaders in Asia – that their conformist, collectivist culture is better suited to nondemocratic forms of government. Support for this position might be gleaned from the public choice literature. If the purpose of democratic participation is to reveal differing individual preferences in a heterogeneous society, then there may be less need for such participation in a society whose members share "common values." Whether Asian societies are all that homogeneous, and whether they will remain so with increasing exposure to not only Western culture, but also the other cultures of the world, is debatable. Less debatable is the fact that Asia's few democracies have tended to be dominated by a single party throughout their short histories.

Thus, as one looks into the 21st century, it is difficult to foresee capitalist and democratic institutions spreading hand and hand around the globe. Of the two, it is certainly capitalism that will march forward more triumphantly. Its rewards are more immediate and apparent. Its institutions and modes of thought can be directly transplanted through the spread of multinationals in ways that are not possible for democracy.

Capitalism has already taken firm root in Asia and Latin America, of course. Indeed, to the extent a conformist, collectivist characterization of Asian culture is accurate, Asia may be a more hospitable soil for capitalism than that of the West – at least for the kind of *corporate capitalism* that is dominant at the close of the 20th century. Conformity to the corporate cultures of large hierarchical organizations may be easier for workers and managers who share the common values of the East, than for those in the West who fancy themselves to be individualists.

---

[9] For example, Buchanan and Tullock (1962) and Mueller (1996).

Even capitalism's triumph is unlikely to be complete, however. The many failed experiments in sub-Saharan Africa suggest that its soil provides a fertile bed for neither capitalism nor democracy with South Africa again the possible lone exception. The same can be said of the sands of the Middle East. Were it not for the impressive economic growth of Indonesia, one would be tempted to hypothesize that Islam and capitalism are somehow antithetical. And recent developments suggest that even Indonesia's economic success may prove to be transitory.

And what of democracy's triumphs? These certainly will be fewer and even less secure. After some 50 or 70 years of repression, one might have expected democracy to take strong hold following Communism's collapse. But it has not done so, or at least not in most cases. Perhaps, this is because the revolutions that ended Communism were too short and too bloodless. No centuries long struggle to wrest power from the crown took place as that which led to democracy's triumph in Great Britain. No armed struggle to wrest power from the crown took place as that which led to democracy's triumph in the United States. As a result, there has been neither the occasion nor the necessity for a John Locke, a John Paine, or a James Madison to make the case for liberty and democracy, and design the institutions to ensure their continued existence. The former Communist countries quickly donned the democratic institutions of their West European neighbors, as a less fortunate family might don the well-worn clothes of its rich neighbors, without pausing to consider how well they fit, or whether new clothes, better tailored to their needs, might not be worth considering. In some cases these borrowed clothes barely concealed the fact that the same persons were governing in much the same way after Communism's fall as before. But even in the most democratic of the former Communist countries, politics lacks the enthusiasm and idealism one might have expected following so many years of dictatorship. Instead, democratic politics in the former Communist countries, where it exists, mirrors politics in the West with all of its rent seeking, corruption and zero-sum game orientation.

Thus, one should not be surprised if democracy succumbs to dictatorship in many of the former Communist countries, as it has with great regularity in Africa, and all too frequently in Latin America. The same is likely to be true in those parts of Asia where democracy is tried. In this essay I have tried to explain why this occurs. Most of us most of the time are creatures of habit responding to the rewards and punishments of the recent past. Democracy in practice means *majoritarian* democracy. Majoritarian democracy tends to reward about as many persons as it punishes with defeat. Many of the benefits that citizens derive from democracy do not arise out of the electoral process as such, but from the institutions that evolve along with free elections – an independent and impartial judiciary, a free press, and the like. Only the most farsighted and forward looking of a country's citizens are likely to appreciate the causal linkages between the existence of these democratic institutions and the quality of their lives.

In practice democracy often does not seem to sustain the habits and loyalty that induce citizens and politicians to behave responsibly. In the most extreme cases, democracy fails to sustain sufficient loyalty to its basic institutions to motivate citizens and politicians to rise to democracy's defense when it is endangered. Thus, although the behavior of many persons in a democracy may not be well *explained* by the rational actor paradigm, a *normative* defense of democracy generally requires that we assume the kind of farsighted, cooperative behavior that only the most sophisticated of rational actors would exhibit. Moreover, without this sophisticated, farsighted behavior on the part of individual citizens, democracy may be unable to survive the many short run challenges it faces. And this may be the most paradoxical of democracy's many paradoxes.

References

Aldrich JH (1997) When is it rational to vote. In: Mueller DC (1997), pp 373–390
Brennan G, Buchanan JM (1984) Voter choice: evaluating political alternatives. American Behavioral Scientist 28: 185–201
Buchanan JM, Tullock G (1962) The calculus of consent. University of Michigan Press, Ann Arbor
Downs A (1957) An economic theory of democracy. Harper and Row, New York
Fiorina MP (1981) Retrospective voting in American national elections. Yale University Press, New Haven
Fiorina MP (1997) Voting behavior. In: Mueller DC (1997), pp 391–414
Hibbs DA Jr (1987) American political economy. Harvard University Press, Cambridge, MA
Hoffman E (1997) Public choice experiments. In: Mueller DC (1997), pp 415–426
Hunington SP (1996) The clash of civilizations and the remaking of world order. Simon & Schuster, New York
Isaac RM, McCue K, Plott CR (1985) Public goods provision in an experimental environment. Journal of Public Economics 26: 51–74
Kuhn TS (1970) The structure of scientific revolutions. 2nd edn. University of Chicago Press, Chicago
Kunreuther H, Ginsberg R, Miller R, Sagi P, Slovic P, Borkan B, Katz, N (1978) Disaster insurance protection. Wiley, New York
Marwell G, Ames RE (1979) Experiments on the provision of public goods. I. Resources, interest, group size, and the free rider problem. American Journal of Sociology 84: 335–360
Marwell G, Ames RE (1980) Experiments on the provision of public goods. II. Provision points, stakes, experience, and the free rider problem, American Journal of Sociology 85: 926–937
Marwell G, Ames RE (1981) Economists free ride: does anyone else? Journal of Public Economics. 15: 295–310
Mill JS (1958) Considerations on representative government. Bobbs-Merrill, New York (first publication, 1861)
Mueller DC (1989) Public choice II. Cambridge University Press, Cambridge
Mueller DC (1996) Constitutional democracy. Oxford University Press, Oxford
Mueller DC (ed) (1997) Perspectives on public choice. Cambridge University Press, Cambridge
Murrell P (1990) The nature of socialism, Princeton University Press, Princeton
Paldam M (1997) Political business cycles. In: Mueller DC pp 342–370
Powell G (1982) Contemporary democracies. Harvard University Press, Cambridge, MA
Schumpeter JA (1950) Capitalism, socialism and democracy, 3rd edn. Harper and Row, New York
Smith A The wealth of nations. The Modern Library, New York (first published 1776)
Staddon JER (1983) Adaptive behavior and learning. Cambridge University Press, Cambridge

A spectre is haunting the world – the spectre of *global* capitalism

William Kingston

School of Business Studies, Trinity College, Dublin, Ireland
(e-mail: wkngston@tcd.ie)

Abstract. Individual property rights are fruitful for economic development because they civilise self-interest by forcing it to serve the common good. The history of previous property rights "cycles," however, shows that their ability to do this deteriorates over time because the laws of property fall under the control of those whom property is meant to discipline. Irresponsible ownership then intensifies inequality until a breaking point is reached. The present cycle is no exception, but its breaking point has been postponed by the growth of the democratically-inspired welfare state.

Globalisation is now eroding the financial basis of this, because mobile capital can escape taxation, leaving labour to carry the burden. The main thrust of this movement is now found in the World Trade Organisation, whose control of intellectual property and commitment to free trade in money as well as goods, can only increase inequality between countries as well as within them. It represents individual property rights which are out of any form of social control, since there is no *global* mechanism for civilising self-interest. Schumpeter's sense of the impending demise of capitalism, if not of its replacement by socialism, may yet be vindicated.

Key words: Property rights – Globalisation – World Trade Organisation – Schumpeter

JEL-classification: A13, F02, K00, P10

Paper presented at the 1998 World Conference of the International Joseph A. Schumpeter Society, Vienna, June 13–16, 1998.

1 Introduction – Schumpeter's wrong prediction

Exactly a century and a half ago as we meet, Marx and Engels published the Communist Manifesto, announcing that "A Spectre is haunting Europe – the spectre of Communism." In 1942, in his "*Capitalism, Socialism and Democracy*," Schumpeter forecast a less apocalyptic future for property-owners by claiming that capitalism would inevitably be replaced by socialism. Social scientists like to think that for them, as in hard science, the test of sound theory is the power to predict; and by this criterion, Schumpeter's theory seems to have been a poor one. The opposite of what he forecast has occurred, even to the extent of the evidence of collectivism's inferiority being hailed as "*The End of History*" (Fukuyama, 1992). The spectre of Communism appears to have been finally exorcised.

However, social science suffers from the disability of not being able to conduct experiments in the ways hard science can, so predictions in it may depend heavily upon the time scale within which hypotheses are considered to be vindicated or disproved. In the case of the prediction which has done Schumpeter's reputation so much damage, there are now a number of indications that the time-scale of at least part of the "experiment" may have been too short. This is not an issue where the jury is still out, therefore, so much as one in which they may have come back from the jury-room with a verdict too hastily.

2 Capitalism in a property rights context

Capitalism is the modern variant of the systems of individual property rights which made the Western world uniquely rich, because they enable individual human creativity to be directed into economic channels (see Rosenberg and Birdzell, 1986). By definition, *Homo economicus* looks only to his own interest, but individual property rights force him to serve social ends in doing so. The tragedy of the commons, whereby freedom of access to a resource held in common results in ruin to all (Hardin, 1968) is avoided. Civil society (including democracy) can emerge from the social space and opportunity which individual property rights provide (cf. Berger, 1993, p. 6). The unique value of such rights, therefore, is that they can *civilise* self-interest. Schumpeter even saw part of the definition of the State in terms of this function:

It is part of its nature that it opposes individual egoism as a representative of a common purpose. Only then is it a separate, distinguishable social entity ([1918] 1991, p. 110).

Individual property rights first emerged fully in Classical times, articulated philosophically by Aristotle, and were characteristically *absolute*, even to the extent of applying to wives and slaves. It was these which made industry and widespread trade possible in Roman times, and it was the same absolute property rights which subsequently underwrote the remarkable effusion of monastic agricultural and technological innovation over several later centuries (cf. Evans, 1996–1997). In fact, Randall Collins has argued most persuasively that Max Weber was wrong to locate the source of modern capitalism in the ethics of the Reformation. Instead,

> the rise of medieval Christendom was the main Weberian revolution, creating the institutional forms within which capitalism could emerge... And there are earlier examples (both in early Christian monasticism and in Chinese Buddhism) where we see the same kind of "Protestant ethic" connection between religiously motivated asceticism and economic productivity, but under quite different theological outlooks (1986, p. 76).

More recently, Lutz Kaelber (1998) has elaborated the same theme.

The medieval period also saw the emergence of a new type of property rights, which were *qualified* instead of being absolute, and these can take credit for much of the growth of urban society, with the wealth and world-wide exploration associated with it, which followed. But after the wars of religion, and justified by the philosophy of the Enlightenment, absolute property rights reasserted the primacy which they had lost. As Lynn White Jr. observed,

> The feudal sense that the enjoyment of wealth is inseparable from public responsibility chiefly distinguishes medieval ideas of ownership from both classical and modern. The vassal class created by the mutation of the eighth century became the ruling element of European society, but throughout all subsequent chaos and despite abuses, it never lost completely its sense of *noblesse oblige*, even when a new and rival class of burghers revived the Roman notion of the unconditional and socially irresponsible possession of property (1964, p. 31, 1968, p. 65).

2.1 Absolute ownership and bourgeois achievement

The revived "Roman notion of the unconditional and socially irresponsible possession of property" is the institutional basis of the economic system which we call capitalism, as Max Weber has correctly shown ([1923] 1961, Part IV; [1904–5] 1976). It was this which made the industrial revolutions possible, in the hands of the "new class of burghers" that Schumpeter saw as the dynamic element in the modern economic world. He noted, too, that "a panegyric upon bourgeois achievement that has no equal in economic literature" is to be found in, of all places, that Communist Manifesto, and concerning this famous document, he urges us to

> observe, in particular, the emphasis upon the *creative* role of the business class. Never, I repeat, and in particular by no modern defender of the Bourgeois civilisation, never has a brief been composed on behalf of the business class from so profound and so wide a comprehension of what its achievement is and what it means to humanity (1949, p. 209).

Indeed, one of the ideas for which Schumpeter himself is best remembered, that of "creative destruction" as the driving force of capitalist economic life, is foreshadowed in Marx and Engels's claim in the Manifesto that

The bourgeoisie cannot exist without constantly revolutionizing the instruments of production...and during its reign of scarce one hundred years, (it) has created more massive and more colossal productive forces than have all previous generations put together... what earlier century had even a presentiment that such productive forces slumbered in the lap of social labour? ([1848] 1950, p. 43).

2.2 Property rights and market power

All this comes about because property rights make markets possible, and the concept of freedom is often benignly associated with the word "market." When owners of property praise the free market, however, they almost always mean freedom from having to subordinate the use of property to external values. This is the source of the "irresponsible" ownership to which Lynn White Jr. referred. In what follows, "socially non-responsible" will be used instead of "irresponsible" to identify this, in case the word "irresponsible" might be taken to indicate that property-owners were altogether predatory in its use. Some of them are, but the more usual objective in using property is the more moderate one of extending its autonomy. At the same time, it is rare for this not to include an element of seeking to escape from co-operating in the social purpose for which the property laws ostensibly exist.

The ethical justification of laws which confer rights of individual property is that the exercise of these rights in a self-interested way is forced into channels which also serve the public good. "Socially non-responsible" is used here simply to indicate that this requirement is absent from the rights in question, so that they can be exercised without seeking or needing justification outside the maximisation of their own value. If this exercise is in any sense unethical, then, blame is rather to be attributed to those who make the laws of property, than to owners of the resulting property rights. As will be seen below, however, part of the problem raised by contemporary property rights is that those who own property are increasingly tending to be the effective law-makers also.

So much for what property-owners mean by the free market. Its alternative – "economists' " – meaning, which is a market with few or no barriers to entry, describes a situation where prices are under constant downwards pressure. This can never be what property-owners want. If profits or rents are to be earned, there must be means of escaping from a market's freedom of entry condition, and all such means of escape amount to market power. Paradoxically, then, market power is not the power to make a market (since this implies freedom of entry) but to *unmake* it, to find ways of escaping the constraints – especially in terms of price – which market forces seek to impose. Simple concepts of property have been greatly extended so that modern property rights now provide a sophisticated range of such escape means. These can be assembled into a market power paradigm (which is a dictionary of terms which will be used subsequently in this paper) along the following lines (Kingston, 1984).

2.3 A market power paradigm

Without exception, all market power can be traced to an identifiable source in positive law, and such sources, which are always laws of property, fall under three headings. The most obvious is Specific market power, where the barriers to entry are immediately identifiable laws or ordinances. Examples are all types of industrial protection, licences and, of course, intellectual property.

Next is the market power of Capability, obtained through investment in productive assets. This largely depends upon the laws which provide for joint stock companies and limited liability. Without these, the large-scale funding which corporations require would not be obtainable, and neither would professional management have evolved, since this depended in its origin on being separated from ownership.

Investment in psychological assets ("reputation") similarly results in Persuasive market power, primarily through developing Brands (granted true monopoly status by Trade Mark *registration* law) and advertising (protected by copyright law). The exclusive right in the registered trade mark allows massive investment to be made in marketing, especially in advertising, to build up knowledge of, interest in and preference for branded products to levels where only a few oligopolistic firms will survive in any product market. It can even be argued that such firms may benefit from massive rents through being members of a *virtual cartel* (Kingston, 1984, p. 66).

An illustration of the economic importance of brands to-day is that when a large firm in a branded goods industry is bought over, the price paid is typically at least 10 times its book value. The difference is the worth of the firm's intangible assets, mainly its brands, whose market power is built upon the legal monopoly of their associated registered trade marks. Nor is it by any means only the industries which are characterised by branded products, particularly those of fast-moving consumer goods, that depend almost wholly for their existence on trade mark registration law. The range of services which these products require, amount to large industries in themselves, and these would simply collapse if there were no brands in the modern sense, that is, those which depend upon having a legally-granted trade mark monopoly. Franchised businesses, from hotels to hamburgers, also depend completely on trade mark registration law. For them, it is essential that ownership of a brand can be legally separate from ownership of the associated physical assets. To-day, too, the media obtain most of their revenue from advertising, and professional sport is so largely financed by sponsorship that it also would be impossible without brands developed on the basis of legal trademark monopoly.

2.4 Earlier property rights "cycles"

All individual property rights give an economic dimension to natural differences in ambitions and aptitudes between persons, and absolute property rights of course intensify the resulting inequalities. This intensification becomes still greater because of what seems to be an inevitable tendency for those who possess property, also to gain control of the institutions and laws which confer and enforce it. Consequently, although individual property rights *can* civilise self-interest, they *need* not do so. In fact, they can *only* be effective in this way to the extent that they are not themselves the expression of self-interest. Because self-interest invariably seeks to capture the forces which can discipline it, the result, as John Stuart Mill (1848, Book II) pointed out, has been that "the laws of property have never yet conformed to the principles upon which the institution of private property rests." In at least three previous historical periods (which might even be designated as property rights "cycles") individual property rights began by underwriting prosperity but ended with power concentrated in relatively few hands, not responsible to anyone nor to any criterion other than its own preservation and expansion.

In the days of its strength, for example, "[T]he Graeco-Roman world was essentially...one of private ownership... a world of private trade, private manufacture" (Finley, 1973, p. 29). But Gibbon ([1776–1778], 1963, Chs. I–III) observed that by the third century A.D., when the Roman Empire was wilting under the attacks of the barbarians, property ownership had become highly concentrated in the hands of those who would not fight to preserve it, because at heart they did not believe that they deserved to have it.

Likewise, the remarkable technical and economic dynamism of the medieval monasteries (especially in their Cistercian mode) was eventually corrupted into privilege and luxury on the basis of their absolute ownership of vast tracts of land and of their involvement in finance, especially in mortgages. (Kingston, 1996; Kaelber, 1998). This lost them popular support and left them fatally vulnerable to predatory kings and nobles. In a still later property rights "cycle," the French revolution set off a widespread reaction to extreme inequalities, similarly caused by individual property rights which were held and used without responsibility.

It seems clear, therefore, that the dynamic energy in individual property rights, which is their ability to civilise self-interest, inevitably deteriorates over time in a way which fits well into Georgescu-Roegen's (1971) description of the growth of entropy in the economic process. The result is growth in parallel of non-responsibility and inequality. Almost any degree of inequality appears to be tolerable, as long as responsibility is present: if the alternative for a medieval peasant is to be expropriated by a predatory warrior, for example, his contribution to the great wealth, power and prestige of his liege lord, who is able and willing to protect him, is a price that will be paid, however grudgingly.

It is equally a matter of common observation that non-responsible behaviour of many different kinds, as long as it does not affect ourselves personally, is quite widely tolerated. But it is the *combination* of the two conditions which seems to be potentially fatal for individual property rights. As an example, for the Soviet expert, Richard Pipes, this explains

> why Russian serfs, who had borne the burdens of serfdom for so long, found them intolerable after 1762 when the Crown freed the gentry from compulsory service and transformed them into a leisure class (1998).

3 Democracy and welfare transfers

The French revolution, and the later revolutions which took their inspiration from it, were reactions to such a combination in the form of the *ancien régime*. Where the inequality and irresponsibility were greatest, as in Russia, such property rights as existed were all but wiped out completely, in the spirit of Proudhon ("Property is theft") and on the basis of Marx's economics. However, in some areas, correlated with the survival of some residual element of Lynn White Jr.'s "feudal sense that the enjoyment of wealth is inseparable from public responsibility," democracy gradually emerged (cf. Huntington, 1991, pp. 72–73, 98). Schumpeter defined democracy in terms of rivalrous competition in the market for votes ([1942] 1950, p. 269). Since every market depends on the existence of property, the vote can consequently be seen as a new type of individual property right, capable of acting as a counterbalance to property of traditional types by giving political power to numbers simply as numbers.

The practical result of this counterbalance has been the welfare state, mitigating the effects of ever-stronger, more concentrated and less "responsible" property rights by correspondingly bigger transfers to those of no or little property. It was such transfers, more than anything else, which falsified Schumpeter's forecast of the replacement of capitalism by socialism. The economic success of the countries which were characterised by them has been in marked contrast to the failure of the countries which tried to operate command economies. By the early 1990s, final economic victory, it appeared, had gone to a system which combines absolute property rights for the production of wealth, with welfare transfers, raised by taxation as a result of democratic pressures, to temper the inevitable resulting inequalities.

3.1 The Welfare State in trouble

More recently, however, Schumpeter's pessimism (because his own preference was for a capitalist system) has begun to be echoed by a new wave of writers, whose concerns are summed up by the theme of Lester Thurow's "*The Future of Capitalism*":

The eternal verities of capitalism – growth, full employment, financial stability, rising real wages – seem to be vanishing just as the enemies of capitalism vanish... in two decades capitalism lost 60% of its momentum (1996, p. 3).

The philosopher, John Gray (1995, 1998) sees what is happening as the collapse of what he calls "the Enlightenment Project." This hoped to create a single, worldwide civilisation, the economic aspect of which was "the inexorable advance of a singular type of western capitalism, the American free market." These two writers share awareness with many others of the emergence of the phenomenon which has been observed towards the end of earlier property rights "cycles," viz. the combination of socially non-responsible ownership with an unacceptable level of inequality.

There are three main reasons why property has become less "socially-responsible" in recent years. Firstly, making the laws which confer property rights has come progressively more under the control of those who benefit from these rights. This trend was noted particularly by Buchanan and Tullock as long ago as 1962:

We may observe a notable expansion in the range and extent of collective activity over the last half-century – especially in that category of activity appropriately classified as differential or discriminatory legislation. During the same period we have witnessed also a great increase in investment in organized interest-group efforts designed specifically to secure political advantage (1962, p. 289).

Since they wrote, the expenses of politics have grown at what looks like an exponential rate in every democratic country. In particular, the coming of television has escalated the costs of getting elected, making politicians correspondingly vulnerable to those who will underwrite those costs. Hence the size and dynamism of the contemporary lobbying industry, and the quite new kinds of property that have been brought into being through its efforts. Many of these extend the value of ownership of shares in corporations or limited partnerships (cf. Korten, 1995, Ch. 10).

Secondly, the growth of branding, based on trademarks, has increased at least as much. Persuasive market power has shown itself to be a particularly effective way of escaping from the discipline of market forces without appearing to do so. Thirdly, and closely associated with both of these developments, has been globalisation of economic activity. This enables property owners to escape from taxation and other controls, since these can only be imposed at the national level.The capacity of states even to maintain their existing levels of welfare transfers, not to speak of increasing them to try to deal with growing inequality, is correspondingly reduced.

3.2 Escalating inequality

The relative gains made by the owners of property in recent years have brought inequalities within sight of pre-French revolution levels. In asking "How far can the system go before it cracks?" Thurow includes the following in his list of indicators from the United States:

Among males, the group most sharply affected, earnings inequalities doubled in two decades. In the decade of the 1980s, all of the gains in male earnings went to the top 20% of the workforce and an amazing 64% went to the top 1%. If incomes rather than earnings are examined, the top 1% gets even more – 90% of total income gains. The pay of the average Fortune 500 CEO goes from 35 to 157 times that of the average production worker... By the early 1990s the share of wealth held by the top 1 per cent of the population (more than 40%) was essentially double what it had been in the 1970s and was back to where it had been in the late 1920s before the introduction of progressive taxation... (1996, pp. 1, 25, 22).

There is evidence, too, that even though there is no longer any possibility that welfare transfers could compensate for growth in the relative advantage of ownership, the rate at which the burden of these transfers is growing is altogether unsustainable. Thurow has calculated that in combination with interest charges they would reach 100% of tax revenues in the US within only 15 years if current laws remain unchanged (1996, p. 98). It is interesting to note that in "*The Crisis of the Tax State*," which contains the germs of several important ideas in "*Capitalism, Socialism and Democracy*," Schumpeter wrote that in the long run, States would not be able to survive "the will of the people to demand higher and higher public expenditures" ([1918] 1991, p. 97).

At the same time as social welfare demands on tax revenues are increasing, globalisation means that national tax bases are being eroded, as firms and individuals take advantage of opportunities to move their activities and their funds to places where they will pay little tax or none at all. Since labour is so much less mobile, it is consequently being forced to carry an increasing share of the burden of taxation. Of all the factors which cause growth in inequality, therefore, globalisation is now the most powerful. This is because even if national laws (including tax laws) can only be partially effective in making property rights "socially responsible," no force *at all* exists to discipline these rights at the world level. There is no *global* mechanism for civilising self-interest.

4 Globalisation – Rodrik's evidence

Hirst and Thompson argue in relation to globalisation that the more extreme descriptions and forebodings are no more than a myth, and they are hopeful that regional arrangements could be developed which "would build up a financial sector dedicated to industrial finance and governed by public policy" (1996, p. 150). A more realistic view, however, is that of Dani Rodrik, who has recently written "*Has Globalisation Gone Too Far*?" (1997) for the Institute of International Economics in Washington, DC, a commission which testifies to unease even in one of the citadels of "free trade" thinking. His conclusions can bring the Institute no reassurance, because his meticulous econometric analyses confirm that globalisation

- can indeed involve an international "race to the bottom" in terms of wages and workers' standards (p. 19);
- makes it more difficult to tax capital (p. 54);
- consequently reduces the ability of governments to spend money on social programs (p. 55); and
- inevitably forces labour to bear a higher share of the total tax burden, including welfare transfers (p. 63).

The importance of these conclusions arises from the clear positive correlation which Rodrik identifies between openness to international trade and government spending, which is so largely made up of welfare transfers, either direct (payments) or indirect (public employment) (Ch. 4). This is a most valuable insight, and it goes a long way towards explaining the growth of big government, especially during the last half-century.

Its impact is further reinforced by a remarkable difference which he notes between the 19 OECD countries and the total of 109 countries for which he was able to obtain data (for 1985–89). The independent variables in his analysis are Openness, Instability in terms of trade, and Exposure to external risk. These together account for 75% of the variation in social security and welfare spending in OECD countries, but have no explanatory power for these countries' government consumption (after excluding income transfers and public investment). In the larger group of countries, however, Rodrik comments that these variables

> do much worse in the regression on social security and welfare spending than they do in the one on government consumption. I attribute this to the fact that social security and welfare spending is rather a mixed bag in lower-income countries, and that most such countries do not have the capacity to run adequate welfare systems. It is plausible that some of the same insurance functions are provided in these countries through government employment and government purchases of goods and services (as captured in government consumption) (1997, p. 60).

4.1 Unemployment aspects

Rodrik's research also allows us to infer why in OECD countries other than the United States, the effect of globalisation has been visible in more unemployment rather than more income inequality. This seems to depend upon the size of the public sector. Employment in this does not carry the stock options and similar devices which differentially boost the earnings of top management so much in privately-owned firms. This inhibits the growth of earnings inequality in the public sector. On the other hand, working for the State or for a State-owned Company, not only carries an explicit or implicit guarantee of a job for life, but also of automatic sharing in economic growth. All the adjustment as a result of globalisation consequently falls on the unsheltered sector of the economy, and when this burden is added to the existing cost of supporting a large public sector, it is hardly surprising that the unsheltered sector shrinks and jobs are lost in it. The social and political consequences of large-scale and prolonged unemployment may be even more serious than greater earnings inequality.

An aspect of the welfare state is that specialised labour as well as worker combinations have "derived market power," which enables them divert rents to themselves out of the primary rents of property-owners (Kingston, 1984, pp. 40–42). For several decades these, together with the welfare transfers which governments were able to make from taxing those same rents, were enough to defuse serious questioning of how the growth in primary market power was being used. To-day, as Rodrik notes (1997, pp. 23–25) to the extent that globalisation enables the primary rents to escape both from derived market power and from taxation, there is every reason for the consensus to break down. In fact, Rodrik reads the sum of his econometric evidence as pointing towards a tension between the consequences of globalisation and the requirements of maintaining the social legitimacy of free trade...Globalisation is not occurring in a vacuum. It is part of a broader trend that we may call marketisation. Receding government, deregulation, and the shrinking of social obligations are the domestic counterparts of the intertwining of national economies. Globalisation could not have come this far without these complementary forces (1997, p. 85).

Rodrik's use of the terms "free trade" and "marketisation" unfortunately clouds the issue, through failure to distinguish between the two meanings of market freedom discussed earlier. What is really at stake in globalisation is market power, and the rents which accrue to it. As already pointed out, the primary "freedom" of markets which depend upon specific legislation to generate and distribute property rights, increasingly consists of the power of the owners of these rights to use them without social responsibility. Freedom *of entry* to such markets is very restricted indeed. The word which Rodrik has coined for the trend he has identified, "marketisation," gives the impression of market forces becoming more widespread. This is the very opposite of what is actually happening, which is the generation of more market power and new forms of it. As the power to escape from market forces, its objective is actually to *prevent* market forces from operating.

4.2 Inequality between countries

Increased inequality within countries is paralleled by growing imbalance between the richer and poorer countries of the world, and for similar reasons, the most important of which is differential levels of market power. International aid programmes ostensibly attempt to redress this imbalance between possessors of market power (predominantly firms in Western countries) and primary producers, on whom market forces bear most heavily. These programmes parallel national welfare transfers, but are even less successful. One reason for this is a widening technology gap between advanced and poor countries. Another is that foreign aid amounts are relatively far smaller in relation to internationally-held property than welfare transfers are in relation to national property. A third is that so much aid is "tied" to purchases from the aid-giving country that it is very largely aid to that country's own firms rather than to the ostensible recipient.

Fourthly, the vulnerability of poorer countries to international flows of speculative funds denies them independence in developing their economies. Estimates of the scale of these mobile funds in the international exchanges vary widely, but none of them place it at less than one hundred times what is needed to finance all international merchandise trade. The surplus is available for raids on currencies. As an illustration, James Tobin recently called attention to how Mexico has been "suffering cruel and painful punishments for crimes of fiscal and monetary policy it did not commit" (uL Haq et al., 1996, p. xiii). A fifth reason, of course, is that the "compensatory" transfers are given to governments, so that they are largely dissipated in uneconomic projects, not to speak of through corruption (Krause, 1997, Ch. V).

5 Institutions for globalisation (1)

5.1 The International Conventions

Just as market power exists at the national level because of clearly identifiable laws, its existence internationally can only be understood in terms of institutional arrangements to spread property rights world-wide. Historically, most Persuasive and Specific market power was internationalised before that of Capability. This was achieved through international Conventions, which were brought into being to replace a large number of bilateral agreements which already existed. The earliest of these, the Paris Convention (1883) covered Trademarks and Patents, and that of Berne (1886) dealt with copyright. The latter was originally intended to cover only literary and artistic works, but it then became much more commercially important as a means of protecting films, advertising and, still more recently, computer programs.

The characteristic method of operation of these Conventions is "National Treatment." This means that while no country is bound to have the same intellectual property regime as others, it agrees to treat citizens of any other Convention country in exactly the same way as its own citizens under any Patent, Trade Mark or Copyright laws it may enact. Later Conventions such as those covering plant variety protection, ornamental designs, phonographic recordings and computer chip mask works, operate in the same way.

As it has developed, the world intellectual property system is strongly associated with concentrated industries, and even within those industries, with relatively few firms. Numerous surveys, such as the Community Innovation Survey in Europe, show that patents are used most by firms with over 1,000 employees. The patent system is used to a disproportionate extent by the chemical industry, which in itself is highly concentrated (Arundel and Kabla, 1998; European Patent Office, 1994).

Patent use also tends to be concentrated by country, notably in the US, Japan and Germany. German patentable invention, for example, is no less than 42 times that of the four poorest EU countries combined. The fast moving consumer goods industries, which are built on the indispensable basis of Trade Marks, are highly concentrated. Copyright has been a most important factor in the world-wide dominance of a single firm, Microsoft, in computer software, to the extent of making that company into the prime target of US anti-trust authorities. Multinational firms are by far the most important users of plant variety protection, and so on.

5.2 Capturing the Conventions' rules

The history of intellectual property provides much evidence of the way in which those who hold property come to gain power over the laws which generate property rights, so as to extend these rights and make them stronger. The principle of "national treatment" on which the Conventions are based, does not require uniformity of intellectual property laws among member countries. However, firms in the more advanced countries, through their governments and with the active cooperation of the Conventions' Secretariat in Geneva, progressively succeeded in developing a standard world system, which contains numerous provisions which are to such firms' advantage.

In the case of patents, the first major change was to remove the requirement to manufacture a product in a particular country in order to maintain a patent there. This made patents into a reinforcement of the market power of capability, because foreign markets could then be supplied by exports from the home market's production units, enabling these to capture economies of scale and scope. Also, it was originally enough that something was new in the country where a patent was being sought, even if it was already known elsewhere, but this was replaced by a criterion of "new in the whole world," to the obvious benefit of the larger and more advanced firms. A further requirement, for what is known as an "inventive step," reinforced this discrimination.

In many countries, Patents will not be granted for any invention that is "against public policy," but Article 7 of the Paris Convention provides in contrast that "the nature of the goods to which a trademark is to be applied shall in no case form an obstacle to the registration of a mark." This prevents member countries from refusing to register trademarks for products which have been proved to be damaging to health, such as cigarettes. Without trademark monopoly, no tobacco firm could invest in building up a brand, and without the resulting sales promotion, consumption would be greatly reduced. In the case of plants, there is no difficulty at all in identifying whose market power a change is intended to boost. Under the 1991 revision of the International Convention for the Protection of New Varieties of Plants, national governments actually have to legislate for explicit *exemption* to allow farmers who use protected varieties to continue the practice of millennia by saving seed from one year's harvest for their own planting the following Spring!

5.3 Value of diverse property rights

When intellectual property becomes a reinforcement of the market power of capability and of persuasion of the largest firms, its function is the exact opposite of what is needed to keep a property rights system healthy. It should instead provide some degree of countervailing market power to smaller firms, since by definition these lack strength in the other two types. Similarly, appropriate specific market power can give poorer countries their best chance of catching up with richer ones. It is therefore in the interest of such countries to develop intellectual property arrangements – as indeed all their laws of property – to suit their own requirements.

Only two countries have done this. One was India, which did not join the Paris Convention because it wanted to develop an indigenous pharmaceutical industry. It judged that it could not do this if the multinational chemical firms could obtain Indian patents. This policy was so successful that its best producers of generic drugs reached the stage of pressing their government to join the Paris Convention, so that they could obtain patent protection abroad for their inventions. The other country was Japan, which did join the Paris Convention as early as 1899, but which regularly changed its patent law (as much as 18 times in the 40 years after World War 2) to suit its own firms. This policy was part of a package to encourage invention and innovation by Japanese firms which has been amazingly successful, as indicated by the fact that no fewer than 7 of the top 10 firms receiving most patents in the United States in 1997 were Japanese.

6 Institutions for Globalisation (2)

6.1 The General Agreement on Tariffs and Trade (GATT)

There was no institutional arrangement for internationalising Capability market power until 1947, and when it did come into existence it was as a result of strong effort by a single country, the United States, rather than through cooperation between a number of countries, as the Paris and Berne Conventions had been. During the nineteenth century, Britain, as the workshop of the world, favoured free trade, but other countries, notably Germany and the United States, were building up their industries behind tariff barriers. However, the US emerged from World War II with unrivalled productive capability, and naturally wanted access to world-wide markets for this. Consequently, it took the initiative within the newly-established United Nations Organisation, of bringing about the General Agreement on Tariffs and Trade (GATT) in 1947. Its primary objective was to eliminate tariffs and import quotas, thus globalising the market power of capability in the same way as the Conventions had earlier globalised specific and persuasive market power.

The GATT's objective of preventing any revival of the world-wide protectionism which had been characteristic of the pre-World war II era, was triumphantly achieved. In its first "round," in 1947, it dealt with 23 countries and freed up trade worth $10 million; in the "Kennedy round," (1962) it was 48 countries and $40 billion; and in the 1973 "Tokyo round," the totals were 99 countries and $155 billion.

6.2 The Conventions and GATT contrasted

The two approaches to internationalising market power differed in several ways. All the Conventions were Europe-driven in origin and allow countries to make their own rules. They are "gentleman's agreements," with no compulsion to join, no substantial commonly agreed minimum level of intellectual property protection, and no effective sanctions for breach. In contrast, the GATT was US–driven, focussed on achieving world-wide free trade in products, with dispute resolution means and strong sanctions against offenders.

From the 1960s, however, the degree of freedom in world-wide access to national markets which had been achieved was undermined through massive growth in *non-tariff* barriers to trade (notoriously in Japan). As well as this, international business spread well beyond trade in physical products, branded goods and publishing, to include services (notably financial) and recorded entertainment. More R & D in firms meant more information in products, and quite new information products *per se*, such as databases, diskettes and C-D ROMS, became commonplace.

In these developments, the United States lost the position of leadership in the production of goods which it had immediately after the war, and which had caused it to take the initiative in establishing the GATT. In the growth of world-wide copying and piracy of information products, US firms were also the main losers. Not surprisingly, this widespread loss of market power caused the US authorities to take a hard look at the institutions by which market power is globalised. What they saw was that GATT's coverage of the fields where US firms wanted to extend their capability market power was very incomplete. It was also clear to them that the Conventions were failing to protect US producers of information, and that the main reason for this was because they had no sanctions against defaulters (as GATT had).

The US had plenty of proof, for example, that the protection its firms obtained in Japan under "national treatment" by no means matched what Japanese firms obtained in the US (for a striking illlustration, see Spero, 1990). The Japanese procedure of opposition before grant of a patent, which was notoriously effective in delaying grants to foreign applicants until local firms had reverse engineered the invention and improved on it, was only one of many devices which seemed to be unfair. Since there was no worthwhile redress under the Paris Convention, the accumulation of experiences of this kind by US firms stimulated their authorities to get the "Uruguay round" of GATT revision negotiations started, with a Preparatory Committee operating between 1982 and 1986. Protection of intellectual property was to be shifted into the GATT.

6.3 "Aggressive Unilateralism"

In his study, Rodrik observed that

> because the social welfare state is the flip side of the open economy...as globalisation proceeds, the social consensus required to maintain domestic markets open to international trade is endangered. With domestic political support for trade eroding, a return to old-style protectionism becomes a serious possibility (1997, p. 53).

A revealing indication of such a change in the US approach to international trade can be seen in the Semiconductor Chip Protection Act of 1984. This arose out of a Court case between Apple Computer and a Japanese firm, on which the very survival of Apple had turned. The Act gives copyright protection to computer programs in microchip form, and this protection could have been brought in through an amendment to the US Copyright Act. It was not introduced in this way, however, because it is through the latter Act that the US was a member of the International Copyright Convention. Consequently, under "national treatment," foreign (especially, of course, Japanese) firms would have to be granted automatic access to the new kind of protection. By writing the chip protection as a separate Act, it was possible to include a condition that its benefit could only be obtained by citizens of States which passed similar legislation to protect US chip producers. Significantly, Japan complied within a year.

Progress in the Uruguay round was very slow, and the rapid compliance of Japan with the 1984 Semiconductor Chip Protection Act convinced the US authorities of the value to them of reciprocity provisions, imposed outside of the existing institutional framework of international market power. In the Omnibus Trade and Competitiveness Act of 1988, various "Section 301" provisions overrode GATT complaint and sanction procedures and replaced them by rapid and severe retaliation when US interests were considered to be damaged. This policy was described by Jagdish Bhagwati, a former policy advisor to the Director-General of the GATT, as one of "aggressive unilateralism... quick fixes on the trade front, using American muscle to extract concessions unilaterally and quickly from others" (Bhagwati and Patrick, 1991, p. 6). It was primarily directed at Japan's erosion of the market power of American firms, and was progressively used more widely by the US until eventually the GATT was reconstructed into the World Trade Organisation (WTO) in 1994. The main difference between the two Institutions is the inclusion of intellectual property (TRIPS) and services (GATS) in the WTO's terms of reference.

7 The World Trade Organisation (WTO)

7.1 TRIPS – the Trade-related Intellectual Property Section

The Trade-related Intellectual Property Section of the WTO agreement (TRIPS), which emerged from the Uruguay round, greatly strengthens the market power of the advanced firms of Western countries. "Special 301" provisions of the US 1988 Act had dealt specifically with intellectual property, but TRIPS definitively shifted it from the toothless Conventions into the GATT-WTO regime of powerful sanctions against breach. As described by Reichman,

The momentum of the multilateral negotiations during the Uruguay Round carried the developed countries well beyond their initial goal, which was to limit the capacity of firms in developing countries to make and export free-riding copies of high-tech goods produced at great cost in the developed countries. Instead, by...1991, the developed countries' strategic goal was to impose a comprehensive set of intellectual property standards on the rest of the world (1998, pp. 585–586).

Even the poorest of the 132 WTO signatory countries are now being forced to adopt minimum standards of intellectual property law and to promise its enforcement. Japan also must abandon its protectionist intellectual property policies and procedures. The secondary group of OECD countries have all joined WTO, which involves accepting TRIPS, as a necessary condition of getting inward foreign investment, especially from multinational high-technology firms. India has joined, so that it will now have to grant patents to Western pharmaceutical firms.

Third World countries have also agreed to accept the obligations of the international intellectual property system, including enforcement provisions, in exchange for promises of better access to the markets of the rich countries for their agricultural produce and for a few traditional manufactures. They and the East European "countries in transition" are given 5 years to comply, and can get longer under certain conditions; the least developed of them have a 10 years' grace period. TRIPS is therefore clearly a vehicle for increasing world-wide specific and persuasive market power. As will be discussed below, this can only result in still more inequality in technology and wealth.

7.2 GATS (the General Agreement on Trade in Services)

By far the most important element in this part of the WTO relates to *financial* services, although this aspect of it was not finally agreed until 1997. Before the Mexican peso crisis of 1994–5, the International Monetary Fund was very active in trying to achieve complete convertibility of the currencies of all its members (Eichengreen and Wyplosz, 1996, pp. 15 and 30, Note 2). This thrust towards freeing the movements of capital around the world has now been taken up by the WTO. Eliminating restrictions on convertibility simultaneously reduces the power of national governments to pursue independent economic policies, and strengthens the power of reserve currencies. This can only widen the inequality between the rich North and the poor South which James Tobin (1974) so deplored.This was not the main reason why he proposed a tax on international transfers, "to throw some sand in the wheels of excessively mobile speculative funds," but experience of the growth of inequality between countries since then certainly explains why that proposal is at last beginning to be taken seriously.

Another almost-lone voice has called attention to how pursuing the cause of international mobility of capital actually destroys the theoretical case for international trade in goods, as this is made by the WTO and similar international bodies. This is because they argue for world trade on Ricardo's principle of comparative advantage. His two-product, two-country model shows that, irrespective of which country has an absolute advantage in the production of particular goods, both countries will be better off if each of them specialises in producing the goods in which it has a comparative advantage, and trades for the others ([1817] 1971, Ch. VII).

7.3 Herman Daly on free trade

However, as Herman Daly has pointed out,

Economists have been giving Ricardo a standing ovation for this demonstration since 1817, as well they should. But in their enthusiasm for the conclusion, modern economists seem to have forgotten one of the premises. Ricardo was very careful to base his comparative advantage argument for free trade on the explicit premise that capital was immobile between national communities... Absolute advantage is the rule for maximizing returns to capital when capital is mobile. Comparative advantage is the rule for maximizing returns to capital subject to the constraint that capital stays at home. This remains true in spite of an improvement in the definition of cost from Ricardo's labor cost to the modern concept of opportunity cost. The difficulty about assumed capital immobility remains. Opportunity cost is the correct concept – but the opportunity set, out of which the opportunity cost (next best alternative) is defined, is the whole world when capital is mobile, and the nation when capital is immobile. When the opportunity set for capital is the whole world, then absolute advantage governs; when it is the nation, then comparative advantage governs... Ricardo would *never* argue that because comparative advantage shows that free trade in goods is beneficial, one can simply extend the argument to show that free trade in capital must yield even more benefits! To appeal to a principle that is premised upon capital *immobility* in order to support an argument in favour of capital *mobility* is too illogical for words (1996, pp. 152, 153, 238).

Elsewhere, Daly (1995) has gone so far as to argue that

the allocative, distributional and scale problems stemming from free trade in to-day's world are sufficient to reverse the traditional default position in its favor. Measures to further integrate national economies should now be treated as a bad idea unless proven otherwise in specific cases. We economists must overcome our habitual devotion to comparative advantage...

Daly's argument has recently received support from Bhagwati on the grounds that instability at the level currently being experienced by the Asian countries threatens the entire world economy, and that the primary cause of this instability is "footloose" money seeking short-term profit. Developing Charles Kindleberger's point that capital mobility has *always* been associated with financial crises, panics and manias, he notes that

The debt crisis of the 1980s cost South America a decade of growth. The Mexicans, who were vastly over-exposed through short-term inflows, were devastated in 1994. The Asian economies of Thailand, Indonesia and South Korea, all heavily burdened with short-term debt, went into a tailspin nearly a year ago, drastically lowering their growth rates (1998, p. 8).

Any advantage that free capital mobility offers, he argues, is not worth the cost of these crises – and in any event, "most of the payoff can be obtained by direct equity investment." This particular type of mobile capital can make labour more productive, transfer management and related skills, and raise living standards.There is little evidence that a country's ability to attract inward foreign investment is significantly reduced by not having freedom of portfolio capital flows, as demonstrated historically by countries as different as Taiwan and Ireland. Japan grew remarkably quickly without capital account convertibility, as mainland China is doing now, and Western Europe's return to prosperity after the war was also achieved without it. Bhagwati's conclusion is therefore that the weight of evidence and logic point...toward restraints on capital flows. It is time to shift the burden of proof from those who oppose to those who favor liberated capital (1998, p. 12).

Economists do not have to abandon their belief in the value of free trade in goods and services, so long as the financial services that are traded internationally are not of a kind which prevents countries from pursuing policies for indigenous development. One of the objectives of GATS, however, is to remove barriers to mobility throughout the world of all kinds of capital. This is incompatible with the WTO's claim to be promoting world trade on the basis of the principle of comparative advantage. If capital is fully mobile, instead of both parties who engage in trade being better off as a result, only the one which is already richer will be, because its absolute advantages will be reinforced. It is hard to imagine more powerful arrangements for widening inequality between countries, in the interest of socially non-responsible property rights. Since in the past it has been the combination of inequality with social non-responsibility which has brought each property rights "cycle" to an end, it is not unreasonable to have a particular fear of the effect on capitalism of the GATS element of the WTO.

7.4 Convergence of GATS and TRIPS

Particular attention should be directed to the parallelism between the GATS and TRIPS components of the WTO. As Daly's argument makes abundantly clear, to the extent that GATS succeeds in bringing about world-wide capital mobility, it replaces comparative advantage by absolute advantage, which is to the benefit of the stronger party in trade, in this case, firms in the rich advanced countries. It is equally clear that to the extent that TRIPS succeeds in establishing high standards of intellectual property protection worldwide, the benefit will be gained by the firms in the advanced countries which are either owners of major Brands or technologically innovative. The extension of market power through TRIPS will keep firms in the poor countries out of both economic areas. This claim needs to be developed further.

8 Institutionalising first-world advantages

8.1 Patents

Making patents more readily available world-wide entrenches the position of firms that are already strong in a particular field of technology. For example, one of several very important managerial innovations of the nineteenth-century German chemical industry was patent "flooding" or "saturation patenting." This was a technique of surrounding an important invention by an impenetrable "thicket" of patents, so that no competitor could provide even a near-substitute for the core, profit-making product. Using it, German firms completely dominated the fine chemical and pharmaceuticals markets of the world until, as a result of the first World War, all their US and British patents were expropriated. Without this, the industries in those countries would have been condemned to remain at their comparatively undeveloped pre-War level, because the German firms would have left no niches unprotected by their patents. In exactly the same way, industries in the poorer countries will have no hope of raising their level of technology in any field where TRIPS will make strong intellectual property protection available to international firms.

8.2 Copying and economic development

A recent thoughtful study of these problems is Yasuske Murakami's "*An Anticlassical Political-Economic Analysis: A Vision for the Next Century*." He argues for free technological transfer because

Technology is knowledge or even thought, more than it is property...[it is] a public good and thus not something optimally allocated through market competition. It is therefore not possible to justify patents or intellectual property rights by the same theory that is applied to market competition in commodities...unless new technology flows in substantial amounts to follower countries, it is highly possible that the basis for the future world system will collapse (1996, p. 250).

Murakami's case for freer technological transfer is especially relevant to his own country, Japan, since so much from its large foreign aid programme is eventually spent on its own firms' products. He underrates how necessary intellectual property is for innovation, but he is certainly right in his view that freedom to copy is essential for international economic convergence. No great economic power, and certainly not the United States nor Germany nor Japan, was able to do without copying freely in its industrial beginnings. The root of the prodigious modern capability of Toyota is Sakichi Toyoda's poor wooden imitation of the fine steel looms from Platt's of Oldham and Draper's of Lowell which he saw at the 1890 Tokyo industrial exhibition. If the best Indian pharmaceutical firms can now face competition from the multinationals, this has only become possible as a result of a learning process through many years of copying their inventions. Indeed, a strong case could be made that if those who make policies for international economic development were really serious, they would abandon all foreign aid, and simply replace it with freedom to copy. This might even go so far as using the former aid funds to compensate the advanced firms that might lose as a result, by subsidising their innovation. The WTO, of course, stands for exactly the opposite approach.

8.3 Branded products

As with other kinds of intellectual property, globalisation of brands reinforces already-existing market power. The market for psychological ingredient, which is exploitable by the market power of persuasion, can only expand from countries with more discretionary income to those with less. Firms in countries with larger home markets have an additional advantage from the acquired experience of their managements in large-scale handling of the special kinds of risk that are associated with decisions about advertising and marketing (Kingston 1984, pp. 54–74). Once every country must grant and enforce trade mark registration, international brands are provided with the legal monopoly basis for their persuasive market power even before they put their products on a market. With all their advantages, nothing can then stop such brands from dominating local ones. Any doubt on this point can be easily resolved by a quick mental comparison of the number of European brands that are strong in the United States and vice versa.

8.4 Bhagwati's "Wall Street-Treasury Complex"

In sum, therefore, the WTO represents the First World acting to trade access to its markets in exchange for world-wide protection for its innovations, and for global free trade in its money. The very existence of this international body testifies to the extent to which the economic policies of Western democratic governments have been captured by those who own and control multinational corporations. A current example is mobilisation of US diplomacy by politicians in the pay of such corporations, to use the WTO to destroy the livelihood of small banana growers in EU former colonies. In coining the phrase, "The Wall Street – Treasury Complex," Bhagwati claimed that

the idea and the ideology of free trade and its benefits – and this extends to the liberalisation of trade in goods and financial and other services at the World Trade Organisation – have, in effect, been hijacked by...lobbies...a power elite...a definite networking of like-minded luminaries among the powerful institutions...(1995, p. 11).

In spite of WTO provisos about compensatory transfers and training for poorer countries, the reality is that the outcomes must be very much to the advantage of property owners, wherever they are. Inequality between the workers in the poorer countries and the governing elites in those countries will be reinforced, leading to continual world-wide instability.

8.5 WTO's misleading statistics

In public statements (for example, Ruggiero, 1998) the WTO tries to give the impression that the poorer countries are benefitting greatly from international merchandise trade, because this has increased 14 times between 1948 and 1997. This is allegedly confirmed by the fact that one-third of the 25 largest trading countries are now developing countries, and that their share of world trade in manufactures has doubled to a fifth of the total in the last 15 years. However, such figures should be read in the context of the reality that the most rapidly growing part of world trade in manufactures is in fact *intra-company* trade, with components or finished goods moving between subsidiary plants or sales offices of multinational firms. Since this type of trade only exists because of the mobility of the multinationals' capital, it reflects the absolute advantage of the countries where the Home Offices of such firms are located, not Ricardian comparative advantage, as the WTO claims would suggest.

9 "The Manic Logic of Global Capitalism"

This is the sub-title of William Greider's recent book, "*One World, Ready or Not*" (1997), which is a very useful complement to the rigour of Rodrik' s econometric studies. It is written with apocalyptic fervour, providing extensive information and reflection, based upon widespread work in the field, on the realities of international business. It also puts flesh on many of Thurow's economic measurements and even pushes many of the latter's more tentative conclusions from his research to their logical end:

[T]he global system of finance and commerce is in a reckless footrace with history, plunging toward some sort of dreadful reckoning with its own contradictions, pulling everyone else along with it... *multinational enterprise is preoccupied with its own imperatives, finance capital consumed by its own search for returns*... The destructive pressures building up within the global system are leading towards an unbearable chaos that, even without a dramatic collapse, will likely provoke the harsh, reactionary politics that can shut down the system (p. 316 (emphasis added)).

9.1 Loosening societal bonds

Greider's phrase "multinational business is preoccupied with its own imperatives, finance capital consumed by its own search for returns" is a powerful expression of the concept of non-responsible property rights discussed above. He sees globalisation causing a "new Luddism" in "the gathering masses of younger people – Europeans call them "marginalised youth" – who have never had a job and perhaps never will" (p. 40). It is destroying the cohesion of societies everywhere, Greider claims, and must therefore in the long run undermine the very possibility of international trade. On this point, it is interesting that one of the questions which Dani Rodrik's investigation had forced him to ask is:

What if, by reducing the civic engagement of internationally mobile groups, globalisation loosens the civic glue that holds societies together and exacerbates social fragmentation?...These developments are afflicting all societies exposed to globalisation, with many developing countries perhaps even more exposed than the advanced industrial countries (Rodrik, 1997, p. 70).

With respect to Indonesia, for example, Greider points out that the "Suharto Miracle" which brought about so much investment and employment from multinational firms, "relied upon a perverse trade-off between government-suppressed wages and government-administered bribery" (1997, p. 396). Because of the violent reaction, Indonesia is now one of the least attractive locations in the world for footloose investment, and this is likely to lead to a vicious cycle of increased poverty and still more violence which all the resources of the International Monetary Fund will not be able to halt.

9.2 Greider's and Thurow's pessimism

Both Greider and Thurow are agreed on what the wider outcome will be. Greider writes that

In various fundamental ways, the United States promotes and props up the global trading system, allowing it to evade many of its gathering contradictions and instabilities. An economic crisis will likely be joined when the United States is no longer able to do this – a climacteric moment that is fast approaching... the American market serves as buyer of last resort for the world... [and] with the Government's blessing, American enterprise facilitates the global adjustments to continuing overcapacity and other market tensions by gradually abandoning elements of its home base of production...

This role cannot continue indefinitely and may soon come to an end. As America's economic dominance has steadily weakened, the nation takes on an increasing volume of foreign indebtedness through its large and persistent trade deficits... At the same time, the nation's broad capacity for mass consumption is being slowly eroded by declining wages and the loss of high-income employment, whether from technological reform or the migration of manufacturing sectors. Thus, the nation's economic resilience is weakening as its debt obligations accumulate (1997, p. 192).

Thurow's comment focusses on the weakness of governments which have been largely captured by property-owners. Indeed, it has an unconscious echo of Gibbon's observation, quoted earlier, about the inability of the Roman system, when it too had become dominated by socially non-responsible property, to cope with the challenges it faced:

Where and when the financial crisis will come and how big it will be, no one knows. That there will at some unknown point in the future be such a crisis is a complete certainty. The most likely crisis involves a run on the dollar...To depend upon America to stop a run on the dollar is to depend upon a preponderance of domestic political interests that simply is not there. Any belief in American actions to stop a run on the dollar that would involve economic pain is a mirage shimmering in the hot desert air (1996, p. 230).

10 Schumpeter's prediction in hindsight

In the light of all this, how does Schumpeter's pessimism about the future of capitalism look to-day? Clearly, he missed four crucial factors. The first of these was the widespread adoption, outside the United States as well as within it, of the management methods which were developed there during World War 2. These had caused the period from 1941 to 1945 in that country to include the most remarkable concentration of output of physical goods (albeit for destructive purposes) that the world had ever seen. The spread of these methods to the rest of the world transformed its productive capacity. Secondly, and partly as a result of this, fossil energy in the form of oil became extremely cheap, and enabled the new management techniques to generate wealth of all kinds at a rate never before achieved. The volume and types of employment associated with this wealth-creation were also unprecedented. Above all, the massive growth of social welfare transfers under democratic pressures mitigated inequality, both really and perhaps even more in public perception.

Schumpeter was also wrong about the role that the intelligentsia would play in causing capitalism to be replaced by socialism, and he himself would probably regard this as his greatest mistake, since he considered that the enmity of this "alienated class" would be the most potent factor in this process ([1942] 1950, p. 151). What he did not foresee was the effect of the massive growth of media which are largely dependent on advertising, itself the result of trade mark registration law, as noted earlier. Inevitably, the editorial content of media financed in this way has been favourable to the economic arrangements which made their existence possible, and this largely stifled negative criticism. The lucrative new markets for the skills of journalists and pundits which these advertising-financed media provided also had a tempering effect on opposition to capitalism from what Schumpeter called "that scribbling set." Highly-paid syndicated columnists, talk-show hosts or panel members are anything but "alienated" from economic arrangements which generate huge demand for their services.

However, on the basic issue of humanity's eventual reaction to excessive inequality combined with socially non-responsible property rights, both historical precedents and present portents are on Schumpeter's side. Loss of a moral basis for property rights played an important part in the decline of the Roman Empire, of the medieval monastic economy and of the *ancien regime* in Europe. Today, David Selbourne (1994) has written most persuasively on how "dutiless rights" are at the heart of the dissolution of civil society which he sees in progress. It is hard to imagine rights that are more "dutiless" than those which are now attached to property which is deployed in world trade.

Schumpeter saw the replacement of the family firm by the large and anonymous corporation as a move away from duty and responsibility in property rights: "Dematerialised, defunctionalised and absentee ownership does not...call forth moral allegiance as the vital form of property did" ([1942] 1950, p. 142). If this is true in respect of the primarily national corporations which Schumpeter knew, how little "moral allegiance" can be expected for absentee ownership of the "dematerialised and defunctionalised" funds that wash around the international foreign exchanges today? Or for the similarly absentee ownership of the "screwdriver" assembly plants of multinational firms, or of the ideas and information which TRIPS is seeking to bring under the World Trade Organisation's control throughout the world?

Most important of all, what moral allegiance would there be for democratic governments which had abdicated legislating for property rights in the interest of the public good, in favour of that of the owners of property? Such governments would then really have become what Marx all along claimed they would be: "executive committees of the exploiting class." A world-wide alienation of electorates is already visible in lower rates of voter participation.

As noted earlier, Schumpeter held that the State can only be a "a separate, distinguishable social entity" as long as it fulfils its function "to oppose individual egoism as a representative of a common purpose." There are warning signs that States are abandoning this role, playing their part instead in a massive growth of inequality between owners and workers, between resources which are internationally mobile and those which are not, between taxation of capital and taxation of labour, and in the widening gaps between rich and poor countries, and between the poor and the elites everywhere.

The new international cutting edge of these forces is the World Trade Organisation, whose origins, objectives and ethos perfectly illustrate how lawmaking for property rights has been captured by those whom that law is meant to discipline in the public interest. Globalisation has made this capture all the more effective in undermining contemporary economic arrangements, because it reduces the tax base and consequently the ability to make social welfare transfers to defuse resentment against excessive inequality.

If a latter-day Marx was now producing a Manifesto against contemporary ills, therefore, what he would see haunting the world is the spectre of *global* capitalism. Against such a background, at least that part of Schumpeter's vision which foresaw an end of the current property rights "cycle," does not seem nearly as implausible as it did even a decade ago.

References

Arundel A, Kabla I (1998) What percentage of innovations are patented? Research Policy 27: 127–141

Berger PL (1993) The uncertain triumph of democratic capitalism. In: Diamond L, Plattner MF (eds) Capitalism, socialism and democracy revisited. Johns Hopkins University Press, Baltimore

Bhagwati J (1995) Free trade, fairness and the new protectionism: reflections on an agenda for the World Trade Organisation. Institute for Economic Affairs, London

Bhagwati J (1998) The capital myth: The difference between trade in widgets and dollars. Foreign Affairs 77 (3): 7–12

Bhagwati J, Patrick HT (eds) (1991) Aggressive unilateralism: America's 301 trading policy and the world trading system. Harvester Wheatsheaf, London

Buchanan JM, Tullock G (1962) The calculus of consent. University of Michigan Press, Ann Arbor

Collins R (1986) The weberian revolution of the high middle ages. In: Weberian sociological theory. Cambridge University Press, Cambridge

Daly HE (1995) Against free trade: neo-classical and steady-state perspectives. J Evol Econ 5: 327–332

Daly HE (1996) Beyond growth. Beacon Press, Boston

Eichengreen B, Wyplosz C (1996) In: ul Haq M, Kaul I, Grunberg I (eds) The Tobin tax: Coping with financial volatility. Oxford University Press, New York

European Patent Office (1994) Eposcript 3: Utilisation of patent protection in Europe. Munich

Evans F (1996/1997) Monastic multinationals: The cistercians and other monks as engineers. Transactions of the Newcomen Society 68: 1–68

Finley M (1973) The ancient economy. Hogarth Press, London

Fukuyama F (1992) The end of history and the last man. Hamish Hamilton, London

Georgescu-Roegen N (1971) The entropy law and the economic process. Harvard University Press, Cambridge
Gibbon E [1776–1778] (1963) The decline and fall of the roman empire. Penguin Books, London
Gray J (1995) Enlightenment's wake: Politics and culture at the close of the modern age. Routledge, London
Gray J (1998) False dawn: The delusions of global capitalism. Granta Books, London
Greider W (1997) One world, ready or not: The manic logic of global capitalism. Allan Lane, London
Hardin G (1968) The tragedy of the commons. Science 162: 1243–1272
Hirst P, Thompson G (1996) Globalisation in question. Polity Press, London
Huntington S (1991) The third wave: Democratisation in the late twentieth century. University of Oklahoma Press, Norman London
Kaelber L (1998) Schools of asceticism: Ideology and organization in medieval religious communities. Pennsylvania State University Press, Philadelphia
Kingston W (1984) The political economy of innovation. Nijhoff, The Hague
Kingston W (1996) Monks, liturgy and labour. Studies 85: 181–189
Korten D (1995) When corporations rule the world. Earthscan, London
Krause M (1997) How nations grow rich. Oxford University Press, New York
Marx K, Engels F [1848] (1950) The Communist Manifesto. Penguin Books, London
Mill JS (1848) Principles of political economy. John Murray, London
Murakami Y (1996) An anticlassical political-economic analysis: A vision for the next century. Stanford University Press, Stanford
Pipes R (1998) Personal communication
Reichman JH (1998) Securing compliance with the TRIPS agreement after US v. India. Journal of International Economic Law 1: 585–601
Ricardo D [1817] (1971) Principles of political economy. Penguin Books, London
Rosenberg N, Birdzell LE (1986) How the West grew rich: the economic transformation of the industrial world. Tauris, London
Ruggiero R (1998) Address of the director-general of the World Trade Organisation to Brookings Institution Forum
Rodrik D (1997) Has globalisation gone too far? Institute for International Economics, Washington, DC
Schumpeter JA [(1918] (1991) The crisis of the tax state. English translation in: Swedberg R (ed) The economics and sociology of capitalism. Princeton University Press, Princeton
Schumpeter JA [(1942] (1950) Capitalism, socialism and democracy, 3rd edn. Harper and Row, New York
Schumpeter JA (1949) The Communist Manifesto in economics and sociology. Journal of Political Economy 57: 199–212
Selbourne D (1994) The principle of duty. Sinclair-Stevenson, London
Spero DW (1990) Patents or piracy? A CEO Looks at Japan. Harvard Business Review 68: 58–67
Thurow L (1996) The future of capitalism. Morrow, New York
Tobin J (1974) 1972 Eliot Janeway Lecture in Honor of Joseph Schumpeter. Princeton University Press, Princeton
ul Haq M, Kaul I, Grunberg I (eds) (1996) The tobin tax: Coping with financial volatility. Oxford University Press, New York
Weber M [1923] (1961) General economic history. [English translation by: Knight FH]. Collier Books, New York
Weber M [1904–5] (1976) The protestant ethic and the spirit of capitalism [English translation by: Parsons T]. Charles Scribner's Sons, New York
White L Jr (1964) Medieval technology and social change. Oxford University Press, Oxford
White L Jr (1968) Dynamo and virgin reconsidered. MIT Press, Cambridge

Reflections on the perspectives of the global economy from the point of view of emerging economies*

Maria Luiza Falcão Silva[1], Joaquim Pinto de Andrade[1], Thomas S. Torrance[2]

[1] Department of Economics, University of Brasilia, Campus Darcy Ribeiro, Asa Norte, Brasilia, DF 70910-900, Brazil (e-mail: mlfalcao@unb.br, jandrade@unb.br)
[2] Department of Economics, Heriot-Watt Business School, P.O. Box 307, Riccarton, Edinburgh, EH14 4AT, UK (e-mail: T.S.Torrance@hw.ac.uk)

Abstract. Recently a number of emerging economies, with high inflation and various kinds of imbalances have experienced what has come to be referred to as *dollarization* – the phenomenon of currency substitution where the dollar gradually replaces the national currency in the performance of its fundamental functions. The phenomenon is most commonly encountered as a component of the exchange-rate-based stabilization programs implemented in a number of emerging economies in Latin America, Asia and the Middle East. The fundamental issue we want to explore is whether this process forces the monetary authorities of emerging economies to act with their hands tied, as if caught in a trap. It is argued that when the expansion of liquidity and domestic credit is determined by the quantity of foreign-exchange reserves, an independent monetary policy vanishes and national sovereignty itself is shackled. Since this scenario typically occurs in a world of increasing globalization of finance, this paper also discusses (with reference to emerging economies) the risks and implications of capital inflows for macroeconomic policy autonomy, economic instability, and vulnerability to external shocks.

Key words: Systemic asymmetries – dollarization – Exchange-rate-based stabilization – Speculative attacks

JEL-classification: G15, 010, 050

Paper presented at the 1998 World Conference of the International Joseph A. Schumpeter Society, Vienna, June 13–16, 1998.

*The authors acknowledge research financial support provided by Brazil's National Research Council (CNP_q) and Professor Dennis C. Mueller for very helpful comments.

1 Introduction

This paper analyzes the macroeconomic adjustment of emerging economies adopting exchange-rate-based stabilization programs (ERBSPs). It provides a brief historical description of the symmetries and asymmetries in the world-wide adjustment mechanism, and concludes that systemic asymmetries are inherent in the international monetary system. This conclusion becomes even more evident when the problems that have arisen while establishing new institutional arrangements, such as a new currency or a policy rule for monetary-base creation, are discussed. In the modern international financial system, the globalization of finance has assumed leadership. The instability of this environment, which lacks co-ordination and where emerging countries' domestic currencies are vulnerable to speculative attacks that threaten national economic autonomy, is emphasized.

In fact, these economies are now highly dependent on foreign capital inflows and have become extremely vulnerable to external shocks, as under the pre-1914 gold standard. As long as capital inflows are highly volatile and dependent on economic conditions in the lending countries (push factors), they possess the permanent potential to inflict a surprise shock. In addition, the fixed-exchange-rate systems widely used by emerging economies are also prone to speculative attacks due to internal disequilibrium and/or contagion effects and self-fulfilling expectations.

This paper is structured as follows: Section 2 discusses whether systemic asymmetries are inherent in the international monetary system. Section 3 presents a brief overview of emerging economies' experience in the aftermath of the Bretton Woods collapse. Section 4 deals with the response of capital flows to disinflation stabilization programs implemented by several developing countries, with examples from Latin America and Asia. And finally, in Section 5, we list the conclusions reached.

2 Are systemic asymmetries inherent in the international monetary system?

When dealing with macroeconomic policy, economists neglect at their peril the absolutely crucial role played by the structural features of the economy and the institutional environment in which policy-making occurs. It is thus important to identify in which relevant respects developing economies differ from industrialized ones, when the adjustment mechanism embodied in different exchange-rate regimes is discussed.

According to Agénor and Montiel (1996) there are at least *four* differences, in this context, worthy of note. *First*, there is a significant difference in the productive structure, with repercussions for the role played by the terms of trade in the adjustment process, specifically for countries that are significantly involved in commodity production. *Second*, in emerging economies prevails a rigid segmentation of markets for goods, capital, labor, and foreign exchange. The *third* difference has to do with the way the open-economy aspects of macroeconomics differentiate between the two groups of countries. And *fourth*, 'political economy' is far more important for the macroeconomics of developing countries than for established industrial countries: indeed, understanding the link between political economy and the structural features of economies is the first essential step to devising successful economic reform.

Ford (1964) argues that to date adjustment in the central global economies has to a considerable extent been effectively transferred to the periphery of the world economy owing to asymmetric relations between the two groups of countries.[1] A wide range of theories of the global growth process suggest that the very success of the developed countries is determined by the existence of developing countries. The most popular of these theories that affected, particularly, the thinking of generations of Latin American economists and policymakers in the 1960s and 1970s are: 'dependency theories', 'growth pole theories' and 'structuralist theories'.[2] Also related to this revival of structuralist ideas, is the new literature dealing with the critical concepts of *pricing to market* and *hysteresis*. *Pricing to market* occurs when firms, rather than pass on exchange-rate changes into export prices, try to retain their market shares by keeping prices constant in the importing country's currency (Martson, 1989). *Hysteresis* embodies the idea that export sales lost when a currency appreciates may not be regained should the currency return to its original level (Baldwin and Krugman, 1989).[3]

Given space limits, however, we restrict our discussion to the adjustment of emerging economies in the globalized economy under alternative exchange-rate arrangements. In this Section we focus briefly on the systemic asymmetries of the pre-1914 gold standard adjustment mechanism before looking at the Bretton Woods period and its immediate aftermath.

Systemic asymmetries in the adjustment mechanism during the Gold Standard Period

The idea that the gold standard enhanced macroeconomic stability in the 'center' countries of the international economy is widely accepted, but the same issue is much less clear when the experience of the 'peripheral' countries is considered. Bordo and Schwartz, for example, point out that:

> for the core countries the balance of payments adjustment mechanism was stable, so few crises occurred; the peripheral countries, by contrast, were subject to shocks imported under fixed exchange rates from abroad and frequently suffered exchange-rate crises and a destabilized growth pattern. (Bordo and Schwartz, 1994, p.1)

Several lines of authoritative research concur in supporting this view of the wider workings of the gold standard mechanism:

---

[1] For a historical approach see Silva (1997).

[2] For a critical synthesis of the literature on "dependency theory" we refer to Chilcote (1974).

[3] See Krugman (1991) for an interesting discussion on this topic. See also Davidson (1993) to a reply on similarities attached to the idea of "hysteresis" in Post-Keynesian economics.

- The first stems from studies by Morgenstern (1959) and Lindert (1969) on the working of the international financial markets during the pre-1914 years. According to them the presence of 'hierarchies' of financial centers, and asymmetries in the responses of exchange-rates to interest rates differentials, provided a rationale for the view that the Bank of England (then the world's dominant central bank), by raising its discount rate, had the power to eliminate reserve losses by attracting short-term capital inflows, thus shifting the burdens of adjustment to the 'extremities' of the system, i.e. to primary producing countries and other emerging economies.
- The second explanation for systemic asymmetries within the gold standard derives from the different adjustment possibilities, in the presence of external shocks, available for creditor and debtor nations. According to Ford (1964):

since Britain was a lending and a creditor country, balance of payments adjustment was immediately the easier for her than a borrowing and debtor country, for it was (and is) always easier to cut a flow of lending abroad than to increase a flow of borrowings in times of difficulties. (Ford, 1964, p. 30)

- A third argument asserts that asymmetries may derive from perverse cyclical patterns of the core economies' capital exports. The classic exposition in this group comes from Triffin (1968). He states that:

the balance of payments of the countries of the so-called periphery would be assisted, over the long run, by large capital imports made available to them from the financial markets of industrial Europe, but these countries would pay for this dependence through perverse fluctuations in the availability of such capital and in their terms of trade over the cycle. The exchange rate instability of most underdeveloped countries...finds here one of its many explanations. (Triffin, 1968, p. 127)

Both Ford (1964, 1983) and Franco (1988) argue, correctly in our view, that the gold standard functioned asymmetrically between creditor industrial economies (like those of nineteenth century Britain, Germany and France) and debtor primary-producer economies (like those of nineteenth century Latin America). The two authors trace this asymmetry to the fact that under the gold standard 'creditors' and 'debtors' possessed an entirely different capacity to overcome external disequilibria. It was much easier to slow down capital exports, in answer to difficulties in the current account, than to raise new loans in times of crisis. In this way, the gold standard enabled the so-called 'center' economies to export macroeconomic instability to the periphery. As Ford (1983) aptly says:

in times of stress or crisis interest rate would rise in London, thereby serving to cut fresh foreign lending (both short and long) by Britain and to encourage the repatriation of British funds employed abroad so that immediate relief was brought to the British balance of payments at the expense of other (borrowing) countries. Again, if such measures brought a decline in primary product prices, British import payments would decline. (Ford, 1983, p. 191)

The reality, for a large part of the world economy, was then, that under the gold standard the automatic adjustment mechanism entailed both: a decline in foreign currency receipts, and in income and imports. These deflationary processes were further reinforced by credit contraction as the drain of gold abroad disrupted the domestic banking sector (Ford 1983, p. 91).

Have emerging and developing economies fared better in the twentieth century? Let us begin to answer this question by looking at the operation of the Bretton Woods regime.

Adjustment mechanism during the Bretton Woods Period

For almost a quarter of a century after World War II, the international monetary system experienced a fixed, but adjustable, exchange-rate regime created by the 1944 Bretton Woods Conference agreement. It collapsed on August 15th, 1971. It is not disputed that the period 1947–71 period was characterized by unprecedented economic growth in both industrial and developing countries. At the same time the world economy experienced extraordinary price stability, even in comparison with the gold standard epoch.

In the end, however, the Bretton Woods scheme proved to be inadequate. From the outset the mechanism involved two primary instruments: (1) the provision of credit facilities to assist members in times of temporary current account difficulties, and (2) clear arrangements for an orderly realignment of exchange rates should 'economic fundamentals' require them. Furthermore, the Bretton Woods regime rested on the US dollar being properly managed as a low-inflation 'anchor' currency, and on other members pursuing monetary and fiscal policies designed to maintain stable exchange rates with the dollar. The Bretton Woods regime was launched and existed in a period characterized by sticky prices and low international capital mobility, which also made it easier for the participating central banks to maintain particular exchange rates through periods of temporary international turmoil.

By the early 1970s, however, the dollar had ceased to be a low-inflation currency, and the ending of gold convertibility at $35 an ounce in August 1971 came as no real surprise. Moreover, by the early 1970s world-wide capital mobility had increased substantially, and capital movements were destabilizing (Obstfeld, 1993). This important change in the international economic environment (which we discuss further in Section 4) coupled with dollar weakness meant that in the summer of 1971 the Bretton Woods agreement and 'instruments' ceased to be either viable or appropriate (in the eyes of the center economies).

On the question of developing countries, some analysts have pointed out that the emergence of the 'third world' as a numerous and influential bloc on the international economic scene dates from the second half of the twentieth century. Earlier in the century, large areas of Africa and Asia were still under European colonial domination – though this was not the case in Latin America where political independence had been gained at the start of the nineteenth century. In the early post-war period, they argue that the developing countries pursued inward-looking strategies limiting their integration into the world economy, and their involvement in managing it. Eichengreeen and Kenen (1994) present several interesting examples in which the developing countries tried, as they put it, to "turn the table on the G-10."[4]

Adjustment mechanism post-1971

Following the Bretton Woods' collapse in 1971, exchange-rate determination in developing countries has been fundamentally different from that in industrial countries. Generally speaking, the industrial countries abandoned efforts to support fixed exchange rates in the early 1970s, and decided to adopt flexible rates (albeit with frequent central bank interventions in times of turbulence), while most developing countries continued to rely heavily on fixed exchange-rates, although no one sort of arrangement universally prevailed (Agénor and Montiel, 1996, p. 191).

More than twenty years after the demise of the Bretton Woods system, the international situation reveals three broad categories of exchange-rate arrangements: (1) pegged or fixed arrangements; (2) flexible or floating arrangements; and (3) various intermediate categories characterized by limited flexibility – 'target-zones' regimes and the Exchange Rate Mechanism (ERM) of the European Monetary System are examples (IMF, 1994).

As of December 1979, 85% of developing countries had some kind of fixed exchange-rate arrangement (IMF, 1979). During the 1980s and early 1990s, however, an increasing number of developing countries moved away from fixed exchange rates to more flexible regimes. By December 1990 the percentage of developing countries with a fixed exchange rate had fallen to 67% – a shrinking, but still a significant percentage (IMF, 1990).

Edwards and Santaella (1993, p. 405) point out that "this movement toward greater flexibility was, to a considerable extent, associated with the debt crisis unleashed in 1982." Having to cope with sudden cuts in external finance they were left with limited policy options. The authors write:

> In an effort to engineer gigantic resource transfers to their creditors, most of these countries adopted adjustment packages that included, as an important component, the abandonment of fixed rate practices. (Edwards and Santaella, 1993, p. 405)

Developing countries quickly adapted to the new circumstances, and during the course of the 1980s and 1990s a large number of developing economies have become more at ease living with 'managed' flexible exchange-rate arrangements.

---

[4] This citation appears in Eichengreen and Kenen (1994, footnote 30). For more details about developing countries activities in matters pertaining to trade or their intention to "turn the table" on issues dealing with allocation of world-wide international reserves, see pp. 30–31 of the paper mentioned above.

3 The emerging economies experience in the aftermath of the Bretton Woods collapse

The process of economic integration among nations has been virtually ineluctable since 1945, with substantial effects on emerging economies. The problems of accommodating to world globalization are magnified when countries simultaneously go through stabilization programs and regional economic integration.[5]

There is, at least, a certain agreement among economists that the actual system of relations among countries is presently in deep crisis, and does not correspond well to the needs of the global economy. In discussing the international macro-system that has emerged since the breakdown of Bretton Woods, Corden (1994, p. 165) points out that "the essential feature is that it is unplanned and uncoordinated, and might be better described as a non-system."

On the critical question of exchange-rate regimes, Davidson (1992/1993) suggests that a stark choice between *rigidly fixed* and *totally flexible* arrangements is not sufficiently refined, when we are searching for a complex mechanism simultaneously to solve disequilibria of current account payments, to promote sustained growth with full employment, and to establish an international standard of reliable monetary value. Hence it is a current imperative for economists to devise and suggest a new economic relationship between countries in which the peripheral economies are not systematically marginalized.

In the immediate aftermath of the Bretton Woods collapse, Latin American economies experienced the shock of the 1970s oil price rises, which both contributed to their external indebtedness and reinforced domestic inflationary tendencies. After the debt crisis which followed Mexico's default in 1982, various attempts to stabilize these economies were undertaken within the context of the 'recovery' programs sponsored by the International Monetary Fund. For its part, the IMF made the adoption of specific macroeconomic stabilization measures a condition (the so-called 'IMF conditionality') for granting or re-financing loans. The stabilization attempts of the early 1980s were, however, largely unsuccessful, and are still the subject of much debate (Silva, 1997).

Recently a number of high-inflation Latin American economies have experienced *dollarization* – a phenomenon of currency substitution where the US dollar comes to replace the national currency as the chief domestic medium of exchange, and at the same time is (voluntarily) adopted as the *anchor* for domestic monetary creation (Salama,1993). This phenomenon can constitute a serious problem. Expansion of domestic liquidity and credit are now determined by the dollar amount of reserves held by the domestic banking system. An independent monetary policy vanishes and national

[5] This is certainly the case of countries like Brazil, Argentina, Paraguay and Uruguay, which constitutes the MERCOSUR whose integration process evolved in the 1980s. MERCOSUR stands for the Spanish expression Mercado Comun del Sur (Common Market of the South).

sovereignty itself is curtailed. The similarities between dollarization and the old gold standard mechanism are striking.

The *conventional approach* to currency substitution assumes that *dollarization* can be easily reversed, when relative rates of return on the competing monies return to their equilibrium levels. This approach, however, ignores *hysteresis*: once an institutional change occurs it may not easily be put into reverse, even if conditions should prevail such that, had they existed earlier, they would have prevented the change happening in the first place. A number of analysts thus reject the conventional 'reversibility' thesis as it applies to *dollarization*.[6]

The question of whether there is any workable means of justly and fairly integrating emerging economies into the global economy is one to which many economists are urgently seeking an answer. The current situation in Latin America is that a group of developing economies appears to be growing more vulnerable to external shocks and to speculative currency attacks. Real growth rates are disappointing and unemployment is rising.

Asia, like Latin America, is suffering enormous economic pain. During the second half of the 1990s several Asian economies were subject to a succession of serious currency crises. The 1997/1998 crises in Malaysia, Indonesia and Thailand, for instance, well examined in Krugman (1998) and IIF (1998), were dramatic with world-wide repercussions. In 1998, even the mighty Japan became a casualty (in her case with a massive asset price deflation). And in Russia, the catastrophic economic disorders that came to a head in August 1998, could yet develop into one of the most serious political and social crises of the twentieth century.

But whether we think of Latin America, Asia or even Russia, the salient fact is that participation of emerging economies in the management of the world economy is strictly marginal. Their currencies are weak and are viewed internationally as 'peripheral monies'. By peripheral money we understand currencies that are perceived to be 'inferior' to those of the center economies, and which are used neither as mediums of exchange in international trade nor as 'reserve' currencies maintained by world central banks.

How is macroeconomic and financial stability to be secured by emerging economies using peripheral monies? How can emerging economies influence the development of the globalization of world trade and finance?

4 The response of foreign capital flows to disinflation stabilisation programmes[7]

Attempts to control the hyperinflation that has plagued many emerging economies, from the 1970s onwards, particularly in Latin America, have led to a variety of disinflation stabilization experiments. The successive failures of these programs have persuaded a number of countries to experiment with so-called exchange-rate-based stabilization programs (ERBSPs). The rea-

[6] See Baldwin (1988) and Baldwin and Krugman (1989, pp. 635–645).
[7] See Silva and Torrance (1998).

soning is that stabilization programs based on the exchange-rate exerting the role of a nominal anchor would act directly on inflationary expectations, which are considered a key determinant of short-run inflation, thus increasing the chances of lowering inflation at minimum cost in terms of unemployment and lost output.

There are at least three common aspects to all recent ERBSPs:

- The first of these is, of course, the use of the exchange rate itself as a monetary anchor. The basic hope is that the adoption of a pre-announced exchange rate emboldens politicians to implement supporting monetary and fiscal policies. Its success is conditional on the credibility of the policy shift and its public acceptability.
- The second aspect relates to a different strand of analysis that by the 1980s stressed disinflation rather than short-run output stabilization, as a choice between money-supply and exchange-rate targeting.
- The third aspect is that ERBSPs have been implemented in a world setting in which the globalization of both trade and finance are proceeding rapidly, with the latter tending to become even more extensive than the former (Kregel, 1996, p. 3).

A serious repercussion of financial globalization, recently highlighted by Edwards (1996), is that short-run capital inflows will tend to appreciate the real exchange rate, which is a result that runs contrary to the long-run goals of social reformers. Also, of course, as long as the commitment to an exchange-rate anchor is held, it encourages investment in domestic financial assets with high exchange-rate-adjusted profits. Nevertheless, once international markets start to suspect the integrity of the anchor, foreign-capital inflows quickly tend to reverse themselves. Such volatility increases countries' vulnerability to credibility problems and to resident capital flight.[8]

Another source of concern is the implication of evidence showing that heavy inflows of foreign capital into emerging markets in the 1990s were motivated mostly by relatively low interest rates in industrialized nations (especially by the US's falling interest rate, in the case of Latin American countries), rather than by confidence in the stabilization programs undertaken by the developing countries and achievements in correcting 'fundamentals'. Calvo et al. (1993) showed that in the last two decades the foreign capital in flows were not restricted to developing countries with good reform records. It follows that, if capital inflows depend more on external factors than on 'correct fundamentals', they may not be sustainable, and could flow out without warning, forcing the recipient countries to incur costly adjustment.

Concern has been expressed in academic and policy circles about the loss of macroeconomic policy autonomy by financial globalization and the

[8] The experience with exchange-rate-based disinflation stabilization programs has not been restricted to Latin America and/or developing countries with chronic high inflation. Detragiache and Hamann (1997) review the experiences with ERBSP of Italy, Ireland, Portugal and Greece during the period 1980–96 and suggest that the main results are not similar to the ones obtained by emerging economies fighting chronic high inflation processes.

unrestricted influx of short-term capital. The concern is correct as far as monetary policy is involved, but is not necessarily true with respect to exchange-rate policy: short-term inflows have allowed, in the initial stages of ERBSPs, the prolongation of an overvaluation policy designed to bring domestic inflation down. This can give governments extra time to implement 'structural adjustments' that may be necessary to make the disinflation policy succeed. In other words: inflation control through monetary stringency is always difficult, but a policy that uses the exchange-rate anchor can last longer provided that domestic interest rates are maintained at a level attractive to foreign capital. However, the costs in terms of fiscal discipline may be high. Financial openness may fail to impose adequate fiscal discipline on governments, or even on the domestic private sector, given the apparent ease with which governmental and private sector deficits can be financed in international financial markets. "Hence, from a domestic point of view, perhaps a case could be made that financial openness brings in excessive domestic macroeconomic policy autonomy!" (Bacha, 1993, p. 10).[9]

Opening an economy extends the range of goods, services and assets available to domestic residents, and the range of potential buyers of domestic goods, services and assets. However, openness may increase the destabilizing power of financial markets. According to Dow (1993) the destabilizing nature depends on the type of economy under consideration:

> Whether exchange rates are more or less flexible determines primarily the limitation put on the supply of finance during an expansion; the more fixed are exchange rates, the greater the scope for capital inflows to continue to finance an expansion. With fixed rates, the responsiveness of supply to changes in expected returns increases; with floating exchange rates, it is demand which becomes more elastic. Since either of these increase the tendency towards financial ease in an expansion and tightness in a contraction, the general statement may be made that economic openness increases the scope of instability. (Dow, 1993, p. 70)

She argues, nevertheless, that "instability in the form of steady expansion is not at all undesirable. Self-sufficient economies, relatively immune from external demand shocks, and particularly those with a history of higher-than-average returns, can enjoy more sustained expansions as a result of external sources of finance" (Ibid, p. 70). However, for export-dependent economies, or in economies that are trying to stabilize, unstable international financial markets can be problematic. When export-led expansions are associated with capital inflows, for instance, exchange-rate overvaluation leads imports to grow relative to exports and the final result may well be the failure of the program.

In economies that have experimented with *dollarization* in the form of a variety of ERBSPs, such as some Latin American countries (Argentina, Brazil, Mexico and Chile), Asian countries (Hong Kong) and Middle

---

[9] Calvo, Leiderman and Reinhart (1993) provide an excellent summary on this issue, adding to the discussion other domestic policy concerns raised by short-term capital inflows.

Eastern countries (Bahrain and Saudi Arabia), the desire to counteract the pressures of exchange-rate overvaluation in situations of large capital inflows, and attempts to limit inflows that are likely to be reversed, have induced the monetary authorities to engage in certain 'back-up' interventionist policies. These activities have taken the form of direct intervention, through exchange controls and taxes, and restrictive domestic credit policy in the shape of sterilization activities.

Central bank sterilized intervention has been one of the most widely used policy response to capital inflows in Latin America. Calvo et al. (1993) point out the main difficulties with this policy: First, sterilization increases the differential between the interest rate on domestic government debt and international reserves, thus creating a quasi-fiscal deficit. Second, by preventing a sharp fall in the domestic relative to the foreign interest rate, sterilization tends to perpetuate capital inflows exacerbating any problems caused by the inflow itself.

Re-evaluating the choice of exchange-rate regimes

When an emerging economy is experiencing stable capital inflows at a desired level, support can reasonably be given to some kind of flexible exchange-rate regime. But on what general considerations should the choice of a regime for a specific country, at a particular point in time, rest?

Dornbusch, in his comments to Bordo's (1993) paper, states:

> a central determination of the direction of capital flows is the interest differential adjusted for exchange rate expectations. Unfortunately, those expectations have no tight link to reality.... Of course, if expectations that are out of touch with market "fundamentals" come to dominate the level of rates, economists and policy makers alike face a conundrum. We can no longer say that markets know best. (Dornbusch comments in: Bordo, 1993, p. 103)

If this line of reasoning is accepted, the debate between fixed *versus* flexible exchange rates boils down essentially to judging which system better lessens the problems with the implementation of the structural change program of the developing country in question.[10]

Despite the erratic fluctuations that have characterized flexible rates, it has until recently been the ruling orthodoxy that markets could determine appropriate exchange rates better than governments. Policymakers in several emerging economies, however, have resisted this conclusion. To them, a more attractive alternative is the adoption of an ERBSP. When the target-bands are wide, they argue, an economy can take advantage of both the short-run flexibility and the long-run predictability of its exchange rate.

---

[10] We are not arguing that the theoretical problems involved when choosing among exchange-rate regimes should be avoided. We are aware that the models dealing with exchange-rate regimes embody assumptions about short and long-run equilibrium of variables, money neutrality, purchasing power parity and other extremely controversial issues that divide economists and have been subject to much academic dispute.

The Exchange Rate Mechanism of the European Monetary System (to be replaced by a fully-fledged currency union on January 1st, 1999) is the world's premier example of a system of target-bands that has, since its creation in 1979, seen several major adjustments of central cross-rates. These adjustments, while often categorized as failures of the system, in reality provided the necessary flexibility for its survival.

The role of foreign reserves

Crockett (1994) analyzes the very interesting and fundamental change of view concerning the role of reserves in the international financial system that occurred between 1965 and 1992. As he puts it:

With the advent of flexible exchange rates, however, an alternative adjustment mechanism became available (at least potentially) which did not require the holding of reserves. At the same time the growth of international markets meant that shifts in the current account no longer had such a direct impact on official reserves. Relatively minor changes in interest differentials could induce short-term capital flows that would protect the reserves against the consequences of movements in the current account position. (Crockett, 1994, p. 88)

Crockett (1994) and Dow (1993) seem to agree that the important change comes on the side of the reserve supply arrangements. The growth of international capital markets has meant that reserve-holding countries face a very elastic supply schedule with the growth and expanding size of the eurocurrency banking market. Monetary authorities can operate in these markets as any other market participant.

However the question of liquidity and reserves as a macroeconomic instrument is particularly relevant when the situation of the developing countries is considered. The entry to the global financial market of countries that have been on the periphery of the international system (including Latin America, Russia, Eastern Europe, etc.) has not been a simple issue.

Dow (1993) critically reviews the conventional finance and development literatures, and summarizes some of its main conclusions. She argues that:

the financial problem facing developing countries is identified as an inadequacy of saving relative to investment demand. Capital inflows constitute one solution to that problem. The implication is that the greater the degree of capital mobility the less likely it is that a shortage of saving will inhibit economic development. The other solution is seen to lie in financial liberalization within developing countries in order to generate saving internally. (Dow, 1993, p. 162)

Further, in her criticism of this traditional view she points out that:

most developing countries lack adequate internal capital markets and are driven therefore to international banks not only for initial financing but also for long-term finance. It is not a shortage of saving which is the problem, but rather the lack of mechanism to turn saving into appropriate funding instruments... the investment should generate the saving to repay the debt. But repayment is made more difficult by virtue of the fact that it must be in the form of foreign exchange. (Dow, 1993, p.163)

Along with Crockett (1994), Dow also suggests that the most important fact not explicitly addressed by the traditional literature is the *endogeneity* of credit creation within modern banking systems. There is no longer any need for prior saving to finance investment when banks create credit to finance investment which generates the savings to fund the credit.[11] Nevertheless, when dealing with exchange-rate-based programs the accumulation of reserves becomes a central issue.

Actually the question of pegging the exchange rate, or letting it float, looked at from the perspective of the developing countries with weak currencies, still remains of crucial importance in the second half of the 1990s. Borrowing credibility from other countries' monies by means of pegging the exchange rate, and delaying or not attempting to correct fundamental macroeconomic variables, can be a very artificial solution that might not last long, and is likely to end in a 'Mexican' breakdown.

Speculative currency attacks

The analysis of circumstances in which a balance-of-payments problem (understood as a persistent loss of foreign-exchange reserves) becomes a balance-of-payments crisis (a situation in which speculators attack the currency), is strongly associated with Krugman's pioneering work of 1979. In the words of one of his later papers:

I have shown that the balance-of-payments crises are a natural outcome of maximizing behavior by investors. When the government's unwillingness to use reserves to defend the exchange rate is uncertain, there can be a series of crises in which capital flows out of the country, then returns, before the issue was finally resolved. (Krugman, 1993, p. 75)[12]

The 'canonical currency crisis model' as developed by Krugman (1979) and by Flood and Garber (1984) explains currency crises in the following manner:

as the result of a fundamental inconsistency between domestic policies – typically the persistence of money-financed budget deficits – and the attempt to maintain a fixed exchange rate. This inconsistency can be temporarily papered over if the central bank has sufficiently large reserves, but when these reserves become inadequate speculators force the issue with a wave of selling. (Krugman, 1979, p. 3)

---

[11] There is today a vast literature on the endogeneity of credit supply. Dow(1993), Chick and Dow (1994) and several Post-Keynesian economists have written several articles related to this topic. We will not discuss it with more detail here since it is not our theme. However it is an important issue to be addressed when analyzing the foreign debt crisis faced by developing countries.

[12] This citation appears in Krugman (1993). That is a copy of the original work initially published in the *Journal of Money, Credit, and Banking* (1979).

The mechanics of the model can be outlined thus: the economy has an external deficit, owns a stock of reserves and pegs the exchange rate. The financing of the debt through monetary base creation leads to a steady growth in the shadow price of the exchange rate. Once the shadow price becomes higher than the price defended by the government, speculators cause a rapid decline in the stock of foreign reserves. The government is unable to sustain the attack, and the system collapses.

The main limitation of this model is the unsophisticated manner in which government policy is portrayed. It is unlikely that any government would stick to this policy once its foreign-exchange reserves started to be exhausted. Furthermore, the recent crises in Latin America, especially the Mexican crisis of 1994–1995, do not support some of the main implications of this model. The rate of interest, for instance, should rise continuously before the attack and not suddenly shoot up, as actually happened.

A second generation of currency crisis models mix the canonical model with Barro and Gordon's (1983a, b) cost-benefit-game approach. Their main element is a trade-off between inflation and unemployment or a trade-off between inflation and public debt. Purchasing power parity links the exchange rate to domestic prices and inflation and the game ultimately leads to a trade-off between fixing the exchange rate (less inflation, more unemployment and a larger debt burden) and devaluing the exchange rate (more inflation, less unemployment and a smaller debt burden).[13] The final equilibrium depends on the expectations of agents, the nature of the shocks and of the initial institutional conditions. The expectation that the government will abandon the fixed exchange rate may increase the cost of defending it and may even precipitate the crisis itself.

One important implication of these models is the possibility of multiple equilibria and with it the possibility of 'self-fulfilling expectations' – a concept much favored earlier this century by Keynes (1936). Contrary to Krugman's standard model in which the speculative attack results from disequilibrium in the 'fundamentals', Obstfeld (1995, 1996) and Velasco (1996), amongst others, advocate the possibility of a currency crisis being the result of self-fulfilling expectations, even when the 'fundamentals' are correct.

This Keynesian notion of self-fulfilling expectations, however, comes from a different conceptual framework. In Keynes' case, the initial institutional and historical conditions are not the deciding factor. To be more specific, the whole 'space' presents multiple equilibria. In that sense there is no place for a determinate relationship between the exchange rate and the 'fundamentals'. According to Keynes (1936), the 'fundamentals' would be dependent on unpredictable market expectations, and, more specifically, on what he described as *animal spirits*. There is thus no clear separation possible between 'fundamentals' and 'bubbles'. In a way, both are part of the same phenomenon, since both depend on the state of expectations.[14] The exchange rate could be affected by the asset prices of the domestic economy

---

[13] Debt burden denominated in domestic currency might lead governments to devalue in order to reduce it.

[14] A very elucidating analysis in this regard is made by Harvey (1996).

as much as by the interest rate. The speculative character of the demand for money that is capable of producing unstable monetary aggregates is likewise liable to affect exchange-rate dynamics.

In this setting currency crises are embedded in general crises as well. In the case of the interest rate, if more economic agents believe that it will increase and sell bonds, the greater will be the actual increase in the interest rate. The same thing could happen with the exchange rate.

Financial instability hypothesis

In addition to these new generation models, we should mention the important contributions of Calvo and Mendoza (1996a, b) and Krugman (1998). Despite the fact that the former develops his model to understand the Mexican 1994 collapse, and the latter analyzes the recent Asian crisis, they have much in common.

In Calvo and Mendoza's (1996a, b) model currency crises are associated with financial crises. Greater foreign capital inflows increase private bank liquidity that becomes domestic lending. Given the expected guarantee of the deposits by the monetary authorities, depositors do not press for prudential regulation of banking lending activities. On the other hand, bankers buy risky assets. As a result, the banking system becomes fragile. Anticipation of devaluation leads to a shift from domestic currency towards foreign currency. Banks are unable to honor their depositors, and are rescued by the Central Bank as the lender of last resort. The consequent increase in the monetary base validates the bank run, and the economy loses reserves. According to Calvo and Mendoza the currency crisis becomes a stock crisis – liquid assets are too high in relation to the stock of reserves.

Krugman's (1998) interpretation is basically the same as Calvo and Mendoza's (1996a, b) with the difference that he views currency crisis as part of a larger financial crisis. Financial deregulation leads to a boom-and-bust situation. Bankers are 'speculators' who have little to lose but a lot to gain from holding highly risky portfolios. The risk-embracing behavior of the bankers is explained by moral hazard, given that the monetary authorities guarantee the depositors. This is the same mechanism alleged by Calvo and Mendoza. The main difference is that Krugman stresses the investment cycle. It is interesting to note that the rate of return taken into account by the financial intermediaries (the 'pangloss' rate of return according to Krugman, 1998) is higher than the expected rate of return. What matters for investors are the positive pay-offs, given that they perceive a guarantee by the government on a minimum pay-off. Moral hazard that favors risky behavior by banks leads to a mass of hopelessly unprofitable over-investment.

These analyses embody complementary arguments. Krugman's scenario is sufficient to produce a financial crisis. Calvo and Mendonza's, on the other hand, emphasizes the complementarity between currency crisis and financial crisis. Krugman's story of financial business cycle is worth reproducing:

So what would a true account of the Asian crisis look like? Let me propose the following story: The problem began with financial intermediaries – institutions whose liabilities were perceived as having an implicit government guarantee, but were essentially unregulated and therefore subject to severe moral hazard problems. The excessive risky lending of these institutions created inflation – not of goods but of asset prices. The overpricing of assets was sustained in part by a sort of circular process, in which the proliferation of risky lending drove up the prices of risky assets, making the financial condition of the intermediaries seem sounder than it was...And then the bubble burst. The mechanism of crisis. I suggest, involved that same circular process in reverse: falling asset prices made the insolvency of intermediaries visible, forcing them to cease operations, leading to further asset deflation. This circularity, in turn, can explain both the remarkable severity of the crisis and the apparent vulnerability of the Asian economies to self-fulfilling crisis – which in turn helps us understand the phenomenon of contagion between economies with few visible economic links. (Krugman, 1998, p. 3)

The three important points in these accounts, particularly in Krugman's 1998 work, are:

(i) A recognition that finance may lead to instability under poorly regulated financial intermediaries.

This is, actually, not a new point. The monetarist argument has always been that monetary mismanagement leads to fluctuations. The interesting issue has to do with the idea of credit-driven fluctuation. The link with the classical economist's view (e.g of J.S. Mill and Alfred Marshall) is clear through the emphasis on the leading role of bank credit. The new point, however, that deserves to be mentioned is the recognition that the endogenous character of credit money lies, ultimately, on the monetary authorities' commitment to bail out banking sector bankruptcies. The commitment of the monetary authorities to bail out domestic banks is the main element behind the elasticity of credit supply and its real effects. Moral hazard is developed from this unregulated 'deposit insurance' policy. Krugman's amendment to the Calvo argument complements the story: banks become over-optimistic during economic booms.

The relationship between these arguments and Minsky's (1976, 1982) approach is striking. Financial intermediation leads via excessive credit creation to an unsustainable expansion in the boom period. What is the difference between the two arguments? A distinction can be made on the basis of the notion of equilibrium and expectation. In Krugman's case, over-expansion comes from the rational behavior of banks and moral hazard. The banks know the pay-offs of the projects and moral hazard allows them to disregard the negative pay-offs. In Minsky's case, the banks have different degrees of confidence in the expected pay-offs of the investment projects.

Krugmans's story amounts to a rational expectations bubble. Credit expansion leads to rising asset prices and the rate of return on financial assets quickly overtakes the rate of return on real assets. This naturally can be explained in terms of speculative bubbles. In contrast, according to Minsky, bubbles arise from the inner dynamics of the economy and the inherent characteristics of financial markets. Expectations about future rates of return are held with different degrees of confidence. Upswings are driven by overconfidence of banks and investors.

(ii) Financial instability leads to real effects.

Money's loss of neutrality during financial crises is noteworthy. According to Krugman, moral hazard leads to changes in the marginal efficiency of capital as perceived by banks. As a consequence, investment projects that did not previously present positive present values are financed. Over-investment and an inefficient allocation of resources *vis-à-vis* equilibrium conditions results. This may lead to temporary and permanent effects. Naturally, in Minsky's case there is no neutrality of money to begin with, and there is no guarantee that the system ever returns to its old resting point.

(iii) Currency crises are a critical part of financial instability.

Krugman's view of the current Asian currency crisis is based on the analysis of financial business cycles. The relationship between currency crises and crises at large is an important insight offered by Krugman (1998). As he says:

> [the] Asian story is really about a bubble in and subsequent collapse of asset values in general, with the currency crises more a symptom than a cause ... (Krugman, 1998, p. 3)

To understand Asia's currency crisis Krugman fashions a model of the business cycle based on financial instability. His implicit view is that after a financial downturn the sudden fall in value of financial assets leads to an outflow of capital and a growing lack of credibility in the domestic currency. In short, a currency crisis is an integral part of a general crisis of the economy.

Herding behavior

To explain the burst of capital outflow that characterizes a currency crisis Calvo (1995) adds to his analysis a psycho-societal concept he calls 'herding behavior'. Global investors systematically disregard economic 'fundamentals', since information is costly, and exhibit instead 'herding behavior'. Investors balance diversification and costly information gathering. The marginal benefits of gathering country-specific information diminishes with geographic diversification and investment becomes highly responsive to very small changes in perceived expected returns. Calvo concludes:

> diversification encourages ignorance, and in this environment even frivolous rumours may trigger massive capital flows that are seemingly inconsistent with a country's "fundamentals"...volatility is an inescapable feature of the global economy that comes along with its advantages for risk-diversification, transfers of technology and enhanced efficiency in resource allocation. (Calvo, 1995, p. 174)

Calvo's argument seems close to what Keynes (1936) viewed as just ordinary human behavior. To overcome uncertainty most economic agents most of the time simply and blindly follow the majority (like the herd of Gadarene swine in the New Testament narrative at St Luke 8: 26–37!). The damaging effects on emerging economies of this kind of non-rational behavior is an ever-present possibility.

5 Concluding remarks

Throughout this paper emphasis has been placed on the special problems of emerging economies attempting to achieve sound money and other attributes of macroeconomic stability.

As far as ERBSPs are concerned, an important weakness is the tendency to highten the economy's exposure to external shocks. Once an economy follows a fixed exchange-rate rule or a narrow-band arrangement, it becomes more vulnerable to external shocks than when it follows a strict floating regime. The time-inconsistency problem rears its head and credibility again becomes a fundamental requirement for the system if it is to survive.

An additional complicating aspect of ERBSPs is that a fixed exchange rate may bring with it a growing disequilibrium of the visible trade balance, if the real or relative-inflation-adjusted exchange rate appreciates as a consequence. Temporary domestic price-level stabilization is not difficult to attain at the cost of a growing distortion of relative prices. This is a characteristic shared by most stabilization programs based on exchange-rate anchors. Relative price distortion exacerbates the problems that these economies have to face, and so increases the possibility of time-inconsistent behavior by policymakers.

External disequilibrium also reflects internal disequilibrium. Emerging economies, in general, inherit from the past oversized and inefficient state sectors in which there are chronic deficits. Excess expenditure over income reduces domestic savings, and this could explain part of the trade deficit.

Inconsistencies in the 'fundamentals' can be partly compensated for by capital inflows. However, this strategy relies heavily on the expectations of foreign investors and the economy could become very sensitive to crises of credibility and to contagious ill effects from external economic sources. An important element of this vulnerability is, certainly, the sustainability of the 'fundamentals'. The government should try to convince foreign investors that it is acting within its intertemporal budget constraint. Disequilibrium of the government sector may lead to financial vulnerability that is closely connected with speculative crises. Governments may even become insolvent, and if this happens it is inevitable that they will seek to monetize their domestic deficits. But once this occurs, it is equally inevitable that there will be hyper-inflation and a consequent drain of official reserves. Investors' expectations of such a disaster may, in some circumstances, bring about the feared disaster as a self-fulfilling prediction.

Bond finance by the government may also lead to speculative crises as suggested by Calvo and Mendoza (1996a, b). Once investors lose faith in the government's ability to defend the domestic currency they seek to exchange domestic-currency denominated bonds for cash dollars. The prophecies may become true: government loses reserves and is forced to permit a devaluation, thereby increasing the cost in domestic currency of the external debt, and leading, eventually, to a monetization of the debt and to further repeated speculative attacks.

Contagious events of undesirable kinds from abroad are likely to damage particular economies. It has been our argument that consistently good 'fundamentals' are not sufficient to insulate emerging economies from speculative currency attacks. On-going present-day crises (in South-East Asia and in Russia, for instance) are startling demonstrations of what can happen when both internal and external factors are ripe for speculative upheaval and turmoil. Our final conclusion, therefore, points to the doleful circumstance that emerging economies are, in reality, currently caught in a network of different traps: currency traps, bad banking traps, 'fundamentals' traps, and exchange-rate traps. Must this be accepted as an inevitable element of the architecture of the economic cosmos?

References

Agénor P-R, Montiel PJ (1996) Development macroeconomics. Princeton University Press, Princeton, NJ

Bacha E (1993) Latin America's re-entry into private financial markets: domestic and international policy issues. Texto para Discussão 299. Departamento de Economia/ PUC, Rio de Janeiro

Baldwin R (1988) Hysteresis in import prices: The Beachhead effect. American Economic Review 78: 773–785

Baldwin R, Krugman P (1989) Persistent trade effects of large exchange rate shocks. Quarterly Journal of Economics 104 (4): 635–645

Barro RJ, Gordon DB (1983a) A positive theory of monetary policy in a natural rate model. JPE 91(4): 589–609

Barro RJ, Gordon DB (1983b) Rules, discretion, and reputation in a model of monetary policy. Journal of Monetary Economics 12: 101–120. Reprinted in: Persson T, Tabellini G (1994) Monetary and fiscal policy, Vol 1. Credibility, chapter 4, pp 99–122. The MIT Press, Cambridge, MA

Bordo MD (1993) The Bretton Woods International Monetary System: An historical overview. In: Bordo MD, Eichengreen B (eds) A restrospective on the Bretton Woods System: Lessons for international monetary reform. The University of Chicago Press, Chicago

Bordo MD, Schwartz AJ (1994) The specie standard as a contingent rule: Some evidence for core and peripheral countries, 1880–1990. National Bureau of Economic Research, Working Paper No. 4860

Calvo GA (1995) Varieties of capital market crises. Center for International Economics, Working Paper No. 15. University of Maryland, College Park

Calvo GA, Leiderman L, Reinhart C (1993) Capital inflows and real exchange rate appreciation in Latin America: the role of external factors. IMF Staff Paper, Vol 40, No 1. The International Monetary Fund, Washington, DC

Calvo GA, Mendoza EG (1996a) Mexico's balance of payments crisis: A chronicle of a death foretold. Journal of International Economics 41: 235–264

Calvo GA, Mendoza EG (1996b) Petty crime and cruel punishment: Lessons from the Mexican debacle. American Economic Review 86 (2): 170–175

Chick V, Dow S (1994) Competition and the future of the European banking and financial system. Discussion Paper 94-16. Department of Economics, University College London, London

Chilcote RH (1974) A critical synthesis of dependency literature. Latin American Perspectives 1 (1): 4–29

Corden WM (1994) Economic policy, exchange-rates and the international system. Oxford University Press, Oxford

Crockett A (1994) The role of market and official channels in the supply of international liquidity. In: Kenen P, Papadia BF, Saccomanni F (eds) The International Monetary System. Cambridge University Press, Cambridge

Davidson P (1992–93) Reforming the World's Money. Journal of Post-Keynesian Economics 15 (2): 153–180

Davidson P (1993) The elephant and the butterfly: or hysteresis and Post-Keynesian economics. Journal of Post-Keynesian Economics 15 (3): 309–322

Detragiache E, Hamann A (1975) Exchange-rate-based stabilization in Western Europe: Greece, Ireland, Itaty and Portugal. International Monetary Fund Working Papers, no 97

Dow SC (1993) Money and the economic process. Edward Elgar, London

Edwards S (1996) Exchange-rate anchors, credibility, and inertia: a tale of two crises, Chile and Mexico. The American Economic Review 86 (2): 176–180 (Papers and Proceedings of the 1996 meeting of the AEA)

Edwards S, Santaella J (1993) The Bretton Woods System, the IMF, and some devaluation controversies in the developing countries. In: Bordo MD, Eichengreen B (eds) A retrospective on the Bretton Woods System: Lessons for international monetary reform, pp 405–460. The University of Chicago Press, Chicago, IL

Eichengreen B, Kenen PB (1994) Managing the world economy under Bretton Woods System: An overview. In: Kenen P (ed) Managing the world economy: Fifty years after Bretton Woods. International Monetary Fund, Washington, DC

Flood RP, Garber PM (1984) Collapsing exchange-rate regimes: Some linear examples. Journal of International Economics 17: 1–13

Ford AG (1964) Bank rate, the British balance of payments, and the burdens of adjustment. 1870–1914. Oxford Economics Papers, no 16

Ford AG (1983) The gold standard 1880–1914: Britain and Argentina. Garland, New York, London

Franco GH (1988) Assimetrias Sistêmicas sob o Padrão Ouro. Texto para Discussão, no 184. Brazil, Department of Economics/PUC, RJ

Harvey JT (1996) Orthodox approaches to exchange-rate determination: a survey. Journal of Post-Keynesian Economics 18 (4): 567–583

Institute of International Finance (1998) Capital flows to emerging market economies. Published on the web at: http://www. iif. com

International Monetary Fund (IMF) (1994) Exchange arrangement and exchange restrictions. Annual Report, Washington, DC

International Monetary Fund (IMF) (1979) International financial statistics

International Monetary Fund (IMF) (1990) International financial statistics

Keynes JM [1936] (1964) The general theory of employment, interest, and money (1936). Harcourt Brace, New York

Kregel JA (1996) Risks and implications of financial globalization for national policy autonomy. Paper prepared for the International Conference: Macroeconomics in the face of globalisation. CORECON, Brasília, Brazil (unpublished manuscript)

Krugman P (1979) A model of balance of payments crises. Journal of Money, Credit, and Banking 11: 311–325

Krugman PR (1991) Has the adjustment process worked? Institute for International Economics, Washington, DC

Krugman PR (1993) Currencies and crises, 2nd edn. Massachusetts Institute of Technology, Cambridge, MA

Krugman P (1998) What happened to Asia? Published on the web at: http://web.mit.edu/krugman/www/ DISINTER.html

Lindert P (1969) Key currencies and gold, 1900-191. Princeton Studies in International Finance, No 24. Princeton University Press, Princeton

Martson RC (1989) Pricing to market in Japanese manufacturing. NBER, Working Paper 2905, National Bureau of Economic Research, Cambridge, MA
Morgenstern O (1959) International financial transactions and the business cycle, NBER and Princeton University Press, Princeton
Minsky HP (1976) John Maynard Keynes. Macmillan, London
Minsky HP (1982) Inflation, recession and economic policy. Wheatsheaf, Brighton
Obstfeld M (1993) The adjustment mechanism. In: Bordo MD, Eichengreen B (eds) A retrospective on the Bretton Woods system: Lessons for international monetary reform. The University of Chicago Press, Chicago
Obstfeld M (1995) International currency experience: New lessons and lessons relearned. In: Brainard WC, Perry GL (eds) Brookings papers on economic activity – 25th anniversary issue. Brookings Institution, Washington, DC
Obstfeld M (1996) Models of currency crises with self-fulfilling features. European Economic Review 40: 1037–1047
Salama P (1993) Câmbio, dolarização e competitividade. In: Santos Filho M (org.) Instabilidade econômica: moeda e finanças. Hucitec, Brazil, SP
Silva MLF (1997) Modern exchange-rate regimes, stabilisation programmes, and co-ordination of macroeconomic policies: recent experiences of selected developing Latin American economies. Unpublished PhD thesis, Heriot-Watt University, Edinburgh, Scotland, UK
Silva MLF, Torrance TS (1998) Exchange-rate-based stabilization plans: the Brazilian experience with a target-zone regime. Economia Aplicada 2 (1): 31–64
Triffin R (1968) Our international monetary system: yesterday, today and tomorrow. Random House, New York
Velasco A (1996) Fixed exchange-rates: credibility, flexibility and multiplicity. European Economic Review 40 (3–5): 1023–1036

Capitalism, profits and innovation in the new techno-economic paradigm*

John Cantwell, Grazia D. Santangelo

Department of Economics, University of Reading, Whiteknights, PO Box 218, Reading, RG6 6AA, UK
(e-mail: J.A.Cantwell@reading.ac.uk, G.D.Santangelo@reading.ac.uk)

Abstract. Innovative profits (of the kind conceptualized by Schumpeter) are today being increasingly created through international corporate networks for technological development. Such profits through innovation are encouraged by newer more flexible organizational forms, and further encouraged (unlike in the conventional perspective on profits and on the incentive to innovate) by knowledge flows between firms. Our empirical evidence, based on US patent data, shows that multinational companies are currently more likely to develop abroad technologies which are less science-based, and less dependent upon tacit knowledge. However, within the science-based industries firms may generate abroad some technologies which are heavily dependent on tacit knowledge, but normally in fields that lie outside their own core technological competencies. We find some evidence of a convergence in corporate technological diversification across large firms, facilitated by the now common spread in the use of information and communication technologies (ICT) as an integrator of formerly separate technological systems. This has led smaller firms to diversify, but giant firms to consolidate activity around those technologies that have become most interrelated.

Key words: Innovation – Profits – Technological diversification – Internationalization

JEL-classification: O31, O32, L11, L60, B25

Paper presented at the 1998 World Conference of the International Joseph A. Schumpeter Society, Vienna, June 13–16, 1998.

* The authors wish to thank the editor for helpful comments on an earlier draft.

1 Introduction

This paper revisits in a modern context three of Schumpeter's concerns, namely, (i) the distinction between the static equilibrium analysis of the circular flow of income and the dynamics of 'entrepreneurial profit' (Schumpeter, 1934); (ii) the understanding of long waves of economic development (Schumpeter, 1939), which modern Schumpeterians have conceptualized in terms of technology paradigms; and (iii) the relationship between the form of economic organization and democratic governance and policy (Schumpeter, 1942).

We distinguish between the standard kind of profits attributable to positions of market power within the existing circular flow of economic activity, and innovative profits that are attributable instead to adding new value and expanding the circular flow. The former type of profits are emphasized in most twentieth century economic analysis, whether neoclassical, Marxist or neo-Ricardian, and involve either the monopolistic power to raise market prices, or the monopsonistic power to lower contracted costs (which in the crucial special case of the labor market, entails a redistribution of income from wages to profits). They can be suitably analyzed through the familiar framework of 'profit maximization'. The latter kind of innovative profits, which add new value to the circular chain through endogenous change (rather than exogenous disturbances), involve principally the development of new technologies of production, defined in the broad sense of new products and processes, and reliant upon the adaptation of social organization. They are best analyzed through the evolutionary approach to the 'search for higher profits' (Nelson and Winter, 1982).

We contend that the relative importance of this second type of profits is rising, and will continue to increase its share of total profits, with the growth in internationalization (which is eroding traditional positions of market power), and the emergence of the new techno-socio-economic paradigm, based upon information and communication technologies (ICT) as an integrator of diverse and hence flexible production systems (Freeman, 1987) reliant on more collective types of organizational form (Lazonick, 1992). In this new paradigm the linkages between science, education and technology have been further increased, and the potential fusion between formerly unrelated technologies through ICT has created major new opportunities for innovation based upon corporate technological diversification. We hold as well that in the longer term this will be associated with more democratic forms of organization, since the creation of innovative profits is essentially a positive sum rather than a zero sum game. While innovation tends to raise productivity and profits ahead of wages, it is not 'exploitative' in that (on average) wages still rise faster than they otherwise would. Governments must also pay increasing attention to education and training, to support a fuller range of scientific disciplines, and to encourage the international transmission of knowledge (the reverse of the conventional concern with 'leakages' which derives from the analysis of technology in terms of the rents associated with market power).

Two aspects of our argument are explored further empirically, using data on patents granted in the US since 1969 to the world's largest firms.

First, we examine the geographical implications of the closer linkages between science and technology in the new ICT-based paradigm. As some technological knowledge becomes more codified, international knowledge flows rise and research communities cross national boundaries, but this may be accompanied by the agglomeration of at least some kinds of technological development in centers of excellence. We ask which types of technology are becoming most locationally concentrated, and most dependent upon local linkages with the indigenous science base in the sites in question; and in which other areas cross-border flows of knowledge, personnel and devices allow innovation to be coordinated more easily across geographically dispersed locations. Second, we investigate the role of ICT in the recent increase in technological interrelatedness and with it corporate technological diversification (Granstrand, Patel and Pavitt, 1997; Cantwell and Piscitello, 1997; Cantwell and Fai, 1999). ICT can be viewed as a 'carrier branch' of the current paradigm (Freeman and Perez, 1988), or as a facilitator of new combinations or a fusion (Kodama, 1992) between formerly separate economic activities within or between firms, in the way in which the capital goods sector provided a linkage between innovation in different industries in the mechanization paradigm of the past (Rosenberg, 1976). We examine how corporate technological diversification has been adapted across firms in recent years in response to the opportunities opened up for innovation by rising technological interrelatedness.

In Section 2 we elaborate further on the distinctiveness of innovative profits, and in Section 3 we relate this notion to changes in the characteristics of technological change in the current paradigm, and some implications for corporate governance and national policies. The data used are described briefly in Section 4. The empirical evidence on the degree of international dispersion of different kinds of technology is discussed in Section 5, while in Section 6 we examine changes over time in the cross-company pattern of corporate technological diversification in selected industries, controlling for variations in such diversification which are attributable to the size of firms. Finally, in Section 7 we draw a few brief conclusions.

2 Alternative views on the origins of profits

Two schools of economic thought can each be grouped together with respect to alternative views on the origins of profits in a capitalist economy. According to the first, profits derive from a search for lower wage costs (either through lower wage rates, or by increasing the intensity of work), and from positions of market power (facilitating higher prices in final product markets, and lower prices in markets for the intermediate products used as inputs). The two are often linked, where for example work is 'put out' to a contractor who is obliged to sell at low prices, and manages to do so by setting low wages and poor working conditions. This perspective on profits dominates much of the economics literature – it is common to most mainstream macroeconomists and industrial economists, to neo-Ricardians, and to most twentieth century Marxist economists.

In this perspective, multinational corporations (MNCs) as well as states lose from global competition. Their protected markets are eroded by international competition, and so profits are everywhere squeezed. The obvious reaction is to pass the squeeze on to others – to workers and contractors, whose security of contract is weakened. This is the perspective as well of the financial markets – to 'make the assets sweat' and to maximize their current value. Overall, this is a zero sum game,[1] in which the gains are limited and of a one-off kind, like in a national context the revenues from privatisation. In classical terms, profits are generated primarily in the realms of exchange and distribution, although there are then consequences for the way in which production is organized.

In the second view profits derive instead from innovation. This is the perspective of Schumpeter and of modern evolutionary economists, but it has strong classical antecedents, especially in the work of Smith and Marx. In this case innovative MNCs and states in the most dynamic centers gain, and not necessarily at the expense of others. Innovation is a positive sum game,[2] in which the gains need not be limited or of a one-off kind. In classical terms, profits are created in production and through continual advances in production, not in the spheres of exchange or distribution – although here, going the other way around, innovation has consequences for the way in which markets are organized.

By and large, the Schumpeterian perspective on the creation of profits is shared by innovative companies based in the most dynamic centers, and by the more internationally integrated MNCs, particularly in sectors at the leading edge of innovation. Note also that the scope for dynamism is not a function of the existing level of productivity or technological capability, although it may be a positive function of the degree of openness of an economy (since the greater incentive to export and compete in world markets increases companies' dynamism). For these purposes innovation is defined as the creation of new products and processes, even where these are not at some notional 'technology frontier'. Innovation consists primarily of the accumulation of tacit capability (a process sometimes termed technological accumulation), which capability is embodied in social organization (mainly in firms), and which is to this extent tied to production in a particular location by a specific set of firms.

---

[1] Strictly speaking, it is zero sum game only with respect to the aggregate income earned from production. There is a social benefit from price competition in the form of higher consumers' surplus. The distribution of income will also be affected by the fall in prices (in favour of those that consume or make further purchases from a higher proportion of their income), and not only by changes in the relative values of wages and profits. We are grateful to Denis Mueller for this qualification.

[2] The qualification here is that technological competition may involve wasteful duplication and hence a net resource cost, as in the patent race analogy. However, even in the pharmaceutical industry in which it might be thought to be most applicable, the patent race analogy has its limitations (Cockburn and Henderson, 1995). As explained further below, in the evolutionary view technological change is localised and differentiated (Nelson and Winter, 1982) and thus, in general, technological competition engenders healthy variety rather than wasteful duplication (Saviotti, 1996; Metcalfe, 1998).

So, in this second view of the origin of profits, what is the mechanism by which innovation leads to a higher share of profits, and hence to greater competitiveness and economic growth? One of us has modeled this mechanism as a process by which wage increases tend to follow productivity increases (including product as well as process improvements that raise the value of products per worker), but with a lag (Cantwell, 1989, 1992a). Owing to this lag, the faster is the rate of innovation or productivity growth, the higher is the share of profits in income. However, if wages do track productivity they will still increase faster with innovation. As in the classical tradition of Smith and Ricardo, a faster rate of economic growth pulls up wages. With innovation, living standards rise despite the low share of wages in income – as remarked earlier, creating profits through innovation is a positive sum game.

However, one response to the erosion of profits of the first kind has been an ever more desparate search for new profits of this kind, through various means of financial restructuring, sub-contracting agreements and the re-negotiation of contracts. Likewise, the current fashion for 'labor market flexibility', if by this is meant the use of contractual flexibility as a means of lowering wages relative to the hours and the intensity of work, as opposed to the creation of greater functional flexibility through the development of facilities for re-training workers for new tasks. Yet ultimately these one-off gains offer little way out. The longer term response must surely be directed principally towards increased efforts for innovation. In this respect internationalization tends to have an extremely beneficial longer term impact on development, by shifting the focus from the first kind to the second kind of profits, whatever the deficiencies might be of the sometimes more immediate impact of the greater intensity of re-contracting in a less regulated environment.

Thus, for example, the new wave of strategic alliances between MNCs has been far more oriented towards joint technological development and inter-firm cooperation in learning, and has been relatively less motivated by the joint exercise of market power, by comparison with the international cartels of the interwar years (Hagedoorn and Schakenraad, 1990; Cantwell and Barrera, 1998). The growing pressures of international competition imply that in a dynamic (as opposed to a static) setting, surviving firms must be increasingly committed to the continuous upgrading of their own capability base, and hence to technological improvement. The distinction between the orthodox kind of profits and the Schumpeterian innovative kind is also analogous to the distinction between static profit maximization (organizing transactions so as to increase current efficiency and market power), and the evolutionary search for higher profits, a somewhat unpredictable search that leads to some mistakes and blind alleys and hence some failures even among 'rational' agents (Nelson and Winter, 1982). The immediate static impact of greater competition is the re-organization of contracts and the re-distribution of income, which might be explained along the lines of the economists' standard conception of profit maximization, while the dynamic impact is that firms must search for higher profits over time through innovation, a search that takes place around an inter-firm variety of viable alternative paths.

Of course, in principle innovation itself might be analyzed in the framework of static profit maximization and market power, and this is what has been done in most standard treatments. Technology is conceptualized as a form of temporary monopolistic advantage, which confers power in an established market and hence profits. Viewed from this standpoint, there is an overriding concern over potential problems of appropriability. If technology leaks freely and can only itself be partially traded, then the regulation of technology through the market fails, reducing the private incentive to invest in new technology. In the alternative Schumpeterian perspective, in which the continual search for high profits and the disruption of established markets necessarily relies upon innovation, the inter-company knowledge flows that accompany creative variety between corporate technological trajectories are more likely to act as a spur to further innovation rather than as a disincentive.

3 Long term development and forms of governance

The relative importance of Schumpeterian profits has increased not just because greater international competition has reduced the scope for the exercise of market power, but also because of changes in the character of technological change. The increased scope for new technological combinations and the international exchanges of knowledge has meant instead that internationalization has created new opportunities for generating innovative profits through a more intensive cross-border interaction in corporate learning processes, and in the establishment of international corporate networks. In addition, the closer connections between science and technology entailed in part by the rising number of applications of newer science-based technologies (ICT, new materials and biotechnology) in most industries, and their greater integration with more traditional technologies, has meant that a higher return can now be earned through skillful learning in the firm, an educated and adaptive work force, and an ability to comprehend and relate to a wider range of potential knowledge inputs.

The role of national governments has begun to change in this view. By supporting education and training systems, governments help to lower the costs and facilitate the creation of tacit capability in firms, which lies at the root of the generation of technological improvements and hence innovative profits and long term growth. That is, governments can help to address the problem of the development of more sophisticated systems of production, which at root is a problem of institutions (or, if you wish, of institutional failure), and not essentially a problem of the malfunctioning of markets. Likewise, by supporting public research, the universities and the science base, governments indirectly encourage firms to invest in their own R&D to be able to tap into a more extensive external network of research, and thereby to increase the returns on their own R&D through suitably adapting their underlying tacit capability. In this event public research is not replacing some 'missing' private research, but instead public research acts as a catalyst for the widening of private research, which in turn supports the preservation of a more sophisticated tacit capability in production. Thus, what innovative companies expect most from local universities is not research with immediate commercial applications in their own sector (which they would normally prefer to conduct in-house), but rather a wider base of knowledge creation and skills with which their own facilities can interact (Pavitt, 1994).

There are two implications of the argument that technology policy should be directed mainly to fostering the formation of tacit capabilities in firms, rather than trying to correct for deficiencies in the market for knowledge. First, firms rather than governments will tend to lead the process of innovation and capability formation, and firms should not be seen as passive actors responding to the external provision of knowledge and skills. However, of course, governments do help to put into place a set of complementary institutions which encourage innovation and knowledge diffusion, especially through their support of education, training and the science and research infrastructure.[3] Second, it is still worth governments backing the local establishment of basic research facilities, even if some of the knowledge generated has spillover benefits abroad, since the greatest and most immediate impact will be concentrated locally, owing to the tendency for the linkages between science and technology to be geographically localized, as has been shown in the literature using patent citations (such as Jaffe, Trajtenberg and Henderson, 1993; Audretsch and Feldman, 1994; Frost, 1996; Almeida and Kogut, 1997).

The problem of building institutions more geared to creating innovative profits tends to be better addressed in national systems of innovation in which governments support science and technology (with the vocal backing of innovative local companies!), as opposed to purely market-based systems. This is especially true in the modern technological paradigm grounded in information and communication technology, computerization, and flexible (more complex) production systems, in which the local linkages between science and technology have become more intensive than they were in the past, and increasingly run across a wide range of formerly separate disciplines. While there need not be 'market failure' in the usual sense, it is inappropriate to follow a laissez-faire ideology in which the public support of research is focused upon the areas of the most direct market potential for local companies. To illustrate the point, a mainstream chemical company increasingly needs to draw on knowledge and skills in many diverse areas, such as electronics and biotechnology, to further develop its own production systems, even if it has no intention of entering markets that are most directly connected with the principal products of these fields.

The national system of innovation is the network of institutions in the public and private sectors of each country that support the initiation, modification and diffusion of new technologies (Freeman, 1987, 1995). The

---

[3] For a detailed discussion of how governments might help to assist institutions in confronting the difficulties of technological learning (as opposed to improving the workings of markets for knowledge) in a developing country context, see Lall (1997).

nationally distinctive features of the system is represented in the particular sectoral patterns of strength or tacit capability that has been developed in private firms in each country (Nelson, 1993; Patel and Pavitt, 1994). The globalization of technological innovation in MNCs, in the sense of an international integration of geographically dispersed and locally specialized activities, tends to reinforce and not to dismantle nationally distinctive patterns of development or national systems of innovation (Cantwell, 1995). Contrary to what is sometimes alleged, globalization and national specialization are complementary parts of a common process, and not conflicting trends [as argued as well by Archibugi and Pianta (1992) and Archibugi and Michie (1997)]. The incentive to organize affiliate specialization is the desire to tap into the locally specific and differentiated stream of innovation in each center, but by specializing in accordance with these local strengths the latter are reinforced. As remarked already, the creation of tacit capability is localized and embedded in social organizations (Nelson and Winter, 1982), and this organizational distinctiveness has a location-specific as well as a firm-specific dimension. The particular path of innovation followed in each country or region has historical origins (Rosenberg, 1976, 1982). In the period of globalization since the late 1960s the general tendency has been for MNCs to become more technologically diversified as they establish newly integrated technological systems, while countries or locations have become more specialized in their technological activity (Cantwell, 1992b).

In what remains we examine evidence on the shape of the internationalization and diversification of corporate technology of the world's largest firms (mainly MNCs). The establishment of international corporate networks for technological development (Cantwell, 1995; Cantwell and Piscitello, 1999) has meant that the creation of some kinds of technology can now be locationally dispersed and coordinated over greater geographical distances, connected by flows of knowledge and personnel. One of us has demonstrated that the growing geographical dispersion of intra-firm networks is linked to an increase in corporate ICT specialization (Santangelo, 1998). Yet there may still be other more complex kinds of technological innovation which remain largely concentrated in a few centers of excellence, and more highly dependent upon the localized contexts provided by these centers. Meanwhile, given the fresh opportunities for new technological combinations due to increased technological interrelatedness and areas of potential fusion often made feasible by ICT, the major companies must adapt their profiles of internal technological diversification accordingly. In some cases this may mean simply broadening their diversification into new (as yet unexplored or little explored) fields; while in other cases it may mean a more intensive effort in certain newly interconnected branches of technology in which the firm has already been engaged. Such areas of research may well have been kept largely separate previously (perhaps being the responsibility of different divisions in the M-form firm), yet can now be beneficially brought together to exploit new economies of scope.

4 The data

The econometric analysis is based upon patents granted to the world's largest industrial firms in the US between 1969 and 1995.[4] Each patent is classified by the year in which it was granted and by the type of technological activity with which is primarily associated, using a classification scheme derived from an arrangement of the classes recorded by the US Patent and Trademark Office (USPTO). Thus, patents from each USPTO class or subclass have been allocated to one of the 56 technological sectors. Patents have been consolidated into corporate groups, initially on the basis of the structure of ownership of groups in 1982. Most of the effects of subsequent merger and acquisition activity (after 1982) are built into the data through the practice of centralizing the patent application procedure in the parent company. However, for some mergers and acquisitions associated with over 100 patents, where patents are not re-directed to an established parent company in this way, the change in ownership structure is incorporated into the data. Sometimes this involves creating a new corporate group (such as Unisys or ABB), and sometimes an expanded consolidation of groups with newly acquired affiliates, in which the affiliates continue with substantial patenting under their own names.

Two sub-datasets were constructed to analyze first the degree of international dispersion of different kinds of technology, and second the changes over time in the cross-company pattern of corporate technological diversification. In the first case, patents assigned between 1969–95 to one of the 10 largest national groups of firms (by nationality of ownership) were grouped by the home country of the parent company, and placed in one of 14 broadly defined industries (as listed in Table 2) on the basis of the primary field of production of the corporate group in question. For all these patents we further distinguish whether the research facilities responsible for the relevant inventions were located in the parent's home country or abroad, to evaluate the extent of the geographical dispersion of technology creation, controlling for differences in the degree of internationalization which are attributable to the country of ownership or the industry of the firm. In the second case, the period 1969–95 was divided into the three sub-periods 1969–77, 1978–86 and 1987–95. A minimum firm size for inclusion was also imposed to ensure meaningful indicators of corporate technological diversification across fields of activity. The threshold chosen was that firms had to have at least 60 patents in each of the three sub-periods. However, only the first and third sub-periods were used in the econometric analysis to allow for adequate time to observe changes in the pattern of technological diversification at the level of individual firms.

---

[4] These data are drawn from the University of Reading database. The use of US patents as a reliable measure of the geographical and sectoral dispersion of innovation in international companies is widely acknowledged in the literature (see Patel and Pavitt, 1991, for brief discussion).

Table 1. Share of US patents of the world's largest firms attributable to research in foreign locations (outside the home country of the parent company), organized by the nationality of parent firm, 1969–1995 (%)

Nationality of the parent company	1969–72	1973–77	1978–82	1983–86	1987–90	1991–95
USA	4.96	5.89	6.40	7.53	7.91	8.62
Germany	12.77	11.05	12.07	14.47	17.05	20.72
UK	43.08	41.24	40.47	47.09	50.42	55.79
Italy	13.39	16.03	13.85	12.59	11.14	16.47
France	8.16	7.74	7.17	9.19	18.17	33.17
Japan	2.63	1.88	1.22	1.26	0.92	1.08
Netherlands	50.40	47.37	47.65	53.99	53.96	55.69
Belgium and Luxembourg	50.36	51.11	49.28	58.15	47.53	53.25
Switzerland	44.36	43.63	43.78	41.59	42.99	52.47
Sweden	17.82	19.90	26.20	28.94	30.60	42.42
Canada	41.19	39.30	39.49	35.82	40.12	43.96
Others	28.21	22.22	26.37	30.34	7.54	3.94
Total (including Japan)	10.04	10.53	10.50	10.95	11.28	11.27
Total (excluding Japan)	10.52	11.59	12.25	13.87	15.76	16.53

5 The international geography of innovation in the ICT paradigm

Before investigating the geographical implications of the closer linkages between science and technology in the new ICT-based paradigm, we briefly describe the trends, as shown in Tables 1 and 2, in the internationalization of corporate technology creation by national and industrial groupings respectively. It is worth investigating in which cases knowledge creation is likeliest to be a locationally dispersed process which crosses national boundaries, and in which cases instead activities are most likely to agglomerate in centers of excellence.

For each national group of the world's largest firms, Table 1 records the share of US patents attributable to research conducted outside the home country of the parent company. These figures show a slight increase in the total average of the share of overseas research activity from 10.04% to 11.27% between the late 1960s and the early 1990s. However, in assessing the pattern of total corporate patenting activity attributable to foreign research, it is worth mentioning the compositional shift in the make-up of total patenting across firms, involving an increase in the share of patenting accounted for by Japanese and Korean firms. As these firms are on average little internationalized in their technological development, this leads, in turn, to a downward pull on the global average foreign share. This argument is illustrated by the figures reported for Japanese firms as well as companies in the category labeled as "others", in which the share of Korean corporate patenting has risen over time. Japan and others are, indeed, the only national groups of firms showing an overall decline in foreign share

Table 2. The share of US patents of the world's largest firms attributable to research in foreign locations (outside the home country of the parent company), organized by the industrial group of the parent firm, 1969–95 (%)

Industrial group of the parent company	1969–72	1973–77	1978–82	1983–86	1987–1990	1991–1995
Food products	16.85	20.72	23.43	24.73	23.70	25.40
Chemicals n.e.s. and pharmaceuticals	12.07	13.72	13.60	13.34	14.49	16.22
Metals and mechanical engineering	11.14	9.93	11.81	12.61	13.49	11.70
Electrical equipment n.e.s. and office equipment	9.15	9.61	9.07	10.21	10.38	10.23
Motor vehicles	4.56	5.11	5.25	6.95	7.13	4.75
Aircraft	1.93	2.01	2.28	2.93	2.47	2.69
Other transport equipment	9.66	3.52	8.23	5.24	6.54	3.09
Textiles and clothing	6.45	8.49	7.10	4.31	3.10	2.40
Paper products n.e.s. and printing and publishing	6.66	9.05	8.03	13.26	16.08	16.06
Rubber and plastic products	7.04	7.46	6.73	6.20	9.12	10.49
Non-metallic mineral products	7.68	8.75	10.73	13.12	14.94	18.38
Coal and petroleum products	18.02	15.21	15.04	16.08	20.32	20.36
Professional and scientific instruments	6.28	4.07	2.97	2.72	1.99	3.61
Other manufacturing	6.86	10.75	13.06	14.14	15.42	20.34
Total	10.04	10.53	10.50	10.95	11.28	11.27

n.e.s. = not elsewhere specified
Sources: US patent database developed by John Cantwell at the University of Reading, with the assistance of the US Patent and Trademark Office

since the late 1960s. Over the whole period 1969–95 the internationalization of research activity grew from 10.52% to 16.53% when excluding Japanese companies. Moreover, the internationalization of the US firms is understated by this measure because of their higher propensity to patent in their own home market from domestically located research. The increase in the internationalization of corporate technological activity occurred mainly in the mid- and late-1980s as a result of a growth in the overseas R&D of German, British, French, Swedish and Canadian firms. This internationalization was achieved in large part through foreign mergers.

In Table 2, the pattern of the internationalization of corporate R&D is, instead, analyzed in terms of the industrial group of the parent company. The overall increase in the internationalization of technological activity was greatest in food products, paper products, non-metallic mineral products and other manufacturing, whilst in science-based industrial sectors the increase in the geographical dispersion of R&D was more contained, although it remained at a level well above average in chemicals and pharmaceuticals, and in petrochemicals (coal and petroleum products). Instead, in the electrical and office equipment industrial sector foreign research was slightly below average, and only marginally more geographically dispersed over the period as a whole (from 9.15% to 10.23%). As will be further argued below, this pattern might be explained by the fact that much science-based technology embodies a greater degree of tacit competencies, which are more difficult to transmit or utilize over longer geographical distances.

To analyze which types of technology continue to remain most locationally concentrated, and most dependent upon local linkages with an indigenous science base, we investigated variations in the extent of world-wide location/dispersion of different types of technology, controlling for country- and industry-specific locational factors in the period 1969–95.

The foreign share (FS) calculated across the 56 technological sectors was used as a proxy for the degree of geographical agglomeration/dispersion. The foreign share is given by the share of US patents of the world's largest firms which are attributable to research in foreign locations. FS is then defined as

$$FS_{ijk} = (FP_{ijk}/P_{ijk}) \tag{1}$$

where P_{ijk} denotes the number of US patents granted in a sectoral activity (j) to a national group of firms (i) in a particular industry (k), whilst FP_{ijk} indicates only the number of US patents granted for research conducted outside the home country of the parent firm to the same national group (i) in the same sectoral activity (j) in the industry in question (k). Country-specific locational factors were taken into account through the use of the foreign share calculated across the 10 principal home countries considered (FSH). Thus, FSH can be written as

$$FSH_i = \Sigma_{jk} FP_{ijk}/\Sigma_{jk} P_{ijk} \tag{2}$$

The foreign patent share calculated across 14 industries (FSI) was, instead, employed to control for industry-specific location factors.

$$FSI_k = \Sigma_{ij} FP_{ijk}/\Sigma_{ij} P_{ijk} \tag{3}$$

In both equations (2) and (3), the subscripts (i), (j) and (k) have the same meaning as in Eq. (1).

In addition, the specialization patterns of national groups of firms across industries were considered through the use of the Revealed Technological Advantage (RTA) index. For each national group of parent companies the RTA was calculated across the 14 industries. Thus,

$$RTA_{ik} = (P_{ik}/\Sigma_i P_{ik})/(\Sigma_k P_{ik}/\Sigma_{ik} P_{ik}) \tag{4}$$

where P_{ik} denotes the number of US patents granted in industry (k) to a national group of firms (i) in the industry in question. By relating the technological advantage in a particular spectrum of activity of each national group of firms to that of other national groups in the same industry, the RTA index varies around unity. Therefore, values greater than one indicate that a group is comparatively advantaged in that industry in

Table 3. Results of the regression in equation (5)

	Coefficient	Standard error	t-ratio
Intercept	−9.590	1.161	−8.259*
FSH_i	0.893	0.024	36.906*
FSI_k	0.752	0.088	8.547*
RTA_{ik}	2.014	0.310	6.494*
Organic chemicals dummy (D_j for j = oc)	−6.816	3.082	−2.212**
Other organic compounds dummy (D_j for j = ooc)	−6.698	3.231	−2.073**
Textiles, clothing and leather dummy (D_j for j = tcl)	12.549	3.642	3.445*
Wood products dummy (D_j for j = wp)	8.379	3.464	2.419**
Building material processing equipment dummy (D_j for j = bmpe)	7.001	3.370	2.077**
R^2	0.341		
Adjusted R^2	0.339		
No of observations	3353		

* Significant at 1% level
** Significant at 2% level

relation to other national groups, whilst values less than one are interpreted as implying a comparative disadvantage.

The extent of the corporate geographical dispersion of technological activity was, then, analyzed with a linear regression model of the following form:

$$FS_{ijk} = \alpha + \beta_1 FSH_i + \beta_2 FSI_k + \beta_3 RTA_{ik} + \beta_4 D_{oc} + \beta_5 D_{ooc} + \beta_6 D_{tcl} + \beta_7 D_{wp} + \beta_8 D_{bmpe} + \varepsilon_i \quad (5)$$

where D_{oc}, D_{ooc}, D_{tcl}, D_{wp}, D_{bmpe} are four sectoral dummy variables ("sector" *j* here being used to mean types of technological activity as defined by the US patent class system, and not the industries of corporate groups *k*), which refer to "organic chemicals", "other organic compounds", "textiles, clothing and leather", "wood products" and "building material processing equipment" respectively. Sectoral dispersion patterns were considered by introducing these dummy variables according to the statistical significance of the relevant sets of residuals of the model (when run initially without any such dummy variables).

As shown in Table 3, this exercise allowed us to indicate technological fields in which the geographical location of activity is the most concentrated or dispersed, having controlled for established firm-level variation in internationalization across countries and industries. Table 3 suggests that the "organic chemicals" and "other organic compounds" sectors are the most geographically concentrated, whilst "textiles, clothing and leather", "wood products" and "building material processing equipment" are the most internationalized, having allowed for the fact that e.g. chemical firms have a relatively high degree of internationalization of technological development,

Table 4. A selection of geographically more concentrated technological sectors, by average residuals, 1969–1995

Technological sectors	Average residuals
Internal combustion engines	−5.76
Power plants	−4.73
Disinfecting and preserving	−4.05
Office equipment and data processing systems	−3.36
Cleaning agents and other compositions	−3.06
Chemical processes	−2.76
Bleaching and dyeing	−2.50
Other electrical communications systems	−2.24
Distillation process	−2.14
Coal and petroleum products	−1.45
Semiconductors	−1.15
Total average	−3.02

Table 5. A selection of geographically more dispersed technological sectors, by average residuals, 1969–1995

Technological sectors	Average residuals
Agricultural equipment	7.86
Woodworking tools and machinery	7.83
Food and tobacco products	5.26
Paper making apparatus	3.88
Mining equipment	3.49
Non-metallic mineral products	2.82
Printing and publishing	2.65
Other specialized machinery	2.37
Textile and clothing machinery	2.22
Total average	4.26

while textile companies are relatively little internationalized. Whilst the regression model selects the strongest cases of either geographically concentrated or dispersed technological fields, somewhat weaker (but still relevant) cases are taken into account in Tables 4 and 5 ranked by the average residual of each sector.

Table 4 lists a selection of geographically more concentrated technological sectors. For these technologies (selected values of j), FS_{ijk} was on average 3% lower than expected from the model, thus implying a relatively low degree of internationalization. In contrast, Table 5 lists a selection of geographically more dispersed technological sectors j, which show a FS_{ijk} on average 4.3% higher than expected from the model. The composition of sectors appears to suggest that at least some core science-based and research-grounded technologies (such as chemicals and computing) are among the geographically most concentrated, whilst those shown in Table 5 suggest that mature technologies are to a greater extent geographically more dispersed. This finding might be explained by the fact that the spatial pattern followed by science-based technologies is highly influenced by the more pronounced tacit character of knowledge in these fields. The more tacit knowledge is, the more spatially concentrated we expect it to be. Since tacitness implies localization of development and greater context-specificity, and requires greater intensity of face to face interaction, knowledge transmission becomes more complex both within and across different organizations (Winter, 1987). The transmission and absorption of knowledge takes on an informal and experimental character, thus requiring higher and more closely complementary technological competencies on the part of co-operating teams. This is the case, for instance, for many computer-based technologies. As argued by Cantwell and Harding (1998), the research strategies of computing multinationals are fairly internationalized, and hence computer technology tends to be so too, since much of it is developed within these specialist companies. In the exercise carried out in this paper, having taken into account the overall internationalization of computer and electrical equipment firms at the industry (i.e. FSI_k) level, computer technology tends to be locationally concentrated at home across the firms of various industries that are involved in its development. Conversely, the transmission of some mature technologies (such as food and tobacco products and textile and clothing machinery) is based on more regularly codified knowledge. This allows for simpler and less context-dependent channels of transmission, thus allowing for the co-ordination of creative efforts over greater geographical distances and, therefore, the spatial dispersion of innovation.

Following Breschi (1997), we can distinguish between two groups of technological sectors, according to the different structure and organization of innovative activity. A first group is represented by traditional and engineering-based sectors, in which innovative activity is geographically more dispersed and is widely developed across the firms of most industries. A second group includes, instead, science-based sectors (e.g. office equipment and data processing systems, semiconductors, chemical process, coal and petroleum products, and other electrical communications systems). These are characterized by geographically more concentrated innovative activity and are developed to a much greater extent by a narrower group of firms primarily in the associated science-based industries.

Of course, beyond the average tendencies revealed by the econometric results, it might still be argued that in some instances even science-based technologies are developed over greater geographical distances, despite their higher tacitness. For this reason in Table 6, we analyze the principal outlying combinations of home country and industry within the spatially more concentrated technological sectors identified in Table 4. For each sector, we considered the most extreme cases of either positive or negative residuals. This allows us to distinguish between the groups which are most representative of a high degree of spatial concentration of these activities, and other less representative groups which have managed to develop a high degree of internationalization of even these kinds of mainly tacit branches of technological development.

The figures clearly reveal that British multinationals prefer to retain their R&D activity at home in the science-based industries. Both UK

Table 6. The largest individual residuals from the geographically more concentrated technological sectors, by nationality of the parent company and industry, 1969–1995

Geographically more concentrated			Geographically more dispersed		
Internal combustion engines					
UK	Food products	−57.54	UK	Textiles	61.69
Netherlands	Chemicals and pharmaceuticals	−48.33	Netherlands	Metals and mechanical engineering	54.00
UK	Chemicals and pharmaceuticals	−43.74	Netherlands	Electrical equipment and computing	42.67
UK	Non-metallic mineral products	−41.99	US	Non-metallic mineral products	41.86
Switzerland	Metals and mechanical engineering	−38.28	UK	Metals and mechanical engineering	30.74
Power plants					
UK	Food products	−57.54	German	Textiles	91.99
UK	Rubber and plastic products	−39.57	Sweden	Chemicals and pharmaceuticals	73.53
Switzerland	Chemicals and pharmaceuticals	−37.22	Sweden	Electrical equipment and computing	46.34
UK	Electrical equipment and computing	−34.54	Belgium and Luxembourg	Chemicals and pharmaceuticals	35.36
UK	Aircraft	−30.58	US	Scientific and professional instruments	32.67
Disinfecting and preserving					
Belgium and Luxembourg	Chemicals and pharmaceuticals	−64.64	Switzerland	Chemicals and pharmaceuticals	49.19
Sweden	Paper products and publishing	−38.62	UK	Food products	42.46
Sweden	Metals and mechanical engineering	−33.55	UK	Oil	32.13
Sweden	Electrical equipment and computing	−23.87	Switzerland	Food products	30.61
France	Oil	−21.73	US	Non-metallic mineral products	16.86
Office equipment and data processing systems					
Netherlands	Metals and mechanical engineering	−46.00	France	Chemicals and pharmaceuticals	55.78
UK	Other manufacturing	−42.01	Switzerland	Food products	50.61
UK	Paper products and publishing	−41.55	UK	Textiles	49.19
UK	Food products	−40.87	Belgium and Luxembourg	Metals and mechanical engineering	36.67
UK	Scientific and professional instruments	−33.84	France	Non-metallic mineral products	35.66

Cleaning agents and other compositions					
Switzerland	Other manufacturing	−44.67	France	Textiles	90.98
UK	Other manufacturing	−42.01	Italy	Metals and mechanical engineering	87.95
UK	Rubber and plastic products	−39.57	Sweden	Rubber and plastic products	78.26
UK	Motor vehicles	−38.05	Switzerland	Non-metallic mineral products	60.68
Belgium and Luxembourg	Oil	−31.71	UK	Paper products and publishing	33.45
Chemical processes					
Netherlands	Food products	−53.70	Germany	Textiles	75.33
Belgium and Luxembourg	Metals and mechanical engineering	−52.22	France	Food products	61.68
UK	Other manufacturing	−42.01	France	Textiles	40.98
UK	Other transport equipment	−36.98	UK	Oil	32.57
UK	Aircraft	−34.75	Italy	Electrical equipment and computing	22.11
Bleaching and dyeing processes					
UK	Non-metallic mineral products	−41.99	UK	Paper products and publishing	58.45
UK	Electrical equipment and computing	−39.54	Italy	Oil	46.33
UK	Chemicals and pharmaceuticals	−38.62	Netherlands	Electrical equipment and computing	44.53
Sweden	Paper products and publishing	−38.62	UK	Oil	39.71
Sweden	Metals and mechanical engineering	−33.55	Belgium and Luxembourg	Chemicals and pharmaceuticals	35.36
Other electrical communications systems					
Netherlands	Metals and mechanical engineering	−46.00	Italy	Oil	79.66
UK	Other manufacturing	−42.01	UK	Textiles	61.69
UK	Paper products and publishing	−41.55	Sweden	Paper products and publishing	44.72
UK	Rubber and plastic products	−39.57	Belgium and Luxembourg	Metals and mechanical engineering	36.67
UK	Other transport equipment	−36.98	UK	Oil	33.01

Table 6 (continued)

Geographically more concentrated			Geographically more dispersed		
Distillation processes					
Switzerland	Chemicals and pharmaceuticals	−46.65	Sweden	Scientific and professional instruments	81.15
Netherlands	Metals and mechanical engineering	−46.00	Sweden	Electrical equipment and computing	76.13
UK	Other manufacturing	−42.01	Sweden	Metals and mechanical engineering	66.45
UK	Chemicals and pharmaceuticals	−34.22	Netherlands	Electrical equipment and computing	50.78
Belgium and Luxembourg	Chemicals and pharmaceuticals	−31.31	UK	Metals and mechanical engineering	32.66
Coal and petroleum products					
UK	Other manufacturing	−42.01	France	Non-Metallic mineral products	80.11
UK	Electrical equipment and computing	−39.54	Sweden	Paper products and publishing	61.38
UK	Chemicals and pharmaceuticals	−28.70	US	Non-metallic mineral products	41.86
UK	Food products	−24.21	Belgium and Luxembourg	Metals and mechanical engineering	36.67
Sweden	Metals and mechanical engineering	−22.44	UK	Metals and mechanical engineering	32.66
Semiconductors					
Switzerland	Other manufacturing	−44.67	Germany	Other manufacturing	85.71
UK	Motor vehicles	−38.05	Switzerland	Chemicals and pharmaceuticals	53.35
UK	Aircraft	−34.75	Germany	Chemicals and pharmaceuticals	52.78
Sweden	Metals and mechanical engineering	−33.55	Sweden	Electrical equipment and computing	35.39
UK	Metals and mechanical engineering	−29.01	UK	Oil	33.80

chemicals and electronics companies show an above-average degree of geographical concentration, having controlled for either industry- and country-specific factors (including the 'British'-specific and the 'chemicals'- or 'electronics'-specific). Conversely, controlling for the same factors, Dutch electronics corporations (i.e. Philips) seem to follow a different R&D locational strategy by dispersing their research activity abroad to an above-average extent, whilst the technological activity of the Dutch chemical industry appears to be spatially concentrated. Instead, the experience of the Swedish science-based industries is less clear-cut in the sense that the geographical dispersion/concentration of research activity varies across the selected fields of technological development.

Therefore, in certain cases the development of science-based technology is dispersed contrary to the trend towards greater concentration, even taking into account industry- and country-specific factors. However, in such cases MNCs seem to locate abroad the development of technology only outside the core of their main activity. To illustrate the point, in the electronics industry R&D is more likely to be dispersed in the chemical or mechanical fields, and not in the electrical equipment and computing technologies themselves. Thus, in this industry, Dutch firms have dispersed innovation in bleaching and dying processes, distillation processes, and engines, while Swedish firms have done likewise in distillation processes and power plants, and Italian firms in chemical processes. Conversely, in the chemicals industry when R&D is more dispersed it tends to occur outside the chemical technologies. This is the case for French chemical companies (e.g. Rhône Poulenc), which locate intensively abroad their research in office equipment and data processing systems, the high locational dispersal of innovation in semiconductors by German and Swiss chemical firms, and in power plants by Swedish and Belgian chemical companies.

Thus, the trend is that MNCs dispersed the development of some science-based technologies only when they lay outside the core of their technology base. However, there are exceptions even to this generalization. In Table 6, the three exceptions are the Swiss chemical industry, which locates heavily abroad innovation in the core technology of disinfecting and preserving, the Swedish electrical industry disperses strongly abroad R&D in semiconductors, and the high geographical dispersal of the development of bleaching and dyeing processes by Belgian chemical firms. These occasional exceptions to the rule deserve closer attention in future research.

6 Corporate technological diversification in the ICT paradigm

Having examined the geography of different fields of innovative activity, we turn now to the relationship between technological diversification and firm size in the light of the apparent rise in the degree of inter-relatedness between formerly distinct fields of technology in the microelectronic era. To do so, we assess the form and extent of the shift in the relationship between firm size and diversification in moving between two distinctive periods (i.e. 1969–77 and 1987–95).

The total accumulated patent stock of each firm (Patot) is used as a proxy for the company's technological size. Since it is well known that the size distribution of firms tends to be approximately lognormal, we use the natural logarithm of the patent stock. The firms' degree of diversification is, instead, estimated by the reciprocal of the coefficient of variation (CV) of the RTA distribution across all 56 technological sectors.

$$CV_{RTAf} = \sigma_{RTAf}/\mu_{RTAf} \tag{6}$$

$$\mu_{RTAf} = \Sigma_j RTA_{fj}/56 \tag{7}$$

$$\sigma_{RTAf} = \{(\Sigma_j(RTA_{fj} - \mu_{RTAf})^2/55\}^{1/2} \tag{8}$$

Where, for each firm (*f*), the RTA index is defined as the share of US patents assigned to it across technological sectors (*j*) relative to the overall share of all US patents assigned to firms in the industry in question. Thus,

$$RTA_{fj} = (P_{fj}/\Sigma_f P_{fj})/(\Sigma_j P_{fj}/\Sigma_{fj} P_{fj}) \tag{9}$$

where P_{fj} indicates the number of US patents granted in a particular sector (*j*) to firm (*f*) in the industry in question.

CV measures concentration of technological activity among sectors for a firm in any particular time period. As shown elsewhere (Cantwell and Fai, 1999), CV is a good measure of concentration for our purposes, and is well related to certain other standard concentration measures.[5] As CV_{RTA} is a positive measure of concentration and, therefore, an inverse measure of diversification, we use $1/CV_{RTAf}$ as our direct measure of diversification, for ease of exposition.

To assess the relationship between size and diversification, the following linear regression model is run:

$$1/CV_f = \alpha + \beta \ln Patot_f + \varepsilon_f \tag{10}$$

where $1/CV_f$ is the inverse of the CV defined in equation (7) for firm f, and $Patot_f$ is the total accumulated patent stock for a firm at the same point in time.

This regression was run for the two periods 1969–77 and 1987–95 for each of the 14 industrial groups of firms listed in Table 2. An adequate number of company observations ensured meaningful results in just five industrial groups (Chemicals and Pharmaceuticals, Electrical Equipment and Office Equipment, Motor Vehicles, Coal and Petroleum Products and Metal and Mechanical Engineering). The regression lines estimated are illustrated for each of the five industries separately in Figs. 1, 2, 3, 4 and 5.

The main point emerging from the Graphs is the apparent "convergence" in overall level of technological diversification across large firms. In the science-based industries (i.e. Chemicals and Pharmaceuticals, Electrical Equipment and Office Equipment, Coal and Petroleum Products) and in

---

[5] The CV is related to the Herfindahl Index (H), which has frequently been used as measure of concentration. $H = (CV^2 + 1)/n$, where n is the number of sectors in the distribution. Thus, here for a fixed n, the use of the CV is in practice equivalent to the Herfindahl Index (see Hart, 1971).

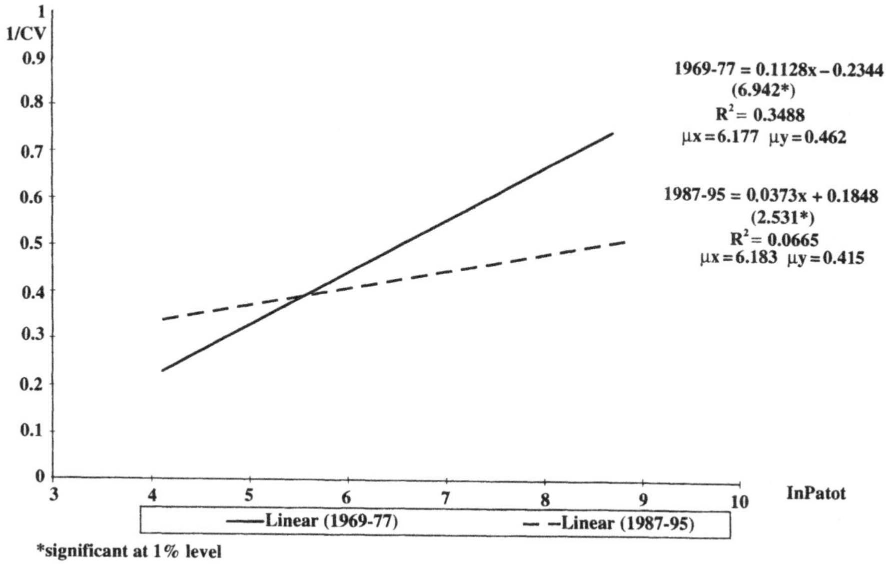

Fig. 1. Estimated regression lines for the chemicals and pharmaceuticals industry, 1969–77, 1987–95

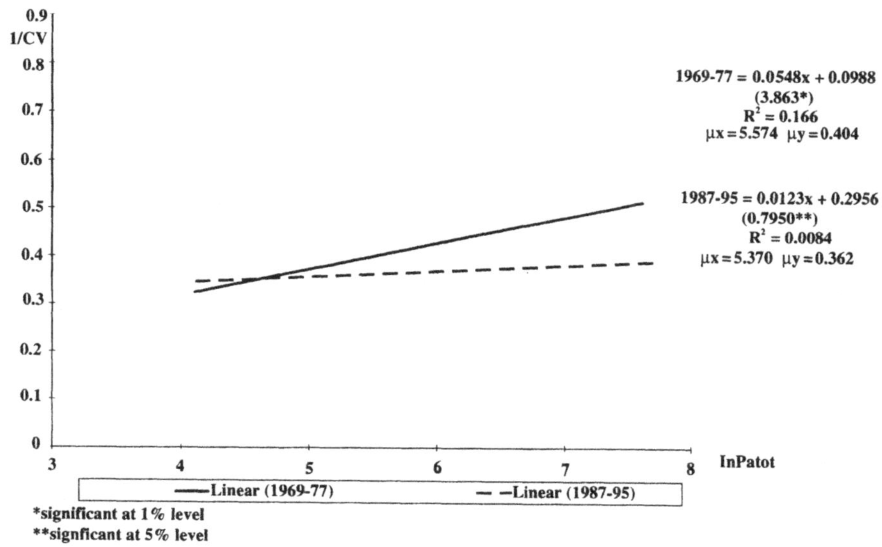

Fig. 2. Estimated regression lines for the metals and mechanical engineering industry, 1969–77, 1987–95

Motor Vehicles, it seems that, whilst many small firms have diversified, "giant" firms have on average rationalized the extent of their technological dispersion. As illustrated in Figs. 1, 3, 4 and 5, in all of these industries we

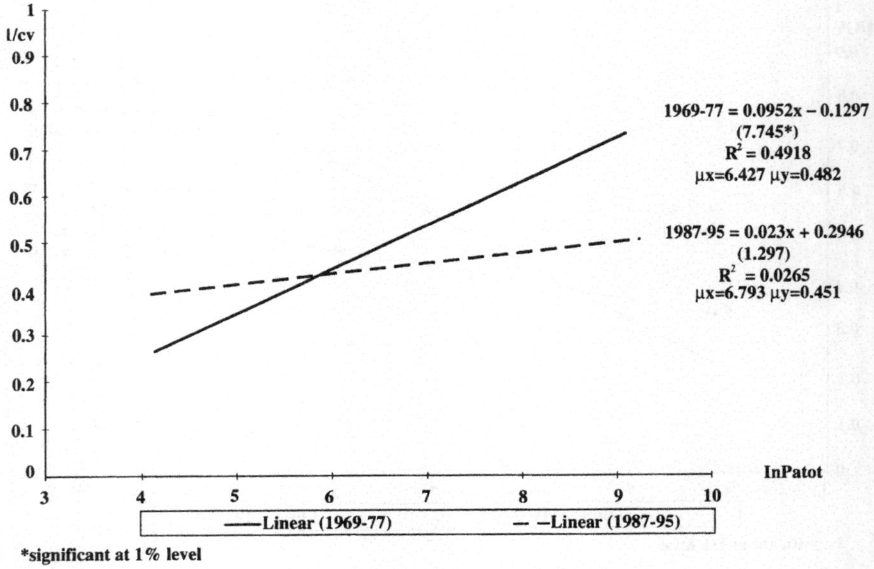

Fig. 3. Estimated regression lines for the electrical equipment and office equipment industry, 1969–77, 1987–95

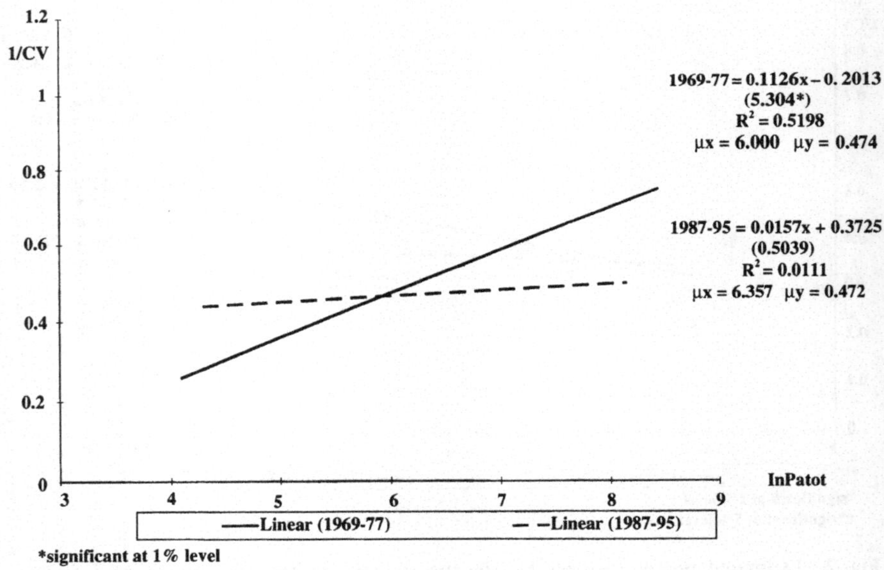

Fig. 4. Estimated regression lines for the motor vehicles industry, 1969–77, 1987–95

observe a rotational shift of the regression line from the first period to the second, thus confirming an average diversification of "smaller" firms but on average the rationalization of technological specialization by "giant"

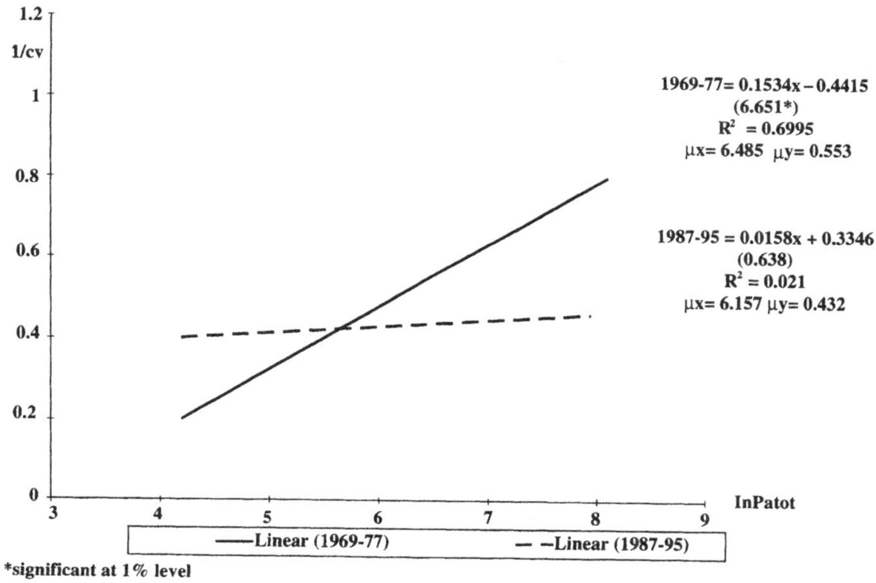

Fig. 5. Estimated regression lines for the coal and petroleum products industry, 1969–77, 1987–95

companies. The pattern is less clear in Fig. 2, in that although there is also a rotational shift in the Metals and Mechanical Engineering industrial group, a greater diversification occurred only at the very lower end of the size categories. Nonetheless, in all these industries there seems to be a clear "target" degree of technological diversification in the later period, to which most firms aspire and which can be identified as occurring at a value of around 0.42%. A similar cross-company convergence in the level of technological diversification has also been found recently by Piscitello (1998), and by Cantwell and Bachmann (1998) in the case of the pharmaceutical industry. Graphically, this argument can be illustrated by considering the intersection point between the two regression lines. Firms lying on the left of the intersection point have diversified, whilst companies lying to the right of this point show a more concentrated specialization pattern. As reported in Table 7, the mean values of the 1/CV and the log of technological size lie just to the right of the intersection point, thus supporting this interpretation of the co-existence of one group of firms with increasing diversification (below size), and another with a greater concentration of effort (above the mean size).

7 Conclusions

We have argued that the creation of innovative profits (as emphasized by Schumpeter) has become increasingly important in the latest technological paradigm, and that such profits are generated by MNCs partly through the

Table 7. The mean values of the regressand variables in the industries selected

Industry	Average 1/CV (1969–77)	Average 1/CV (1987–95)	Average lnPatot (1969–77)	Average lnPatot (1987–95)
Chemicals and pharmaceuticals	0.46	0.42	6.18	6.18
Metals and mechanical engineering	0.40	0.36	5.57	5.37
Electrical equipment and office equipment	0.48	0.45	6.43	6.79
Motor vehicles	0.47	0.47	6	6.36
Coal and petroleum products	0.55	0.43	6.49	6.16
Total average	0.48	0.43	6.13	6.17

establishment of international corporate networks for technological development. However, we have shown that the geographical dispersion of innovation tends to be achieved more readily in some fields than others; the creation of some technologies remains more highly concentrated in local centers of excellence. The technological fields that have continued to be relatively concentrated are those in which tacitness is greatest and linkages with a local science base (and the face to face interaction that this entails) are most significant. Part of the reason for this is that the science-based technologies are developed primarily by firms in the science-based industries (chemicals and electronics) and, although these firms have certainly internationalized their innovation activity, they have tended to retain the generation of their core technologies at home, while dispersing other related R&D efforts abroad. Yet the other consideration is simply that for firms in all industries (even those that are not science-based), the creation of technologies in which tacit knowledge carries a greater weight is harder to coordinate across longer distances. Furthermore, we have shown that in the exceptional cases in which the development of science-based technologies has been locationally dispersed, this is usually attributable to firms in the science-based industries developing a few non-core technologies over distance – chemical firms that develop some electronic technologies abroad, or electrical equipment companies that innovate in chemical technologies over a greater geographical distance. It will be of interest to examine these exceptions more carefully in further research.

Large firms have been obliged not merely to internationalize their technology base, but for similar reasons to exploit new areas of technological interrelatedness through corporate technological diversification (Cantwell and Piscitello, 1999). The overall move towards diversification of "smaller" and hence initially less diversified firms might be explained as a result of technological "fusion" between formerly unrelated technologies, for which process ICT has been both an agent and a catalyst. Technological fusion facilitated by ICT has created new opportunities for diversification for firms that were relatively little diversified before, while at the same time encouraging a greater focus of effort in the largest firms, in and around those sectors which have become most closely interrelated to one another and to the core strengths of the firm. As argued by Kodama (1992), technological fusion is a necessary condition for technological diversification, since it enables companies to establish new and closer technological complementarities between different fields of innovation. In this process, ICT is likely to play a particular role in establishing new areas of interconnectedness in the current paradigm. Information and Communications Technology can be viewed as a "carrier branch" (Freeman and Perez, 1988) or "transmission belt" and a core connector for innovation between formerly separate economic activities, in the way in which the capital good sector was in the mechanization paradigm of the past (Rosenberg, 1976).

References

Almeida P, Kogut B (1997) The exploration of technological diversity and the geographic localization of innovation. Small Business Economics 9: 21–31

Archibugi D, Michie J (1997) Technological globalisation and national systems of innovation: an introduction. In: Archibugi D, Michie J (eds) Technology, globalisation and economic performance. Cambridge University Press, Cambridge New York

Archibugi D, Pianta M (1992) The technological specialization of advanced countries. Kluwer Academic Publishers, Dordrecht

Audretsch D, Feldman MP (1994) Knowledge spillovers and the geography of innovation and production. Centre for Economic Policy Research Discussion Papers, No. 953, London

Breschi S (1997) The geography of innovation: a cross-sector analysis. CESPRI Working Paper, Universita Commerciale Bocconi, No. 95

Cantwell JA (1989) Technological innovation and multinational corporations. Basil Blackwell, Oxford

Cantwell JA (1992a) Japan's industrial competitiveness and the technological capabilities of the leading Japanese firms. In: Arrison TS, Bergsten CF, Graham EM, Harris MC (eds) Japan's growing technological capability: Implications for the US economy. National Academy Press, Washington, DC

Cantwell JA (1992b) The effects of integration on the structure of multinational corporation activity in the EC. In: Klein M, Welfens PJJ (eds) Multinationals in the New Europe and global trade. Springer, Berlin Heidelberg New York

Cantwell JA (1995) The globalisation of technology: what remains of the product cycle model? Cambridge Journal of Economics 19(1): 155–174

Cantwell JA, Bachmann A (1998) Changing patterns in technological leadership – evidence from the pharmaceutical industry. International Journal of Innovation Management 2(1): 45–77

Cantwell JA, Barrera MP (1998) The localisation of corporate technological trajectories in the interwar cartels: cooperative learning versus an exchange of knowledge. Economics of Innovation and New Technology 6(2): 257–290

Cantwell JA, Fai F (1999) The changing nature of corporate technological diversification and the importance of organisational capability. In: Dow S, Earl P (eds) Economic knowledge and economic coordination: Essays in honour of Brian J. Loasby. Edward Elgar, Aldershot (forthcoming)

Cantwell JA, Harding R (1998) The internationalisation of German companies' R&D. National Institute Economic Review 163: 99–115

Cantwell JA, Piscitello L (1997) Accumulating technological competence – its changing impact upon corporate diversification and internationalisation. Discussion Paper in International Investment and Management, University of Reading, No. 232

Cantwell JA, Piscitello L (1999) The emergence of corporate international networks for accumulation of dispersed technological competencies. Management International Review 39: forthcoming

Cockburn I, Henderson R (1995) Racing to invest? The dynamics of competition in ethical drug discovery. Journal of Economics and Management Strategy 3(3): 481–519

Freeman C (1987) Technology policy and economic performance: Lessons from Japan. Frances Pinter, London

Freeman C (1995) The 'National System of Innovation' in historical perspective. Cambridge Journal of Economics 19(1): 5–24

Freeman C, Perez C (1988) Structural crises of adjustment, business cycles and investment behaviour. In: Dosi G, Freeman C, Nelson RR, Silverberg G, Soete LLG (eds) Technical change and economic theory. Frances Pinter, London

Frost T (1996) From exploitation to exploration: the geographic sources of subsidiary innovations and the evolutionary theory of the multinational enterprise. Paper presented at the EIBA Annual Conference, Stockholm

Granstrand O, Patel K, Pavitt KLR (1997) Multi-technology corporations; why they have 'distributed' rather than 'distinctive core' competencies. California Management Review 39: 8–25

Hagedoorn J, Schakenraad J (1990) Inter-firm partnerships and cooperative strategies in core technologies. In: Freeman C, Soete LLG (eds) New explorations in the economics of technical change. Frances Pinter, London

Hart PE (1971) Entropy and other measures of concentration. Journal of the Royal Statistical Society 134: 74–895

Jaffe AB, Trajtenberg M, Henderson R (1993) Geographical localisation of knowledge spillovers, as evidenced by patent citations. Quarterly Journal of Economics 58(3): 577–598

Kodama F (1992) Technology fusion and the new R&D. Harvard Business Review

Lall S (1997) Coping with new technologies in emerging Asia, paper prepared for the Asian Development Bank's 'Emerging Asia' study

Lazonick W (1992) Business organisation and competitive advantage: capitalist transformations in the twentieth century. In: Dosi G, Giannetti R, Torinelli PA (eds.) Technology and enterprise in a historical perspective. Oxford University Press, Oxford

Metcalfe JS (1998) Evolutionary economics and creative restructuring. Routledge, London

Nelson RR (ed) (1993) National innovation systems: A comparative analysis. Oxford University Press, Oxford New York

Nelson RR, Winter SG (1982) An evolutionary theory of economic change. Harvard University Press, Cambridge, MA

Patel P, Pavitt KLR (1991) Europe's technological performance. In: Freeman C, Sharp ML, Walker W (eds) Technology and the future of Europe: Global competition and the environment in the 1990s. Frances Pinter, London

Patel P, Pavitt KLR (1994) National innovation systems: why they are important, and how they might be measured and compared. Economics of Innovation and New Technology 3(1): 77–95

Pavitt KLR (1994) Try business class worldwide. Times Higher Educational Supplement

Piscitello L (1998) Coherence in technological and product diversification of the world's largest firms. Mimeo, Politecnico di Milano

Rosenberg N (1976) Perspectives on technology. Cambridge University Press, Cambridge New York

Rosenberg N (1982) Inside the black box: Technology and economics. Cambridge University Press, Cambridge New York

Santangelo GD (1998) The impact of the information technology revolution on the internationalisation of corporate technology. Discussion Paper in International Investment and Management, University of Reading, No. 246

Saviotti PP (1996) Technological evolution, variety and the economy. Edward Elgar, Aldershot

Schumpeter JA (1934) The theory of economic development: An inquiry into profits, capital, credit, interest and the business cycle. Oxford University Press, Oxford New York
Schumpeter JA (1939) Business cycles: A theoretical historical and statistical analysis of the capitalist process. McGraw Hill, New York London
Schumpeter JA (1942) Capitalism, socialism and democracy. Allen and Unwin, London
Winter S (1987) Knowledge and competencies as strategic assets. In: Teece DJ (ed) The competitive challenge strategies for innovation and renewal. Ballinger, Cambridge

Debt, growth and inflation in large European economies: a vector auto-regression analysis

Majid Taghavi

Economics Division, University of Northumbria at Newcastle,
Newcastle upon Tyne NE1 8ST, UK (e-mail: majid.taghavi@unn.ac.uk)

Abstract. This paper attempts to empirically test the hypothesis that whether debt matters in the EU. This has been performed by examining the potential adverse effects of debt in large European economies on investment, inflation and growth. Using the hybrid cointegration and vector autoregressive models, the findings, based on the period 1970–97, suggest that debt causes significant adverse effects on investment, but its impact on growth is not clear-cut. Moreover, debt appears to be inflationary in most cases in the long run, though produces no clear short run pattern on inflation.

Key words: Cointegration – Convergence – Debt ratio – Deficit ratio – Vector autoregression

JEL-classification: H6, C3

1 Introduction

The recent sharp rises in public debt of most OECD members have reached unprecedented levels that had only been observed in the aftermath of major wars. Large debt has been primarily related to (a) adverse external supply shocks and, (b) weaker/coalition governments since the early 1990s.[1] It is

---

Paper presented at the 1998 World Conference of the International Joseph A. Schumpeter Society, Vienna, June 13–16, 1998.

[1] Roubini and Sachs (1989) have shown that coalition governments tend to have been less efficient in reducing their budget deficit and net public debts than those stable and majority-party governments.

now generally believed that abnormal debts in large economies not only do disturb the workings of their markets, but can also have an adverse effect on the economies of their trading partners.[2]

The Maastricht Treaty has specifically identified debt and deficits as major areas, which the member states need to control. The Treaty has urged members to bring their debt ratios down to around 60% – a rather difficult task for Belgium and Italy in particular, where the ratio currently stands at around 130% and 120% respectively. The concern was expressed in the Treaty that large debts could be inflationary and hamper real growth. Moreover, most market economists have for long argued that large government spending can seriously cause crowding-out effects, damage growth and be inflationary.

Whilst a large number of researchers (Alesina et al., 1990, 1997; Barro, 1992; Blanchard, 1985; Button and Pentecost, 1993, 1994; O'Leary, 1997; Tanzi and Schuknecht, 1994) have examined processes of fiscal and debt adjustment/convergence in OECD countries, this paper attempts to empirically investigate the real consequences of large debts over the short and long terms in the four large European economies: France, Germany, Italy and UK. The paper aims to answer this fundamental question: does debt matter at all. We explore whether debt causes inflation, hampers growth or slows down private investment. For the purpose of empirical investigation, the hybrid techniques of co-integration and vector auto-regression (VAR) are applied to macro data on price inflation, real GDP growth, real debt ratio, and real gross fixed capital formation in the four economies.

The rest of the paper is organised as follows. Part 2 provides a background to the extent of debt and deficits in Europe; whilst Part 3 introduces the methodological issues relating to unit-root, co-integration and VAR, and the data used for the estimations. Part 4 examines the overall empirical findings of the research. Concluding remarks are provided in Part 5.

2 Background

Barro (1979, 1987) has demonstrated that over a span of roughly 200 years in both the US and the UK, public debt ratios have fallen during peacetime, and jumped during wartime. However, since the 1970s, Barro's hypothesis has been rather weakened as the debt ratio in almost all OECD countries has escalated to new high values in spite of no major wars. The recent unprecedented rises in debt ratios in large economies of Europe have been a matter of concern amongst Eurocrats who have seen this as a major factor hampering a speedy convergence process. As European markets are becoming more integrated, it is now almost generally agreed that public debt, depending on its depth and magnitude, in a given European economy could have negative externalities on the rest of the Community. In particular, it is believed that large debts can be inflationary, reducing growth and discouraging investment. Panel A of Table 1 shows debt ratios in the large European economies over the period 1970–97. Although over the 1970s and

[2] In particular, see Alesina and Perotti (1995, 1997) and Raynold et al. (1991).

Table 1. Debt, deficit, growth and inflation in large European economies

	1970	1980	1990	1997	Percentage change over period		
					1970–80	1980–90	1990–97
A. Gross public debt as % of GDP at market prices							
France	15	20	35	58	33	75	66
Germany	18	32	44	62	78	37	41
Italy	38	58	98	122	53	69	24
UK	80	54	35	55	−32	−35	57
EU11	29	37	62	71	27	67	14
B. Deficit as % of GDP at market prices							
France	0	0	2.4	2.3	0	inf	−4.2
Germany	0	2.9	3.1	2.5	inf	6.8	−19.0
Italy	3.7	8.5	11.8	5.0	129	38.8	−57.6
UK	0	3.5	2.9	2.5	inf	−17.1	−13.4
EU11	0.5	3.6	2.5	2.1	620	−30.5	−16.0

	1970–79	1980–89	1990–97	AVG
C. Real GDP growth rates (%)				
France	3.7	2.3	1.9	2.6
Germany	3.1	1.7	2.0	2.3
Italy	3.8	2.3	1.8	2.6
UK	2.4	2.4	1.4	2.1
EU11	3.0	2.5	1.6	2.4
D. Consumer price inflation (%)				
France	9.2	7.4	2.3	6.3
Germany	5.0	2.9	2.8	3.6
Italy	12.8	11.2	3.2	9.0
UK	13.3	6.7	4.4	8.1
EU11	3.0	2.5	1.6	2.4

Sources: OECD and Eurostat

1980s one observes greater percentage rises in the debt ratio, the 1990s show that the ratio in all the large economies had reached levels that have never been experienced before.

On the other hand, when deficit ratios are examined, as shown in panel B of Table 1, Italy with a history of larger deficits than that of the EU average, has managed to reduce the ratio significantly over the period 1990–97. In fact, whilst the 1970s and 1980s have been regarded as the periods of large growth in the ratio, the 1990s see tremendous improvements in the deficit ratio in all the EU economies. A general examination of panel B appears to indicate that the four economies have exercised much greater control over deficit than over debt. Nevertheless, as cumulative deficits represent debt, it is misleading to compare flows with stocks. However, one can argue that deficits appear to be falling within the recommended EU rate and hence is of no potential threat to the economies.

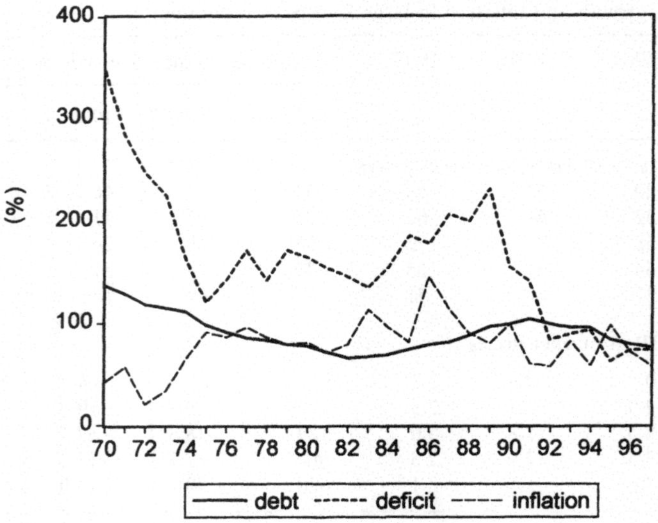

Fig. 1. Convergence based on coefficient of variation large european economies

Moreover, as shown in panel C of Table 1, real GDP growth rates over the period 1990–97, relative to their historic averages, have fallen in all four economies, as well as in the rest of the EU countries. These lower growth rates across EU may have something to do with higher debts. On the other hand, when considering movements in consumer prices, as given in panel D of Table 1, inflation has been declining significantly over the period 1990–97, with the current rates of inflation in all EU being much lower than their historic averages. On the whole, this preliminary examination of these tables tend not to offer any concrete conclusion as whether debt could have caused any disturbance to the system.

Some studies of economic convergence[3] have emphasized that if debt is significant, then economies would fail to converge as smoothly and as speedily as expected. Based on a single statistical measure, the coefficient of variation (*cv*), applied to relevant macro indicators, these studies have attempted to measure the extent of any convergence overtime. For example, if price inflation has converged on similar figures in most economies of the EU, then the estimated value of *cv* will approach zero. Based on this *cv* technique, Fig. 1 depicts the extent of convergence/divergence in debt ratios, deficit ratios, and the consumer price inflation in the large European economies. This figure indicates that, although *cv* estimates are still around 70%, there has been significant convergence in all areas since the early 1990s.

A major drawback with this technique is that it considers only one factor at a time with no regard to causality amongst the variables. More-

[3] In particular see O'Leary (1997), Barro and Sala-I-Martin (1991, 1992), Bernard and Durlauf (1995), and Button and Pentecost (1994) for the technique and findings based on coefficient of variation as a measure of convergence.

over, this technique fails to distinguish between convergence to a large value or to a small value. For example, although there appears to be a relatively small value of *cv* in 1997 on the debt ratio amongst the four economies, these economies, as seen in Table 1, have approached high values of debt ratios away from the Treaty's set value of 60%.

3 Methodological issues and data

Considering what has been shown so far, it is fair to argue that deficit ratios do not appear to be of serious threat to the EU members. On the other hand, debt (the historic cumulative sum of deficits) in most EU member states has gone well beyond that of the recommended rate. To test whether large debts can cause inflation, growth and crowding-out effects, we apply the co-integration technique for detecting any linear relationship amongst these variables. If the findings suggest that there are no such strong linear combinations amongst these variables, then one is led to adopt and apply the vector auto-regressive technique (VAR). This is because VAR is a system of simultaneous auto-regressive equations allowing for non-linear relationships amongst variables in a multi-variate setting. However, prior to such applications, one needs to test for the stationarity property of the variables.

The unit root test proposed by Dickey-Fuller (1979) for stationarity postulates that most macro variables move over time with a non-constant variance, making modelling a difficult task. Assume a variable X which is modelled as:

$$X_t = \mathrm{a} + \mathrm{bt} + \mathrm{u_t} \tag{1}$$

where

$$\mathrm{u_t} = \rho \mathrm{u_{t-1}} + \varepsilon_t \quad \varepsilon_t \sim \mathrm{NID}(0, \sigma^2) \tag{2}$$

Substituting (2) into (1) and re-arranging gives the reduced form expression:

$$X_t = \gamma + \beta \mathrm{t} + \alpha X_{t-1} + \varepsilon_t \tag{3}$$

In expression (3) if $\alpha = 1$ then X is said to be stationary of order 1 that is:

$$\Delta X = \varepsilon_t \tag{4}$$

With ε_t being white noise, ΔX will be a random walk variable with a finite variance. For any value of α less than unity, X will be stationary; while any value of α greater than unity will lead to an explosive variance of X.

The augmented Dickey-Fuller (ADF) test, on the other hand, tests the hypothesis that, in the general model,

$$\Delta X_t = \gamma + \beta \mathrm{t} + \Sigma \alpha_i X_{t-i} + \varepsilon_t \tag{5}$$

$\alpha_i = 1$ for every lag of X.

The concept of co-integration follows from stationarity.[4] Assume that there are two variables, X and Z, each being stationary of order 1. If there exists a linear combination so that

$$Z_t = a + bX_t + \varepsilon_t \quad \varepsilon_t \sim NID(0, \sigma^2) \tag{6}$$

then X and Z are said to be co-integrated of order 1. In this case as developed by Engle and Granger (1987), a test for the presence of co-integration is performed by simply running an OLS regression of Z on X and subjecting the residual of equation (5) to a unit root test. In general, variable Z could be regressed on k variables, producing a vector of k coefficients, better known as vector co-integration.

In the absence of any co-integration amongst our variables, one may resort to the vector auto-regressive model (VAR), a dynamic time series simultaneous system of equations. A general form of an augmented VAR may be given as follows:

$$Z_t = a_0 + a_1 t + \Sigma\Phi_i Z_{t-i} + \Psi X_t + u_t \tag{7}$$

where Z_t is an (m × 1) vector of jointly determined dependent variables and X_t is an (q × 1) vector of exogenous variables. Finally, the (m × 1) vector of disturbances satisfies all the classical assumptions.

Although the VAR technique is a reduced form procedure, it has several advantages over competing methods. As has been noted by Raynold et al. (1991), the VAR technique imposes no spurious *a priori* constraints or assumptions on variables, and hence allows the data to determine the model. Moreover, as has been pointed out by Fischer (1981) and Runkle (1987), since few restrictions are imposed on the way in which the system variables interact, the VAR appears to be well-suited for examination of the channels through which a variable operates.[5] Finally, the moving average part of expression (7) embodies the so-called *historical decompositions* (HDs) and *variance decompositions* (VDs) of the model, which will enable us to work out the size and the life length of impulses produced by variables as a result of shocks to the system.[6]

For the purpose of estimation, an annually based data set consisting of consumer price inflation (P), real GDP growth (Y), real public debt-GDP ratios (D), and real fixed capital formation-GDP ratios (K) is used. All the data are collected from OECD and Eurostat and cover the period 1970–97.[7]

[4] In particular, see McKinnon (1990) and Schwert (1987) for detailed analyses of unit root and cointegration.

[5] For some relevant applications, see, for example, Caines et al. (1981), Hasan and Taghavi (1996) and Litterman (1986).

[6] For a detailed analysis of VAR and estimation procedure and derivation of HDs and VDs, see Pesaran (1997) and Watson (1994).

[7] The redefined version of debt ratio (based on the Maastricht Treaty) offered by data sources go only as far back as 1970.

Table 2. Results of stationary test

Variable	Level		First Diff.		Second Diff.	
	t_1	t_2	t_1	t_2	t_1	t_2
France						
D	−1.267	−1.044	−2.504	−3.245	−5.015**	−4.867**
P	−1.262	−2.867	−3.149	−3.197	−4.823**	−4.733**
Y	−3.615*	−3.401	−4.721**	−4.775**	–	–
K	−3.009	−2.946	−4.343**	−4.283**	–	–
Germany						
D	−0.167	−1.976	−2.803	−2.776	−5.052**	−4.861**
P	−2.662	−3.327	−3.277	−3.119	−4.626**	−4.225**
Y	−3.719*	−3.655*	−5.581**	−5.483**	–	–
K	−3.564*	−3.601*	−4.426**	−4.325	–	–
Italy						
D	−0.389	−2.424	−3.296	−3.326	−5.545**	−5.508**
P	−1.562	−3.067	−3.591*	−3.875*	−7.038**	−6.923**
Y	−4.032**	−4.890**	–	–	–	–
K	−4.731**	−4.622**	–	–	–	–
UK						
D	−2.316	−2.204	−2.435	−2.586	−4.121**	−4.001**
P	−1.725	−3.167	−3.902*	−3.917*	−4.784**	−4.673**
Y	−3.893*	−3.816*	−5.271**	−5.138**	–	–
K	−3.729*	−3.696*	−4.843**	−4.743**	–	–

* 5% significance level, ** 1% significance level, t_1 equation with constant, t_2 equation with trend and constant

Table 3. Results of co-integration test* (Engle-Yoo statistic)

Variable	France	Germany	Italy	UK
D	−1.67	−2.67	−2.21	−2.12
P	−1.98	−2.18	−2.12	−2.45
Y	−2.03	−2.32	−2.32	−2.13
K	−2.14	−2.17	−2.41	−2.56

* Based on the 5% critical value being −4.43 (source: McKinnon, 1990)

4 Empirical results

The data were first checked for stationarity by using the ADF test. With the exception of P and Y, all variables are expressed in logs. The results are shown in Table 2, giving detailed tests based on two linear stationary models – expressed as equation 5 – (t_1: with constant; and t_2: with constant and trend) at level, and two orders of differencing. The overall results here suggest that most variables possess one unit root, whilst P and D in all countries exhibit two unit roots.

Table 3 presents the results of co-integration tests with lags of orders 1, 3 and 5 years, all based on a general debt ratio model of the order (D, K, P, Y). The overall results indicate no co-integration amongst variables, as

Table 4. Results of the Granger causality test*

Number of lags	1	3	5
France	D ≠> P	D ≠> P	D => P
	<≠	<≠	<≠
	D ≠> Y	D ≠> Y	D => Y
	<≠	<≠	<=
	D => K	D ≠> K	D ≠> K
	<≠	<≠	<=
Germany	D => P	D => P	D => P
	<≠	<≠	<=
	D => Y	D ≠> Y	D => Y
	<≠	<≠	<=
	D => K	D ≠> K	D ≠> K
	<≠	<≠	<≠
Italy	D => P	D => P	D => P
	<≠	<≠	<=
	D => Y	D ≠> Y	D => Y
	<≠	<≠	<=
	D => K	D => K	D ≠> K
	<≠	<≠	<≠
UK	D ≠> P	D => P	D => P
	<≠	<≠	<=
	D => Y	D => Y	D ≠> Y
	<≠	<≠	<≠
	D => K	D ≠> K	D ≠> K
	<≠	<≠	<≠

* Based on the estimated F-statistic at the 5% significance level

the critical value of 4.43 at the 5% level exceeds the values estimated through the Engle-Yoo procedure.

To further our investigation, the Granger causality tests are performed to determine whether there is any pair-wise causality amongst our variables.[8] Such findings are offered in Table 4 based on the estimated F-statistic at the 5% significance level. The pair-wise causality between debt ratio and other variables suggests that in most cases debt Granger causes inflation under 3 and 5 year lags in all countries. There remains very little support in favour of any causality between investment and debt ratios. Though no conclusive support is found of any causality between growth and debt, growth in France and Germany is seen to be sensitive to debt in the longer run. Finally, in most cases there appears to be relatively little support for bi-causality amongst variables. In most cases, it is the debt ratio, which Granger causes other variables.

These important findings suggest that pair-wise causality leads to a limited and hence incomplete verdict, and that one should proceed with multivariate VAR on the stationary induced pre-filtered data.[9] The general

[8] Analytical aspects of the original thoughts on causality can be found in Granger (1969).

[9] The cointegration tests were also performed by pairing the variables in turn. The results provide similar inference.

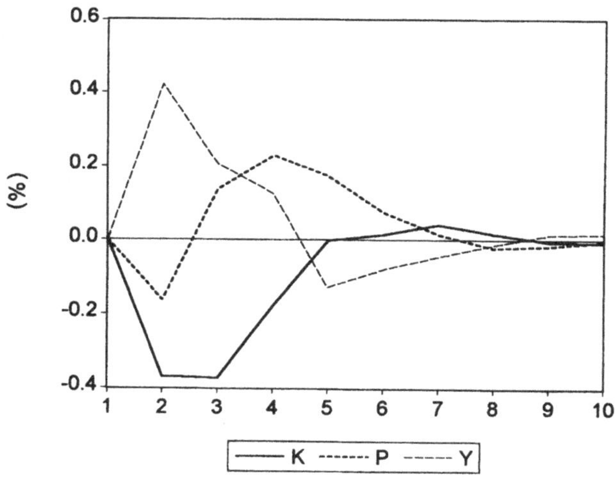

Fig. 2. France: Impulses caused by 1% increase in French debt ratio

model of debt, of the orders mentioned earlier, running from debt to investment, inflation and then growth, is applied again. After several trials, the best VAR estimates were found to be of the lag order 2 for all the countries.[10] An effective way of presenting and evaluating the likelihood of any correlation and causality is to examine the extent of response made by variables as a result of a shock in another variable in a multivariate setting. Response functions are, therefore, the by-products of the VAR application, and can be treated as predictions.

The resulting impulses produced on investment, inflation and growth as a result of a 1% increase in debt ratios for each country are given in Figs. 2 to 5. In addition, Figs. 6 to 9 depict the impact of each of the four countries' debt on the overall EU economy. The impulse functions, here, give the magnitude (in percentage) and length (in years) of a response by a macro variable, as a result of one percent increase occurring at the base year in the debt ratio. As appears from these Figures, in most cases a shock of this nature tends to last for nearly ten years.

Based on these figures, Table 5 presents the short run (one year), and the cumulative magnitude of these responses supported by the statistical significance of the latter.

A careful examination of these findings leads to the following conclusions:

(i) Changes in debt ratios in all four countries appear to deteriorate investment in the short run, and significantly undermine investment in the longer run. As shown in Table 5, the cumulative impact of debt on investment in Italy and France is much higher than in the other two countries, standing at −1.34% and 0.95%, respectively. Moreover, debt in any of the four economies seems to exhibit similar outcome, though different in

[10] Detailed tests are available to readers on request.

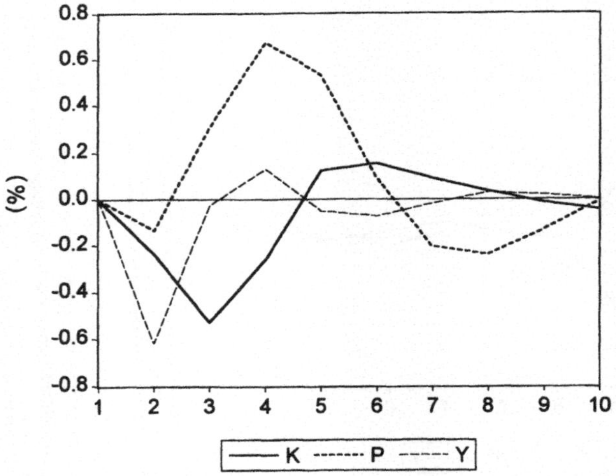

Fig. 3. Germany: Impulses caused by 1% increase in German debt ratio

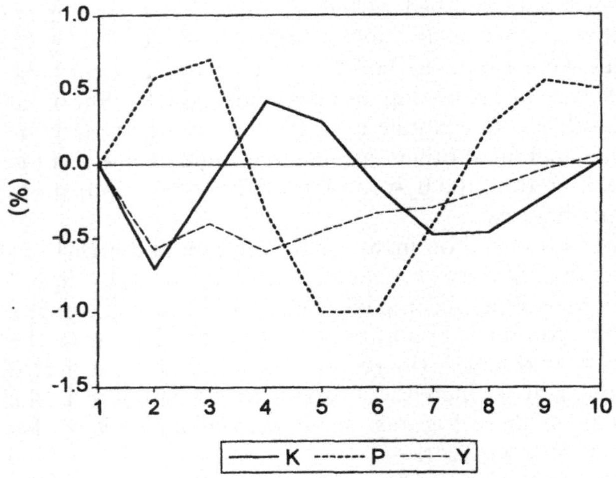

Fig. 4. Italy: Impulses caused by 1% increase in Italian debt ratio

magnitudes, on the EU as a whole. Once again, a 1% increase in the Italian debt ratio tends to have a cumulative impact of as much −1.66% on the EU investment.

(ii) The short run impact that debt generates on growth varies quite substantially from one country to another. Whilst in France and UK a one percent debt leads to nearly 0.4% growth in the short run, Germany and Italy experience negative short run growth rates of around 0.65%. Similarly, as the cumulative figures suggest, whilst Italy experiences a substantial fall in its growth of about 2.2%, the UK enjoys a significant improvement in growth of around 1.2%. Nevertheless, the cumulative impact of debt on

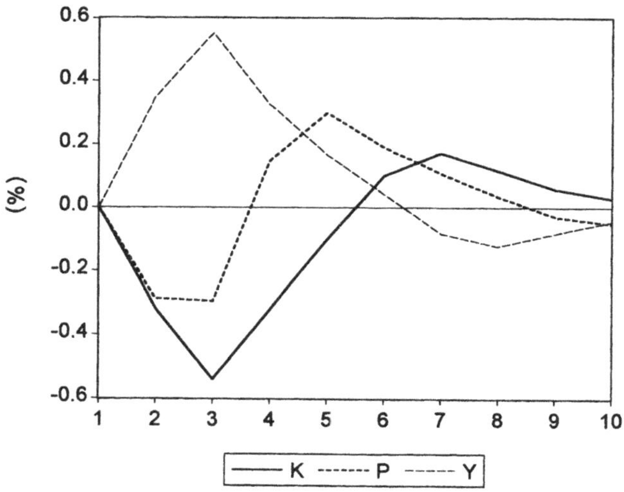

Fig. 5. UK: Impulses caused by 1% increase in UK debt ratio

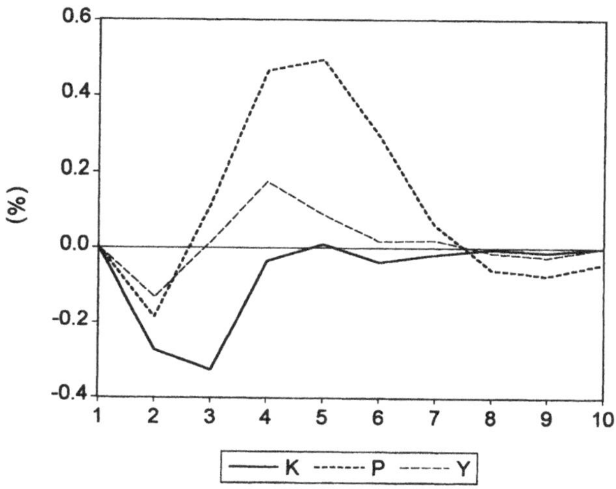

Fig. 6. EU: Impulses caused by 1% increase in French debt ratio

growth tends to support the view that debt could, though not significantly in all cases, induce growth in each of the four countries and the EU in the longer term.

(iii) Inflation impulses, caused by changes in debt ratios, give rather unclear and inconclusive, and differing pictures in these four countries. Whilst inflation in the short run is seen to decrease – though fractionally – in France, Germany and the UK, in Italy the experience appears opposite. The cumulative impact of debt on inflation, on the other hand, suggests that debt could be significantly inflationary in all the four countries and the EU as a whole. As these figures suggest, a 1% increase in debt ratios in

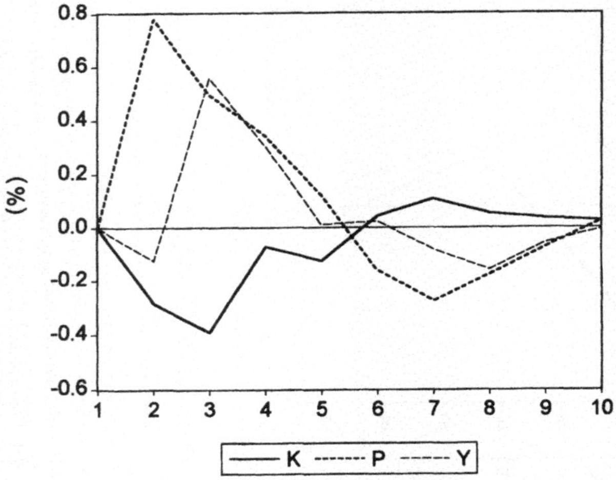

Fig. 7. EU: Impulses caused by 1% increase in German debt ratio

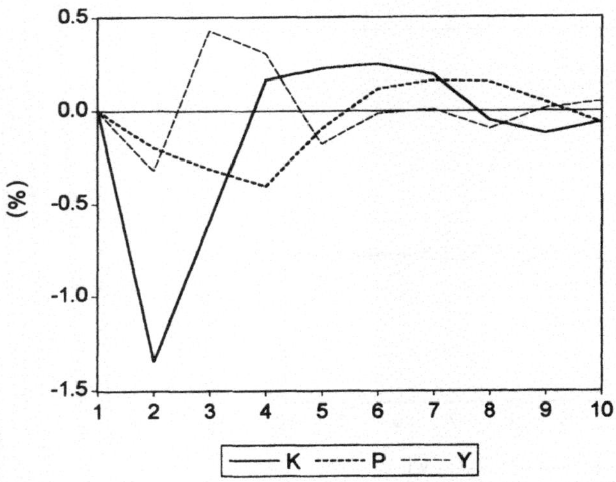

Fig. 8. EU: Impulses caused by 1% increase in Italian debt ratio

Germany and the UK could lead to an EU cumulative inflation of between 1.18% and 1.03%.

5 Conclusions

This paper has made an attempt at investigating whether debt ratios in the large European economies matter at all. The extent and severity of debt ratios have been considered in relation to their potential adverse impacts within a given economy, as well as their spillover effects on the rest of the EU. Tests based on co-integration and causality have indicated that a

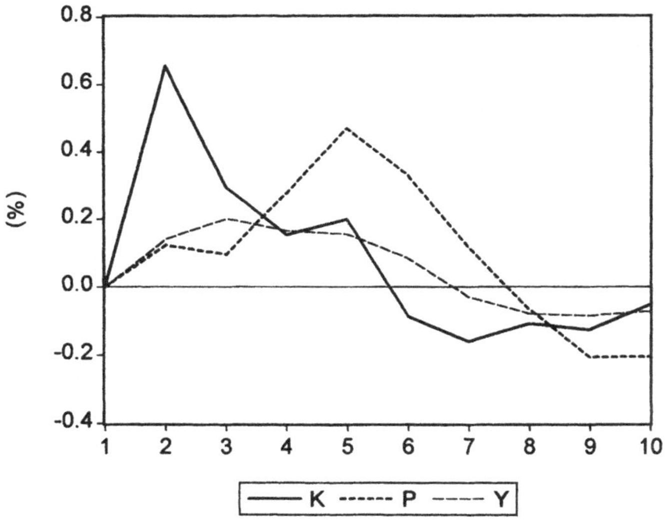

Fig. 9. EU: Impulses caused by 1% increase in UK debt ratio

Table 5. Short run and cumulative impulses due to 1% change in debt ratio[a] (%)

	Investment		Inflation		Growth	
	SR	CUM	SR	CUM	SR	CUM
Fig. 2.	−0.37	−0.95** (.322)	−0.17	0.49* (.212)	0.44	0.87* (.453)
Fig. 3.	−0.52	−0.76* (.315)	−0.12	0.96** (.287)	−0.63	−0.67* (.311)
Fig. 4.	−0.74	−1.34** (.424)	0.63	−0.16 (.113)	−0.65	−2.21** (.503)
Fig. 5.	−0.31	−0.79* (.411)	−0.29	0.22* (0.105)	0.37	1.16** (.376)
Fig. 6.	−0.27	−0.47* (.215)	−0.18	0.74* (.304)	−0.16	0.11 (.099)
Fig. 7.	−0.31	−0.61* (.307)	0.78	1.18** (0.235)	−0.13	0.44* (.222)
Fig. 8.	−1.35	−1.66** (.453)	−0.21	−0.64* (.347)	−0.36	0.07 (.112)
Fig. 9.	0.65	0.98* (.487)	0.15	1.03** (.324)	0.16	0.17 (.124)

[a] Numbers in brackets represent standard errors
* Statistically significant at the 5% level
** Statistically significant at the 1% level

vector auto-regressive model is best suited for our empirical investigations. The overall findings based, therefore, on VAR impulse functions yield rather similar patterns in both intra- and inter-country analyses.

Debt has found to substantially deteriorate investment in the short run and in the long run, with a rather sluggish adjustment process. Therefore, debt can cause significant crowding-out effects in the European economies. Growth is slightly and insignificantly enhanced by changes in debt in the long run, but gives no clear picture in the short run. Finally, the impact of debt on inflation offers no clear-cut patterns in the short run. However, our empirical findings, based on cumulative effects, suggest that debt could have significant adverse effects on inflation.

References

Alesina A, Perotti R (1995) Fiscal expansions and adjustments in OECD countries. Economic Policy 21: 205–240

Alesina A, Perotti R (1997) Fiscal adjustments in OECD countries: composition and macroeconomic effects. IMF Staff Papers 44: 210–248

Alesina A, Prati A, Tabellini G (1990) Public confidence and debt management: a model and case study of Italy. In: Dornbusch R, Draghi M (eds) Public debt management: Theory and history. Cambridge

Barro RJ (1979) On the determination of public debt. Journal of Political Economy 87: 940–971

Barro RJ (1987) Government spending, interest rates, prices, and budget deficits in the United Kingdom, 1701–1918. Journal of Monetary Economics 20: 221–247

Barro RJ, Sala-i-Martin X (1991) Convergence across states and regions. Brookings Papers on Economic Activity 1: 107–182

Barro RJ, Sala-i-Martin X (1992) Convergence. Journal of Political Economy 100: 223–251

Bernard AB, Durlauf SN (1995) Convergence in international output. Journal of Applied Econometrics 10: 97–108

Blanchard OJ (1985) Debt, deficits and finite horizons. Journal of Political Economy 93: 223–247

Button KJ, Pentecost EJ (1993) Regional service sector convergence. Regional Studies 27: 623–636

Button KJ, Pentecost EJ (1994) Regional economic convergence in Great Britain and Germany. CREEF Research Papers 94/5, Loughborough University

Caines PE, Keng CW, Sethi SP (1981) Causal analysis and multivariate autoregressive modelling with an application to super-market analysis. Journal of Economic Dynamics and Control 3: 267–298

Dickey DA, Fuller WA (1979) Distribution of the estimators for autoregressive time series with a unit root. Journal of the American Statistical Association 74: 427–431

Engle RF, Granger CWJ (1987) Cointegration and error correction: representation estimation and testing. Econometrica 55: 251–294

Engle RF, Yoo BS (1987) Forecasting and testing in cointegrated systems. Journal of Econometrics 35: 143–159

Fischer S (1981) Relative shocks, relative price variability and inflation. Brookings Papers on Economic Activity 2: 381–441

Granger CWJ (1969) Investigating causal relations by econometric models and cross-spectral methods. Econometrica 34: 541–551

Hasan M, Taghavi M (1996) Money, output, price and causality in mainland China. Applied Economics Letters 2: 101–105

Litterman R (1986) Forecasting with Bayesian vector autoregressions – five years of experience. Journal of Business and Economic Statistics 4: 25–38

McKinnon JC (1990) Critical values for cointegrating test. University of San Diego Working Paper, California

O'Leary E (1997) The convergence performance of Ireland among EU countries: 1960–90. Journal of Economic Studies 24: 43–58

Pesaran MH (1997) The role of economic theory in modelling the long run. Economic Journal 107: 178–191

Raynold P, McMillin WD, Beard TR (1991) The impact of federal government expenditure in 1930s. Southern Economic Journal 58: 15–28

Roubini N, Sachs J (1989) Government spending and budget deficits in the industrial countries. Economic Policy 8: 99–132

Runkle DE (1987) Vector auto-regression and reality. Journal of Business and Economic Statistics 5: 437–442

Schwert GW (1987) Effects of model specification on tests for unit roots in macroeconomic data. Journal of Monetary Economics 20: 73–103

Tanzi V, Schuknecht L (1995) The growth of government and the reform of the state in industrial countries. IMF Working Paper, 95/130

Watson, M.W (1994) Vector auto-regression and co-integartion. In: Engle RF, MacFadden D (eds) Handbook of econometrics. North Holland, Amsterdam

Uncertainty and the size distribution of rewards from innovation*

F. M. Scherer[1], Dietmar Harhoff[2], Jörg Kukies[3]

[1] John F. Kennedy School of Government, Harvard University, Cambridge, MA 02138, USA (e-mail: mike_scherer@harvard.edu)
[2] Universität München, D-80539 München, Germany
[3] Graduate School of Business, University of Chicago, Chicago, USA

Abstract. Previous research has shown that the distribution of profit outcomes from technological innovations is highly skew. This paper builds upon those detailed findings to ask: what stochastic processes can plausibly be inferred to have generated the observed distributions? After reviewing the evidence, this paper reports on several stochastic model simulations, including a pure Gibrat random walk with monthly changes approximating those observed for high-technology startup company stocks and a more richly specified model blending internal and external market uncertainties. The most highly specified simulations suggest that the set of profit potentials tapped by innovators is itself skew-distributed and that the number of entrants into innovation races is more likely to be independent of market size than stochastically dependent upon it.

Key words: Innovation – Risk – Uncertainty – Skew distributions – Gibrat's Law

JEL-classification: O31, C15

1 Introduction

For two years the authors have been compiling and analyzing several new data sets on the profit returns to inventions and high-technology startup

---

Paper presented at the 1998 World Conference of the International Joseph A. Schumpeter Society, Vienna, June 13–16, 1998.

* Financial support from the Sloan Foundation and the Center for European Economic Research, Mannheim, at earlier stages of this project is gratefully acknowledged.

enterprises. The data, combined with evidence available earlier, exhibit striking regularities. The size distribution of rewards from technological innovation is highly skew, with an extended tail on the high-value side. A log normal distribution provides in most instances the best fit. Having pinned down with considerable confidence the structure of rewards ensuing from innovative activity, we advance now to the stage of formulating what Ijiri and Simon (1977, p. 109) called "extreme hypotheses," attempting to determine what behavioral processes, undoubtedly stochastic, led to the observed distributions. In this paper we summarize the empirical evidence and then explore, mainly through simulation exercises, plausible alternative stochastic processes to see which ones conform most closely to the size distributions actually encountered in the world of innovation.

2 The empirical evidence

Our research has focused on eight sets of data, seven of which are new to the economics literature (see Scherer, 1998; Harhoff et al., 1999). The most ambitious effort involved collecting useable survey and interview evidence on 772 German and 222 U.S.-origin inventions, on all of which German patent applications were filed in 1977, leading to issued German patents considered sufficiently valuable by their holders to warrant paying annual renewal fees totalling DM 16,075 until their expiration at full term in 1995. These will be called the German and U.S. patent data sets. Two other data sets pertained also to invention patents, one tallying the royalties received between 1977 and 1995 on the 118 invention patent "bundles" licensed by the Harvard University Office of Technology Licensing, the other royalties received in the years 1991 through 1994 by six research-oriented U.S. universities on 350 to 466 licensed patent bundles. These will be called the "Harvard" and "Six University" data sets respectively. Two other data sets tallied the asset value appreciation (or loss) experienced on a total of 1,053 investments in startup companies by U.S. venture capital firms between 1969 and 1988. One sample, covering 383 investments, was compiled by Venture Economics Inc.; the other, covering 670 investments, by Horsely Keogh Associates. They will be referred to by the names of the compiling firms. Still another analysis of startup company experiences was carried out by the authors. It followed the common stock values of 131 high-technology companies previously nurtured by venture capital firms from the time they made initial public stock offerings (IPOs) between 1983 and 1986 through (at least, for 52 surviving entities) 1995. This is called the IPO survey. Finally, we used the data compiled and analyzed previously by Henry Grabowski and John Vernon (1990, 1994) on the discounted present value of profits (or more exactly, quasi-rents) realized on two sets of new pharmaceutical chemical entities marketed in the U.S. market – 98 introduced in the 1970s and 66 between 1980 and 1984. These will be called the "Grabowski-Vernon drug" data sets.

Table 1 characterizes in two main ways the reward outcome distributions observed for these eight samples. The second numerical column estimates the fraction of total observed sample profits, royalties, or market

Table 1. Paremeters of the observed innovation reward size distributions

Data set	Number of observations	Percent of value in top 10 percent	Slope estimates α	
			All obs.	Right tail[a]
German patents	772	88%	.42	$.87_{(81)}$
U.S. patents	222	81–85%	.32	$.43_{(63)}$
Harvard patents	118	84	.41	$.71_{(30)}$
Six university patents				
1991 Royalties	350	93	.50	$.64_{(153)}$
1992 Royalties	408	92	.51	$.65_{(186)}$
1993 Royalties	466	91.5	.51	$.61_{(214)}$
1994 Royalties	411	92	.52	$.65_{(233)}$
Venture economics startups	383	62	.60	$.97_{(136)}$
Horsley-Keogh startups	670	59	.77	$.90_{(285)}$
IPOs – 1995 value	110	62	.44	$.82_{(13)}$
Grabowski-Vernon				
1970s drugs	98	55	.43	$1.22_{(23)}$
1980s drugs	66	48	.41	$1.36_{(17)}$

[a] The number of right-hand tail observations covered is indicated in subscripted parentheses. For the IPOs, the sample includes only 53 firms surviving at the end of 1995.

value captured by entities ranked among the top ten percent of reward earners. For samples on which the distributional data were available only by class intervals, the Top Ten Percent share was estimated by nonlinear interpolation, assuming a log normal distribution of rewards.[1]

The third and fourth columns in Table 1 summarize the distribution parameters using the Pareto-Levy distribution, which has the particularly simple form:

$$N = kV^{-\alpha} , \tag{1}$$

where V is the value of the profits or other rewards from an innovation, N is the number of cases with value V or greater, and k and α are parameters. For data sets on which individual observations were available, the log-linear fit implied by the Pareto-Levy distribution did not emerge; the distribution was characteristically concave to the origin, as illustrated (despite one extreme billion-Mark value) for the German patent data in Fig. 1. However, in many instances, observations in the right-hand (most valuable) tail exhibited a fit close to log linear, and in any case, information on α slope values for the entire set of observations and those in the right-hand tail conveys a good sense of both the distribution's skewness and the degree of

[1] For the most valuable U.S. patents, a range of estimates is presented, assuming alternatively that patents in that open-ended interval averaged $200 million and $250 million. For values in closed distribution intervals, geometric means of the interval bounds were used to estimate interval average values.

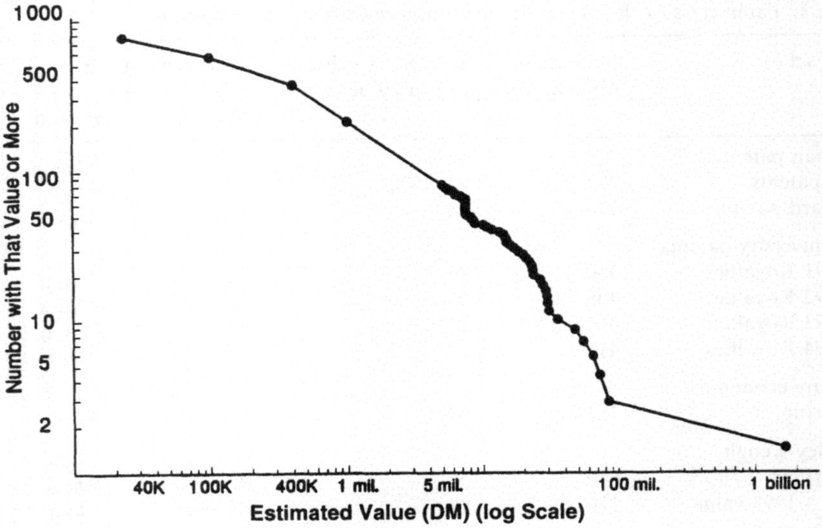

Fig. 1. Plot of German renewed patent values on Pareto coordinates

concavity. Therefore, we report in Table 1 values of α estimated by ordinary least squares regression for all available observations and for a subset conforming as closely as possible to the most valuable 25 percent of those observations. For data available only by class intervals, the right-hand tail α values were estimated by reaching out to the include the class boundary including (and over-reaching) the 25 percent point.[2]

Two generalizations stand out. First, in all cases, a relatively small number of top entities accounted for the lion's share of total invention or innovation value. The highest concentration of value is unambiguously for the patents, which tend to cover the narrowest range of innovative subject matter.[3] (Many new products and processes are protected by multiple patents.) The fraction of total portfolio value attributable to the top ten percent of business entities is quite similar for the two sets of venture-fund-

[2] For the German patents, we include only right-hand tail observations on which detailed interview data were available.

[3] A simulation analysis revealed that when there are complementarities or substitution effects among patents, a distribution that was purely Paretian ignoring those effects became concave when the effects were introduced. Three sets of 200 observations were generated, assuming a Pareto distribution with $\alpha = 0.5$. The observations were then randomized, and observation values were assumed to be affected by the values of their nearest neighbors, mediated by some random number. For example, the value of observation V_i became $V_i^* = V_i + (NORM_i\, V_{i+1}) + (NORM_i\, V_{i-1})$, where $NORM_i$ was a normally distributed random variable with mean zero and standard deviations of 0.2 and 0.33. Distinct concavities appeared in the double-log distribution of observations so transformed, e.g., as the largest original values appreciably augmented or reduced the value of smaller neighbors but were little affected by those neighbors' values. A simulation permitting only rectangularly distributed positive complementary effects induced only slight concavity.

backed startup companies and for the IPO companies (whose value gains occur at a later life cycle stage, since venture funds typically liquidate their positions shortly after the companies they have backed launch initial public offerings). The smallest share of total portfolio value, and hence the least skewness, is found for the new drug samples, perhaps because many drugs are protected by multiple patents but possibly also because of biases in the way the estimates were made.[4]

Second, substantial skewness is shown both by large fractions of total sample value attributable to the top 10 percent "winners" and by relatively flat Pareto function slope estimates (i.e., low absolute values of the slope parameter α). The simple correlation between top 10 percent value shares and right-hand tail α estimates for the twelve samples is −0.83. Only for the two new pharmaceutical product samples, with the lowest top ten percent value shares, are the right-hand tail α estimates greater than unity – the threshold above which Pareto distributions have asymptotically finite means (see Mandelbrot, 1963; Scherer, 1998). For right-hand tail slope values below unity, reducing risk by forming ever-larger portfolios is problematic, since, in the pure Pareto case, means do not converge, following the weak law of large numbers, toward stable values with rising sample size. The near ubiquity of slope values below unity in absolute value reveals a high degree of skewness indeed.

3 Further insights from the IPO sample[5]

Because the stock market values of firms included in our IPO sample could be tracked monthly over a period of from nine to 13 years following the initial issuance of shares between January 1983 and December 1995, particularly rich insight into the evolution of high-technology enterprises' early economic success could be achieved. The 131 IPOs were believed to be an exhaustive sample of IPOs launched during 1983–86 that had been backed previously by venture capital funds and that operated in pre-specified high-technology industries, excluding health care provision. Monthly stock prices were obtained, initially from the Center for Research on Securities Prices files and, to fill numerous gaps, by manual search. No record of actual market transactions was found for 21 of the IPOs, and so the final sample included only 110 companies. Of those 110, 52 survived to the end of 1995, 23 disappeared by merger (only five of which outperformed the NASDAQ index prior to their acquisition), and 35 were delisted, often accompanied by bankruptcy. Our basic analytic approach was to set aside $1000 for investment in each IPO, parking the funds in the NASDAQ index

[4] The estimates were based upon sales data, to which a non-varying quasi-rent margin fraction was applied before returns were discounted back to the date of product introduction. If the best-selling drugs (the "blockbusters") carried higher profit margins, which seems plausible, the degree of distribution skewness will be underestimated.

[5] Joerg Kukies was primarily responsible for the data collection on this sub-project. He was assisted by Jesus Viejo Gonzales, Christopher Choi, and Anne Sohns. Valuable leads to data sources were provided by Josh Lerner.

from January 1, 1983, until the time of IPO. Stock splits and dividends were tallied, and cash dividends (a fairly rare event) were reinvested (with no allowance for tax) at the time of payment. When companies exited by merger or delisting, the cash proceeds were parked in the NASDAQ index until December 1995.[6] The total value of the 110 investments as of December 31, 1995, was as follows:

52 surviving companies	$ 417,002
23 acquired companies	96,400
35 delisted companies	21,178
Total terminal value	$ 534,580

Had the same initial $110,000 been invested in the NASDAQ index in January 1983, investors would have had $501,908. Thus, our sample of high-technology companies fared only slightly (and statistically insignificantly) better than the NASDAQ index generally (compare Brav and Gompers, 1997).

Figure 2 illustrates how company investment values evolved between June 1986 and December 1995. It is confined to ten companies, including the five most successful full-term survivors and five others selected randomly. The share values for the random choices cluster so closely in the $0–2000 range that they are for the most part indistinguishable. Had one invested $1000 in Adobe Systems, Concord Computing, or Amgen, on the other hand, one would have had shares valued at $77,565, $74,130, and $55,980 respectively by the end of 1995.

Figure 3 shows how cross-sectional value distributions on doubly logarithmic coordinates evolved between 1987 and 1995. To the 52 full-term survivors from our main sample, one additional high-technology IPO backed by a venture fund but missed by our initial search – Microsoft – has been added for the analysis that follows.[7] As time advances, the distribution becomes increasingly skew, as shown by slope (α) coefficients for the entire cross-sectional distribution falling in absolute value from 0.96 at the end of 1987 to 0.47 by the end of 1995. For the top 13 companies (i.e., the top 25 percent) at any given point, the slope values declined from 1.25 in 1987 to 0.95 in 1991 and 0.72 in 1995.

The value trajectories shown in Fig. 2 follow quite "noisy" paths between 1987 and 1995, among other things with frequent rank order changes. That what occurred approximated a random walk is shown by estimating

---

[6] The value of delisted companies is almost surely over-estimated, since it was based upon the last reported end-of-month value, and since later quotations probably fell, it is doubtful that investors could have liquidated and reinvested their stakes at the reported price.

The top ten percent company share tallied in Table 1 includes the reinvested proceeds from one company that merged on particularly attractive terms along with 12 full-term company values.

[7] Microsoft "went public" in March 1986. A parked 1983 investment of $1000 accumulated to $129,958 by December 1995. Adding it was important to our test for path dependence.

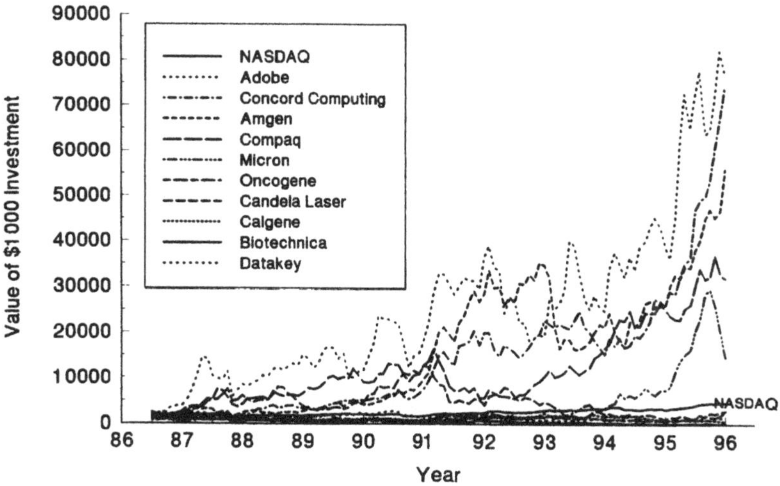

Fig. 2. Evolution of the value of $1000 investments in ten IPOS

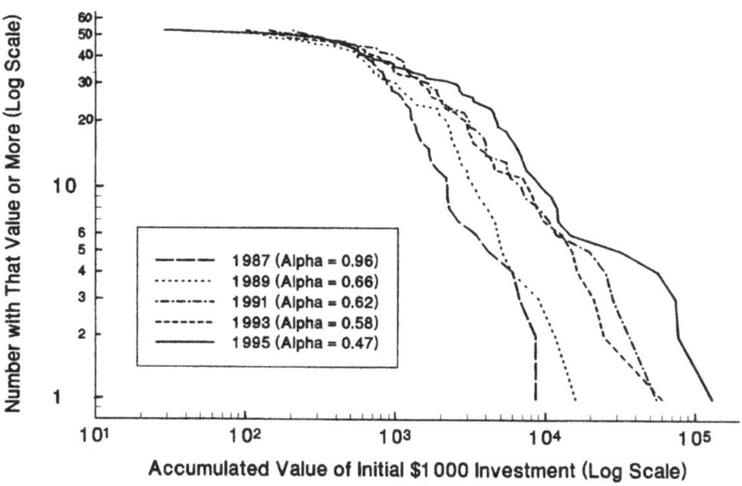

Fig. 3. Pareto plot of 53 IPO values, 1987–1995

for each of the 53 full-term companies a simple monthly market model regression of the form:

$$\delta P_t = a + \beta(\delta NASDAQ_t) + e_t \ , \tag{2}$$

where δP_t is the month-to-month percentage change in a company's stock value, $\delta NASDAQ_t$ is the corresponding change in the NASDAQ index, e_t is a random error, and β measures the stock's market risk. The mean value of β was 1.16, showing that the new high-technology stocks on average exhibited more systematic risk than the overall NASDAQ market portfolio. The Durbin-Watson coefficients for the 53 price change regressions averaged 2.13, with a standard deviation of 0.22. Only nine of the 53 regressions had Durbin-Watson coefficients outside the 1.64 to 2.36 range, beyond which one might infer at the 95 percent confidence level negative autocorrelation (eight cases) or positive autocorrelation (one case).[8] Thus, the visual impression of value changes that exhibit much "white noise" is confirmed.

Since value evolutions governed by path dependence can also generate highly skew distributions (see DeVany and Walls, 1996), further tests for possible path dependence were conducted.

An intercept term *a* in equation (1) significantly different from zero in equation (1) implies systematic upward or downward price drift. Only four of the 53 market model regressions had t-ratios on *a* (all positive) of 2.00 or more. Thus, there was little evidence of significant upward drift, although four of the most successful companies (in descending t-ratio order, Microsoft, Concord Computing, Adobe, and Compaq) were exceptions.

As an additional test for path dependence, price levels (not percentage changes) during months 2 through 37 were regressed on an integer time variable. Extrapolated predictions from that regression were then added to regressions for the months remaining through December 1995 of price levels on the value of the NASDAQ index. In 34 out of 53 cases, addition of the extrapolated trend series variable led to R^2 increments significant in F-ratio tests at the 5 percent level. Among 19 cases with positive first-three-year price trends, the trend variable had significant positive explanatory effects for two computer-oriented companies (Microsoft and Compaq) and four biotech companies (Amgen, Chiron, Molecular Biosystems, and AL Pharmaceuticals) and significant negative effects (indicating a reversal of the early trend) in 13 cases. Among nine cases with negative first-three-year trends, a significant continuation of the downward trend was found in six cases and a significant reversal in three cases. Altogether, only six of the 53 regressions exhibit significant continuation of a positive initial trend consistent with the type of path dependence that would increase skewness over time. Since random walks produce what appear in hindsight to be cycles or trends, some incidence of correlated growth between early and later periods is almost inevitable. Thus, we are led to conclude that the incidence of path dependence was at best modest. It almost surely existed in the case of Microsoft because of the cumulative software lock-in effects resulting from the Microsoft operating system's early selection for IBM's personal computers.

4 Technical uncertainty vs. product market uncertainty

Initial public stock offerings are seldom made until one or more products have been shown by research and development to be technically feasible (although for pharmaceutical products, clinical testing often continues with funds raised through IPOs). The skew distributions that emerge following an IPO suggest that there must be substantial risks associated with consumers' (and regulators') response to new products.

[8] Negative autocorrelation implies non-random alternation between high and low changes; positive autocorrelation non-random sequences of positive or negative price changes.

Insight into this point can be sharpened by re-examining the findings from pioneering research by the late Edwin Mansfield and his students (1977, pp. 22–32). He and his colleagues secured information on the outcomes of individual R&D projects in 16 chemical, pharmaceutical, electronics, and petroleum corporations. They quantified three different success probabilities: (1) the probability that a project's technical goals will be met; (2) the probability that, given technical success, the resulting product or process will be commercialized; and (3) the probability that, given commercialization, the project yields a return on investment at least as high as the "hurdle rate" applied by the firm's decision-makers on investment projects. For all 16 companies combined, the average conditional probabilities were:

Probability of technical success	0.57
Commercialization, given technical success	0.65
Financial success, given commercialization	0.74

The firms' overall average success rate is found by multiplying the three conditional probabilities, i.e., $0.57 \times 0.65 \times 0.74 = 0.27$.

The question arises, could a three-stage stochastic process with these average success probabilities lead without more to the kind of skew reward distributions revealed by our data? As one source of insight, a Monte Carlo simulation model was tested. Each of 156 "firms" was assumed to make three successive stochastic draws from rectangular distributions, one with mean probability 0.57 and range 0.14 to 1.00, one with mean probability 0.65 and range 0.30 to 1.00, and one with mean probability 0.74 and range 0.48 to 1.00. The product of the three probability draws was multiplied by a uniform profit potential of 1000. The resulting distribution of profits was highly concave on doubly logarithmic coordinates, with a slope coefficient (corresponding to the Pareto α) of -1.21 over all observations and -4.33 over the most profitable 39 observations. Top 10 percent outcomes accounted for 23.8 percent of total profits. Thus, the distribution was much less skew than any we have observed for cross sections of firms or individual inventions.[9] This could be because the simulation here abstracts from possible skewness in the size distribution of projects sampled by Mansfield et al. and perhaps also because the projects, mostly from large, well-established corporations, were less risky on average than those covered by our various surveys.

5 Gibrat processes

When the market value of a representative company grows or declines randomly from month to month (or year to year) by a stochastic multiplier, some version of a Gibrat process may be operating (see Gibrat, 1931; Ijiri

[9] Even less skewness emerged when the sampling distributions around Mansfield's three means were symmetrically normal (and bounded above at unity) rather than rectangular, e.g., with a Paretian slope of 6.65 for the most profitable 25 percent of sample observations.

and Simon, 1977). With the simplest Gibrat process, an initial value V_0 is altered sequentially over time by a string of random and independent multipliers $\epsilon_i, i = 1, T$, so that in the final period the value V_T is:

$$V_T = V_0 \, \epsilon_1 \ldots \epsilon_i \ldots \epsilon_T \; . \tag{3}$$

Taking logarithms, one obtains:

$$\ln V_T = \ln V_0 + \ln \epsilon_1 + \cdots + \ln \epsilon_i + \cdots + \ln \epsilon_T \; . \tag{4}$$

Under the central limit theorem, the sum of a string of random variables is asymptotically normally distributed. Thus, following what is called Gibrat's Law, $\ln V_T$ should be normally distributed, given sufficiently large T.

The weight of evidence from our innovation reward samples is that a log normal distribution fits the data better than plausible alternatives. The time series evidence from our IPO study suggests that a random walk of the Gibrat type operates. The two pieces of evidence together point toward some kind of Gibrat process as a source of differing innovation payoffs, and in particular, as the source of the observed skew distribution of market values resulting from equal-sized investments in individual high-technology IPOs.

We must nevertheless inquire whether there are sufficiently many independent random shocks ϵ_i to satisfy the "large numbers" requirement for asymptotic log normality. From the estimation of equation (2) above for 53 companies, the mean standard deviation of month-to-month stock value growth (in percentage terms) was found to be 18.61 percent, with a range of from 10.1 to 30.8 percentage points. This reveals a value evolution process that was on average quite noisy.

To see whether a strict Gibrat process with monthly random shocks of that magnitude would yield the observed IPO value distributions, a Monte Carlo experiment was conducted. An initial investment of $1000 was made in 100 hypothetical IPOs. Each investment thereupon grew on average by 1.03 percent per month, plus or minus a normally distributed error term with mean zero and standard deviation of 18.6 percent, for a total of 120 months.[10] The shares of the ten value leaders were computed and Pareto α slope values were estimated for all 100 companies and the 25 value leaders for each two-year interval, with results as follows:

	Top 10 Value Share	Pareto α $N = 100$	Pareto α Top 25
After 24 months	31.3%	0.93	2.29
After 48 months	48.7%	0.63	1.23
After 72 months	57.6%	0.51	1.07
After 96 months	62.0%	0.47	1.09
After 120 months	67.0%	0.41	1.00

Plainly, considerable skewness emerges as the Gibrat process unfolds. At the end of ten years, the firms comprising the top ten percent of the value

[10] I.e., the monthly multiplier was $1.0103 + \epsilon$, where ϵ was normally distributed with mean zero and standard deviation 0.186.

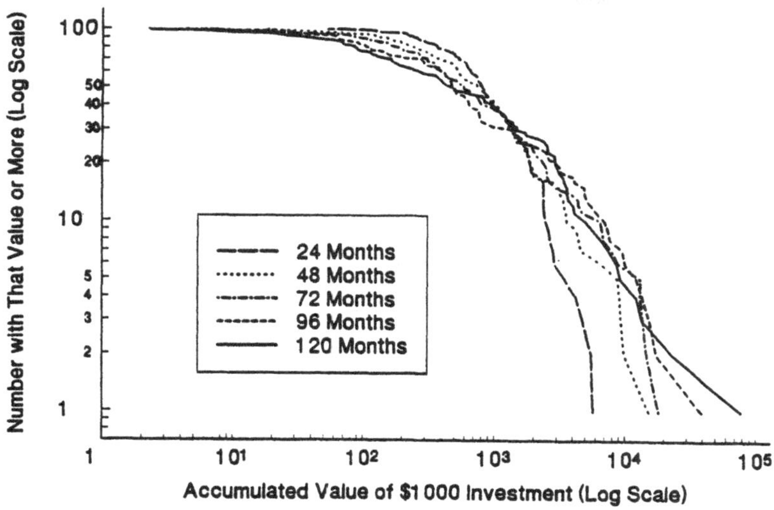

Fig. 4. Plot of Gibrat experiment outcomes on Pareto coordinates

distribution account for 67 percent of total sample value, compared to 62 percent for our IPO sample in 1995 when the universe is considered to be all 110 firms or 61 percent (for five firms) when only the 52 full-term survivors are included. The evolution of full-sample α estimates for the Monte Carlo experiment tracks closely the experience of the actual IPO companies. Slopes for the most successful 25 percent differ somewhat more, e.g., 0.72 for the actually observed full-term IPOs in 1995, compared to 1.00 after the experiment has run its course. Considerable similarity (but not identity, especially in the high-value tail) of distribution evolution patterns is suggested by comparing Fig. 3, which tracks 53 IPOs at five time benchmarks, and Fig. 4, which summarizes the Gibrat experiment's cross-sectional distribution.

If the distribution of company values resulting from the experiment were in fact log normal, the skewness parameter $\sqrt{\beta_1}$ would be insignificantly different from zero and the kurtosis parameter β_2 would be insignificantly different from 3.0 when logarithms are taken of the resulting value observations.[11] For the Gibrat experiment and 53 actual IPOs (including Microsoft), the measured parameters at roughly comparable time points were as follows:

	Gibrat experiment		53 actual IPOs	
	Skewness	Kurtosis	Skewness	Kurtosis
6 years, 1991	−0.27	3.33	0.27	2.85
10 years, 1995	−0.22	2.91	−0.03	3.09

[11] Where μ_k is the kth distribution moment, the coefficient of skewness is defined to be $\sqrt{\beta_1} = \mu_3/\mu_2^{3/2}$. The coefficient of kurtosis is defined as $\beta_2 = \mu_4/\mu_2^2$.

Table 2. Evolution of individual firm values in the Gibrat experiment

Firm rank at month 48	Firm value at month				Firm rank at month 120
	48	72	96	120	
1	15,150	18,064	15,270	22,934	2
2	9,748	13,489	7,555	1,715	28
3	9,181	14,454	38,848	76,848	1
4	8,987	12,915	13,475	5,528	9
5	8,610	12,931	9,850	8,437	6
6	6,455	6,502	5,912	3,517	14
7	4,513	1,453	758	1,433	30
8	4,369	2,221	6,869	3,256	17
9	4,150	7,846	3,123	2,801	22
10	3,493	2,464	4,803	1,034	38
11	3,456	6,312	1,361	933	40
12	3,342	1,289	2,564	4,022	11
13	3,292	2,440	1,429	12,016	4
14	3,101	1,565	571	459	50
15	3,022	8,758	2,404	2,833	20
16	2,702	843	1,381	1,090	37
17	1,951	4,228	4,743	2,098	27
18	1,932	4,661	4,964	3,501	15
19	1,899	132	64	66	86
20	1,833	1,323	743	917	41
21	1,830	6,754	9,400	4,847	10
22	1,821	388	962	3,583	13
23	1,663	1,879	7,245	9,055	5
24	1,655	1,189	2,899	2,920	19
25	1,655	975	748	241	61

For both the experiment and the actual IPO data, the measured skewness and kurtosis coefficients lie well within the 95 percent confidence bounds consistent with normality of the underlying distribution (see D'Agostino and Stephens, 1986, pp. 376–385). Thus, we conclude that, given the observed month-to-month changes in high-technology IPO market values, an approximately log normal cross sectional distribution of company common stock values could and plausibly did emerge after six to ten years of random growth in the marketplace.

Table 2 focuses on the 25 most valuable Gibrat experiment companies after 48 months have transpired, ranked in descending market value order, and shows how the market values of those companies evolved in the experiment's remaining years. Three of the top four companies at the 120-month mark had already emerged among the top 13 at the 48-month mark. Path dependence is suggested, when in fact what happened is that some companies experienced an early run of good fortune, after which there was (by the assumption of independent random growth draws in any given month) an equal probability that they would continue to grow as rapidly as other firms. The Pearsonian correlations among full-sample company values at various experimental time points were as follows:

	24 months	48 months	72 months	96 months
48 months	.500	1.000	.908	.654
72 months	.432	.908	1.000	.735
96 months	.276	.654	.735	1.000
120 months	.197	.537	.587	.852

All inter-correlations exceed 95 percent statistical significance thresholds; and the correlations between distributions separated by two years increase systematically after the first 24-month sorting-out has occurred. This facet of the experiment reveals that one must be wary of inferring path dependence causation after-the-fact when an early growth spurt is followed by continued rank leadership (see Feller, 1957, pp. 77–85; Scherer and Ross, 1990, pp. 141–142).

6 A more structured model

It would be premature, however, to conclude that the skew distributions observed in our various data sets arise solely from Gibrat processes of the simple form modelled thus far. The closest consonance has been found to the stock market performance of companies during the ten years after they have floated initial public offerings. Because of disclosure lags, the connection between the underlying events determining company profitability and common stock prices may be erratic. Many of the IPOs included within our sample sold numerous products, not always closely related, during the later years covered by our analysis, but most of our data cover single well-defined inventions or innovations. And at bottom, the Gibrat process is a "black box" under which random events of unspecified origin affect company value. We ask therefore, is it possible to identify stochastic models that yield invention and innovation reward size distributions like those we have observed, but that have a richer underlying structure reflecting the kinds of technical and market events known to occur when new products and processes are developed and commercialized?

To address this question, a much richer stochastic model was developed and tested in 20 initial variants covering some 2,400 innovation histories involving approximately 10,000 simulated company participants.[12] Extensions were then tested in 20 further runs. The model is essentially Gibratian in flavor, with a series of random draws affecting innovating and imitating firms' profit realizations multiplicatively. However, the stochastic events have been structured to conform as closely as possible to what has actually been recorded in numerous histories of patented inventions and innovations. By way of introduction, a profit potential of varying size comes into existence, firms compete through research and development to tap the profit potential, some succeed more rapidly than others and enter the market in a stochastic order that determines market shares, price competition may or

[12] All simulations were performed using FORTRAN programs modified for each set of varying assumptions.

may not appear to erode profit realizations, and new technologies emerge to render the subject technology obsolete.

6.1 The model parameters

Profit potential. The logical starting point for any realistic model is an annual profit potential that can be tapped by firms through innovation. Two quite different assumptions were modelled. In eight first-stage cases, the ith innovation's potential was determined by random draws from a rectangular distribution over the range 0–1. Each sampled variate was multiplied by \$1000 to determine the annual profit (or more exactly, quasi-rent) potential. However, draws of less than 0.1 were multiplied by 10 so that only about one case in 100 had a profit potential of less than \$100. Thus, most of the values were distributed rectangularly over the range \$100–1000. In 12 cases, random draws with replacement were made from a skew distribution replicating the distribution of {value added less payroll outlays} reported for four-digit manufacturing industries in the 1987 U.S. *Census of Manufactures*. Fifty "NEC" (not elsewhere classified) industries and 109 other industries below a specified size threshold were deleted, leaving 298. After rescaling, the range of annual skew quasi-rent potentials was from \$40 to \$2590, with mean of 210. The distribution was nearly log normal, with skewness coefficient of 1.00 and kurtosis coefficient of 3.56. However, it was less skew than any of the innovation reward distributions from our empirical samples; the top 10 percent of observations by number accounted for only 45 percent of total sample potential profits, and for the top 25 percent, the Pareto slope coefficient was 1.41.

Number of competing firms. Two approaches, exogenous and endogenous, were used to determine the number of firms seeking to exploit the profit potential. With exogenous entry, the number of firms was independent of quasi-rent potential, being set as 5.0 plus a normally distributed random variable with mean zero and standard deviation of 2.0. Values below 1.0 were truncated at 1.0 and values above 12.0 were truncated at 12.0. With endogenous entry, the number of firms N varied stochastically with the size of the innovation's quasi-rent potential. In rectangular potential cases, $N = (1.33 + .00667 \text{ POTENTIAL})\Phi$, where $\Phi = (1 + \sigma/4)$, σ being a normally distributed variate with mean 0 and standard deviation 1. Figure 5 illustrates the distribution of firm numbers as a function of the potential from simulation run 13. The number of firms per thousand dollars of quasi-rent potential increases less than proportionately with the potential, i.e., with an elasticity of roughly 0.75, reflecting the tendency (not modelled explicitly) for R&D costs per firm to rise when more firms are contending for a prize (see e.g. Reinganum, 1989). In the skew potential case, $N = (1.75 + .00625 \text{ POTENTIAL})\Phi$, where $\Phi = (1 + \sigma/4)$.

Date and order of entry. The dates T at which firms begin to tap the profit potential, and hence the order of entry, were determined, consistent with

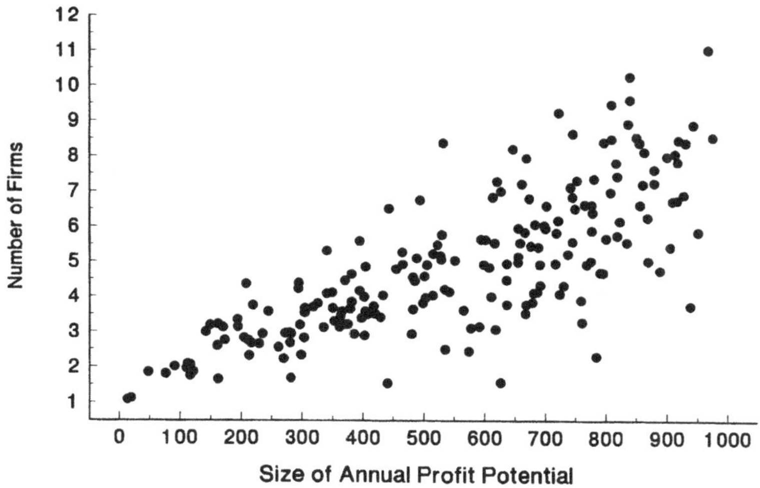

Fig. 5. Illustration of endogenously determined firm numbers

many models of research and development rivalry (see e.g. Reinganum, 1989, pp. 855–856), as the expected value of a hazard function $T = 1/h$, where h is 0.667 times a rectangularly distributed random variate over the interval 0–1. Before addition of one-half year for production startup, rounding, and truncation, T lay in a 90 percent confidence interval from 1.58 years to 30 years. Fractional values were rounded downward to the nearest integer.

First mover advantages and market shares. Firms were ranked according to their time of innovation (before rounding), and the earliest entrants enjoyed first mover advantages whose strength depended upon a random draw from a rectangular distribution. For the first 20 runs, strong first mover advantages applied with probability 0.1; middling advantages with probability 0.5; and weak advantages with probability 0.4. In the strongest first mover case, the market (and hence profit potential) share of a firm ranked $j + 1$ was 36.8 percent of firm j's share; with intermediate first mover advantages, 60.6 percent; and with the weakest advantages, 77.9 percent. Market shares were normalized to sum to unity in each time period. No changes in entry ranks were effected during any given 20-year run for the first 20 runs, although all firms' shares fell as additional firms entered.

Profit potential penetration rate. Most models of R&D rivalry have assumed that the full profit potential is appropriated as soon as at least one firm completes its R & D (for an exception, see Scherer, 1967). This is highly unrealistic; it takes time to penetrate a new product's potential market. Thus, in all runs, the rate of quasi-rent potential penetration for market participants following innovation by the first firm was determined by the function $(1 - e^{-pt})$, where p is a random variable drawn from a rectangular distribution bounded between 0.3 and 0.75 and t is a running time variable initialized at the first entrant's R&D completion date. Thus, if p = 0.5, the fraction of quasi-rents appropriated is 39.3 percent in the first year of sales, 63.2 percent in the second year, 91.8 percent in the fifth year, etc.

Market structure and price competition. Price competition among market participants can deplete the market's profit potential. For each year in which firms participated in an innovation market, a Herfindahl-Hirschman index was calculated. For HHI values greater than 0.333, joint profit maximization was assumed, with no depletion of the quasi-rent potential. For lower HHI values, firms were assumed to engage in Cournot rivalry, with the quasi-rent potential being dissipated more, the lower the HHI index. Thus, with a numbers-equivalent structural index (1/HHI = 0.250) implying four equal-size firms, 43.8 percent of the maximum profit potential is appropriated; with a numbers-equivalent of 12, 15.6 percent of the potential is appropriated.

Obsolescence. Paralleling the firm entry approach, the impact of competition from superior outside goods (Schumpeter's "creative destruction") was modelled in two ways. In the first ten runs, obsolescence was stochastically exogenous. From year six on, random draws were made from a 0–1 rectangular distribution, and in the first year with a value less than or equal to 0.1, obsolescence commenced. From that time on, the quasi-rent pool was eroded by $e^{-0.15\tau}$, where τ is the number of years elapsing from the onset of outside goods competition. On average, erosion started in year 11, but with considerable dispersion.[13] In the next ten runs and later variants, obsolescence was endogenous. Both the date at which outside competition commenced (but not earlier than year 3) and the rate at which it eroded the subject innovation's profitability were assumed to rise stochastically with the size of the potential (undissipated) profit pool. Figure 6a,b illustrates for Monte Carlo run 13 the dependence of starting years and erosion rates (vertical axis) upon the size of the quasi-rent potential (horizontal axis).

Discount rate. In all runs, individual firm quasi-rents were discounted to present value as of year zero at a 10 percent real interest rate.

6.2 Results

Table 3 summarizes the results of the first 20 Monte Carlo experiments embodying various combinations of the assumptions described above. In each run, 120 innovation histories were simulated. Some innovations, especially those with only one or two participating firms, dropped out because no firm completed its R&D project in time to have a discounted

---

[13] No explicit assumption is made concerning the source of outside innovations. They could come from outside firms or from one or more of the modelled firms.

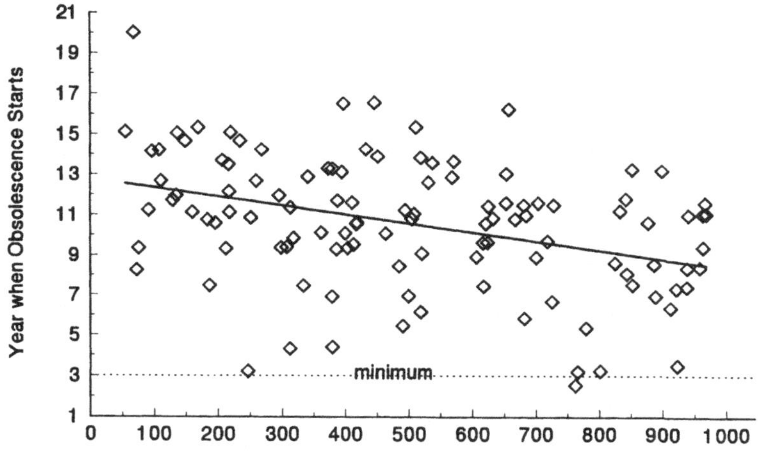

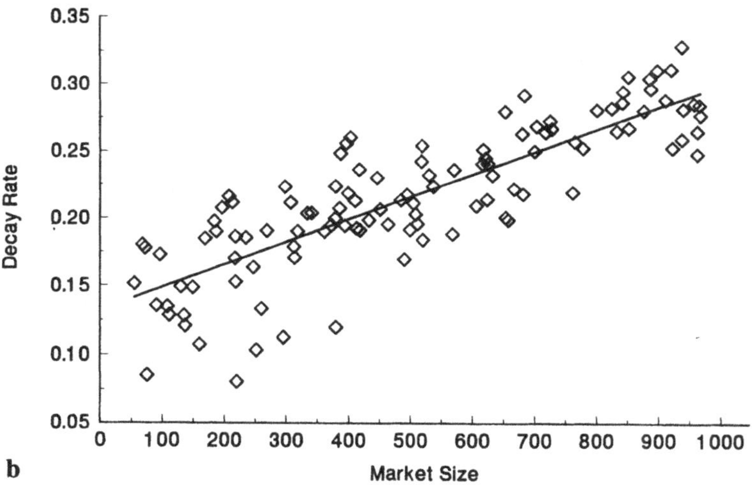

Fig. 6. a Endogenous determination of obsolescence starting year. **b** Endogenous determination of obsolescence decay rate

quasi-rent present value of 5 or more. (The maximum DPV for a first mover was 11,144; the mean 783.)

In Table 4, the discounted present value of quasi-rents for the first firm into the market is taken as dependent variable in an ordinary least squares regression with key experimental parameters as explanatory variables. The sample comprises 940 observations from eight runs, each representing the first run embodying a particular constellation of assumptions. The most powerful explanatory variable by a substantial margin, with a partial r^2 of 0.500, is the size of the quasi-rent potential firms competed to tap. The second-highest t-ratio (and partial r^2) is for the Herfindahl-Hirschman index (measured at midpoint year 10), in part because higher HHI values imply higher market shares for leading firms and also because values below

Table 3. Summary of the first 20 Monte Carlo experiments

Run	Potential	Entry	Obsol.	Parameters for first firm to innovate					
				No.	Top 10%	α_{ALL}	$\alpha_{25\%}$	Skew	Kurtosis
1	Rect.	Exog.	Exog.	120	27.3%	1.02	3.08	−0.15	2.44
2	Rect.	Exog.	Exog.	118	27.1%	0.90	3.19	−0.40	2.50
3	Rect.	Endog.	Exog.	119	24.9%	1.56	2.77	0.29	2.50
4	Rect.	Endog.	Exog.	118	23.5%	1.39	3.41	−0.35	4.02
5	Skew	Exog.	Exog.	118	54.5%	0.80	1.10	0.61	3.38
6	Skew	Exog.	Exog.	120	44.9%	0.87	1.31	0.29	3.57
7	Skew	Exog.	Exog.	118	50.5%	0.85	1.12	0.41	3.69
8	Skew	Endog.	Exog.	114	36.0%	1.11	1.53	0.38	4.24
9	Skew	Endog.	Exog.	115	40.2%	1.11	1.49	0.66	3.94
10	Skew	Endog.	Exog.	111	28.8%	1.27	2.67	0.04	3.61
11	Rect.	Exog.	Endog.	118	27.0%	0.88	2.82	−0.95	4.91
12	Rect.	Exog.	Endog.	118	24.2%	0.90	4.23	−0.48	2.32
13	Rect.	Endog.	Endog.	117	23.8%	1.61	2.87	−0.06	3.56
14	Rect.	Endog.	Endog.	118	22.8%	1.63	3.12	0.01	2.95
15	Skew	Exog.	Endog.	118	42.1%	0.85	1.61	0.35	2.44
16	Skew	Exog.	Endog.	118	31.8%	0.97	2.18	−0.14	2.62
17	Skew	Exog.	Endog.	118	44.8%	0.88	1.37	0.38	2.84
18	Skew	Endog.	Endog.	116	28.9%	1.45	2.19	0.49	3.21
19	Skew	Endog.	Endog.	115	25.7%	1.47	2.50	0.06	3.20
20	Skew	Endog.	Endog.	115	30.0%	1.24	2.26	0.10	3.14

Codes: Rect. = rectangular profit potential distribution, Endog. = endogenous, Exog. = exogenous.

0.333 precipitated profit-eroding price competition.[14] HHI values at year 10 fell below the 0.333 threshold in 42 percent of the cases. Thirteen percent of the first movers remained pure monopolists at that milestone. The third-highest t-ratio emerges for the year at which obsolescence began to set in. A variable measuring the erosion rate due to obsolescence is also significant. Together, the two variables imply an important role for Schumpeterian creative destruction. Because in most cases some firm's hazard function outcome let the firm complete its innovation and enter the market at year two or three, variations in initial starting dates had only a modest impact on quasi-rent values.[15] A year's delay implies a sacrifice amounting to 12.5

[14] The strength of first mover advantages was highly correlated with HHI indices and had little incremental explanatory power once HHI indices were included in the regression. A regression relating the HHI values to the number of firms and the strength of first mover advantages was as follows:

$$\underset{}{\text{HHI}} = \underset{(81.42)}{0.979} - \underset{(33.59)}{0.067}\ \text{NFIRMS} - \underset{(24.99)}{0.120}\ \text{FIRSTMOVE},\ R^2 = 0.716;$$

where NFIRMS is the number of firms participating in an innovation rivalry and the FIRSTMOVE index is scaled at 1 for the largest market share differential between first-moving and lower-ranked firms and 3 for the smallest. For pure monopoly cases (NFIRMS = 1), FIRSTMOVE was scaled at zero.

[15] The mean first-completion date, excluding values above 20, was at year 2.67; the median at year 2.30; the mode at year 2.01.

Table 4. Regression of firm 1's discounted present value on model parameters

Variable	Coefficient	t-ratio	Mean
Intercept	−465.48	3.72	–
Profit potential	1.79	30.51	391
Starting date	−98.07	5.44	2.67
Penetration rate	431.33	3.29	0.53
Obsolescence date	32.48	7.17	11.12
Obsolescence rate	−1591.94	4.20	0.17
HHI index, year 10	1514.21	17.72	0.45
Endogenous entry	−166.62	4.83	0.50
Skew distribution	−4.98	0.14	0.50

N = 940; mean dependent variable value = 783; standard deviation = 808; R^2 = 0.607

percent of average first mover discounted quasi-rents for the full sample. With endogenous entry, quasi-rents are reduced on average by 21 percent relative to the full-sample mean value, all else equal. Skew profit potentials reduce first-mover discounted present values by about one quarter relative to full-sample means, but with considerable variance.

We return to Table 3 to inquire which experimental conditions led to quasi-rent size distributions most closely consonant with those we have observed empirically. For each run, innovations were ranked in descending order of the quasi-rents realized by the first mover. Examining first the shares of total discounted quasi-rents in any given run appropriated by the most profitable ten percent of the first movers, we find results approaching those observed empirically only in runs 5–7, 15, and 17 – all with skew profit potentials and exogenous entry. In only two cases (runs 5 and 7) did the leading firms secure 50 percent or more of total sample quasi-rents, i.e., roughly the same share as the drug innovators, and five to eleven percentage points less than the high-technology venture investments and IPOs (compare Table 1). Those five cases, and especially the skew potential, exogenous entry cases, are the only ones with Pareto slope coefficients for firms in the right-hand quarter of the size distribution anywhere near those observed empirically – i.e, in the range of 1.10 to 1.37. None of the simulations yielded right-hand tail slope coefficients as low as those observed for the venture startups and IPOs. Both endogenous entry and endogenous obsolescence (Schumpeterian creative destruction) reduce leading firm quasi-rent shares and steepen distribution function tail slopes.

When logarithms are taken of discounted first-mover quasi-rents, the skewness coefficients for their size distributions scatter fairly tightly about the zero value consistent with a log normal distribution.[16] The average skewness coefficient over 20 runs is +0.08. The distributions exhibit a slight tendency toward higher kurtosis coefficients than the 3.0 value that would prevail if the size distributions were strictly log normal (last column of Table 3).

[16] A 90 percent confidence interval around the zero expectation extends to plus or minus 0.36 with 118 observations.

None of the 20 simulations generated a concentration of quasi-rents as high as was observed empirically for individual patents or related patent bundles. To explore whether some important stochastic element was overlooked, 20 additional runs embodying three changes were computed.

One possible limitation may have been the assumption that first movers' relative market positions persisted throughout the experiment, with no displacement from later movers offering marginally superior products or sustaining more effective marketing campaigns. To pursue this lead, runs 21 through 28 accepted the basic parameter assumptions of runs 13–14 and 18–20, but added a variant of Gibrat-like random growth. For each year after at least one firm completed its R&D project, the individual firm market shares determined on the basis of first-mover principles were subjected to a random annual multiplier $(1 + \mu)$, where μ was normally distributed with mean zero and standard deviation 0.1. The altered market shares were then normalized to sum to unity. Random growth increments or shortfalls experienced in any given year were carried forward into later years, so the Gibrat effects were cumulative. The results are presented in the first panel of Table 5. If anything, less skewness emerges than in otherwise similar runs 13–14 and 18–20. The top ten percent shares are lower on average, especially for the runs tapping a skew quasi-rent potential, and the right-hand tail distribution slopes are steeper on average. The highest first mover share and the least steep slope are found in each category among the simulation runs without random market share changes. Evidently, Gibrat processes do not necessarily increase skewness when high concentration materializes at the outset as a result of first mover advantages and/or random sampling of quasi-rent potentials. For the most dominant firms in such cases, the probability of *further* market share gains through particularly lucky random draws is small.

In some of the Gibrat runs, the market shares of first movers were eventually exceeded by those of the second or third movers. Despite discounting, later movers' total discounted quasi-rents exceeded those of first movers in from one to eight cases per run. Because of such rank changes and also because firms that are not the first to complete their R&D projects can make significant innovative contributions, quasi-rents were merged and arrayed in seven cases for both the first and second movers, and in two illustrative cases, for the first three entrants. The results are summarized in the second and third panels of Table 5. The total quasi-rent share of first- and second-moving firms ranked among the combined top ten percent increased in every case relative to the top ten percent shares for first movers only. For upper quartile slopes, on the other hand, the differences between first-mover-only and combined first and second mover distributions were erratic.

In runs 1–20, the probability that first movers would achieve the largest proportional disparity between their market shares and those of later movers was 0.1. Six additional runs, numbers 29–34, increased the probability of the most extreme disparity to 0.3, with assignment to the intermediate and weakest first mover cases each accorded probabilities of 0.35. These stronger first mover assumptions were simulated for analogues

Table 5. Summary of further simulation run results

Run	Potential Entry		Obsol.	Parameters for first firm to innovate					
				No.	Top 10%	α_{ALL}	$\alpha_{25\%}$	Skew	Kurtosis
With Gibrat growth process added									
21G	Rect.	Endog.	Endog.	119	22.2%	1.37	3.28	−13.51	152
22G	Rect.	Endog.	Endog.	119	21.5%	1.07	4.04	−2.58	18.9
23G	Rect.	Endog.	Endog.	120	25.1%	1.08	3.35	−0.71	4.35
24G	Rect.	Endog.	Endog.	120	22.4%	1.28	3.85	−0.40	3.22
25G	Skew	Exog.	Endog.	120	35.5%	0.95	2.00	0.16	2.64
26G	Skew	Exog.	Endog.	120	40.1%	0.89	1.60	0.21	2.83
27G	Skew	Exog.	Endog.	120	38.9%	0.95	1.54	0.14	2.92
28G	Skew	Exog.	Endog.	119	32.4%	0.95	2.11	−0.08	2.56
First and second entrants									
5–2	Skew	Exog.	Exog.	229	56.1%	0.78	1.15	0.49	3.64
13–2	Rect.	Endog.	Endog.	226	25.4%	1.22	2.83	−1.16	9.61
14–2	Rect.	Endog.	Endog.	230	25.5%	1.10	2.71	−1.68	11.92
17–2	Skew	Exog.	Endog.	228	45.6%	0.90	1.41	0.46	2.89
25–2	Skew	Exog.	Endog.	233	39.1%	0.97	1.96	0.37	2.79
26–2	Skew	Exog.	Endog.	231	42.1%	0.88	1.61	0.16	3.22
27–2	Skew	Exog.	Endog.	230	40.0%	0.91	1.62	0.13	3.02
First three entrants									
14–3	Rect.	Endog.	Endog.	317	30.0%	1.00	2.65	−1.02	6.62
17–3	Skew	Exog.	Endog.	320	48.6%	0.81	1.38	0.28	3.20
Stronger first mover advantages									
29	Rect.	Exog.	Endog.	118	25.4%	0.96	3.44	−0.55	3.08
30	Rect.	Exog.	Endog.	119	24.9%	1.04	3.53	−0.41	2.66
31	Skew	Exog.	Endog.	118	39.1%	0.84	1.77	0.03	2.75
32	Skew	Exog.	Endog.	119	37.0	0.97	1.68	0.16	3.06
33G	Skew	Exog.	Endog.	119	32.5	0.98	2.23	0.00	2.51
34G	Skew	Exog.	Endog.	120	37.6	0.79	1.86	0.01	2.40
PIMS market share determination									
35	Rect.	Endog.	Endog.	116	21.0	1.66	4.00	−0.27	2.88
36	Rect.	Endog.	Endog.	119	21.2	1.38	3.82	−0.90	5.60
37	Rect.	Endog.	Endog.	118	19.7	1.29	4.87	−1.19	6.12
38	Skew	Endog.	Endog.	113	27.9	1.25	2.10	−0.12	3.69
39	Skew	Endog.	Endog.	115	26.6	1.30	2.98	0.04	2.65
40	Skew	Endog.	Endog.	116	29.8	1.25	2.48	0.22	3.13
35–3	Rect.	Endog.	Endog.	313	28.6	0.87	3.00	−0.70	4.07
38–2	Skew	Endog.	Endog.	210	32.3	0.83	2.25	−0.48	3.42

of runs 11–12, 15–17, and 25–28. The results are presented in the fourth panel of Table 5. Surprisingly, there was very little difference in top ten percent quasi-rent shares or upper quartile slopes between the averages for runs 29–34, with stronger first mover advantages, and their earlier counterparts.

Finally, a referee suggested that an implausibly high number of innovation participants resulted from the endogenous innovation race participation equation and that the distribution of market shares might be more realistically determined by using an empirical formula derived from PIMS (Profit Impact of Market Strategy) studies:[17]

$$MS_j = \left(\frac{1}{n}\right)\sum_{i=j}^{n}\left(\frac{1}{i}\right); \quad j = 1,\ldots,n \ , \tag{5}$$

where MS_j is the market share of the jth firm among a total of n firms. To explore these possibilities, the coefficients on POTENTIAL in the endogenous firm number determining equations were reduced by 30 percent for the rectangular case and 20 percent for the skew case, leading to decreases in both the maximum and average number of firms.[18] Market shares were determined precisely according to equation (5) with probability 0.5. To allow differences in the strength of first mover advantages, market shares generated by equation (5) were raised to the exponent 0.8 with probability 0.25 (reducing the asymmetry of normalized market shares) and to the exponent 1.25 with probability 0.25 (increasing the asymmetry of shares). Other assumptions were as in simulation runs 13–14 and 18–20. The last panel of Table 5 reports the first mover quasi-rent results of six simulation runs embodying these changes, three for rectangular profit potential cases and three for skew potential cases. Data for two representative runs including the first, second, and third entrants are also presented. The runs for first movers alone exhibit less skewness than their original counterparts. The three-firm simulations (including those not reported in Table 5) had full-sample α values as low as those obtained in earlier simulations, but right-hand tail α values were higher and top ten percent share values were lower. Thus, the revised assumptions did not provide a superior approximation to observed real-world innovation reward size distributions.

Figure 7a–d graphs on Pareto coordinates four representative size distributions from the first 20 simulation runs – three with distribution parameter outcomes most closely approximating those observed empirically and one (from run 13) with one of the lowest top ten percent first mover quasi-rent shares. All are concave to the origin, as were all distributions constructed from actual data. None exhibits an outlying value some distance removed from the main cluster of observations, as emerged with the detailed German patent value data (Fig. 1) and also the Harvard University patent royalty and drug profit distributions reported in Scherer (1998). However, such outliers appeared in earlier trial simulations (not explicitly reported here) and cannot be ruled out for alternative random draw constellations. Endogenous entry run 13 stands out for its consistently steep right-hand tail slope.

---

[17] See e.g. Buzzell and Gale (1987), who do not, however, report the market share formula identified by the referee.

[18] As a result, the average number of firms was reduced to 3.52 in the rectangular case and 2.42 in the skew case, compared to 4.47 and 2.63 in comparable previous simulations.

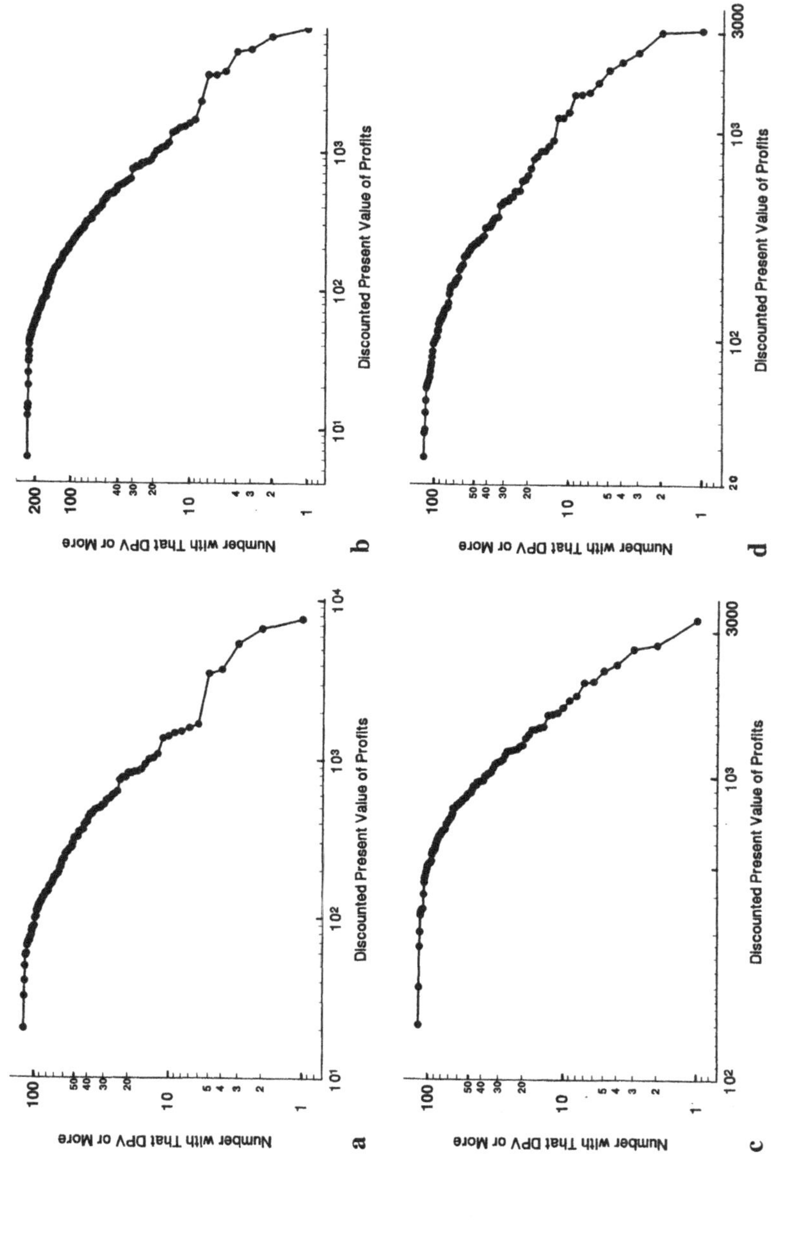

Fig. 7. a Plot of run 5: Exogenous entry, skew potential, first firm profits only. **b** Plot of run 5: exogenous entry, skew potential, first and second firm profits. **c** Plot of run 13: endogenous entry, rectangular potential, first firm profits only. **d** Plot of run 17: exogenous entry, skew potential, first firm profits only

6.3 Evaluation

To the extent that the simulation runs track with reasonable fidelity the kinds of uncertainties encountered in real-world innovation histories, it would appear that ex ante innovation profit potentials are more likely to be skew-distributed than rectangularly distributed, and entry into innovation "markets" appears to be approximated better by the assumption of exogeneity than endogeneity.

Skewness of the innovation profit potentials seems eminently plausible. The distributions of manufactured product sales at the four- or five-digit level of disaggregation are known to be skew, and although most innovation markets are probably narrower subsets of five-digit product categories, skewness appears to persist at the quite narrow seven-digit level of disaggregation.

Because inventive and innovative efforts are known to be responsive to the pull of demand (see Schmookler, 1966; Scherer, 1982) and because would-be innovators plainly search aggressively for profit-earning opportunities, our finding that an endogenous entry assumption yields less realistic size distributions than an exogenous entry assumption merits deeper critical scrutiny. If innovative profit potentials are skew-distributed and contests to appropriate them are of a winner-take-all character, skew outcome distributions could result even if innovation races attracted sufficiently many entrants to leave zero ex ante profit expectations, as a large class of theoretical models postulates (see Reinganum, 1989). However, empirical studies by Mansfield et al. (1981, p. 627), Gort and Klepper (1982, p. 629), and Utterback (1994, Chapter 2) reveal that in the great majority of cases, first movers do not appropriate all the profits from an innovation race. It is frequently possible to invent around first movers' patents, and most innovations attract a stream of rival firms, some early, some late, offering variants and imitations. Two phenomena appear to explain the apparent failure of entry to rise systematically (even if stochastically) with the size of an innovation profit potential. For one, it may be so difficult to predict in advance the existence and size of an innovation profit potential that matching of entry attempts to profit prospects operates quite imperfectly – so much so that little or no correlation exists between the profit potential and the number of firms, holding R&D costs constant (see also on this problem Richardson, 1960). Second, as Henderson and Cockburn conclude from a detailed analysis of rivalry in new drug development (1994a, b), firms' capabilities to undertake innovations are often heterogeneous and specialized. An imperfect match between capabilities and opportunities undermines the correlation between profit potentials and entry.

7 Conclusion

From our research and research by others, e.g., on invention patent renewal rates (see e.g. Lanjouw et al., 1996), it is clear that strong regularities pervade the size distribution of rewards realized on technological innovations.

The distribution is highly skew, so that a relative handful of successful innovators reap the lion's share of profits from innovative efforts. For the richest data, a log normal distribution provides the best overall fit. In this paper we have attempted to determine what stochastic processes might lie behind the observed size distributions. Some kind of iterated proportional stochastic growth process of the sort first proposed by Robert Gibrat seems the most plausible candidate. The simplest Gibrat processes yield over plausible time intervals log normal distributions with parameters approximating those we have observed in the real world. However, the stochastic events experienced in the evolution of a technological innovation almost surely have a richer stochastic structure than does the simplest Gibrat process. In this paper we have attempted to characterize that structure and determine through simulation experiments whether realistic size distributions emerge. Some of the experiments, and especially those which tap skew profit potentials and assume stochastically exogenous entry into innovation rivalries, yield size distributions approximating those observed in the real world. The simulated distributions, however, do not probe the extremes of skewness found for patented inventions. To approximate even more closely what occurs in the uncertain world of innovation rivalry, further stochastic elements may have to be identified.

References

Brav A, Gompers PA (1997) Myth or reality? The long-run underperformance of initial public offerings: Evidence from venture and nonventure capital-backed companies. Journal of Finance 52: 1791–1821

Buzzell RD, Gale BT (1987) The PIMS principles: Linking strategy to performance. Free Press, New York

D'Agostino RB, Stephens MA (eds) (1986) Goodness-of-fit techniques. Marcel Dekker, New York

DeVany A, Walls WD (1996) Bose-Einstein dynamics and adaptive contracting in the motion picture industry. Economic Journal 106: 1493–1514

Feller W (1957) An introduction to probability theory and its applications, 2nd edn. Wiley, New York

Gibrat R (1931) Les inegalities economiques. Recueil Sirey, Paris

Gort M, Klepper, S (1982) Time paths in the diffusion of product innovations. Economic Journal 92: 630–653

Grabowski H, Vernon J (1990) A new look at the returns and risks to pharmaceutical R&D. Management Science 36: 804–821

Grabowski H, Vernon J (1994) Returns on new drug introductions in the 1980s. Journal of Health Economics 13: 383–406

Harhoff D, Scherer FM, Vopel K (1998) Exploring the tail of patent value distributions. Working paper, Center for European Economic Research, Mannheim

Harhoff D, Narin F, Scherer FM, Vopel K (1999) Citation frequency and the value of patented inventions. Review of Economics and Statistics 81: 511–515

Henderson R, Cockburn I (1994a) Racing to invest: The dynamics of competition in ethical drug discovery. Journal of Economics and Management Strategy 3: 481–519

Henderson R, Cockburn I (1994b) Measuring competence? Exploring firm effects in pharmaceutical research. Strategic Management Journal 15: 63–84

Ijiri Y, Simon H (1977) Skew distributions and the sizes of business firms. North-Holland, Amsterdam

Lanjouw JO, Pakes A, Putnam J (1996) How to count patents and value intellectual property: Uses of patent renewal and application data. Working paper, Yale University, New Haven

Mandelbrot B (1963) New methods in statistical economics. Journal of Political Economy 71: 421–440

Mansfield E, Wagner S et al. (1977) The production and application of new industrial technology. Norton, New York

Mansfield E, Schwartz M, Wagner S (1981) Imitation costs and patents: An empirical study. Economic Journal 91: 907–918

Reinganum JF (1989) The timing of innovation: Research, development, and diffusion. In: Schmalensee RL, Willig RD (eds) Handbook of industrial organization, vol I, pp. 849–908. North-Holland, Amsterdam

Richardson GB (1960) Information and investment. Oxford University Press, Oxford

Scherer FM (1967) Research and development resource allocation under rivalry. Quarterly Journal of Economics 81: 359–394

Scherer FM (1982) Demand-pull and technological innovation: Schmookler revisited. Journal of Industrial Economics 30: 225–238

Scherer FM (1998) The size distribution of profits from innovation. Annales d'Economie et de Statistique no. 49/50: 495–516

Scherer FM, Ross DR (1990) Industrial market structure and economic performance, 3rd edn. Houghton-Mifflin, Boston

Schmookler J (1966) Invention and economic growth. Harvard University Press, Cambridge, MA

Utterback J (1994) Mastering the dynamics of technological innovation. Harvard Business School Press, Boston

The determinants of pharmaceutical research and development expenditures

Henry Grabowski, John Vernon

Department of Economics, Duke University, Durham, NC 27708, USA
(e-mail: grabow@econ.duke.edu)

Abstract. Since the late 1970s, pharmaceutical R&D has grown at a rapid rate relative to sales and other variables. In this paper, we examine the determinants of pharmaceutical R&D using a pooled data sample of 11 major drug firms over the period 1974 to 1994. We find that expected returns and cash flows are important explanatory variables of firm research intensities during this period. This is consistent with our results for an earlier sample period characterized by very different growth patterns on R&D.

Key words: Pharmaceuticals – R&D – Innovation – Cash flow – Expected returns

JEL-classification: L65, O31, O33

1 Introduction

In an earlier paper, we examined the determinants of pharmaceutical R&D outlays in the United States for the period spanning the early 1960s through the mid 1970s (Grabowski and Vernon, 1981). This period was characterized by a dramatic decline in new drug introductions together with relatively stagnant growth in R&D expenditures. The drug industry was adjusting to increased regulatory controls and other factors during this time. In our regression analyses, we found that lagged returns on R&D and cash flow availability were important determinants of R&D investment

---

Paper presented at the 1998 World Conference of the International Joseph A. Schumpeter Society, Vienna, June 13–16, 1998.

behavior. In particular, we found that lagged R&D returns exhibited a significant downward overall trend during this period and this, in turn, exerted an important restraining effect on R&D investment outlays.

In this paper, we examine the determinants of pharmaceutical R&D for the more recent time period 1974 to 1994. In contrast with the earlier one, this period has been characterized by a rapid growth in industry R&D expenditures. Since the late 1970s, R&D expenditures have grown at more than 10% annually in real terms (PhRMA, 1997). Furthermore, R&D-to-sales percentages have increased by several percentage points. We wish to examine the factors underlying these dramatic changes in R&D investment behavior. For this purpose, we utilize an analytical model with the same basic structure as the one employed in our earlier paper.

The plan of the paper is as follows. In the next section, we review past work, together with recent trends and developments. The following sections present our model and the empirical findings. The final section considers policy implications and discusses important issues for continuing academic research.

2 Evolution of pharmaceutical R&D: prior work and current trends

2.1 The post-1962 period

In our earlier paper, we examined the determinants of firm research intensities (R&D-to-sales ratios) for a pooled sample of ten drug firms over the period 1962–1975. This was a period in which firm research intensities exhibited a moderately declining overall trend. This was in contrast to the earlier post-World War II period in which firm research intensities were expanding over time.

A major event in 1962 was the passage of Kefauver-Harris Amendments to the Food, Drug and Cosmetic Act. This occurred in the aftermath of the Thalidomide incident.[1] This 1962 law created the investigational new drug (IND) process and the requirement that all new drugs demonstrate proof of efficacy as well as safety before FDA approval (Wardell and Lasagna, 1975). The FDA took several years to implement fully all of the changes from the 1962 law. Several academic studies were performed analyzing industry development times and R&D costs during this period. They found that development times increased by several years after 1962, and R&D costs per new drug introduction also increased several fold (Baily, 1972; Wardell and Lasagna, 1975).

A key determinant of research intensities in our model is the expected return on R&D. With R&D times and costs per NCE rising significantly during the post-62 period, it is plausible to postulate the returns on R&D would be falling. In our earlier analysis of R&D determinants, we utilized a proxy measure of the expected returns on R&D. The numerator of this measure was a firm's sales of its recent new drug introductions and the

[1] Thalidomide was a drug which produced fetal deformities in pregnant women. It had been introduced in several European countries but not in the US.

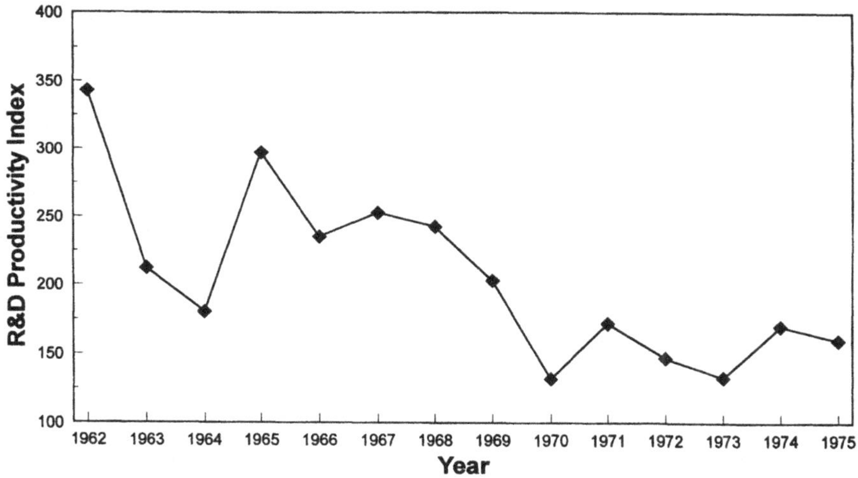

Fig. 1. Aggregate R&D Productivity Index, 1962–1975

denominator was its lagged R&D expenditures. We labeled this as an R&D productivity index.

Figure 1 shows a plot of the aggregate trend in the R&D productivity index variable for the ten firms in our sample over the period 1962–1975. It indicates that new product sales per R&D investment dollar fell rather significantly during this period. This pattern of declining returns is consistent with the finding of several other studies for the post-62 period (see for example, Baily, 1972; Schwartzman, 1976).

The other major explanatory variable of R&D in our earlier work was the availability of cash flows. We found that cash flows remained relatively stable relative to overall sales over most of the post-62 period. This expanding supply of internally generated funds helped to buffer the observed decline in R&D intensities. However, as the lower returns on the new drug introductions cumulated over time, cash flow margins were also starting to be affected adversely. By the early 1970s many major drug successes of the earlier post-war era were also coming off patent and subject to increasing competitive pressures.

In subsequent work, we analyzed the distribution of returns on new drug introductions in the 1970s and 1980s (Grabowski and Vernon, 1990, 1994). We found that this distribution is highly skewed.[2] In particular, a small number of drugs in the right hand tail of the distribution have a disproportionate effect on the mean returns realized by particular firms and the industry as a whole in any period. These top decile drugs are often referred to in the industry as "blockbusters," and the search for them is a key driver of the R&D process.

The period between the end of World War II and the early 1960s saw the introduction of many important advances that were also big winners from

[2] This skewness of returns is a characteristic of returns distribution in several other research-intensive industries (Scherer, 1998).

an economic perspective. There were many significant new antibiotic drugs, but this period also witnessed the introduction of hydrocortisone and several other corticoids, the thiazide diuretic drugs, major and minor tranquilizers, and the initial birth control products (Pharmacy Times, 1976).

After the passage of the 1962 Amendments, the industry was faced not only with adjusting to more stringent regulatory requirements, but also the prospect of diminished technological opportunities in many of therapeutic classes that had previously experienced major advances. There were certainly important drug innovations in the post-62 period, most notably the first cephalosporin antibiotics in 1964 and the introduction of the beta blockers in 1968 (Wardell and Lasagna, 1975).[3] However, the main approach to drug R&D in this era was random screening of candidates. The ability to find new drugs that were advances over established ones became increasingly harder and costlier in many therapeutic classes.

The first half of the 1970s was characterized by fewer major new drugs, and a decline in the mean returns to R&D (Grabowski and Vernon, 1990). The leading firms began to focus their R&D activities on new therapeutic targets and approaches. As the 1970s progressed, it was clear that the industry was facing a crossroads with respect to its R&D performance. Some observers saw the drug industry as perhaps entering a period of technological maturity (Scherer, 1978).

2.2 Drug innovation since 1975

The period of the late 1970s represented a turning point with respect to the innovative performance of the industry. In particular, an important milestone was the introduction of Tagamet (cimetidine) by SmithKline. This drug not only represented a major advance in the treatment of ulcers but also was seen as an important validation of the emerging "rational drug design" approach to drug discovery and development. In particular, the Tagamet molecule was designed to block specific cell receptors (histamine H_2 receptors) known to affect the process of acid secretion. Tagamet was the first of the histamine H_2 receptor inhibitors, and it yielded high private and social returns (Geweke and Weisbrod, 1981; Grabowski and Vernon, 1990). By 1980, it had become the largest selling drug worldwide. It was replaced as the top-ranked selling drug by Zantac in 1987, another H_2 blocker that claimed certain advantages relative to Tagamet in terms of drug interactions and dosage convenience.

The new rational drug design approach and expanding disease targets produced many new drugs that could be classified as both major therapeutic and economic successes. Table 1 provides a list of significant compounds

---

[3] The adverse effects of increased US regulatory controls during this period are illustrated by the differential behavior of US and UK regulatory authorities toward propranolol (Inderal), the first of the beta blockers class. This compound was initially approved in the UK in 1965 with indications for hypertension, angina and arrhythmias. It was approved 2.5 years later in the United States, but only for the very narrow indication of arrhythmias (Wardell and Lasagna, 1975). It was not until July 1976 that it was approved in the United States for hypertension, the indication with the largest number of patients.

Table 1. Significant drug innovations, 1978–1994

Year	New drug	Primary use	Mode of action
1978	Tagamet	Ulcers	H_2 receptor antagonist
1981	Capoten	Hypertension	ACE inhibitor
1982	Zovirax	Herpes Virus	Nucleoside
1982	Procardia	Hypertension	Calcium channel blocker
1983	Sandimmune	Transplantation	Interleukin-2 inhibitor
1984	Augmentin	Antibiotic	Beta lactam inhibitor
1985	Seldane	Allergies	H_1 receptor antagonist
1986	Cipro	Antibiotic	DNA gyrase inhibitor
1987	Mevacor	Cholesterol reduction	HMG-C_oA reductase inhibitor
1987	Retrovir	AIDS	Nucleoside/RT inhibitor
1988	Prozac	Depression	Serotonin Re-uptake inhibitor
1989	Epogen	Anemia	Erythrocyte growth factor
1989	Prilosec	Ulcers	Proton pump inhibitor
1990	Diflucan	Antifungal	Structural inhibitor
1990	Clozaril	Schizophrenia	Atypical tricyclic
1991	Biaxin	Antibiotic	Protein synthesis inhibitor
1991	Zofran	Nausea/vomiting	5Ht3 antagonist
1991	Neupogen	Cancer adjunct	Neutrophil growth factor
1993	Taxol	Ovarian cancer	Anti-microtubule
1993	Imitrex	Migraine	5HT1 agonist
1994	Risperdal	Schizophrenia	D2/5HT2 antagonists

introduced between 1978 and 1994. The drugs on this list represent a new mode of action for treating particular diseases. They were also major commercial successes, given that they all achieved global peak sales of at least one half billion dollars (measured in 1998 dollars). The primary indications for these drugs include many categories which previously had little or no adequate drug treatments (herpes, transplantation, AIDS, migraine headaches, schizophrenia, etc.). Other drugs in this table provided benefits in terms of better side effect profiles and patient tolerability for the treatment of widespread medical problems (i.e., hypertension, cholesterol reduction, depression, etc.).

In most cases, the drugs listed in Table 1 were the first movers in a new chemical family of drug products (Green, 1998). Competition in these classes center around new product introductions and is subject to both incremental and generational advances over time. Many follow-on introductions in a new class also achieve sales in the top deciles of the returns distribution. Indeed, while strong first-mover advantages exist in pharmaceuticals, the second or third introduction in a class sometimes overtakes the pioneering one as the drug of choice.[4]

It is clear that the past two decades have witnessed an impressive renaissance in drug innovation and R&D competition that was very broad in its scope. The main hypothesis of the present paper is that R&D intensities in pharmaceuticals have increased over time because major new drug introductions have generated favorable expected returns to R&D investment,

[4] For analyses of competition in two major therapeutic classes, see Suslow (1996) and Ellison et al. (1997).

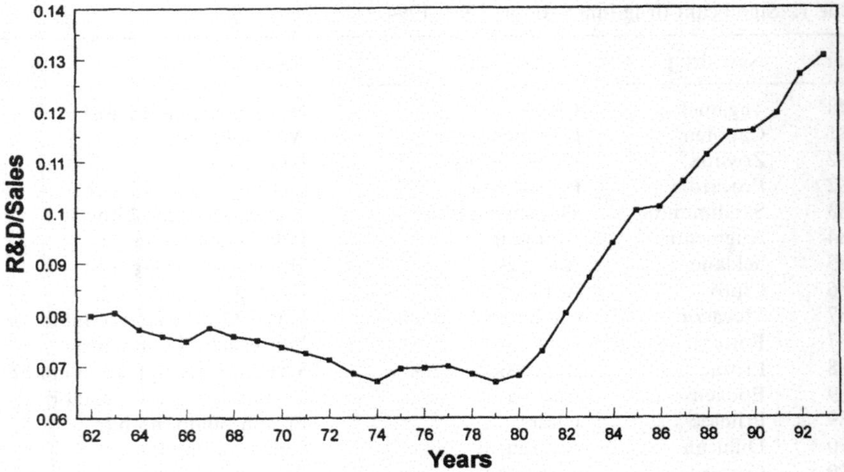

Fig. 2. Aggregate R&D/Sales, 1962–1993

and expanding industry cash flows have provided a readily available (and relatively low cost) source of funds to finance R&D. This will be examined in terms of a regression model that is discussed in the next section.

The dramatic changes in research intensities that have occurred over time in this industry are illustrated in Fig. 2. This shows the trend in the aggregate R&D-to-sales ratios for seven firms that reported R&D data over the full 33-year period, 1962 to 1993.[5] This graph shows that R&D intensity was generally declining in the period 1962 to 1974, that it stabilized in the 1975 to 1980 period, and it has increased almost in a linear fashion since 1980. The value achieved in 1993 is close to double what it was at the minimal point in 1974. We will examine the determinants of firm R&D intensities for the 1974 to 1994 period using an economic model that is similar in structure to our earlier work.

3 The R&D investment decision

In accordance with basic economic theory, the R&D investment decision is determined by the intersection of the marginal rate of return on investment schedule (mrr) and the marginal cost of capital schedule (mcc). The mrr schedule is obtained by arranging potential R&D projects in order of decreasing rates of return, and the mcc schedule reflects the opportunity cost of alternative investments for the firm.

Figure 3 shows the determination of the optimal amount of investment, R*. The mcc schedule here consists of two horizontal segments, representing a lower cost of internal funds and a higher cost of new equity financing, and

[5] The seven firms are Abbott, Bristol Myers, Lilly, Merck, Pfizer, Schering Plough and Upjohn. They are the seven firms common to our prior and current regression analyses (as discussed in Section 4).

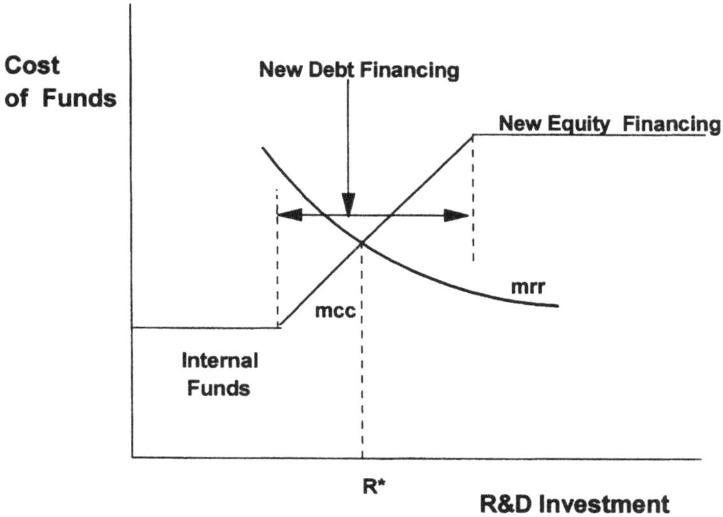

Fig. 3. The R&D investment decision

a rising connecting segment that represents the cost of new debt financing. Recent work on firm investment behavior supports the hypothesis shown here that the cost of internal funds is less than that for new debt and equity financing. There have been many theoretical reasons given for the difference in the cost of internal and external funds. They include transaction costs, tax advantage, agency problems, costs of financial distress, and asymmetric information (for a recent survey, see Hubbard, 1998).

In the pharmaceutical industry, the problems of great uncertainty about the outcome of R&D, the length of the R&D process (12–14 years), and asymmetric information combine to make the difference between internal and external funds especially important. In addition, unlike fixed investment in plant and equipment, the outcome of drug R&D is simply new knowledge, which may or may not have value.[6]

Algebraically, the optimal level of investment, R*, is obtained by solving the equation,

$$\mathrm{mrr}(R,X) = \mathrm{mcc}(R,Z) \qquad (1)$$

where R = investment expenditures in R&D; X = a vector of variables influencing the return from new drug R&D; and Z = a vector of variables

[6] The extremely difficult problem of raising funds for R&D in small biotech firms with little or no cash flow highlights this point. The head of one such biotech firm indicated that in order to obtain venture capital, a new project must have the ability to generate a 25–35 percent annual rate of return (US House of Representatives Hearings, 1995). In addition, suppliers of venture capital must see a viable exit strategy for getting their money out of the company – that is, through an initial public offering, a merger, or a corporate partnership with an established company. Many such corporate partnerships are now taking place in the industry where established companies with large cash flows supply funds to small biotech firms.

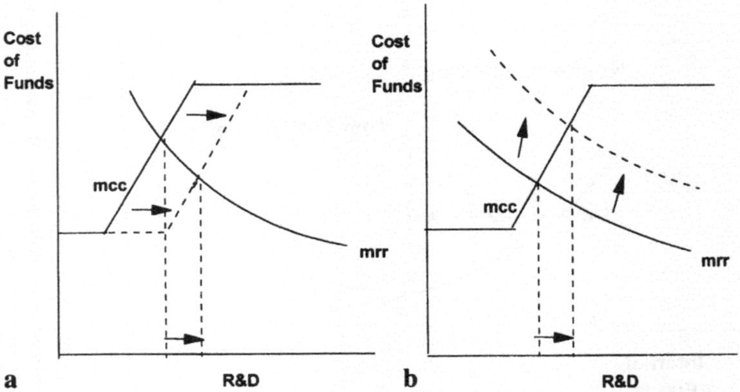

Fig. 4a, b. Two effects on R&D investment. **a** Increased cash flow. **b** Increased expected returns

influencing the opportunity cost of investing in new drug R&D. The reduced form solution is therefore,

$$R^* = f(X,Z). \tag{2}$$

This is the basic equation that will be estimated in the regression analysis to be described in the next section.

Figure 4 provides a simple graphical analysis of the two major determinants of R&D investment that we have found in our earlier work, and that we also find in the current study. First, in Fig. 4a we show that increased availability of internal funds, or cash flow, leads to a positive effect on optimal R&D investment. Second, in Fig. 4b, we show that an increase in expected returns shifts the mrr schedule upward and also leads to a positive effect on optimal R&D investment.

4 Regression model

Data on firm financial variables were obtained from Standard and Poor Compustat files. The data are taken from consolidated income and balance sheet statements which include the firm's total sales and expenditures for all products and services on a global basis. Two major considerations in selecting the sample of firms were the availability of R&D expenditures for the complete 1974–1994 period and a high degree of specialization in ethical drugs. This led to a sample of eleven firms.[7]

The eleven firms in our sample accounted for 42.3% of ethical drug sales in the United States in a middle year of our sample, 1989. Also, for the

[7] The eleven firms are Abbott, American Home Products, Bristol Meyers, Johnson & Johnson, Lilly, Merck, Pfizer, Schering Plough, Syntex, Upjohn, and Warner-Lambert. Seven of these firms were included in our early analysis of R&D determinants (footnote 4). We excluded three firms from our prior sample due to merger and data consistency problems and added four firms that were not available previously because of incomplete R&D expenditures data.

period 1985–1989, they accounted for just over half of the innovative output of the industry in that period. Innovative output is measured as the sum of the first three years' sales of all new chemical entities (NCEs) introduced in the United States during the period.

Based on the general discussion in the last section, we specify the regression model shown below:

$$RDS_{it} = f(E\pi_t, CFS_{it-1}, D_i) \quad (3)$$

where RDS_{it} = R&D divided by sales for each firm for each year

$E\pi_t$ = index of expected returns to R&D in pharmaceuticals in year t

CFS_{it-1} = cash flow divided by sales for each firm in year $t-1$

D_i = dummy variable for firm i

For the $E\pi_t$, variable two measures were used. The first measure is the Newsal variable. It is defined as the total new product sales (first three years) for industry NCEs introduced in years 0, −1, −2, −3, and −4, all divided by real R&D expenditures in year −2. It is therefore a rough "productivity of R&D" variable, at the industry level.

The basic idea underlying this formulation is that firms are well aware of the new products being introduced throughout the industry, and that their expectations depend not only on their own recent successes, but also on the success of the industry as a whole. Many firms pursue parallel paths in their R&D activities, and there are strong spillover opportunities across firms in pharmaceuticals (Henderson and Cockburn, 1996). In addition, competitors are often able to appropriate some of the knowledge from new approaches to drug research and apply them to different medical problems and therapeutic areas. It should be noted that we tried a firm level version of the Newsal variable in early specifications, but perhaps because of its high degree of volatility at the firm level, this formulation was only marginally statistically significant.[8]

Figure 5 shows the plot of the Newsal variable for the sample period. As noted earlier it has a generally rising trend. This is a dramatic contrast to the behavior of the Newsal variable between 1962 and 1974 that exhibited a strong downward trend (Fig. 2).

Because of the obvious difficulty of capturing firms' expected returns through a "past success" variable, we also report the results for a second $E\pi_i$ variable, Imarg. This is a measure of the industry margin, which is defined as the weighted average of pre-tax profits divided by sales for the pharmaceutical divisions of the eleven drug firms in our sample. Figure 6

[8] In our prior study of R&D determinants, this variable was measured at the firm level, and it was significant at normal confidence levels. In this regard, it is relevant to point out that there is evidence that spillovers were more narrow in scope and took longer to realize when the random screening approach to drug discovery was dominant (Sykes, 1997; Henderson and Cockburn, 1996).

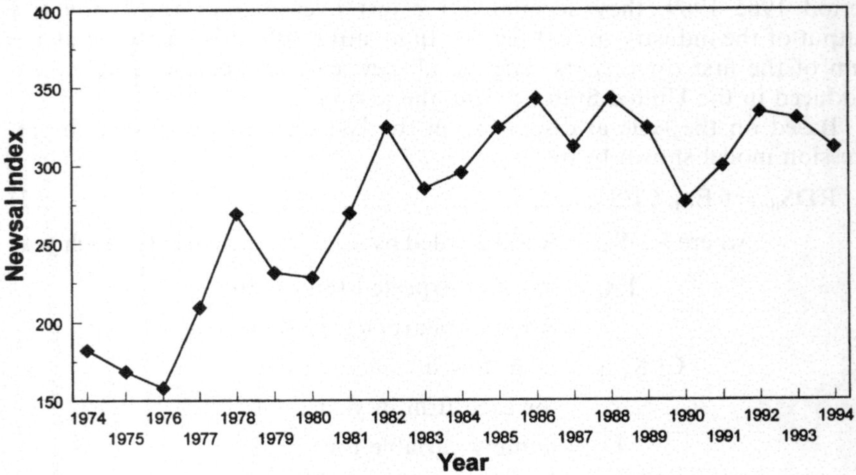

Fig. 5. Newsal Index, 1974–1994

plots the Imarg variable and shows that it was declining during the 1970s and increasing after 1981.[9]

The two variables, Newsal and Imarg, can be viewed as substitutes. However, it is also possible to think of them as capturing different aspects of expected returns to R&D. That is, Newsal captures the productivity of recent R&D in terms of the amount of sales of new introductions. On the other hand, Imarg is the profit margin of the industry, and therefore captures the price-cost margin on current sales (i.e., both for new as well as established products). While IMARG is a function of R&D performance, it also reflects broader economic forces impinging on the industry. For this reason, we report regressions that include both Newsal and Imarg together, and regressions in which each is used alone.

The CFS_{it-1} variable is designed to measure the firm's internally generated funds before investment in R&D, other capital assets, and before the payment of dividends. It consists of the sum of after-tax income, depreciation, plus after-tax R&D. R&D is expensed for tax purposes and receives an implicit subsidy compared to other capital assets. Hence, one must add back "after-tax R&D outlays" to after-tax income and depreciation to obtain pre-investment cash flows (Hall, 1992; Grabowski and Mueller, 1972). For this purpose, we used a flat tax rate of 33%.[10]

[9] As discussed in our earlier study, the declining trend in industry profit margins during the 1970s reflects the fact that drug prices lagged the producer price index substantially during the 1970s, while the reverse was true during the 1980s (Grabowski and Vernon, 1990). An Office of Technology Assessment study (1993) also pointed to increased insurance coverage during the 1980s as an important factor positively affecting industry sales and profit margins.

[10] "After-tax R&D" is computed as 0.67 times R&D expenditures. We used 33 percent as the average effective tax for pharmaceutical firms based on the analysis of this issue undertaken in Grabowski and Vernon (1994).

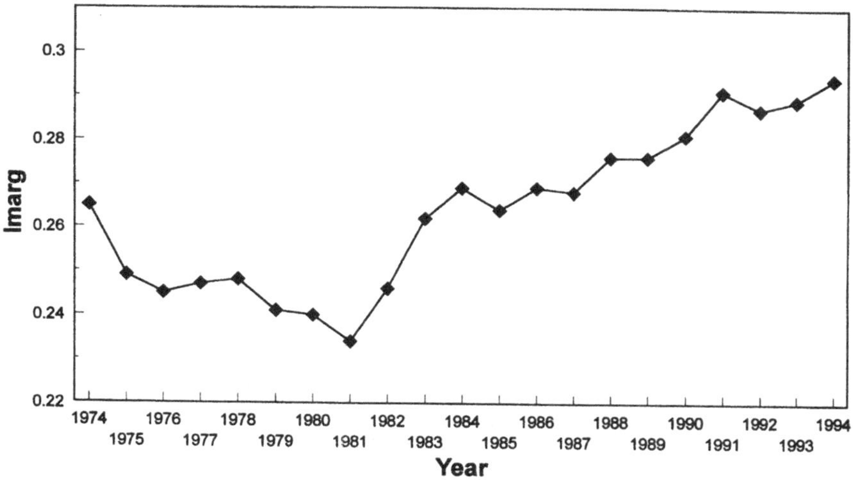

Fig. 6. Imarg, 1974–1994

Theoretically, RDS is a complicated function of all past cash flows. Although we experimented with alternative lag formulations for this variable, the one year lag appeared to perform marginally better in terms of statistical performance. The CFS variable aggregated over all firms is plotted in Fig. 7. Note that it was generally flat until it began to increase in 1983.

Firm dummy variables were introduced for ten of the eleven firms to capture all firm differences between firms and over time. We tested the null hypothesis that the firm dummies were simultaneously all equal, and it was easily rejected. In the regression results, we do not report the coefficients of individual dummy variables.

Two tables of regression equations are reported. Table 2 covers the complete time period of 1974 to 1994. Table 3, containing the same specifications as Table 1, covers the shorter period 1980 to 1994. Generally, the equations are quite similar although the t-statistics are slightly lower for the shorter period. Even so, the t-statistics indicate highly significant effects of both expected returns and cash flow variables in all equations. All variables also have the theoretically expected positive algebraic signs.

Equation 1 in Table 2 uses the Newsal version of expected returns, and both Newsal and CFS are highly significant with the expected signs. The coefficient of the cash flow variable, CFS, is 0.31 and can be interpreted as implying that a $1 million increase (decrease) in cash flow will lead approximately to a $310,000 increase (decrease) in R&D expenditures. This compares to coefficients of 0.26 in Grabowski's 1968 study and a range of 0.22–0.27 in our 1981 study. On the other hand, when we turn to equations 2 and 3, the coefficients are much lower, equal to 0.12 and 0.13 respectively. These comparisons are summarized in Table 4.

Inclusion of both Newsal and Imarg in equation 2 seems to support the idea that they do capture somewhat different aspects of expected returns, as discussed earlier. When Imarg is included in equations 2 and 3, however,

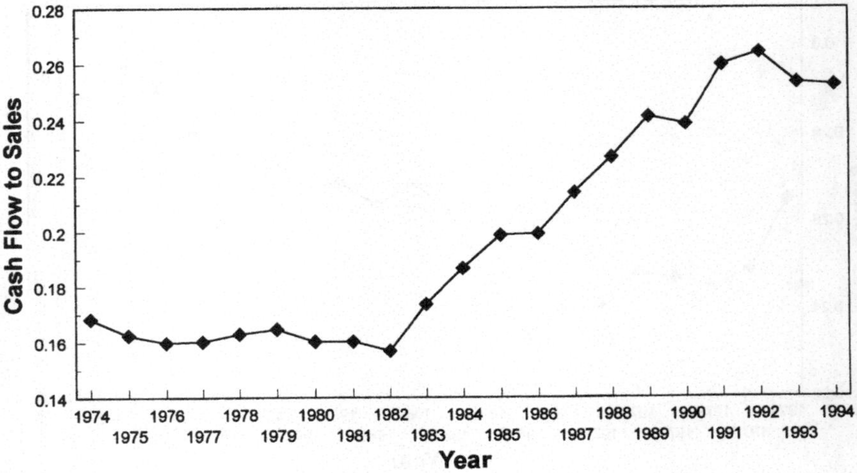

Fig. 7. Cash flow to sales, 1974–1994

Table 2. Linear regression explaining R&D-to-sales ratio for eleven firms, 1974–1994

Equation[a]	1	2	3
Intercept	−0.03 (6.46)	−0.19 (12.40)	−0.21 (12.47)
Newsal	0.19 (10.42)	0.12 (7.81)	–
Imarg	–	0.73 (10.59)	0.94 (12.98)
CFS	0.31 (13.73)	0.12 (4.74)	0.13 (4.61)
$\hat{R}$sq/F	0.87/124.5	0.91/182.4	0.89/150.8
N	230	230	230

[a] Firm dummies also included in these equations.

Table 3. Linear regression explaining R&D-to-sales ratio for eleven firms, 1980–1994

Equation[a]	1	2	3
Intercept	−0.04 (3.35)	−0.18 (10.32)	−0.18 (10.02)
Newsal	0.20 (5.45)	0.08 (2.49)	–
Imarg	–	0.77 (9.47)	0.85 (11.24)
CFS	0.32 (13.41)	0.12 (4.14)	0.11 (3.89)
$\hat{R}$sq/F	0.87/91.48	0.92/141.0	0.92/147.16
N	164	164	164

[a] Firm dummies also included in these equations.

the coefficients of CFS fall in magnitude and have lower t-statistics than when only Newsal is included (in equation 1). This is probably due to the higher correlation between Imarg and CFS ($r = 0.51$) than between Newsal and CFS ($r = 0.33$), as would be expected given their definitions.

To summarize the findings, there is strong evidence that both expected return and cash flow variables are important determinant factors for

Table 4. Cash flow and drug R&D consistency of estimates over time

Study	Period	Coefficient[a]
Grabowski (JPE 1968)	1958–62	0.26
Grabowski and Vernon (AEI 1981)	1962–75	0.22–0.27
Grabowski and Vernon (1998)	1974–94	0.12–0.31

[a] Variable has somewhat different definitions and lag structures in prior studies.

pharmaceutical R&D. However, it is difficult to untangle the two effects in a precise fashion from econometric analyses. This is consistent with analyses of R&D determinants performed on broad cross-sectional data samples (Hall, 1992; Grabowski and Mueller, 1972).

5 Policy implications and future research issues

The empirical analysis undertaken in this paper indicates that expected returns and cash flow are important determinants of pharmaceutical R&D. The rapid growth in the R&D intensities of drug firms since the late seventies reflects the strong positive effects of both of these factors. These findings are in accordance with the model illustrated in Figs. 2 and 3. The results are also consistent with our earlier analysis that focused on a period of declining rather than rising research intensities.

The analysis has a number of important applications. In particular, it provides a conceptual framework to analyze the effects of proposed policy actions on pharmaceutical R&D. Government interventions affect R&D returns and the supply of funds to undertake pharmaceutical R&D in a multitude of ways. These include pre-market regulatory controls, drug price and reimbursement controls, product formularies, tax policy, patents, technology transfer policies, etc. (Towse, 1995). It is important to gauge the effects of these different government policies on drug industry R&D, given the evidence from medical and econometric studies that drug innovations have yielded high social returns (see, for example, Lichtenberg, 1998; Cutler et al., 1997).

One example of how this general framework can be utilized to study R&D impacts is our recent analysis of the Vaccines For Children Program (Grabowski and Vernon, 1997). In 1993 the Clinton Administration created this Program to increase the government's purchases of pediatric vaccines. One estimate from the Department of Health and Human Services was that the government would eventually account for approximately 80% of the US vaccine market purchases at prices significantly below the private sector. Our analysis indicated that if the program were implemented in accordance with these initial plans and projections, it would have had very significant negative impacts on the returns to and the cash flows available for new vaccines. As a consequence, vaccine suppliers would be expected to shift R&D investments to adult vaccines and other biopharmaceutical R&D projects.

The most far-reaching government proposal affecting pharmaceuticals in recent years was the 1994 Clinton Health Reform Act. This Act would have extended government price controls over a large segment of the U.S. pharmaceutical market. While analyses were commissioned by the Administration concerning its effects on the demand for pharmaceuticals and drug budget implications, the authors of the Act gave little attention to its potential long-run effects on drug R&D or innovation. A partial analysis of this issue was eventually undertaken by the Congressional Budget Office (CBO, 1994). Given the essential role that R&D plays in economic growth and welfare, it would seem important that prospective analyses be undertaken of the effects of policy changes on R&D in this and other research-intense industries.

In this paper, we have focused on the determinants of total R&D outlays. Other microeconomic issues regarding drug R&D investment behavior also warrant further academic research. For example, the allocation of R&D funds between discovery and development activities and across different therapeutic areas remains an important area that has received little formal study. In addition, the multitude of recent R&D partnership agreements between universities, start-up biotech firms and major pharmaceutical firms raise a number of intriguing issues concerning the future evolution of the pharmaceutical R&D process.

References

Baily MN (1972) Research and development costs and returns: the U.S. pharmaceutical industry. Journal of Political Economy 80: 70–85

Congressional Budget Office (1994) How health care reform affects pharmaceutical research and development. U.S. Congress, Washington

Cutler D, McClellan M, Newhouse J (1997) The costs and benefits of intensive treatment for cardiovascular disease. AEI/Brookings Institution, Conference on Measuring the Prices of Medical Treatments

Ellison SF, Cockburn I, Grilliches Z and Hausman J (1997) Characteristics of demand for pharmaceutical products: An examination of four cephalosporins. RAND Journal of Economics 28: 426–446

Geweke JF, Weisbrod BA (1981) Some economic consequences of technological advance in medical care: the case of a new drug. In: Helms RB (ed) Drugs and health. AEI Press, Washington

Grabowski HG (1968) The determinants of industrial research and development: a study of the chemical, drug and petroleum industries. Journal of Political Economy 76: 292–306

Grabowski HG, Mueller DC (1972) Managerial and stockholder welfare models of firm expenditures. Review of Economics and Statistics 54: 9–24

Grabowski HG, Vernon JM (1981) The determinants of R&D expenditures. In: Helms RB (ed) Drugs and health. AEI Press, Washington

Grabowski HG, Vernon JM (1990) A new look at the returns and risks to pharmaceutical R&D. Management Science 36: 804–821

Grabowski HG, Vernon JM (1994) Returns to R&D on New Drug Introductions in the 1980s. Journal of Health Economics 13: 383–406

Grabowski HG, Vernon JM (1997) The search for new vaccines: the effects of the Vaccines for Children Program. AEI Press, Washington

Green DG (1998) Is price regulation necessary? A summary of arguments. Pharmacoeconomics 14, Supp.1: 137–142

Hall BH (1992) Investment and research and development at the firm level: does the source of financing matter. Working Paper no. 4096, NBER, Cambridge, Mass, June

Henderson R, Cockburn I (1996) Scale, scope and spillovers: The determinants of research productivity in drug discovery. RAND Journal of Economics 27: 32–59
Hubbard RG (1998) Capital-market imperfections and investment. Journal of Economic Literature 36: 193–225
Lichtenberg FR (1998) Pharmaceutical innovation as a process of creative destruction. Working Paper, Columbia University
Office of Technology Assessment (1993) Pharmaceutical R&D: Costs, risks and rewards. Congress of the United States, Washington
Pharmacy Times (1976) Compilation of new drugs: 1940 through 1975
PhRMA (1997) 1997 industry profile. Pharmaceutical Research and Manufacturers of America
Schwartzman D (1976) Innovation in the pharmaceutical industry. Johns Hopkins University Press, Baltimore
Scherer FM (1998) The size distribution of profits from innovation. Annales d'Economie et de Statistique
Scherer FM (1978) Technological maturity and waning economic growth. Arts and Science 1: 7–11
Suslow VY (1996) Measuring quality change in the market for anti-ulcer drugs. In: Helms RB (ed) Competitive strategies in the pharmaceutical industry. AEI Press, Washington
Sykes R (1997) The pharmaceutical industry in the new millennium: Capturing the scientific promise. Centre for Medicines Research International Publications, Carshalton, Surrey, UK
Towse A (1995) (ed), Industrial policy and the pharmaceutical industry. Office of Health Economics, London
U.S. House of Representatives (1995) Hearings before the Subcommittee on Health and the Environment
Wardell WW, Lasagna L (1975) Regulation and drug development. AEI Press, Washington

Industrial policy, competence blocs and the role of science in economic development*

Gunnar Eliasson

The Royal Institute of Technology (KTH), S-10044 Stockholm, Sweden

Abstract. Government is studied as supporter of science and of the transformation of scientific discoveries into new technology and firm formation. The importance of scientific discovery outside academe is recognized as is the experimental nature of the transformation process entailing frequent business failure. Competence bloc theory is used to understand the minimum set of actors with competence needed for the incentive structure to be complete and the risk of losing the winners minimized. Competence bloc analysis also helps clarify the theoretical foundations of industrial policy and useful roles for science parks. I find that to succeed as a catalyst for industrial competitiveness park management should be less concerned with science and technology and more with the economics of the transformation process.

Key words: Competence bloc – Experimentally organized economy – Spillovers – New industry formation – Organization of production – Industrial policy – Science parks

JEL-classification: D2, L6, L8, O12, O14, O3, M13

1 The problem

Alfred Marshall (1890, 1919) had a great intellectual problem with the Walrasian model which he had contributed to developing and for which he

---

Paper presented at the 1998 World Conference of the International Joseph A. Schumpeter Society, Vienna, June 13–16, 1998.

* Earlier versions of parts of this paper were presented at two OECD meetings OECD/CERI in Tokyo Nov. 11–12, 1997 and in Paris May 14–15, 1998.

for a long time had been a prominent academic representative (Laestadius, 1999). The evidence of increasing returns was everywhere visible, but accepting them shattered the very foundation of the then established Walrasian model. The profession was not pleased with Marshall's preoccupation. Marshall's book *Industry and Trade* (1919), where this problem was explored in depth as a problem of reality,[1] was not even reviewed in some major economic journals.[2] To solve his problem Marshall (1919) created the concept of an "industrial district" within which firms suffered decreasing returns individually, but the district as a whole functioned as an "externality", creating large total factor productivity gains within the district. This was, however, too radical a proposition to be absorbed by the most conservative of all professions.[3]

In 1944 Frank Knight came back to the same problem suggesting that observed increasing returns must depend on some invisible (unmeasured) factor of production that he called "knowledge". This proposition I take as *the first* cornerstone for my analysis. Romer (1986) and Lucas (1988), unaware of the fact that Marshall had said it much better already in 1919, made the Marshall knowledge externality the foundation of what they almost 60 years later called the "new growth theory".

In this paper I identify the role of science and the policy maker in creating Marshallian knowledge externalities through the spontaneous or designed creation of industrial districts, notably around university campuses (science parks). For this I need a theoretical structure that captures the growth process in sufficient detail to make the roles of the policy maker and the science park identifiable. To that end I introduce the *competence bloc*, that explicitly *creates the increasing returns to innovative search* of Marshall's theory (Eliasson and Eliasson, 1996; Eliasson, 1998b). Silicon Valley is the most well known case of a spontaneously created competence bloc, but it would not have come about were it not for the presence of certain institutional circumstances. The competence bloc only defines the requisite actors with competence, and the principles for sharing profits (incentives) for the innovative and entrepreneurial selection process to take place. The competence bloc, therefore, is not sufficient to set the selection process in motion. For this we also need the competitive push of the *experimentally organized economy* (Eliasson, 1987, 1991, 1996a, Chapter II) and a model to link the outcomes of experimental innovative search to the macro economy.

The increasing returns to innovative business experiments embodied in the competence bloc create the three distinguishing (from the neoclassical model) features of the experimentally organized economy; (1) non trans-

---

[1] Alfred Marshall is in fact credited by Joseph Schumpeter (1954) with being the first economist to attempt to make business reality part of economics.

[2] See Laestadius (1992).

[3] After Marshall's death the critique of him continued (Laestadius, 1999). For Sraffa (1926) the perfect information, equilibrium properties of the Walrasian model were not to be questioned or replaced by a monopoly situation. It did not help intellectually that Young (1928) sided with Marshall in observing that the static Walrasian model was of little use for understanding economic progress. Such heresy, John Hicks (1939) observed, was not to be allowed.

parency from any position in the investment opportunity set, (2) bounded rationality, and (3) tacit knowledge due to critical incommunicable competencies. Together (*first*) this makes (Eliasson, 1991, 1992) business or entrepreneurial mistakes a normal feature of the dynamic economy and a standard cost for economic development. Innovative entry and forced competitive exit become necessary and important elements of economic growth.

Science parks on university campuses, industrial parks and technological incubators are all artificial policy devices designed to be part of national industrial policy programs to support economic growth. Most of these parks have been instituted around a university with the express purpose of facilitating for firms to draw on research generated there. Causality, however, (*second*) often goes the opposite way (Eliasson, 1995, 1997d), advanced firms unintentionally spilling research results that diffuse to other industries and academe, therefore, unintentionally functioning as technical universities. Ignoring this private externality as a fact means misunderstanding the nature of technical change. Efficient policy, hence, also means both recognizing and facilitating the diffusion of such privately generated spillovers to other industries. This requires that the spillover generating firms be compensated for the positive externalities created.[4] *Third*, we are not talking about abstract bits and pieces of information that can be separately traded in the market, but of people with knowledge who diffuse through the labor market. Hence, functioning labor markets are a necessary requisite for the competence bloc and the efficient commercialization of research carried out there. *Fourth*, significant parts of new industry creation based on innovation occur through new establishment, entrepreneurs in university labs or in advanced firms jumping ship to establish their own business. The *fifth* circumstance to recognize is that the flow of knowledge that becomes useful in firms is industrial, embodying an integration of technical knowledge with economic considerations, mostly in the form of a selection of those technological solutions that meet profitability criteria. This selection and integration requires a certain (*receiver*) *competence* in the firm that can rarely be acquired in a university environment (Eliasson, 1986, p. 46 f., 57 f., 1990a, p. 277). Hence, to understand new industry formation it is necessary to specify all the competencies needed to build an industry on a certain selection of scientific knowledge and make sure that all factors needed to achieve that are in place. But the knowledge capital needed for growth is much more than the knowledge created in and around universities and science parks. When these factors have been introduced in terms of the *competence bloc* we can derive possible roles for the policy maker. This analysis will take us through the world of the *Knowledge Based Information Economy* (Eliasson, 1990b).

2 Spillovers, competence blocs and economic selection: Theory I

It has long been recognized (see for instance Nelson, 1986; Stankiewicz, 1986; Jaffe, 1989) that science contributes somehow to industrial progress.

---

[4] E.g. in aircraft industry (Eliasson, 1995).

Fundamental principles of science are eventually converted into engineering applications. The universities and engineering schools are conventionally thought of as the creators of the principles of these applications. Literature, therefore, often places the core of the industrialization process in science and the scientific institutions. More critical voices, however, suggest that scientists and university engineers have really done little more than encode the principles of the applications (innovations) long before created, understood and implemented in practice. The university environments, furthermore, some argue, are not sufficiently creative to support truly innovative discovery. The minds there are rather inclined to encode and document and be critical of everything they do not understand. Hence, new business ideas should rather be looked for in the experimental industrial and business environments, where actors have to be innovative to survive. Since new empirical studies support that view, an ambition of this analysis will be to give the roles of science and the university in industrial development reasonable dimensions.

From technology to industrial spillovers

Spillovers are industrial rather than technological (see Eliasson, 1996b). To reach successful industrial application a new technology has to be commercially selected and filtered through a competitive market process. This filtering creates economic value and the filtering itself embodies complex competencies. Studies reporting on the presence of strong and significant technological spillovers, furthermore, are based on data that have been filtered through and selected in competitive markets (Eliasson, 1995, 1997c, d). These studies do not support the idea that expanding resources to science and new technology development will automatically enhance industrial competitiveness in other environments. It may rather be so that attending to the transformation process embodying the economic filtering will be the most efficient way of putting industrial life into dormant innovations in academia or business. This, as we will demonstrate, is a matter of attending to institutions.

The competence bloc

The competence bloc is the configuration of actors that together initiates and stimulates the growth of an industry (see Table 1). It is *defined in terms*

Table 1. Actors in the competence bloc

1. Competent and active customers
2. Innovators who integrate technologies in new ways
3. Entrepreneurs who identify profitable innovations
4. Competent venture capitalists who recognize and finance the entrepreneurs
5. Exit markets that facilitate ownership change
6. Industrialists who take successful innovations to industrial scale production

Source: G. Eliasson and Å. Eliasson (1996)

of end results, a bundle of functionally related *products in the market*, not in terms of technologies or physical inputs[5], and its dominant function is the selection of winning technical and economic solutions. This selection involves the joint minimization of the two errors; (1) to allow losers to survive for too long and (2) to reject winners. The competence bloc also has to function as an attractor that benefits and attracts competent investors in such a way that only investors who also contribute positively to the attractiveness of the competence bloc are selected. Under such circumstances the competence bloc will develop faster than the sum of outputs of its constituent actors. This is Marshall's synergy discussed in terms of externalities or increasing returns to innovate search associated with the bloc, rather than with individual actors. Hence, a minimum *critical competence mass and variety* is needed before a competence bloc becomes self propelled into a growing industry. The policy problem to be discussed below is whether *policy catalysts can be inserted to initiate* a competence bloc and/or induce it *to reach critical mass faster* and/or whether such catalysts are to be found in the science community.

The competence bloc can be defined (as in Table 1) by its actors. The innovative quality level of the output selected and produced within the competence bloc is always limited by the competence of the customers. *Competent customers* are always present in innovative and advanced industries. We define the *innovator* as the actor who integrates different (new and old) technologies in an innovative way. The *entrepreneur* searches actively for, and identifies commercially viable innovations and prepares them for initiation in the market.[6] But the entrepreneur needs financing from understanding and *competent venture capitalists* who provide risk (equity)

---

[5] The competence bloc differs from Dahmén's (1950) *development bloc,* which is concerned with synergies in physically defined manufacturing and distribution systems, and from Carlsson's (1995) *technological system* which is input determined around the use of a generic technology (a factor input like robots) in many types of production. While the technological system concerns the use of one general technology in many industrial applications, the competence bloc presents all actors with competence needed to integrate different technologies (competencies) to create and develop an industry. We also have the concept of a *national system of innovation* (Nelson, 1988; Lundvall, 1988, 1992) which (as used by Lundvall and Nelson) is close to a technological system, being defined geographically and in terms of technological inputs. The innovation system approach has two not so appealing sides in that it gives a central role to the policy maker and imposes a national dimension by prior assumption. Since our main point is to identify, within the competence bloc, a meaningful role for the university and for the policy maker we cannot simply make the Government and the nation the central actor by assumption. Such assumptions will make the analysis misleading. The competence bloc, on the other hand, imposes no such prior assumptions, and is closer to Marshall's notion of an *industrial district*.

[6] The literature is not clear about the distinction between the *innovator* and the *entrepreneur*. Each usually is a little bit of the other. For my purpose I want to keep the two concepts theoretically apart, identifying the innovator with the engineer who integrates new and old technologies into something new and unexpected, and the entrepreneur with the person who sees the commercial opportunities of some particular innovation. Von Mises (1949) is one of the few who uses that definition explicitly. It is quite another thing that the two actors often mix in practice.

financing at reasonable rates. Reasonable rates require that the venture capitalist is capable of understanding the new business proposed, and such competent capitalists are extremely rare when innovations occur outside the technology range of traditional industry (Eliasson, 1997a). The venture capitalist in turn may want to unload his or her investment at a good return and return to new venture financing. Hence, a functioning second-hand (IPO) *exit market* is necessary to prop up *incentives* all the way down to the innovator. Finally, *industrial competence* is needed to move the winners up to industrial scale production and distribution. This whole chain of competent actors is a necessary condition for the creation of viable new industry and the range of variation of industrial knowledge represented by the actors at each step is part of the competence specification of the economy. Together all actors create the situation (within the competence bloc) of *increasing returns to innovative and entrepreneurial search*. The competence bloc, hence, incorporates an institutional theory of efficient economic selection and industrial policy.

The customers play an important role in defining the quality of the products designed and produced.[7] In the long run the quality of output is always limited by the quality of the customers, and customers will decisively influence the direction of technical change. Hence, for industrial leaders marketing strategy, more than anything else, is to capture the most competent customers in order not to be locked into inferior product technologies. The competence bloc can also be seen as an extended firm (Eliasson, 1997a). IBM, for instance, integrated all actors of the competence bloc within its corporate structure well into the 1980s, and for a long time very successfully so (Eliasson, 1996a, pp. 175 ff). It was even competent customer to itself. This hierarchical – non-market – integration, however, was not innovative enough and did not achieve the radical technological transformation needed to move mainframe and individual PC technology into the new world of integrated computing and communications.

While incentives require many agents with a varied competence for winners to be identified, the larger the number of actors and the more varied their competence, the greater is *competition*, and the more efficient and successful the selection of winners. The increasing returns to innovative search should, hence, be taken to mean that the risks of losing a winner are minimized.

The prime *function of the competence bloc*, hence, *is to guide the selection* of *successful innovations through its competence filter*, *induced by incentives and enforced by competition*, and to move the innovations as fast as possible towards industrial scale production and distribution. To summarize;

(a) The *competence* of the actors determines the quality of the selection.[8]
(b) *Incentives* are determined within the competence bloc and depend on the presence and competence of all actors (*completeness*).

---

[7] This captures the Burenstam-Linder (1961) argument that domestic consumption patterns constitute a form of trade protection.

[8] In Quattro Cento Florence (G. Eliasson and U. Eliasson, 1997) the quality of the art produced.

(c) *Competition* is determined within the competence bloc and depends on the number, variety and character of actors, or the success of the selection of winners.

Economic incentives all the way down depend on the presence of all legs in this competence bloc, and they all have to be substantiated by a well structured property rights system) that minimizes the risks of predatory imitation (patent and copy rights etc.; Eliasson, 1998a).

3 The experimental order and growth through competitive selection: Theory II

Increasing returns to innovative search is synonymous to a nonlinear economy with phases of unpredictable "chaotic" behavior. The extent of such behavior depends on the organization of the economy, the variety of its knowledge base, incentives to search in it and the intensity of competition. The organization of the competence bloc defines the nature and variety of the knowledge base, or the investment opportunity set. Other institutions define the incentives to act commercially on the opportunities and together define the intensity search and of competition. Depending on the organization of the competence bloc the long-term macro outcomes vary widely (Eliasson and Taymaz, 1999).

In the vast and nontransparent competence bloc of a successful industry no actor can feel safe from devastating competitive entry into their markets. Incumbent firms constantly have to take precautionary action (through reorganization and rationalization) in anticipation of such unpredictable competitive entry, or risk business failure and exit. In doing so they also subject other incumbent actors to increased competition, and force additional exits. It is most risky to make the wrong decision, but in general it is more dangerous for the firms not to act, than to act (Eliasson, 1990a). Thus, economic growth in the experimentally organized economy takes place through competitive selection through the four investment growth mechanisms in Table 2; *innovative entry*, *reorganization*, *rationalization* and forced *exit*. In the experimentally organized economy no actor can ever feel safe (Eliasson, 1996a, p. 45). This model of growth through competitive selection in the experimentally organized economy allows us (1) to explicitly identify roles for science and the policy maker in the endogenized growth process and (2) to characterize differences in terms of different types of industries. What roles can the policy maker play and what roles can science play in the new types of industries developing. To complete the theoretical part of the paper we have to introduce the different channels through which

Table 2. The four mechanisms of economic growth

1. Entry
2. Reorganization
3. Rationalization
4. Exit (shut down)

Source: G. Eliasson (1993a, 1996a, p. 45)

Table 3. New technology is diffused

1.	When people with competence move (labor market)
2.	hrough new establishment by people who leave other firms (innovation and entrepreneurship)
3.	When subcontractors learn and vice versa (competent purchasing)
4.	When competitors learn from technological leaders (imitation)

Source: G. Eliasson (1995)

new technology is diffused and how these diffusion mechanisms interact with the four investment growth mechanisms in Table 2.

Diffusion of innovations around technical universities and advanced firms (spillover sources) follows four principally distinct paths (see Table 3). The most important diffusion mechanisms involve the movement of people (items 1 and 2) with competence. If the labor market does not work or the conditions for entrepreneurship are not well developed one should expect little radically new industry formation. Technology diffusion through subcontracting networks and simple imitation belong to the mature industries based on an established and fairly well known body of knowledge, notably engineering. In aircraft industry diffusion along channels 2 and 3 dominates, in C&C industry 1 and 2.

The entire selection machinery of the competence bloc is necessary for the creation of a radically new industry, and especially a viable, varied and competent venture capital industry. When missing, as in many industrial countries, therefore, little entrepreneurship is exhibited outside the existing industry. Without a varied venture capital competence in place new industry formation will be restricted to technologies close to those of existing industry, which will also provide the bulk of venture capital (Eliasson, 1997a). Public risk capital, influenced by political decisions tends to be even more incompetent here.

4 Industrial knowledge creation and the role of science parks – policy

Sources of industrial and scientific knowledge differ. Science does not normally concern itself with the commercial value of its discoveries. For innovative technical knowledge to become industrial and commercially viable in terms of Table 1 the other actors of the competence bloc are needed.

The firm as a technical university

Once technological spillovers from advanced firms have been recognized, we have embraced the idea (Eliasson, 1994a, 1995, 1996d, 1997d) of the advanced firm as a technical research institute and university. The empirical evidence is overwhelming. Practically the entire IT and communications industry in the US has been founded on spillovers from firms (see further Sect. 5). While science thrives on specialization, industry derives new technology from *integrating* different technologies into new composite technologies with an industrial and commercial potential (innovation item 2 in Table 1). Hence, industry thrives on organizational competence. While the business manager or leader works through other people, the idea of being managed is rarely appreciated by academics, and the less so the more time they have spent in academe (Eliasson, 1996d). As a consequence very different traditions and attitudes to work have developed in the two environments. They are difficult to break or bridge. Hence, the industrial usefulness of academic research is more limited than we might like to believe.

Few academically developed technologies have formed the base for a new business, especially if we move outside biotech industry, one of the very few genuinely science-based industries (see under case 5.3 in Sect. 5). Biotech, on the other hand, is all based on entrepreneurship around academic laboratories (for a survey see G. Eliasson and Å. Eliasson, 1996, 1997), notably involving what Zucker and Darby (1996) call "academic stars", with very extensive publishing in academic journals. This industry, in its modern form, furthermore, is based on three fundamental scientific breakthroughs around 1975.[9] The academic and industry laboratory environments in biotech are similar and scientists move rather freely between academia and business. It is unclear whether this "exception", that is rapidly becoming an industry in the US, depends on the technology itself, or whether we are witnessing the first stage in a new industry formation. While the main role of academe is the provision of educated young people in engineering and natural sciences, biotech is based on entrepreneurship on discoveries in academic labs, and a liberal political and academic rule system that supports such entrepreneurship. Here California, notably Silicon Valley, stands out as an example of a competence bloc where all the necessary actors (of Table 1) have been present and actively contributed to the activation and commercialization of scientific discovery.

The role of science parks

With proper definitions the role of science and academic research in industrial knowledge formation and development is significantly reduced. Universities appear mostly as teaching and talent filtering institutions, even though very importantly so. New industries like biotech that draw directly on academic research will, however, become increasingly important in the future development of industry. Industrial laboratories, furthermore, will increasingly recruit academically trained people with research experience to develop the new technologies, where the wealthy industrial nations have to excel, compared to developing economics, and rapidly leave their old trades to stay competitive and rich. To succeed this will have to involve a radical overhaul of existing attitudes, organization and practices in western universities.[10] Against this backdrop I now turn to industrial policy and the ambitions of policymakers to commercialize the results of the large investments in academic research and teaching.

---

[9] Namely (1) recombinant DNA technology or genetic engineering, (2) the hybridoma technique to construct antibodies and (3) protein engineering.

[10] Many studies, furthermore, have observed a strong skill bias in technological change underlying the need for support of education, and possibly academic research (Eliasson, 1986, 1994b, 1996d; Berman, Bound and Machin, 1997).

Science parks are the fashion in industrial policy discussion, mostly instituted to create jobs and, perhaps, exports, but more recently also with the express purpose to create technological spillovers to support long term economic growth. Sometimes these parks are called "industrial", sometimes "technological incubators", signifying a more or less "science" or "industrial" orientation. Most of them are predominantly "technical" in their orientation, and in so far as industry creation is the ultimate ambition, the prerequisites for success, as we have characterized them, are typically missing. The physical and *regional dimensions* dominate the literature on science parks, a focus that suppresses the awareness of important economic factors. Innovations or new technologies are often assumed to diffuse mechanically at no cost. This is completely wrong.

A competence bloc may coincide with a region. This would be the case if Bavaria and Baden Wûrtenberg (Munich and Stuttgart) were specialized in making only luxury cars. This is not the case. Bavaria also holds the German C&C competence bloc and sophisticated biotech industries are significantly present. And Silicon Valley holds the world's dominant C&C and biotech competence blocs. Furthermore, while geographical proximity matters (Mercedes, BMW, Porsche Audi and Bosch are all within fast autobahn commuting distance), technological and competence integration increasingly occurs over geographical distances and through artificial C&C intermediation (for instance virtual design), and the more so the closer to standardized industrial scale production and distribution the activity is. Hence, a geographical definition of an industrial park is not appropriate. It shuts out awareness of a number of important aspects by assumption.

The rationale for a science park is as a spillover source (an externality) in Marshall's (1890) original meaning. The spillovers may, however, be dormant and have to be activated, or entrepreneurs to carry them on to industrial applications may be lacking. Hence, the role of a science park is that of an "intermediator", or catalyst, between universities and industry of services produced in universities. This intermediation has to range over the entire competence bloc in Table 1 and complement universities with competencies it lacks. Many, perhaps most of those intermediating tasks turn out to be business propositions requiring business knowledge and experience.

Organization and management

Since Arrow (1962) academic literature has increasingly reflected the view that the innovative output of R&D is independent of the organization of R&D. Most of the spillover literature in fact assumed that innovations are the output of a production process with the sole input of R&D (Eliasson, 1997d). Hence, the conclusion goes, R&D can be placed in Government laboratories and the innovative results distributed freely, thus seemingly solving Arrow's (1962) welfare dilemma of monopolized knowledge through patents etc., a problem that derives from the neoclassical economic model.

So called R&D races are another theoretical notion in innovation research that originates in the neoclassical model. Actors race into a tiny state space, at no, or negligible search costs to find the only and best innovation. The winner takes all and the system settles down in one predictable equilibrium. These theoretical implications, although familiar to the theoretical economist, are utterly at variance with our theoretical conclusions as well as the experience of the industrial manager[11]. But most writing on science parks is based on such neoclassical notions. The interesting question is; can results from academic research, oriented towards presentation and citation be useful in an environment oriented towards doing things and capturing a profit? Our theory suggests no, and there is evidence supporting this inference.

Strategic or spontaneous spillovers

Furthermore, we should distinguish between *deliberate* (planned or strategic) and *spontaneous* spillovers, for instance from the defense industry. The strategy of a science park is to support the generation of spillovers. Are strategic spin-offs "better" than spontaneous ones? They have often failed dramatically. It might be better practice to improve conditions for spontaneous spillovers rather than try to select and commercialize particular technologies; picking winners. And it may be far more important for growth to attend to the diffusion, than the generation of spillovers. This is all "administered" within the competence bloc. Our conclusion is that *it is more efficient policy to make sure that all institutions of the competence bloc are in place than to encourage and/or support particular high-tech industries or to attempt to pick winners and commercialize particular technical innovations*. To link academia and the science park to economic growth we, thus, have to go by way of the competence bloc and the four fundamental investment mechanisms of economic growth (in Table 2).

5 Cases

The best way to give credibility to the conclusions above is to support them by case presentations. The previous presentation, in fact, can be seen as a structured exhibit of the results of a large number of case studies in which I have been involved. I present cases from the engineering, C&C, biotech and financial services industries. The case of Helium recycling (under 6.4) has not been published elsewhere and is, therefore, reported on in some detail. Five different types of production (1) draw more or less directly on scientific knowledge and (2) figure differently in terms of the endogenous growth model stylized by the four investment growth mechanisms in Table 2 and the four diffusion channels in Table 3. It is particularly interesting to clarify the differences between industries developing through new entry and exit

[11] Arthur (1994, 1996) has improved modeling reality by allowing for the possibility of being locked into one of two possible equilibria. Only under the more realistic assumptions of a complete firm based macro model with learning capacity of individual firms is it, however, possible (Ballot and Taymaz, 1998) to show theoretically that several more or less inferior solutions can live long competitive parallel lives.

and industries growing through reorganization and rationalization. We choose:

A. New, entering production

(1) *Computing and communications (C&C) industry*	A new, well established, but still rapidly innovating and expanding industry and a technology that has dramatically reconfigured the industrial landscape over the last couple of decades.
(2) *Financial services industry*	An old industry that has been completely restructured through the integration of academic research and C&C technology.
(3) *Biotech and health care industry*	A new, in its modern form some 20 year old industry with great potential, that is firmly based in science.

B. Mature and potential crisis production (Reorganization, rationalization or exit)

(4) *Engineering industry*	A mature industry with its technological roots 200 years back in the industrial revolution. The industrial backbone of the industrialized world, notably in Europe and Japan. Very limited academic foundation.
(5) *Education and research industry*	An old industry in need of *product innovation and reorganization*

The knowledge base of the firms of each of these industries will be characterized in turn and the factors (existing and lacking) needed to reorganize and develop production clarified.

A. New, entering production

5.1 Computer and Communications (C&C) industry – the paradoxical case of indigenous new establishment in a typical intelligence industry

C&C industry has several origins, some of which may be academic, some spillovers from the US defense industry but most of them indigenous to the industry itself. Bell Labs is a semi-academic institution where a team headed by William Shockley developed the transistor in 1947. Jay Forester from MIT designed the magnetic core memory in 1953. Shockley founded Shockley Semiconductor Laboratories in Palo Alto in 1955, which became the seed bed for Fairchild Semiconductor 1959 which in turn was the seed bed for a sequence of later new establishments, including *Intel* in 1968. Intel introduced the microprocessor (the fourth generation of computing) in 1971. From the second half of the 1980s computing and communicating have been gradually integrated into the Computing & Communications (C&C) industry, or the fifth generation of computing, largely a US creation, and, as it now looks, the result of indigenous new firm establishment around advanced industrial firms that has been greatly facilitated by the selective supply of young and well educated talent from elite US universities, first MIT and Harvard, then Stanford and Silicon Valley (Eliasson, 1996d). A particularly interesting observation concerns the change in (item 1, Table 1) competent customer input in the industry. As the role of defense industry has diminished and the entire industry "fragmented" into a complex of specialist developers and producers, the sophisticated and competent customers have increasingly become civilian and indigenous to the industry. While the indigenous industrial origin is fairly obvious by inspection it was more surprising to observe the fairly low intensity of highly educated (Ph.D. level) people with research experience in the production throughout this industry. Particular talent appeared to be more important than education, and even though most firms interviewed (in Eliasson, 1996d) believed that Ph.D's represented more talent than people with lower degrees, this was not sufficient. Phil.dr recruiting was mostly in areas where radically new technology was being introduced. For instance, the development of parallel computing required innovative talent in mathematics and computer science, a quality that was normally only available at the Ph.D. level. It is, therefore, paradoxical to note that the most academic and abstract of all intelligence industries appears to have made relatively little use of highly educated people with a research experience.

5.2 Dramatic product development in financial services

Financial services, like C&C industries, constitute a rapidly expanding service industry moved by fast product development in the ivory towers of academe. Financial technology operating through the resource allocation mechanisms has exercised a profound influence during the last decade on the world economy. Technology in financial services draws on two critical sources: the C&C technology and academia. The fifth generation computing (Eliasson, 1996a) has been particularly important for the global influence of financial services and its related technological development, but academics have been instrumental in new financial product development. The securitization of global financial services (see Day, Eliasson and Wihlborg, 1993) carries the signum of academic research, and several of its representative stars have recently received the "Nobel prize" in economics. Markowitz (1952) formulated the portfolio theory which soon turned into financial practice. Modigliani and Miller (1958) demonstrated that if separate markets for risks could be established the old rules of thumb from corporate finance would become irrelevant or misleading. By formulating the Capital Asset Pricing (CAP) model and a way of pricing risks through the estimated beta coefficients Sharpe (1964) established the foundation for exactly those markets. When Black and Scholes (1973) and Merton (1973) developed a pricing formula for an option at a given level of risk the very foundation for the derivatives markets had been laid. These theories were rapidly turned into new financial products that, when combined with modern C&C technology, notably in the 1980s, has gradually and dramatically changed the financial system of the industrial world, and the rest of the economy with it, radically redefining and reducing the roles of national policymakers. This case is interesting because the products traded in these markets are pure abstractions ("algorithms"), that integrate with C&C technology to exercise this economic potential. The novelty of these academic abstractions, furthermore, were first appreciated by the commercial community and only later generally understood in academe. And the product range is rapidly expanding in even more sophisticated directions, further undermining the monetary sovereignty of the national state (see Eliasson and Wihlborg, 1998).

5.3 Health care – an emerging industry

Health care is old, but is emerging through technological and commercial change as a radically new industry. It is conventionally thought of as consisting of; (1) hospital care, (2) pharmaceuticals, (3) medical instruments and laboratory equipment and (4) biotech that all integrate to substitute for, or complement care. To be complete, however, (5) health insurance should be added as a fifth supporting industry, establishing a peculiar three dimensional customer (patient, insurer and hospital) that strongly influences the composition and quality of demand. Care and health insurance have conventionally, notably in Europe, been seen as a public, non commercial responsibility, but the US is a clear exception and the care sectors in European countries are beginning to develop into profit driven industries, exhibiting increasing innovativeness. Pharmaceuticals constitute a technological input in care services, often substituting for hospital care, and the biotech industry is, in turn, increasingly becoming a technology supplier to pharmaceutical industry. Similarly, medical instruments are a technological input in care services increasingly involving a significant privatization and reorganization of care services. Typical illustrations are the growing number of outcontracted private laser-based eye surgery and dialysis clinics that keep patients out of costly hospital care.

Competent customers (item 1 in Table 1), notably hospitals and insurance providers, are critical in influencing the direction of technological development of the entire industry, but all actors in the entire competence bloc have to be involved for the industry to develop. Health care industry uses highly educated labor with research experience intensively. For hospital care this is so almost by definition, as in pharmaceutical industry, but biotech is perhaps the only really science founded industry which has been created around university research labs by university researchers forming closely knit teams as new firms (see G. Eliasson and Å. Eliasson, 1996).

Swedish health care is a competence bloc with great industrial potential, albeit heavy up front in Table 1 and deficient in the later commercialization stages (Eliasson, 1997c). There are extremely competent customers (the hospitals), and technology throughout hospital care, pharmaceuticals, biotech and medical instruments is very advanced. The health care industry suffers, however, from the European problem in two ways. It lacks a broad and competent venture capital industry to support the selection of commercially viable projects, and its core is solidly grounded in the public sector, exhibiting strong internal reluctance for turning good ideas into profit making ventures. Above all, the technological development of health care is influenced by the extent to which exclusive luxury production is allowed, luxury services that primarily raise the quality of life, not necessarily prolonging it, that eventually develop into standard lower cost practice. For the health care industry to become a sophisticated, growing and competitive industry luxury customers will have to be part of the market to move innovative product development[12] and here the US, with a large private health care industry, has a decisive competitive advantage over Europe (Eliasson, 1997c). Without a radical change in mentality, including significant privatization of the care sector the industry will not take off in proportion to its local potential. It is interesting to note that the most successful commercializations of health care technology are occurring exactly where Swedish industry exhibits strong competitive advantages, namely in the intersection of health care and mechanical engineering; the medical instrument and laboratory equipment industries.[13] The interesting thing is that the public hospital care sector is not exhibiting a corresponding interest in outsourcing part of their production in the market. As already concluded, the "technical" competence is advanced but critical commercial competencies are lacking, slowing the transformation of the technological potential of the health care sector in Sweden into a new industry.

Biotech, and health care, are the only industries of any size founded directly in academic labs (G. Eliasson and Å. Eliasson, 1996, 1997). Biotech is an old industry, including beer and wine making. In its modern form it is, however, based on three methodological discoveries in university laboratories, the invention of two of which have been awarded Nobel prizes. Practically all of this new industry has been established through new firm entry on a new idea developed by a group of researchers around an "academic star", who is also, as a rule, a well known academic with a CV of many publications (Zucker and Darby, 1996). Zucker and Darby found that top academic quality is really what matters for successful entry in biotech, and that the possibilities for participating academics to become rich are great. A more elaborate econometric study finds that a research focus on human genetics tends to shorten the stay of a star academic at the university (Zucker, Darby and Torero, 1997). This star scientist also moves faster to establish a firm, or to a firm, the more nearby scientists have successfully done the same thing. Again we have the reverse paradox (to

[12] As in luxury car production.

[13] Both Gambro (now Incentive), specializing in dialysis equipment and treatment and Elekta (specializing in radiation brain surgery) are making inroads into the care market by building specialized, private treatment clinics.

that in the C&C industry). In biotech, the most practical, applied and lab oriented of the two industries, higher academic education and research experience, really matter.

Swedish KaroBio is a recently founded (1987) private biotech company that internalizes (for profit) several functions of a competence bloc or a science park (see G. Eliasson and Å. Eliasson, 1997, p. 151 ff). The big pharmaceutical companies have been notoriously bad – despite very large R&D investments – at generating innovative new substances. Small pharmaceutical or biotech labs are much more innovative but lack financial resources, notably in Europe with its deficient venture capital markets. In addition, university labs lack the innovative and entrepreneurial spirit and experience to realize the commercial potential of what they are doing in the lab. KaroBio has established itself as an intermediator between the small business lab, or the university lab and the big pharmaceutical companies. Within its narrow range of specialties it develops, identifies (discovers) and helps screen potential substances and promising candidates for clinical testing in a large pharmaceutical company. In one sense KaroBio, therefore, performs commercially a task that a science park might very well take on, also for profit.

Biotech ins an input in the pharmaceutical industry. Pharmaceutical and medical instrument industries are input industries in hospital care, reducing the need for costly treatments there. Two potential developments stand out. First, new drugs and new technologies offer the potential of effective preventive medication, keeping patients out of costly care. Second, however, new technology of the same kind also offers radically improved but costly treatments that keep patients in much better health for much longer than before, even though his or her life is not necessarily prolonged. It appears that "surging" medical costs in the US are to a large extent not a matter of inflation, but the result of radical increases in the quality of health care as demanded by the customers (Eliasson, 1997c).

B. Mature, possibly crisis production (reorganization, rationalization or exit)

5.4 Aircraft industry at the helm of engineering industry

Airplanes are products with a very long life[14], that excel in complexity and are developed and manufactured under very complex circumstances. Today airplanes cannot be designed, developed and manufactured within one firm (hierarchy). Production has to be outcontracted over the market and organized in ways that in the aircraft industry is often called *integrated production* (Eliasson, 1995, 1996b). Integrated production thus requires a holistic approach and the system's productivity potential associated with choosing the right organizational mix is large. Since airplanes are mod-

[14] Development of the Swedish JAS-Gripen fighter plane began in 1981 and the last fighter planes are planned to be retired between 2030 and 2040.

ernized at least two or three times over their life cycle, their design has to allow for easy repair and modernization to make the use of the product cost efficient over its entire life cycle. This means that the customer plays a critical role both for the direction of technology development chosen and for financing (items 1, 2 and 4 in Table 1). The industry is not typically small scale entrepreneurial, but rather part of innovative industrial scale production (item 6). Aircraft producers, furthermore, are top of the line integrators of advanced forms of three technologies; the mechanical, electronics and new materials technologies. This organizational technology in the production of large and complex products with long lives constitutes premier engineering knowhow that is experience based, and has been developed and implemented in advanced firms. Leading firms, furthermore, always develop their core technologies internally because if transferable from the outside it can also be accessed by competitors. While some component specialties can be taught in classroom, the critical holistic organizational competence is always transferred on the job. Here technical universities play a limited role as knowledge suppliers. The complexity of the integration, furthermore, makes it virtually impossible for competitors to directly *imitate* successful solutions (item 4, Table 2). Both advanced competence per se and the relatively satisfactory protection from easy imitative competition suggest that successful industrial countries will orient their production in this "complex" direction and increase both the role of advanced engineering firms as a "university" supplying experienced engineers to related down-stream industry (item 1 in Table 3), and the diffusion of specific competencies through subcontracting networks (item 3).

Direct entrepreneurial new establishment based on new technology is not typical of engineering industries. The separation of subcontractors (outsourcing), yes, but there are few examples of new establishments based on radically new innovations around engineering industry, compared to IT and communications industry. One reason may be that advanced engineering firms excel in integration and organization. which is inherently large scale. Another reason may be a conservative, non-entrepreneurial culture in large engineering firms and the use of standardized technology. On the other hand, the Swedish computer industry began within Saab (the Swedish aircraft and automobile producer) in the early 1960s, and was successfully developed within Saab, but then effectively destroyed when incorporated in a large scale, misconceived strategic venture into business information systems by Ericsson (Eliasson, 1996a, pp. 196 ff). Ericsson, on the other hand, with good luck, but also some serendipitous capacity captured sophisticated digital radio technology from its military electronics and moved rapidly to become the big player in the mobile phone market. As a second generation spillover Ericsson military electronics was taken further successfully into telephone systems control, which is now (together with Hewlett Packard) a 1000-employee operation. Aircraft engines are another spin off – that would not have occurred without the presence of a military aircraft industry. Volvo Aero is now a global competitor in advanced aircraft engine components. There is also a third generation of spin offs in the form of a global aircraft engine modernization and maintenance company

(Volvo Aero Engine Services) and a separate hydraulic engine operation (VOAC).

Recycling of super cooled Helium – an academic spillover in engineering and medical instrument industry (a US case)[15]

Super frozen helium (close to the absolute freezing point) is an expensive coolant used to create very strong magnetic fields to obtain very clear pictures in medical imaging. The powerful magnetic field shakes the hydrogen atoms in the body. When the field is suddenly stopped one can measure the decay of hydrogen atom vibration. The technology is very complicated. But the magnets have to be super cooled to achieve sufficiently strong magnetic fields.

Significant skepticism about the possibility of putting expensive frozen helium into a closed recycled system existed when this company was started 1988 by a young MIT Ph.D. This founder came from an entrepreneurial family. He had passed high school and college with honors grades, took his masters degree at the MIT Cryogenic department in 1982, and was encouraged to continue with a Ph.D. thesis. He did so on the promise that his thesis problem would be oriented towards an industrial application; in this case a project that was at the time considered impossible to solve for industrial practice, recycling of frozen helium. In 1988 he realized that he had a product in his thesis work. Thanks to his professor's reputation and connection with General Electric[16] and the MIT brand name, the licensing office at MIT managed to get some venture capitalists interested. The new MIT Ph.D. got a seed grant from the Small Business Administration in Washington DC in 1988, and half a million dollars plus venture funding in 1989 to build a firm on his thesis. In early 1991 the company had a "working proof of concepts" and more venture capital soon arrived. In 1993 the first prototype was ready. Government venture funding was, however, considered too slow to keep imitators behind. More private venture capital was secured and by 1995 demand for the new product was running ahead of supply. Very few people were employed at the company (in 1995). Despite its technological complexity as a product (the closed recycling system), most manufacturing work can be outcontracted. Only assembly takes place at the firm, and, surprisingly, welding, the quality of which is critical for product functions.

The inventor/entrepreneur owns less and less of the firm, since venture investors continually acquire equity, but the value of what he owns has, nevertheless, increased significantly. At the time of the interview (in 1995) he thought his entrepreneurial role would soon be over. He would not necessarily stay on to take the project to industrial scale production (item 6, Table 1). If the price was right he would sell.[17]

---

[15] Based on an interview for Eliasson (1996d, 1997a) in 1995.

[16] Together with Siemens the big name in superconductive magnetic imaging.

[17] When I checked back one and a half year later the firm had been acquired by a large company.

5.5 Education and research – an industry in need of innovative product development

During the postwar period education has become a dominant resource user and an increasingly important economic force, not least as a filter of talent. Education at all levels suffers from lack of contact with the markets it is increasingly supposed to serve. As all industries protected from competition it lacks the experimental product development associated with commercial production. The protection in Europe is provided by regulators that have shifted "product development" to the political level, resulting in an even more pronounced alienation of the educational system from its ultimate customers. The industry is, therefore, deficient in the market competence that it will need in the future. The most serious effects of this absence show up in secondary education in many industrial countries where the supply of well educated young people, intellectually equipped for efficient life-long learning is becoming an increasingly important asset for future industrial development. Combined with badly functioning labor markets, ill-equipped to filter and allocate human capital and talent advanced economies may rapidly lose their previously privileged position of competence (Eliasson, 1994a,b,c).

Higher education is primarily engaged in advanced vocational training. It trains teachers and researchers, and teachers for its own training of teachers and researchers. Such production tends to develop internal resistance to change and be solidified in its own traditions. The universities, however, carry the important responsibilities (see Table 4); (1) to supply educated and talented people (the training and filtering task), (2) to supply research results and (3) to supply university entrepreneurs. The first task has always been dominant and will continue to be. The second and hard task is becoming increasingly important through (3), but the third (university entrepreneurship), by its very nature, often clashes with tradition.

Universities have conventionally taken for granted that it is sufficient for production simply to add resources to higher education and turn out more of the same. With increasing numbers of students taking jobs in industry, rather than in public services or in teaching or research, its old product

Table 4. The role of the science park

Role of universities (Academia)	Role of science park	Needed
1. Supply of educated and talented people		(1) Functioning markets for competence ("labor market")
2. Supply of research results	↓ **Intermediation** – creation – diffusion – introduction	(2) Efficient property rights Institutions (Incentives) – patents – consulting – imitation
3. Supply of University entrepreneurs (New establishment)		(3) Functioning complete competence bloc

specification is no longer adequate. New engineering and trade universities have an advantage over the old universities, since they do not suffer from tradition. Their students also get preferential treatment in industry recruiting (Eliasson, 1997b). New industries emerging in the very advanced economies (like the US) need highly educated people with a research experience, but young people who are not too indoctrinated by academic values (Eliasson, 1996d). The university industry at large, furthermore, has to exhibit a broader range of academic and potential industrial competencies than the industrial base. This is particularly so in the small industrial nations. This means that many talented young students with a high academic degree in some field not directly represented in industry will have difficulties landing a job in their field. Conservative recruiting practices in mature industries, a practice that is negative for the long-run development of local industry reinforces this problem. In general, the same recruitment practices and difficulties of assessing talent prior to a test period, mean that the most talented students will enter the job market at inefficiently low positions. To effectively exploit the great talent and knowledge potential residing in the university community, entrepreneurship around the institutes for higher learning has to be radically raised. And this is even more important in Europe with badly functioning labor markets and a large population of the students stranded in the wrong jobs (Eliasson, 1994a,b, 1997b).

6 The bridges between technology and economic growth – necessary institutions

For new technologies to contribute to industrial competitiveness and economic growth the passage of many bridges has to be arranged. Some of these bridges have not yet been built, some range over the internal hierarchies of firms, some bridge different markets. The ranges over which choices have to be made are vast and varied and a profound micro, interior firm to macro understanding is needed to say anything credible on policy (Eliasson, 1984). Rather than beginning with the mistaken assumption that the technical university is a natural supplier of advanced industrial technology, we have studied the nature of industrial technology; its creation, diffusion and application. We have identified roles in that process for the (technical) university, the advanced firm and the science park. The analysis implies a considerably diminished role for academic institutions as creators of new technology and a relatively enhanced role as a teaching and talent filtering institution. The competence bloc theory took us part of the way towards an understanding of innovative activity, the competitive selection of projects and the efficient organization of the experimentally organized market economy. The next and last step, therefore, is to go macro to explain economic growth and the role of policy, using the conceptual structure of the Swedish micro (firm) based macro model (Eliasson, 1977, 1991). Here macroeconomic growth is generated through competitive selection among firms by way of the four investment mechanisms (Table 2); *entry*, *reorganization*, *rationalization* and *exit* (Eliasson, 1996a, c; Eliasson and Taymaz, 1999). The quality of this selection is determined by the quality of the actors in the competence bloc. It is largely experimental and the industrial landscape is littered with failed projects; a standard cost for coming out with some winners. However, we have also understood that (1) radically new industry is needed to move the mature industrial economies onto long-run growth paths that maintain their relative wealth positions, that (2) this radically new industry formation occurs through a viable entry and forceful exit process and that (3) this only occurs if all the actors of the competence bloc and required incentives are present to support competition and the selection of potential winners. The complexity of that experimental selection process is extreme and, hence, has to be decentralized to the locally competent actors at the micro level who are coordinated through the competence bloc. Our analysis shows that attempts to ambitiously "guide" the selection process centrally through policy instruction or to direct it through particular bridging institutions will reduce the efficiency of the use of competence in the selection of projects. Successful policy making should rather be concerned with the efficiency and completeness of the competence bloc, and this focus of industrial policy becomes more important the larger the policy ambition to "create new industry".

In clarifying the role of university based innovative activities we have to recognize that the most important task of academe is teaching and the filtering of talent to jobs (Table 4, item 1) and only to some extent the supply of research results. Here the efficiency of the labor market matters for making higher education productive, and it is by no means clear that industries in the rich western world need its large research establishment to be supplied with necessary research output (item 2), except in one particular dimension; *long run viable growth requires a broad and varied supply of new technology beyond the technology supplied by the indigenous industry*. Much of it is available internationally, some of it in the form of spontaneous spillovers from indigenous industry and some of it may have originated in university labs. But in the latter case there is a long and resource demanding way before it is even close to becoming useful industrial technology. To transform such new technology, unrelated to incumbent industry into industrial scale production *viable university entrepreneurship* is key, and for university entrepreneurship to result in new firm formation and growth a *complete and viable competence bloc is needed*; i.e. to move production out of the confines of its existing technologies. Industrial policy and the role of science parks should, therefore, always be defined in terms of completeness of the competence bloc. This looks as the traditional policy role; remedying a market failure when it comes to the ability of markets to identify and commercialize existing technologies. We have already pointed to the general lack of competent venture capital[18], and to the high level technology but

[18] The role of a science park has to be defined in the context of a competence bloc and it will be different if placed in an advanced industrial economy or in an industrializing economy. Catching up by introducing technology already applied in an advanced economy (the policy of the Hsinchy industrial park in Taiwan; see Larson, Lembre and Meldahl, 1997) is fundamentally different from creating radically new technology, the distinctive attribute of Silicon valley. Europe lies somewhere in between, many of its industries being in a catch-up situation.

lack of commercial spirit in the provision of health care services in Sweden. But it would be both unfair and incorrect to call the absence of commercial activity a market failure, when the absence can be explained by Government activities (regulation, taxes etc.). We should rather be talking about Government failure. The policy problem, hence, is to stimulate market activity through the removal of those obstacles both to support the creation, diffusion and introduction of new viable technology and the import of existing technology, perhaps through supporting foreign direct investments. Both tasks place the *science park in an intermediating position between the innovators and the channels of diffusion to the users*. A fundamental conclusion of this paper is that *most of these intermediating tasks will be business propositions*. Furthermore, if looking only at academia as a possible creator of new technology we are narrowing our attention down to an actor that is less significant than it has been believed to be, but an actor that may become increasingly important for the future economic well being of already rich industrial economies. Let me, therefore, look more carefully at the science park as an intermediator between academe and industry using Table 4.

The roles of universities are, in order of importance: (1) to supply educated and talented people, (2) to supply research results and (3) to supply university entrepreneurs. All three diffusion channels (to the right in Table 4) have traditionally been the responsibility of Government. The science park, therefore, comes out of this analysis as an agent for policy tasks that have traditionally belonged to Government, i.e. to support a functioning market for competence, efficient institutions and a complete and efficient competence bloc. The science park, however, does not have to be a public entity. Many, perhaps most, of its tasks might be more efficiently organized as private profit motivated activities, improving the requisite infrastructure for a functioning growth process; notably through innovative entry of new firms. In this growth process science and academia take part primarily as suppliers of educational services and secondarily, and perhaps increasingly, as suppliers of new technology. For this, however, *a strong entrepreneurial reorientation of the academic community*, away from its ingrained academic traditions *is required*. Here the US, and notably California, appear to be far ahead of the rest of the world (Saxenian, 1994; Eliasson, 1996d; Larson, Lembre, and Meldahl, 1997). To succeed as a policy instrument or a catalyst for industrial competitiveness and economic growth, the park administration should be less concerned with science and technology and the physical facilities of the park, and more with the economics of, and the commercial incentives supporting the diffusion process. In this reorientation away from science and technology towards a more commercial academic life science parks appear to have an important role to play. However, by definition and charter they do not seem to have been asked to play that role.

References

Arrow KJ (1962) Economic welfare and the allocation of resources for invention. In: Nelson R (ed) The rate and direction of inventive activity: economic and social factors. NBER, Princeton University Press, Princeton, NJ

Arthur B (1994) Increasing returns and path dependence in the economics. The University of Michigan Press, Ann Arbor, MI
Arthur B (1996) Increasing returns and the new world of business. Harvard Business Review 74 (4)
Ballot G, Taymaz E (1998) In: Eliasson G, Green C (eds) Human capital, technological lock-in and evolutionary dynamics. The University of Michigan Press, Ann Arbor, MI
Berman E, Bound J, Machin S (1997) Implications of skill-biased technological change. International evidence. Working Paper 6166 (Sept.), NBER, Cambridge, MA
Black F, Scholes M (1973) The pricing of options and corporate liabilities. Journal of Political Economy 81: 637–659
Burenstam-Linder S (1961) An essay on trade and transformation. Wiley, New York
Carlsson B (ed) (1995) Technological systems and economic performance: the case of factor automation. Kluwer, Boston Dordrecht London
Dahmén E (1950) Svensk industriell företagarverksamhet (Entrepreneurial activity in Swedish industry, 1919–39). IUI, Stockholm, also published in 1970 by the American Economic Association Translation Series under the title Entrepreneurial Activity and the Development of Swedish Industry, 1919–1939
Day RH, Eliasson G, Wihlborg C (eds) (1993) The markets for innovation, ownership and control. IUI, Stockholm, North-Holland, Amsterdam
Eliasson G (1977) Competition and market processes in a simulation model of the Swedish economy. American Economic Review 67 (1): 277–281
Eliasson G (1984) The micro-foundations of industrial policies. In: Jacquemin A (ed) European industry, public policy and corporate strategy. Oxford University Press, Oxford; also IUI Booklet No. 173, Stockholm
Eliasson G (1986) Kunskap, information och tjänster – en studie av svenska industriföretag (Knowledge, information and service production – a study of Swedish manufacturing firms). IUI, Stockholm
Eliasson G (1987) Technological competition and trade in the experimentally organized economy. Research Report No. 32. IUI, Stockholm
Eliasson G (1990a) The firm as a competent team. Journal of Economic Behavior and Organization 13 (3): 275–298
Eliasson G (1990b) The knowledge-based information economy, Chapter 1. In: Eliasson G, Fölster S, et al. (eds) The knowledge-based information economy. IUI, Stockholm
Eliasson G (1991) Modeling the experimentally organized economy. Journal of Economic Behavior and Organization 16 (1–2): 153–182
Eliasson G (1992) Business competence, organizational learning, and economic growth: establishing the SmithÄSchumpeterÄWicksell (SSW) connection. In: Scherer FM, Perlman M (eds) Entrepreneurship, technological innovation, and economic growth. Studies in the Schumpeterian tradition. The University of Michigan Press, Ann Arbor
Eliasson G (1993a) Företagens, institutionernas och marknadernas roll i Sverige. Appendix 6 In: Lindbeck A (ed) Nya villkor för ekonomi och politik. SOU 1993: 16
Eliasson G (1994a) Högre utbildade i företag. Rapport Nr. 14, Ds 1994: 119, Agenda 2000, Ministry of Education
Eliasson G (1994b) Markets for learning and educational services – a micro explanation of the rôle of education and competence development in macroeconomic growth. OECD, DEELSA/ED/CERI/CD (94) 9 (4 Nov), Paris
Eliasson G (1994c) Educational efficiency and the market for competence. European Journal of Vocational Training 2/94: 5–11
Eliasson G (1995) Teknologigenerator eller nationellt prestigeprojekt? Exemplet svensk flygindustri (A technology generator or a national prestige project? The Swedish aircraft industry). City University Press, Stockholm
Eliasson G (1996a) Firm objectives, controls and organization – the use of information and the transfer of knowledge within the firm. Kluwer, Dordrecht Boston London
Eliasson G (1996b) Spillovers, integrated production and the theory of the firm. Journal of Evolutionary Economics 6: 125–140

Eliasson G (1996c) Endogenous economic growth through selection. In: Harding A (ed) Micro-simulation and public policy. North Holland, Amsterdam
Eliasson G (1996d) The use of highly educated people in production. KTH, TRITA-IEO R, 1996: 10
Eliasson G (1997a) The venture capitalist as a competent outsider. Mimeo, KTH, INDEK, Stockholm
Eliasson G (1997b) International management, education and leadership. European Journal of Vocational Training 10/97
Eliasson G (1997c) Hälso – och sjukvrdsindustrin – ett kompetensblock med stor affärspotential. KTH, INDEK, TRITA IEO R 1997: 03
Eliasson G (1997d) In: Carlsson B (ed) General purpose technologies, industrial competence blocs and economic growth, pp 201–253. Kluwer, Dordrecht Boston London
Eliasson G (1998a) From plan to market. Journal of Economic Behavior and Organization 34: 49–68
Eliasson G (1998b) Competence blocs and industrial policy in the knowledge based economy. In: OECD Science Technology, Industry (STI) Revue, No. 22
Eliasson G, Eliasson Å (1996) The biotechnological competence bloc. Revue d'Economie Industrielle, 78-4° (Trimestre)
Eliasson G, Eliasson Å (1997) In: Carlsson B (ed) The biotechnological and pharmaceutical competence bloc, pp 139–168. Kluwer, Dordrecht Boston London
Eliasson G, Eliasson U (1997) Företagandets konst – om konstproduktionen i renässansens Florens (The art of entrepreneurship – on art production in renaissance Florens). City University Press, Stockholm
Eliasson G, Green C (eds) (1998) The micro foundations of economic growth. University of Michigan Press, Ann Arbor, MI
Eliasson G, Taymaz E (1999) Institutions, entrepreneurship, economic flexibility and growth – experiments on an evolutionary model. KTH, INDEK, TRITA
Eliasson G, Wihlborg Cl (1998) Electronic money – new markets for banks, markets for new banks or markets for non-banks. Paper presented at the International Joseph A. Schumpeter Society Conference in Vienna, June 13–16, 1998
Hicks JR (1939) Value and capital. The Clarendon Press, Oxford
Jaffe AB (1989) Real effects of academic research. American Economic Review 79(5): 957–970 (Dec.).
Knight F (1944) Diminishing returns from investment. Journal of Political Economy LII: 26–47
Laestadius S (1992) Arbetsdelningens dynamik. Studentlitteratur, Lund
Laestadius S (1999) Marshallian dynamics and new growth theory. Trita-IEO R 1999: 1, KTH, Stockholm
Larson A, Lembre P, Meldahl C (1997) Science parks and industrial development – a competence bloc analysis of Swedish, Taiwanian and US Industrial Districts. Masters thesis. KTH, Stockholm
Lucas RE, Jr (1988) On the mechanics of economic development. Journal of Monetary Economics 22 (1): 2–41
Lundvall B-Å (1988) In: Dosi F, Freeman C, et al. (eds) Innovation as an interactive process. Pintner, London
Lundvall B-Å (1992) National systems of innovations. Pinter, London
Markowitz HM (1952) Portfolio selection. Journal of Finance 7: 77–91
Marshall A (1890) Principles of economics. Macmillan, London
Marshall A (1919) Industry and trade. Macmillan, London
Merton RC (1973) An intertemporal capital asset pricing model. Econometrica 41: 867–887
Von Mises L (1949) Human action. Contemporary Books, Chicago
Modigliani F, Miller MH (1958) The cost of capital, corporative finance and the theory of investment. American Economic Review 48 (3): 261–297
Nelson R (1986) Institutions supporting technical advance in industry. American Economic Review 76: 186–189

Nelson R (1988) In: Dosi G, Freeman C, et al. (eds) Preface to Part B. National systems of innovation. Pintner, London
Romer PM (1986) Increasing returns and long-run growth. Journal of Political Economy 94 (5): 1002–1037
Saxenian A (1994) Regional advantage, culture and competition in silicon valley and route 128. Harvard University Press, Cambridge, MA London
Schumpeter JA (1954) History of economic analysis. Oxford University Press, Oxford; (1986) Allen & Unwin, London Boston Sydney
Sharpe WF (1964) Capital asset prices: a theory of market equilibrium under conditions of risk. Journal of Finance XIX (3): 425–442
Sraffa P (1926) The laws of return under competitive conditions. The Economic Journal XXXVI: 535–550
Stankiewicz R (1986) Academia and entrepreneurs. Developing university-industry relations. Pintner, London
Zucker LG, Darby MR (1996) Star scientists and institutional transformation: patterns of invention and innovation in the formation of the biotechnology industry. Proceedings of the National Academy of Sciences 93 (23): 12709–12716
Zucker LG, Darby MR, Torero M (1997) Labor mobility from academe to commerce. Working Paper 6050 (May), NBER, Cambridge, MA
Westerman J (1768) On Svenska näringarnes undervigt emot de utländske, förmedelst en trögare arbets-drift (On the inferiority of the Swedish compared to foreign manufacturers because of a slower work organization). Lars Salvius, Stockholm
Young A (1928) Increasing returns and economic progress. The Economic Journal VIII: 527–542

Multimarket contact and inter-firm cooperation in R&D*

Nicholas S. Vonortas

Center for International Science and Technology Policy and Department of Economics, The George Washington University, 2013 G Street, N.W., Suite 201, Washington, DC 20052, USA (e-mail: vonortas@gwu.edu)

Abstract. Research joint ventures (RJVs) have been widely acclaimed for their alleged ability to restore private incentives to undertake R&D. Economists have, however, also sounded the alarm concerning the opportunities RJVs may create for collusion between partners. The danger of anti-competitive behavior increases significantly when repeated R&D collaboration occurs between firms that also "meet" in many product markets. This phenomenon is shown to be present in a large set of U.S.-based RJVs. The question is about the incentive trade-off: Are the alleged advantages of RJVs in terms of enhancing incentives for R&D sufficient to overcome the potential disadvantages in terms of decreasing incentives for R&D due to simultaneous multiproject and multimarket contact? Significant foreign participation, high technological and market uncertainties, and the set up of "porous" RJVs may operate as a check to anti-competitive behavior.

Key words: Research joint ventures – Cooperation in research and development – Multimarket contact – Multiproject contact

JEL-classification: L2, L4, O3

Paper presented at the 1998 World Conference of the International Joseph A. Schumpeter Society, Vienna, June 13–16, 1998.

* The research underlying the results reported in this paper was supported by the U.S. National Science Foundation (grant SRS-9510909). The skilled assistance of Yongsuk Yang, a doctorate candidate at The George Washington University, is greatly acknowledged.

1 Introduction

Research joint ventures (RJVs) – defined here as organizations, jointly controlled by at least two participating entities, whose primary purpose is to engage in research and development (R&D) – have acquired a strong reputation among policy analysts in the United States and the European Union as part of the cure for a number of failures in innovation markets. It has been frequently argued in the economics and business literature, for example, that RJVs have the potential to restore private incentives to undertake R&D in cases where the costs and uncertainties are prohibitively high for individual firms and the appropriability of technological knowledge is low.[1] RJVs are said to provide a useful mechanism for firms to acquire complementary resources and to exploit economies of scope in technologies with infrastructural characteristics and imperfectly defined technological paradigms such as information technology, advanced materials and biotechnology. One of the primary objectives of many firms participating in RJVs seems to be the creation of new investment "options" in emerging technology fields (Vonortas, 1997a).

As far as policy is concerned, however, RJVs may also have disadvantages. These disadvantages can generally be of two kinds. On one hand, some have been skeptical about the extent to which collaboration is compatible at all with individual firm interests. For example, by limiting research duplication, RJVs can actually restrict the use of parallel approaches to solve uncertain technical problems (Fusfeld, 1994; Nelson, 1961), thus, potentially hurting social welfare. Moreover, the presence of moral hazard when cooperative R&D is publicly subsidized raises doubts about whether companies will invest public money in the best interest of the taxpayer. I have addressed this issue elsewhere (Vonortas, 1998) and will have very few things to say about it here. On the other hand, the danger remains that RJVs could potentially be used to co-opt competition. A concern, in this respect, has been whether technology information sharing can be effectively separated from production collusion (Clarke, 1984). Another concern has been whether large diversified firms use RJVs simply to create links to competitors and facilitate collusion across many markets (Scott, 1993).[2] This paper concentrates on the latter.

I draw on an extensive database of RJVs registered with the U.S. Department of Justice and the Federal Trade Commission under the

[1] The relevant literature has literally exploded. A few examples include Contractor and Lorange (1988), Coombs et al. (1996), D'Aspremont and Jacquemin (1988), De Bondt et al. (1992), Dodgson (1993), Kamien et al. (1992), Katz (1986), Link and Bauer (1989), Martin (1994), Simpson and Vonortas (1994), Suzumura (1992), Teece (1992), Vonortas (1994). For an extensive literature review, see Vonortas (1997a).

[2] This should also be interpreted to include links to actual and potential competitors. One kind of risk that firms regularly try to brace against is having someone else come up with a great product that may knock them out of the market completely. In principle, at least, cooperative R&D could be used to avoid being knocked out of the market by enticing competition (actual and anticipated) to participate. This could well lead to the reduction of R&D investment and the retardation of the rate of innovation. I would like to thank Dennis Mueller for this observation.

National Cooperative Research Act (NCRA) and, its extension, the National Cooperative Research and Production Act (NCRPA) since the mid-1980s. For brevity, all these organizations will be called NCRA RJVs for the rest of the paper. This information is used to illustrate the intensity of inter-firm cooperation and shed some light on the question of whether extensive antitrust tolerance of cooperative R&D has resulted in the formation of complex "constellations" of firms that may limit market competition.

I also draw on the literature on multimarket contact for some of my arguments. This literature has been around at least since the mid-1950s but has not played a significant role in the debate concerning cooperative industrial R&D in either the United States or the European Union. Still, its basic message is particularly relevant in this case. RJVs – and, by extension, all types of inter-firm technical alliances – offer platforms for firms to "meet" (make a contact). For large diversified firms, frequent ("multiproject") contact is additional to the usual contact in multiple product markets (multimarket contact). The more frequently firms meet, the theory goes, the better they can learn each other's strategies, the larger their incentive to collude, and the more effective the mechanisms for enforcing collusion. Is multiproject contact through RJVs a cause of concern? Are there any safeguards against the potential anti-competitive behavior?

The evidence points at positive answers to both questions. Significant multiproject contact in NCRA RJVs is observed. In many cases this is accompanied with significant multimarket contact outside of the specific RJVs. However, extensive participation of foreign-based organizations, high technological and market uncertainty in the focus areas, and member mobility in a non-negligible number of RJVs may dampen the possible anti-competitive impact of this contact.

The rest of the paper is organized as follows. The following (second) section summarizes the multimarket and multiproject contact argument as it relates to RJVs. The third section illustrates the extent of cooperation in the examined set of NCRA RJVs. The fourth section presents the evidence on multiproject contact in these RJVs and discusses the safeguards against potential anti-competitive behavior. Finally, the fifth section concludes.

2 Multimarket contact

John Scott summarized a popularly held view when he argued that "...public policy in the United States has moved toward promoting cooperation among firms as a means to effectively cluster complementary resources." (Scott, 1993, p. 3). Such clustering frequently drives technological advance (Kodama, 1995; Teece, 1987). The urgency U.S. policy makers felt to "level the playing field" and allow American firms to compete on equal terms with their Japanese (and European) counterparts led, according to Scott, to the NCRA without careful consideration of all anti-competitive possibilities. In particular, he focuses on the additional possibilities RJVs offer to member firms to "meet" in various industries. Given, on one hand, the belief of economists that multimarket contact facilitates the enforcement of collusive arrangements and, on the other, the indication that his sample of NCRA RJVs from the mid-1980s more or less replicated similar types of diversification observed in individual firms, Scott concluded that these RJVs could have easily had socially detrimental results.

Elsewhere, I have argued against the second half of Scott's conclusion (Vonortas, 1997a). My evidence from a larger set of NCRA RJVs (announced between 1985 and 1995) shows that the patterns of "virtual" diversification achieved in these RJVs have been significantly different than the patterns of internal diversification in individual firms. Thus, NCRA RJVs have apparently enabled firms to try new combinations of complementary competencies. In that respect, at least, RJVs demonstrated a real potential to raise private and social returns.

In contrast, the first half of Scott's argument, relating to the opportunities offered by RJVs to their members to meet in many markets, and the consequent collusive implications that this might entail, deserves serious consideration. His observation that the anti-competitive dangers of multimarket (and multiproject) contact were not considered in relation to NCRA is right on the mark. Such dangers were neither taken into account in the case of the Framework Programmes established by the European Community in the early 1980s to support cooperative R&D (Mytelka, 1995; Van Wegberg and Van Witteloostuijn, 1995).

The industrial organization literature has provided both theoretical and empirical support to the argument that multimarket contact may facilitate collusion. Edwards (1955) appears to have been the first to discuss multimarket collusion.

"The interests of great enterprises are likely to touch at many points, and it would be possible for each to mobilize at any one of these points a considerable aggregate of resources. The anticipated gain to such a concern from unmitigated competitive attack upon another large enterprise at any point of contact is likely to be slight as compared with the possible loss from retaliatory action by that enterprise at many other points of contact.... Hence there is an incentive to live and let live, to cultivate a cooperative spirit, and to recognize priorities of interest in the hope of reciprocal recognition." (Edwards, 1955, p. 335 – quoted in Van Wegberg and Van Witteloostuijn, 1995, p. 84.)

In fact, Edwards (1955) argued that "technological partnerships" may facilitate series of agreements for mutual market accommodation. More recently, Harrington (1987) and Bernheim and Whinston (1990) have appraised theoretically the potential for collusion due to multimarket contact. According to Bernheim and Whinston, the danger arises only if firms and markets are asymmetric since multimarket contact is then used to allocate market power according to spheres of influence that firms establish. In practice, however, both conditions are satisfied. Not only markets are asymmetric, firms are asymmetric too (Nelson, 1994).[3] Thus, for all practical purposes, one should consider at least the possibility of collusion as a result of multimarket contact.[4]

In short, the argument as it relates to RJVs is as follows. Multimarket contact can lead to tacit agreement between oligopolists by permitting rivals to achieve cooperative outcomes while behaving noncooperatively. By definition, an RJV creates a mechanism for firms to meet in order to carry out R&D jointly. The proliferation of RJVs has offered the opportunity to participating firms to meet multiple times, thus creating two dangers. First, it is quite possible that multiple project meetings allow firms to learn to coordinate their market interests. Second, frequent meetings to conduct R&D means that the technological interests of two firms overlap to a large extent, which may open an effective avenue for punitive action against a defector: shunning from a technological area(s) or from a technical standard over a period of time. In industries and technologies like those prominent in NCRA RJVs (Section 3), even a delay of a few months when bringing a new product to market can be deterministic for success.

3 NCRA RJVs

The enactment of the NCRA in 1984 and the NCRPA in 1993 created an invaluable source of information on U.S.-based RJVs. The parties of an RJV seeking the antitrust protection provided by the NCRA and NCRPA are required to file notifications with the U.S. Department of Justice and the Federal Trade Commission disclosing the composition and principal research content of the RJV. Subsequent notifications of changes in membership or the research objectives of RJVs are also required. Both kinds of filings are being posted in the Federal Register and have been used in building my data set.

An extensive database of RJVs has been constructed at The George Washington University on the basis of these filings (NCRA-RJV database). Its unique characteristic is that it combines information on joint venture characteristics with information on the characteristics of the participants. The NCRA-RJV database will be used in this section to briefly describe the general characteristics of the RJVs registered during 1985–1995 and of RJV participants.[5] The latter comprise U.S. and foreign organizations, including firms, universities, and government agencies/laboratories. Additional information from this database will be used in the next Section to illustrate multiproject contact in NCRA RJVs.

The term "membership" defines every reported entry to the RJVs in question. Although useful for some purposes – e.g., for determining how

[3] The resource-based view of the firm has provided a host of arguments to support the existence of such discretionary differences (Penrose, 1959).

[4] The empirical evidence is less conclusive. For example, Feinberg (1985) and Scott (1982) found evidence of collusion as a result of multimarket contact; Alexander (1985) did not.

[5] For more extensive descriptions of the NCRA RJVs and of their participants see Vonortas (1997a, b).

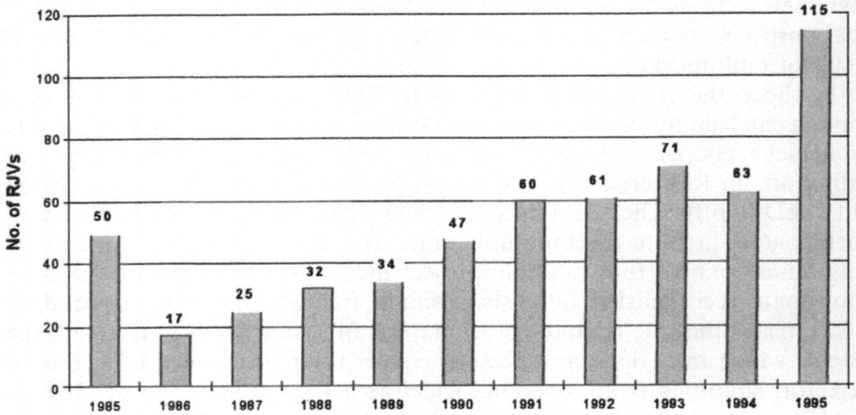

Fig. 1. New RJV announcements

inclusive RJVs have been – membership is less appropriate for others – e.g., for determining the number of organizations participating in NCRA RJVs. Since RJV members are announced at different levels of organizational aggregation one will often encounter consistency problems (e.g., divisions of the same company may be counted separately). Thus, the term "entity" is used to denote an independent organization. For business participants, this is the company level. Universities, government labs and agencies are also considered to be entities. Double counting is eliminated at this level of aggregation: participants are counted only once regardless of how many RJVs each has engaged in.

Five hundred and seventy five new RJVs were announced between January 1, 1985 and December 31, 1995. The number of registered RJVs steadily increased in this time period, with the exception of 1986 and 1994 which apparently reflected the reaction to the legislation changes in 1984 and 1993 (Fig. 1). Cooperation has involved high technology activities. The technical concentration of these 575 RJVs is shown in Table 1.[6]

Telecommunications RJVs have outnumbered RJVs in any other field. Significant activity was also registered in the environment, advanced materials, energy, transportation, software, and chemicals. These were followed by subassemblies and components (including semiconductors and other electronic components), manufacturing equipment, factory automation, photonics, test and measurement, and computer hardware at a lower level. Relatively little activity was recorded in areas with well-enforced intellectual property rights (biotechnology, medical equipment, pharmaceuticals).[7] Very few RJVs were classified as relatively low tech (N/A).

[6] The classification system suggested by the compilers of the CorpTech (Corporate Technologies) database was used here. The CorpTech technical areas can be transformed into SIC code-based industrial activities.

[7] Other forms of inter-firm alliances predominate in these sectors, including licensing, technology swaps, marketing agreements and mergers and acquisitions.

Table 1. Primary technical areas of RJVs

Technical area	1985	1986	1987	1988	1989	1990	1991	1992	1993	1994	1995	Total RJVs	%
Telecommunications	8	1	6	8	10	15	17	17	23	15	11	131	22.78
Environmental	9	1	3	2		6	9	3	5	6	12	56	9.74
Advanced materials	3	5	3	4	5	2	2	5	6	5	13	53	9.22
Energy	5	1	2	1	4	6	9	14	7		1	50	8.70
Transportation	8	3	2			1	4	3	5	9	9	44	7.65
Software	1		1	2	4	2	3	1	4	3	18	39	6.78
Chemicals	2	2	2	2	7	5	8	4	1	3	2	38	6.61
Subassemblies and components	5		1	2		1	1	1	3	6	7	27	4.70
Manufacturing equipment	1	2	2	1	2	3	1	1	1	3	9	26	4.52
Factory automation	2		1	3	1	2		5	3	3	2	22	3.83
Photonics	1		1			2	1	2	3	2	9	21	3.65
Test and measurement		1	1	2	1		4	4	1	1	6	21	3.65
Computer hardware	1			1			1	1	4	1	4	13	2.26
N/A	1	1		1					1	2	5	11	1.91
Biotechnology	1			3		1			1	1	3	10	1.74
Medicals	1					1			2	3	3	10	1.74
Pharmaceuticals	1								1		1	3	0.52
Total RJVs	50	17	25	32	34	47	60	61	71	63	115	575	100

Table 2. Cooperative activity of all identified entities

No. of memberships	Memberships	Entities	% (entities)
1	2388	2388	69.28
2	1058	529	15.35
3	540	180	5.22
4	284	71	2.06
5	260	52	1.51
6 to 10	922	123	3.57
11 to 20	902	64	1.86
21 to 50	946	30	0.87
More than 50	806	10	0.29
Total identified memberships	8106		
Total memberships	9246		
Total identified entities		3447	100

More than two thirds of all identified entities have participated in only one RJV (Table 2).[8] However, almost half (44 percent) of all identified memberships were accounted for by approximately 7 percent of the identified entities (entities with five or more memberships), indicating a significant level of concentration in RJV participation. These very active organizations have tended to be large corporations which should not be surprising given that the primary reason for RJV registration is to benefit from antitrust protection (Table 3).

Business firms clearly dominated the identified U.S.-based entities (86 percent of a total of 2,343 entities). About half of them are private companies, almost 43 percent are public firms, 1 percent are joint ventures, and less than 0.3 percent are partnerships. The remaining firms are "unclassified" in terms of ownership; it is almost certain that most are privately held. Overall, then, quite a significant share of all U.S. business entities that have participated in the listed RJVs have been private and, on average, small or medium sized firms.

Finally, Fig. 2 categorizes the examined RJVs on the basis of their membership. A full 45 percent have had more than five members. It should be mentioned that the number of RJVs with only two members is inflated by the presence of Bellcore, the most active entity in the database (Table 3). Bellcore, the research arm of the seven regional Bell companies during the examined time period, is a joint venture itself. Eighty-seven of the 115 RJVs involving Bellcore have reported only one other partner and are included in the two-member category in Fig. 2. If Bellcore is considered as seven en-

[8] Eighty-eight percent (8,106) of all announced memberships have been identified. In the case of business firms, making up close to nine-tenths of member entries, the following sources the following sources were used for identification: CompuStat, Corporate Technologies (CorpTech), Thomas' Register, Standard & Poor's Corporate Records, Moody's Directory, World Business Directory, Ward's Business Directory, Million Dollar Directory, and Directory of Corporate Affiliations. The remaining unidentified memberships (1,140) correspond to participants that engaged in only one RJV; they are likely to be small privately owned companies and nonprofit organizations.

Table 3. Most active identified entities

No.	Entity	Type	Country	Memberships
1	BellCore	JV	US	115
2	GM	Public	US	105
3	Chevron	Public	US	80
4	Amoco	Public	US	79
5	Du Pont	Public	US	76
6	AT & T	Public	US	75
7	Exxon	Public	US	74
8	IBM	Public	US	69
9	Texaco	Public	US	67
10	Mobil	Public	US	66
11	HP	Public	US	48
12	BP	Public	US	46
13	GE	Public	US	46
14	Shell	Public	Netherlands	44
15	DEC	Public	US	44
16	Ford	Public	US	42
17	Atlantic Richfield	Public	US	41
18	Rockwell International	Public	US	37
19	Siemens AG	Public	Germany	35
20	Kodak	Public	US	34
21	Lockheed Martin	Public	US	34
22	TI	Public	US	33
23	Allied Signal	Public	US	31
24	Phillips	Public	US	31
25	Motorols	Public	US	30
26	USX-Marathon	Public	US	29
27	United Technologies	Public	US	29
28	Boeing	Public	US	28
29	UNOCAL	Public	US	27
30	Unisys	Public	US	26
31	3M	Public	US	26
32	Fujitsu	Public	Japan	24
33	Morthern Telecom	Public	Canada	24
34	Northrop Grumman	Public	US	23
35	NEC	Public	Japan	23
36	Honeywell	Public	US	23
37	Chrysler	Public	US	23
38	GTE	Public	US	22
39	Dow Chemical	Public	US	22
40	Sun Microsystems	Public	US	21
41	Hitachi	Public	Japan	20
42	Caterpillar	Public	US	20
43	Apple Computer	Public	US	20
44	U. of California	University	US	20
45	Novell	Public	US	20
46	Cable Television Labs.	JV	US	19
47	Philips N.V.	Public	Netherlands	19
48	Bristol-Myers Squibb	Public	US	19

Table 3 (continued)

No.	Entity	Type	Country	Memberships
49	Thomson-CSF	Public	France	18
50	Toshiba	Public	Japan	18
51	Groupe Bull	Public	France	18
52	Bell Atlantic	Public	US	18

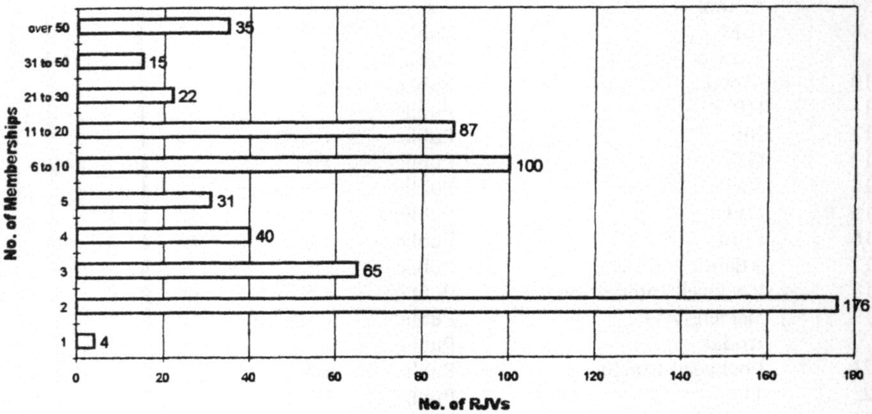

Fig. 2. RJVs classified by total number of members

tries, the number of RJVs with more than five members increases dramatically to 68 percent of the total.[9]

4 Multiproject contact in NCRA RJVs

4.1 Contact

The NCRA-RJV database was searched for evidence of multiproject and multimarket contact. Some of the results are presented in Tables 4 and 5. A few examples are presented in the Appendix (Fig. A1–A4).

Table 4 (multiproject contact) lists the pairs of firms that met in twenty or more NCRA RJVs between 1985 and 1995, together with the firms' primary industries and the area of technical concentration of the respective

[9] Figure 2 contains four RJVs with only one member. Three of them are similar cases to Bellcore: two involve the (10) members of the Motor Vehicle Manufacturers Association of the United States and one involves the member financial institutions of VISA International (a very long list). The fourth RJV was initially announced as open to participation. However, there were no subsequent announcements of joining members until the end of 1995.

Table 4. Multiproject contact in NCRA RJVs

Collaborating firms				MPC[a]	SIC of NCRA-RJVs																	
Firm 1	SIC1	Firm 2	SIC2		13	23	28	29	30	35	36	37	38	44	46	48	49	60	73	80	87	95
Amoco	2911	Chevron	2911	56	15	1	2	26	1	2		3	1	1	1		3					
Chevron	2911	Exxon	2911	51	11	1	3	23	1	2		4	1	1	1		1		1			1
Exxon	2911	Mobil	2911	51	10	1	4	21	1	2	1	4		2	1		1		2			1
Amoco	2911	Exxon	2911	50	13	1	3	23	1	1		3	1	2	1		1					
Amoco	2911	Mobil	2911	50	12	1	2	24	1	2		3		2	1		2					
Chevron	2911	Mobil	2911	50	13	1	2	21	1	2	1	4		1	1		2					1
Chevron	2911	Texaco	2911	50	15	1	2	21	1	2	1	3		1	1		1					1
Mobil	2911	Texaco	2911	48	14	1	1	20	1	2	1	3		2	1		1					1
Amoco	2911	Texaco	2911	47	15	1	1	22	1	1		2		2	1		1					
Exxon	2911	Texaco	2911	47	12	1	2	20	1	1		3	1	2	1		1		1			1
BP	2911	Chevron	2911	36	10		1	19			1	3		1								1
Amoco	2911	BP	2911	35	13			18				2		2								
Amoco	2911	DuPont	2820	34	11	1	1	13		2		1	1	1	1		1				1	
Amoco	2911	AR	2911	33	12	1	1	15		1		2			1							
AR	2911	Chevron	2911	33	9	1	1	15		1	1	3			1							1
Chevron	2911	DuPont	2820	33	9	1	2	13		1	1	1	1	1	1		1		1			
Ford	3711	GM	3711	33			2			5	4	14				1			6		1	
BP	2911	Mobil	2911	32	7		1	16			1	3		2					1			1
BP	2911	Texaco	2911	32	10			16			1	2		2								1
DEC	3570	IBM	3570	32	1		1			3	5					4		1	16		1	
DuPont	2820	Texaco	2911	32	10	1	1	13		1	1	1		1	1		1		1			
AT & T	4813	IBM	3570	31			1			2	8					4		1	14		1	
BP	2911	Exxon	2911	31	6		1	17				3		2					1			1
DuPont	2820	Exxon	2911	31	6	1	3	11			1	1	1	1	1		1		4			
AR	2911	Mobil	2911	30	8	1	1	12		1	1	3			1				1			1
Chevron	2911	Shell	2911	30	10		2	11		1		3		1					1			1

Table 4 (continued)

Collaborating firms				MPC[a]	SIC of NCRA-RJVs																	
Firm 1	SIC1	Firm 2	SIC2		13	23	28	29	30	35	36	37	38	44	46	48	49	60	73	80	87	95
AR	2911	Texaco	2911	29	10	1	1	12			1	2			1							1
Exxon	2911	Shell	2911	29	5		5	9		1		3		2					3			1
Amoco	2911	Shell	2911	28	9		2	11		2		2		2								
DuPont	2820	Mobil	2911	28	5	1	3	10		1	2	1		1	1		1		2			
AR	2911	Exxon	2911	27	7	1	2	10		1		3			1				1			
AT & T	4813	DEC	3570	27			1			2	4					3		1	14	1	1	
DEC	3570	HP	3570	27	1					2	3					4		1	15	1		
Mobil	2911	Phillips	2911	27	7	1	2	14			1	1							1			
Mobil	2911	Shell	2911	27	6		4	9		1		3		2					1			1
Exxon	2911	Phillips	2911	26	6	1	2	14				1	1						1			
HP	3570	IBM	3570	26	1					2	3					4		1	15			
BP	2911	DuPont	2820	25	9		1	10			1	1		1					1		1	
GM	3711	IBM	3570	25	1					4	4					5			9		2	
Texaco	2911	UNOCAL	2911	25	4	1		15				2	1				1					1
AR	2911	BP	2911	24	8		1	9			1	3							1			1
AR	2911	DuPont	2820	24	8	1	1	10			1	1			1				1			
BP	2911	Shell	2911	24	7		1	9				2		2					1		1	1
Chevron	2911	Phillips	2911	24	7	1	1	13			1	1										
Amoco	2911	Phillips	2911	23	7	1		14				1										
Amoco	2911	USX-Marathon	2911	23	11	1	1	8				1			1							
AT & T	4813	HP	3570	23						1	4					3		1	13		1	
Chevron	2911	UNOCAL	2911	23	4	1		14				2					1					1
Shell	2911	Texaco	2911	23	7		1	8				3		2					1			1
Chevron	2911	USX-Marathon	2911	22	10	1	1	8				1			1							
DEC	3570	GM	3711	22	1					3	3					4			10		1	

DuPont	2820	Shell	2911	22	6		4	5		1		1		1					3		1	
GM	3711	HP	3570	22	1					2	4					4			11			
Phillips	2911	Texaco	2911	22	7	1	1	10			1	1	1									
Amoco	2911	UNOCAL	2911	21	4	1		14				1					1					
AT & T	4813	Motorola	3663	21			1			1	5					3		1	10			
Chrysler	3711	GM	3711	21			2			1	2	13				1					2	
Exxon	2911	UNOCAL	2911	21	3	1		11				2	1				1		1			1
Mobil	2911	UNOCAL	2911	21	3	1		12				2					1		1			1
DEC	3570	Motorola	3663	20			1			1	5					2		1	9	1		
GM	3711	Rockwell	3760	20						3	4	1	1			2			7		2	
GM	3711	TI	3674	20						2	6		1			2			8		1	
Texaco	2911	USX-Marathon	2911	20	8	1	1	7				1	1		1							
		Total		1900	425	34	81	676	10	66	85	130	14	43	24	46	24	8	190	3	17	24

[a] MPC: Multiproject contact

RJVs (by year). A SIC classification was used for the technical area of the RJVs.[10] Sixty-three pairs of firms are shown to have cooperated between twenty and fifty-six times. A casual look confirms that the dominant parent industry is petroleum refining (SIC 2911): out of the 1,900 total contacts registered by all sixty-three pairs, 1,332 (70 percent) were accounted by pairs with both firms declaring their primary activity in petroleum refining. A further 207 contacts (11 percent) involved meetings between one petroleum refining firm and DuPont (SIC 2820), the only chemical firm in the table. Other frequent pairs were those between General Motors (SIC 3711) and: (i) the other two large U.S. motor vehicle manufacturers (54 contacts); (ii) three computer companies (IBM, DEC, HP (SIC 3570)) (69 contacts); (iii) Rockwell (SIC 3760), a missile and space vehicles producer (20 contacts); and, (iv) Texas Instruments (SIC 3674), a semiconductor producer (20 contacts). DEC met with five other companies 128 times in total. Hewlett-Packard met with four companies 98 times in all.

Appendix Fig. A1–A4 present the maps of multiproject contact in NCRA RJVs of four large, very active corporations during the examined time period with their main activity in four different sectors: chemicals (SIC 28), computer and office equipment (SIC 357), electronic and other electrical equipment (SIC 36), and telecommunications (SIC 481). Note that the maps present links between companies only if they met ten or more times. Many other similar maps with comparable density could also be drawn.

Table 5 (multimarket contact) lists the same 63 pairs of firms as Table 4 but adds a column showing the number of common 4-digit SIC industries between the firms in each pair. Only one pair involves two firms with no common business lines (General Motors and Hewlett Packard). Three more pairs involve two firms each with two common business lines – General Motors linking with DEC, IBM, and Texas Instruments. Six additional pairs involve firms with three common business lines – all including Texaco and another petroleum refining (Amoco, BP, Mobil, Phillips, Shell) and a chemical firm (DuPont). Four pairs involve two firms each with four common business lines. The remaining 49 pairs involve two firms each with five or more common business lines, with the highest of sixteen business lines shared by Amoco and DuPont.

The evidence in Tables 4 and 5 and Appendix Fig. A1–A4 is overwhelming that large diversified corporations have met in NCRA RJVs much more frequently than commonly understood. Many of these corporations also "meet" each other in many product markets. The combination of extensive multiproject and multimarket contact strengthens the possibility of collusive play with potentially detrimental effects for the main policy objectives of the NCRA and NCRPA: the promotion of industrial

[10] In these calculations, the joint ventures that have participated in NCRA RJVs as members were treated as single entities. This was necessary in order to isolate the multiproject contact induced by NCRA RJVs from the multiproject contact induced by joint ventures outside the NCRA set. This means, however, that information on multiproject contact between individual members of these joint ventures and other partners in NCRA RJVs is omitted. The multiproject contact reported on Table 4 must thus be considered as the minimum between the specific pairs of firms.

Table 5. Multimarket contact between firms with high multiproject contact in NCRA RJVs

Collaborating firms				MPC*	MMC*
Firm 1	SIC1	Firm 2	SIC2		
Amoco	2911	Chevron	2911	56	9
Chevron	2911	Exxon	2911	51	6
Exxon	2911	Mobil	2911	51	5
Amoco	2911	Exxon	2911	50	8
Amoco	2911	Mobil	2911	50	8
Chevron	2911	Mobil	2911	50	7
Chevron	2911	Texaco	2911	50	5
Mobil	2911	Texaco	2911	48	3
Amoco	2911	Texaco	2911	47	3
Exxon	2911	Texaco	2911	47	4
BP	2911	Chevron	2911	36	9
Amoco	2911	BP	2911	35	10
Amoco	2911	Dupont	2820	34	16
Amoco	2911	AR	2911	33	10
AR	2911	Chevron	2911	33	10
Chevron	2911	Dupont	2820	33	9
Ford	3711	GM	3711	33	7
BP	2911	Mobil	2911	32	12
BP	2911	Texaco	2911	32	3
DEC	3570	IBM	3570	32	10
Dupont	2820	Texaco	2911	32	3
AT&T	4813	IBM	3570	31	5
BP	2911	Exxon	2911	31	6
Dupont	2820	Exxon	2911	31	8
AR	2911	Mobil	2911	30	10
Chevron	2911	Shell	2911	30	7
AR	2911	Texaco	2911	29	5
Exxon	2911	Shell	2911	29	6
Amoco	2911	Shell	2911	28	9
Dupont	2820	Mobil	2911	28	8
AR	2911	Exxon	2911	27	8
AT&T	4813	DEC	3570	27	4
DEC	3570	HP	3570	27	8
Mobil	2911	Phillips	2911	27	9
Mobil	2911	Shell	2911	27	6
Exxon	2911	Phillips	2911	26	6
HP	3570	IBM	3570	26	8
BP	2911	Dupont	2820	25	9
GM	3711	IBM	3570	25	2
Texaco	2911	UNOCAL	2911	25	6
AR	2911	BP	2911	24	10
AR	2911	Dupont	2820	24	10
BP	2911	Shell	2911	24	7
Chevron	2911	Phillips	2911	24	10
Amoco	2911	Phillips	2911	23	10
Amoco	2911	USX-Marathon	2911	23	7
AT&T	4813	HP	3570	23	4
Chevron	2911	UNOCAL	2911	23	9

Table 5 (continued)

Collaborating firms				MPC*	MMC*
Firm 1	SIC1	Firm 2	SIC2		
Shell	2911	Texaco	2911	23	3
Chevron	2911	USX-Marathon	2911	22	8
DEC	3570	GM	3711	22	2
Dupont	2820	Shell	2911	22	9
GM	3711	HP	3570	22	0
Phillips	2911	Texaco	2911	22	3
Amoco	2911	UNOCAL	2911	21	7
AT&T	4813	Motorola	3663	21	7
Chrysler	3711	GM	3711	21	5
Exxon	2911	UNOCAL	2911	21	5
Mobil	2911	UNOCAL	2911	21	8
DEC	3570	Motorola	3663	20	4
GM	3711	Rockwell	3760	20	7
GM	3711	TT	3674	20	2
Texaco	2911	USX-Marathon	2911	20	4
Total				1900	428

MPC: Multiproject contact
MMC: Multimarket contact

R&D and the speeding up of technological innovation. If the problem was pervasive, the long-term results could be felt in the form of lower economic competitiveness and loss in consumer welfare.

What's more, the NCRA linkages should not be viewed in isolation from a much wider phenomenon. Linkages through these RJVs are only part of a larger set of contacts through strategic alliances of various kinds taking place at the national and international levels. The density of this activity has prompted analysts to argue that alliances have been changing the meaning of rivalry in some industries (Gerlach, 1992). "As this happens, competition increasingly takes place among constellations of allied firms. In this new style of group-based competition, who wins and who loses depends on the competitive advantages that each group of firms creates through collective action." (Gomes-Casseres, 1996, p. 108).

Is our antitrust regulation system sophisticated enough to deal effectively with inter-firm cooperative agreements? Is the scale tilting toward limiting competition and possibly slowing down the rate of technological advance? Nobody knows without further systematic empirical appraisals of the antitrust implications of multimarket contact and multiproject collaboration.

4.2 Safeguards against anti-competitive behavior

There are three possible checks against potential anti-competitive behavior through this activity.

1. Foreign participation in RJVs may dilute efforts to restrict competition in a particular geographic area.

2. Technological and market uncertainty may dilute efforts to restrict competition in a particular technological area.
3. The creation of "porous" constellations of firms – i.e., groupings whose composition changes frequently – may dilute efforts to restrict competition in a geographic or technological area.

A *check to potential anti-competitive effects* of frequent collaboration in RJVs can be foreign participation. In their discussion of the collusive dangers from multiproject contact through the E.U. Framework Programmes on R&D, Van Wegberg and Van Witteloostuijn (1995) suggested low-entry barriers to non-European firms exactly for that reason. As Fig. 3 shows, almost a quarter of the identified participants in the examined NCRA RJVs were foreign based.[11]

The identified foreign-based entities in the first eleven years were 1,092 (32 percent of the total), accounting for 2,129 memberships (about 26 percent of the total). By and large, this extensive presence reflects the activity of foreign multinational corporations (Table 6). Similarly to large diversified American firms, these corporations come on board in search of new technology options and in expectation of technological and market complementarities.

Foreign participants were spread out in about half of all 575 NCRA RJVs; 289 RJVs registered foreign participation of some kind (Table 7). Although they tended to concentrate on small and medium size RJVs with only business participants, a careful look indicates that almost all large RJVs (54 out of 56 RJVs with more than 25 members) have had foreign participants.

RJVs with foreign participants engaged mostly in information technologies. The sum of RJVs pursuing research in electronics, communications, software, computer equipment, and photonics were over half of all RJVs with international participation (149 out of 289 RJVs with foreign participation). Chemicals, petroleum refining, oil and gas mining, and automobiles were the other areas with significant foreign participation.[12] All in all, foreign-based participants have had a significant presence in terms of the research links achieved in the examined RJVs. About 40 percent of all identified links – unique pairs of identified member entities – involve at least one foreign party (135,369 out of 336,590) (Vonortas, 1997a).

Does the extensive participation of foreign-based firms mean that potentially collusive behavior has been dissipated? Or does this aspect of foreign participation turn innocuous in an increasingly internationalized economic environment? One can easily think, for example, of large diversified multinationals with global strategies, meeting in many geographical and product markets, whose willingness to compete more or less vigorously in any single market is closely related to what happens in other markets. Put differently, widespread foreign participation in certain technological fields

---

[11] Foreign-based participants include U.S. operating firms whose ownership could be ultimately traced abroad.

[12] Foreign government agency and university participants account for about a third of all government and university memberships in the database. They participate mostly in RJVs on software and oil and gas mining.

Country	Entity	Membership	%
US	2343	5964	73.7
UK	175	343	4.2
Japan	161	418	5.2
Canada	130	209	2.6
Germeny	115	233	2.9
France	78	200	2.5
Italy	48	85	1.1
Australia	46	53	0.7
Sweden	40	83	1.0
Netherlands	35	106	1.3
Switzerland	32	76	0.9
Taiwan	20	28	0.3
Norway	19	36	0.4
Korea	18	34	0.4
Mexico	18	19	0.2
Finland	14	37	0.5
Denmark	13	18	0.2
Singapore	13	15	0.2
Belgium	13	14	0.2
Israel	11	12	0.1
India	10	10	0.1
Spain	9	14	0.2
Hong Kong	7	10	0.1
South Africa	7	9	0.1
Brazil	6	11	0.1
Austria	6	6	0.1
China	5	5	0.1
New Zealand	5	5	0.1
Hungary	4	5	0.1
Greece	4	4	0.0
Ireland	4	4	0.0
Portugal	4	4	0.0
Saudi Arabia	3	3	0.0
Venezuela	2	3	0.0
Colmbia	2	2	0.0
Argentina	1	1	0.0
Costa Rica	1	1	0.0
Czechoslovakia	1	1	0.0
Estonia	1	1	0.0
Europe	1	1	0.0
Indonesia	1	1	0.0
Kenya	1	1	0.0
Luxembourg	1	1	0.0
Malaysia	1	1	0.0
Russia	1	1	0.0
Rwanda	1	1	0.0
Tanzania	1	1	0.0
Turkey	1	1	0.0
West Indies	1	1	0.0
Yugoslavia	1	1	0.0
Total	*3435*	*8093*	*100*

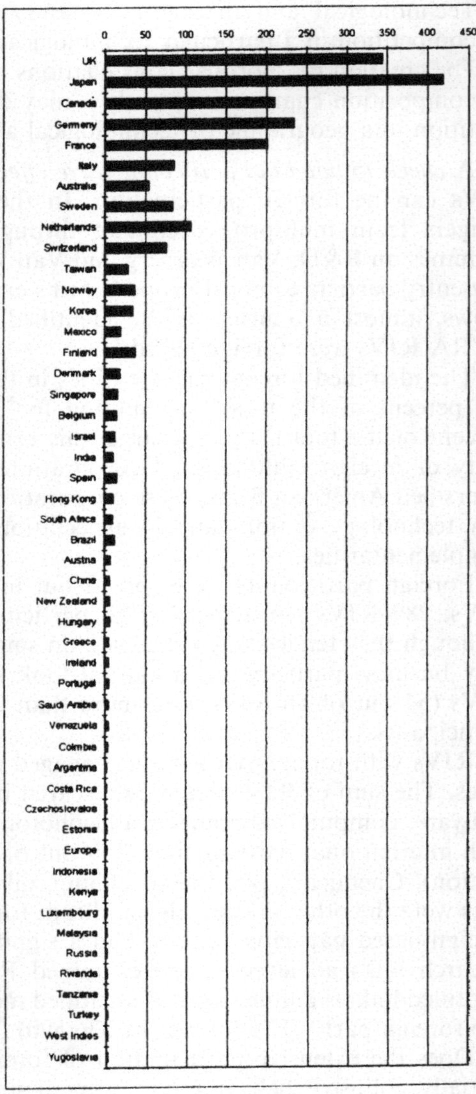

Fig. 3. Identified entities by country

may also hide attempts to restrict competition at a global scale. Only inconclusive answers can be given without further research.

Another *check to potential anti-competitive effects* from repeated collaboration in RJVs, this time for a particular technological area, can be technological and market uncertainty. The NCRA-RJV database was also searched for evidence of strategic motives of firms for participating in these RJVs. Elsewhere, I have shown that the "virtual" diversification achieved in the RJVs in question has tended to be different in the aggre-

Table 6. Most active foreign identified entities

No.	Entity	Type	Country	Memberships
1	British Petroleum PLC	Public	UK	46
2	Shell Oil Co.	Public	Netherlands	44
3	Siemens AG	Public	Germany	35
4	Fujitsu Ltd.	Public	Japan	24
5	Northern Telecom Ltd.	Public	Canada	24
6	NEC Corp.	Public	Japan	23
7	Hitachi, Ltd.	Public	Japan	20
8	Philips N.V.	Public	Netherlands	19
9	Groupe Bull	Public	France	18
10	Thomson-CSF	Public	France	18
11	Toshiba Corp.	Public	Japan	18
12	Alcatel Answare	Public	France	17
13	L.M. Ericsson Tel	Public	Sweden	15
14	Nippon Telegraph and Telephone Corp.	Public	Japan	15
15	ABB Asea Brown Boveri, Ltd.	Public	Switzerland	15
16	Pritish Telecom PLC	Public	UK	15
17	Bayer AG	Public	Germany	14
18	Sony Corp.	Public	Japan	13
19	Mitsubishi Corp.	Public	Japan	12
20	Societe Nationale Elf Aquitaine	Public	France	12
21	Fiat S.p.A.	Public	Italy	12
22	Honda Motor, Ltd.	Public	Japan	11
23	Volvo AB	Public	Sweden	11
24	ICL PLC	Public	UK	11
25	OKI Electric Industries Co., Ltd.	Public	Japan	11
26	Pacal, PLC	Public	UK	11
27	Matsushita Electric	Public	Japan	10
28	Daimler-Benz AG	Public	Germany	10
29	Nissan Motor Co., Ltd.	Public	Japan	10
30	Hoechst AG	Public	Germany	10
31	Nokia Corp.	Public	Finland	10
32	Sharp Corp.	Public	Japan	9
33	Samsung Group	Public	Korea	9
34	Roussel UCLAF	C	France	9
35	Isuzu Motors, Ltd.	Public	Japan	9
36	Renault Vehicles industries	Public	France	9
37	GEC PLC	Public	UK	9
38	Yokogawa Electric Corp.	Public	Japan	8
39	Ciba, Ltd.	Public	Switzerland	8
40	Ing. C. Olivetti and Co. S.p.A.	Public	Italy	8
41	Zeneca Group PLC	Public	UK	8
42	Saab-Scania AB	Public	Sweden	8
43	Petro-Canada Inc.	Public	Canada	7
44	SmithKline Beecham PLC	Public	UK	7
45	Agip S.p.A.	Public	Italy	7
46	BASF Aktiengesellschaft	Public	Germany	6
47	Norsk Hydro A.S	Public	Norway	6
48	Newbridge Networks Corp.	Public	Canada	6
49	Telefonica De Espana, S.A.	Public	Spain	6
50	Elf Aquitaine, Inc.	Public	France	6
51	Mitsubishi Motors Corp.	Public	Japan	6
52	Gandalf Technologies, Inc.	Public	Canada	6

Table 7. Size and type of RJVs with foreign participants

RJV size[a]	Firm only	Firm-gov.	Firm-gov.-univ	Firm-univ.	Total
1–3	75	1	0	1	77
4–10	74	2	2	2	80
11–25	59	9	3	7	78
26–50	10	6	1	2	19
51–100	8	1	4	2	15
Over 100	2	5	10	3	20
Total	228	24	20	17	289

[a] Number of memberships

gate than the internal diversification of individual companies, an indirect indication that many firms join to do things they cannot, or are not willing to, do on their own (Vonortas, 1997a, forthcoming). For our purposes, it would also be of interest to observe where the specific linkages have taken place – that is, we would like to know who-collaborates-with-whom-on-what in NCRA RJVs.

This will be done here with the help of two "technology maps" based on the core (primary) activities of RJV business participants. The first map, shown in Fig. 4, interlocks the technological fields of RJVs and the core industrial activities of the RJV participants at the two-digit SIC level. This clustering addresses the who-collaborates-on-what part of the question. The second map, shown in Fig. 5, interlocks the core industrial activities of participants in all RJVs at the two-digit SIC level.[13] The information is then presented across industries. This clustering addresses the who-collaborates-with-whom part of the question.[14]

Figure 4 can be considered as the graphical illustration of a technology input-output table where the rows – corresponding to the core industrial activities of RJV participants – are the inputs and the columns – corresponding to the technological fields of RJVs – are the outputs. The number in a cell of such a table would represent the number of memberships by all firms whose primary industry is indicated at the beginning of the corresponding row to all RJVs classified in the industry indicated at the top of the corresponding column. The diagonal cells would indicate the number of memberships by firms whose core industrial activity coincides with the technological field of the RJVs these firms participate in.[15]

The most densely populated technological fields for NCRA RJVs have been business services (basically computer software) (SIC 73), communi-

[13] Classification of large diversified firms by their primary industry is admittedly not entirely appropriate. The primary industry classification was maintained on two considerations. First, the numbers in the cells of the Tables supporting Figs. 4 and 5 become very large and unwieldy when secondary industries are included. Second, these numbers are of dubious interpretation anyway in the absence of industry weights for individual firms. The large number of entries was expected to help average out misrepresentations.

[14] In constructing both Figs. 4 and 5, all joint ventures participating in the examined RJVs were broken up into their respective members.

[15] Note that different memberships of the same firm may be included in different cells.

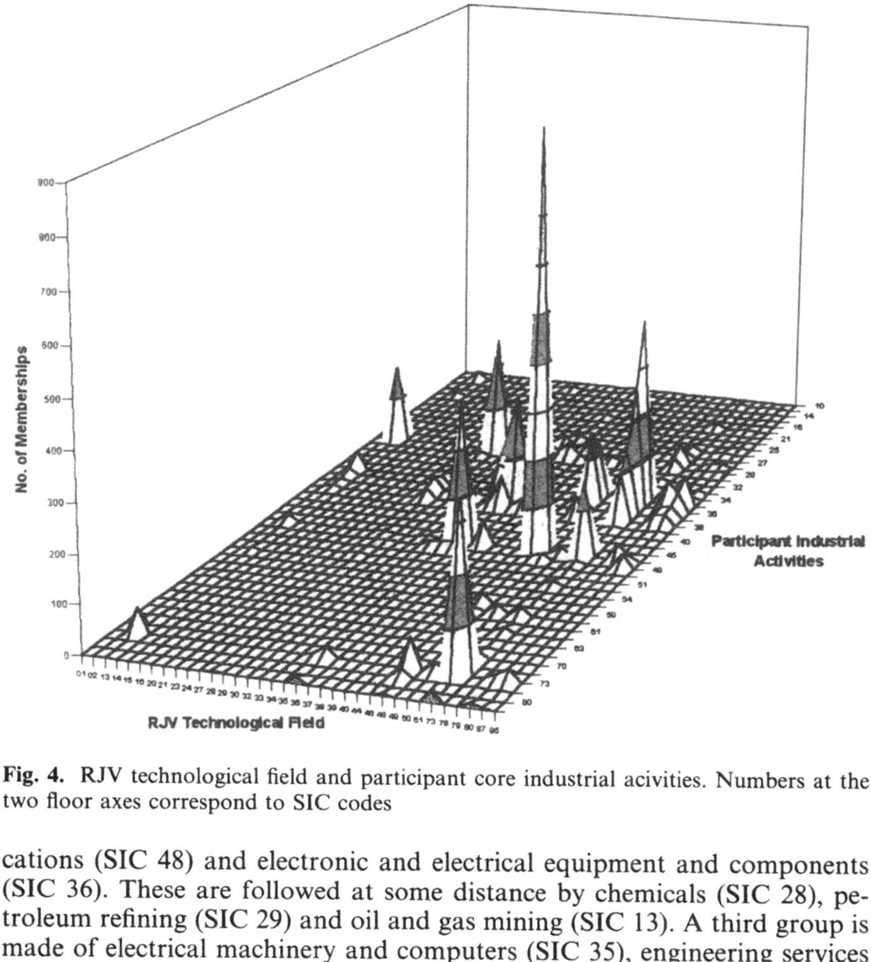

Fig. 4. RJV technological field and participant core industrial acivities. Numbers at the two floor axes correspond to SIC codes

cations (SIC 48) and electronic and electrical equipment and components (SIC 36). These are followed at some distance by chemicals (SIC 28), petroleum refining (SIC 29) and oil and gas mining (SIC 13). A third group is made of electrical machinery and computers (SIC 35), engineering services (SIC 87), and health services (SIC 80).

Firms in communications (SIC 48), machinery and computer equipment (SIC 35), and electronic and electrical equipment (SIC 36) have been the most active participants in NCRA RJVs. Firms in transportation equipment (SIC 37), software (SIC 73), petroleum refining (SIC 29), chemicals (SIC 28), and scientific instruments (SIC 38) have also been very active.

The clearly distinguishable spike in Fig. 4 corresponds to communications firms (SIC 48) participating in RJVs in the same field (843 memberships).[16] Machinery and computer equipment (SIC 35) and electronic and electrical equipment (SIC 36) producers have also been significantly active in communications RJVs. The most diverse and significant participation,

[16] This number reflects the very extensive participation of Bellcore in the examined RJVs. As in the case of all joint ventures in this section, Bellcore was broken up into its constituent members (seven local Bell companies).

however, has been in RJVs focusing on software (SIC 73) which drew large numbers of participants with core activities in SIC 73, 35, 36, 48, 37, and 38.

The pattern of collaboration differs from industry to industry. Firms in chemicals (SIC 28), petroleum refining (SIC 29) and software (SIC 73) have been very own-sector oriented in terms of the technological field of the RJVs they chose to participate in. On the contrary, firms in machinery and computer equipment (SIC 35) and electronic and electrical equipment (SIC 36) spread out their collaborative R&D effort to many fields. Firms in transportation equipment (SIC 37), instruments (SIC 38) and communications (SIC 48) have tended to be fairly narrowly focused to a few other fields beyond their own core industrial activity.

I now turn to the who-collaborates-with-whom question. Figure 5 can be considered as the graphical illustration of a "cooperation table" whose rows and columns correspond to the core industrial activities of the RJV business participants. Only half of such a table (including the diagonal) has entries to avoid double counting. The number in a cell represents the number of times firms whose primary industry is indicated at the beginning of the corresponding row met with firms whose primary industry is indicated at the top of the corresponding column. Diagonal cells correspond to horizontal cooperation. Off-diagonal cells correspond to vertical cooperation.

Two more observations concerning the construction of the "cooperation table" underlying Fig. 5 must also be pointed out. First, all industrial links are

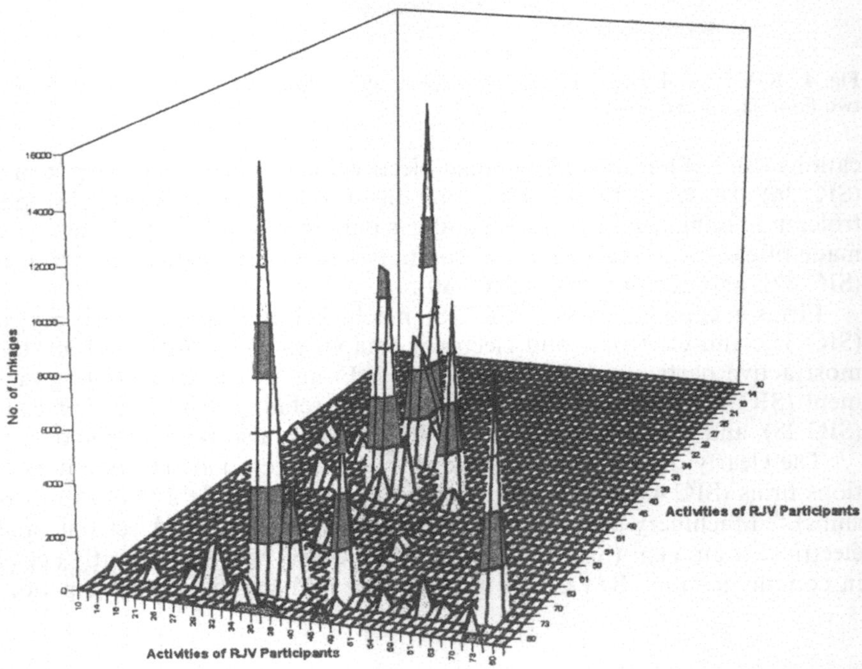

Fig. 5. Linkages of Industrial Activities in NCRA-RJVs. Numbers at the two floor axes correspond to SIC codes

weighed equally. For example, if an RJV lists firms A, B, and C as members, all three possible linkages in this RJV (AB, AC, BC) are counted and are given the same weight. This essentially assumes that all three firms cooperate equally extensively in this RJV.[17] Second, linkages between two industrial activities are counted as many times as they have occurred in an RJV. If, for example, firms A and B in the RJV have the same primary industry which differs from that of firm C, both the AC and BC linkages are counted even though they are the same. This procedure is followed because we are interested in observing how many times two industrial activities have met in RJVs.

Firms in machinery and computer equipment (SIC 35), electronic and electrical equipment (SIC 36), communications (SIC 48), and software (SIC 73) have registered most cooperative activity. The same industries also had the highest rates of horizontal cooperation. Significant activity (more than 1,000 linkages) has also been registered by firms in chemicals (SIC 28), petroleum refining (SIC 29), transportation equipment (SIC 37), and instruments (SIC 38).

The closest cooperative relationship has been between software (SIC 73) and machinery and computer equipment (SIC 35). Other strong cooperative relationships include machinery and computer equipment (SIC 35) and electronic and electrical equipment (SIC 36), electronic equipment (SIC 36) and software (SIC 73), communications (SIC 48) and computer equipment (SIC 35), communications (SIC 48) and software (SIC 73), and electrical machinery and computer equipment (SIC 35) and scientific instruments (SIC 38).

If intra-sectoral cooperation is added to inter-sectoral cooperation, one easily reaches the conclusion that the production and application of information technologies have led cooperation in NCRA RJVs. Advanced materials (spread out primarily in the group of chemicals due to the peculiarities of SIC classification) have also played a major role. A third area, but at a significant distance from the other two, is biotechnology and medicals, primarily in conjunction with information technology applications. It is no secret to business analysts that these three technology areas offered the highest technological opportunities during the examined time period.

In addition, these technological areas share two important characteristics that make them good candidates for cooperative R&D. One common characteristic is the lack of well-defined technological trajectories – routes of technological advance (Dosi, 1988) – save for narrow product ranges. This has been most visible in information technology, largely due to technology convergence in a digital environment. It could be argued that the areas of biotechnology and advanced materials have also been undergoing equally important redefinition of their technological trajectories with the newly acquired capabilities for DNA/RNA sequencing and gene manipulation, on the one hand, and capabilities for building materials atom by atom to exact

[17] Clearly, this is an oversimplification. The RJV type, RJV size, the type of the participants, the status of the participants within an RJV, and the technological field of an RJV may have a significant impact on the individual industrial linkages. In addition, our focus on the primary industrial activities of the participating firms is also not entirely satisfactory; see footnote 13.

specifications, on the other. The second common characteristic of these technological areas is their "infrastructural" nature: the underlying technologies affect a wide array of industries ranging from agriculture, to mining, to manufacture, and services. Information technology is the most "infrastructural" of the three, but the other two follow closely behind.

The combination of very high technological opportunities, imperfectly defined technological trajectories, and infrastructural characteristics seems to make information technology, advanced materials and biotechnology primary candidates for inter-firm cooperation in R&D. If so, the evidence indicates that many firms join RJVs focusing on these areas to "hedge their bets" against very high technological and market uncertainties. This, in fact, agrees with my other finding reported above that the "virtual" diversification achieved in these RJVs is significantly different on average than the internal diversification of individual firms, indicating partners who join in order to experiment with new forms and markets. One is led to the conclusion that firms have viewed the examined RJVs as a less costly (and less risky) way of pursuing longer term, uncertain R&D that will create the technological options of the future.

These conclusions are important for implying that cooperation in NCRA RJVs is part and parcel of the more general trend of inter-firm cooperation through strategic alliances of all kinds, driven by the rapidly rising costs, increasing complexity, and heightened awareness of the importance of certain "core technologies" in contemporary industry (Hagedoorn and Schakenraad, 1990). The market and technological uncertainties inherent in the application of these technologies can operate as a check to potential anti-competitive behavior from widespread collaboration.

Uncertainty could also, however, provide an incentive for "locking-in" proprietary technologies by creating tight agreements between most (all) major players in an area with clauses limiting partners to the technologies and corresponding standards arising from these agreements (see also footnote 2). Hence the relevance of the *third check of potential anti-competitive effects* from repeated collaboration: the creation of "porous" constellations. The term "porous" is used here as a metaphor for relatively short-living, flexible agreements with partners who can easily change constellations. The U.S. legislation has explicitly requested that the registered RJVs do not contain unreasonable limitations of participation that might lead to industry monopolization.

I searched the NCRA-RJV database for evidence of mobility between joint ventures. Membership has not remained stable throughout the lifetime of all examined RJVs. Over a quarter of the recorded joint ventures (161) had reported membership changes by the end of 1995. Of these, 93 recorded new member entries but no exits; 27 recorded member exits but no new entries; and 41 RJVs recorded both entries and exists. The time trends of RJV member entries and exits throughout the examined 11-year period, as reported by the end of 1995, are shown in Fig. 6. Total entries are broken down in two classes: founding members of newly registered RJVs (initial members) and new members joining RJVs (added members).

Overall, there had been considerable mobility in and out of more than a quarter (161) of the recorded RJVs by the end of 1995. Subtracting from the

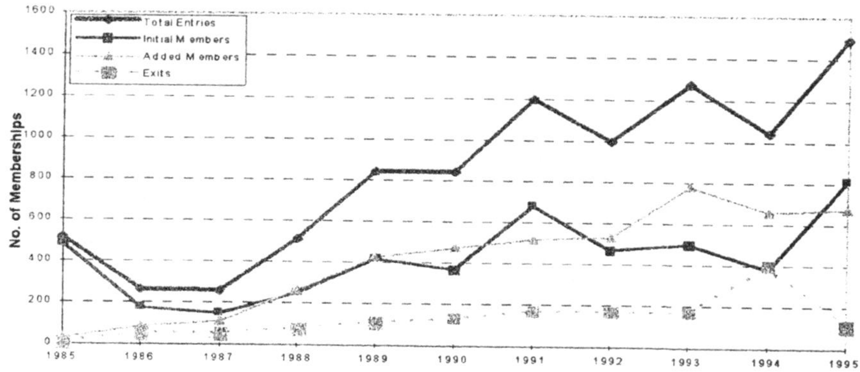

Fig. 6. RJV membership changes. Total entities = Initial Members + Added Members. Initial members are the members when RJVs are launched. Added Members are the new members of existing RJVs. Exits are the terminated memberships

total also the newly formed RJVs in 1995 (115) – for which it was too early to expect announcements of changes – we are left with 299 RJVs with no reported changes. Is that bad? Not necessarily. Among others, the answer would depend on whether: (i) the R&D in question would have been undertaken by any firm in the absence of the RJV; (ii) all potential players in the specific technology have participated in the RJV; (iii) nonparticipants are excluded from the technology. Unfortunately, it is very difficult to come across such detailed information for every single of these RJVs.

5 Concluding remarks

The discussion in this paper adds a cautionary note to the euphoria often expressed with respect to the prospects of inter-firm cooperation in R&D in opening new technological frontiers and speeding up innovation. Besides the ongoing debate on whether RJVs and other technical alliances can indeed play a central role in the strategic outlook of firms, there is the broader policy issue of whether the alleged advantages of RJVs in restoring incentives to undertake R&D – when the costs and uncertainties are high and the appropriability of technological knowledge is low – are sufficient to counterbalance the danger of anti-competitive behavior that may be facilitated through collaboration. On these grounds, a number of economists have opposed greater regulatory leniency towards RJVs without careful consideration of the contingencies. The material presented herein, based on evidence from a large number of RJVs formed in the United States from the mid-1980s to the mid-1990s, suggests that they should be listened to carefully.

An area that requires the urgent attention of economic analysts and policy makers alike is the crossroads of multimarket and multiproject contact. Antitrust authorities must be alert to the enhanced possibility of market concentration in the presence of repeated collaboration in R&D between firms that also "meet" in many product markets. While the dangers of multimarket contact are generally understood by industrial economists, it is now the case that increasing numbers of technical alliances (including

RJVs) provide platforms for firms to "meet" and align their future technological interests. The effects of the latter are not well understood.

Cooperation in R&D is not anti-competitive in principle. One could, for example, argue that such practice may facilitate the establishment of technology standards leading to R&D and market economies, new firms and new technology applications. It could turn anti-competitive, however, if these standards are not the best that could arise from market processes and if they are "enforced" through collusive arrangements. Since, on one hand, multimarket contact raises both the incentives to collude and the enforceability of collusion while, on the other, multiproject contact facilitates the coordination of long-term technological interests and again enhances the enforceability of agreements, the danger of anti-competitive behavior increases when the two are combined in an asymmetric market environment with asymmetric firms.

Three kinds of safeguards against market concentration through R&D cooperation were pointed out: (i) foreign participation in RJVs; (ii) the presence of technological and market uncertainty in the technological area(s) of focus; and, (iii) the establishment of porous inter-firm agreements, that is, agreements that do not lead to air tight constellations of firms. While none of these safeguards can guarantee full protection against the possibility of anti-competitive behavior induced/facilitated by the frequent collaboration between diversified firms, they do have the potential to operate as a check against it. In the least, they can operate as guiding posts for both antitrust authorities and prospective collaborators weighing the advantages and disadvantages of specific cooperative agreements in R&D.

Appendix

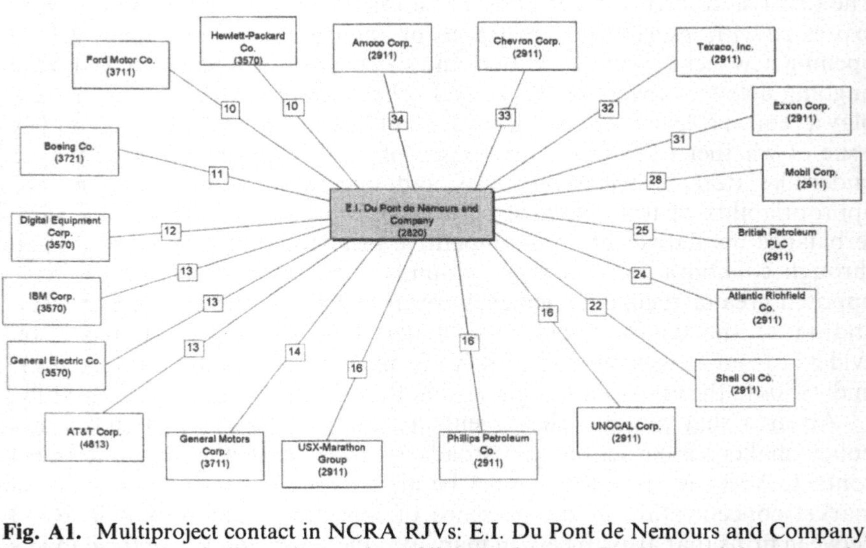

Fig. A1. Multiproject contact in NCRA RJVs: E.I. Du Pont de Nemours and Company. Numbers in squares indicate the number of linkages between Du Pont and the companies in the outer boxes. Numbers in parentheses indicate the primary line of business of the respective company

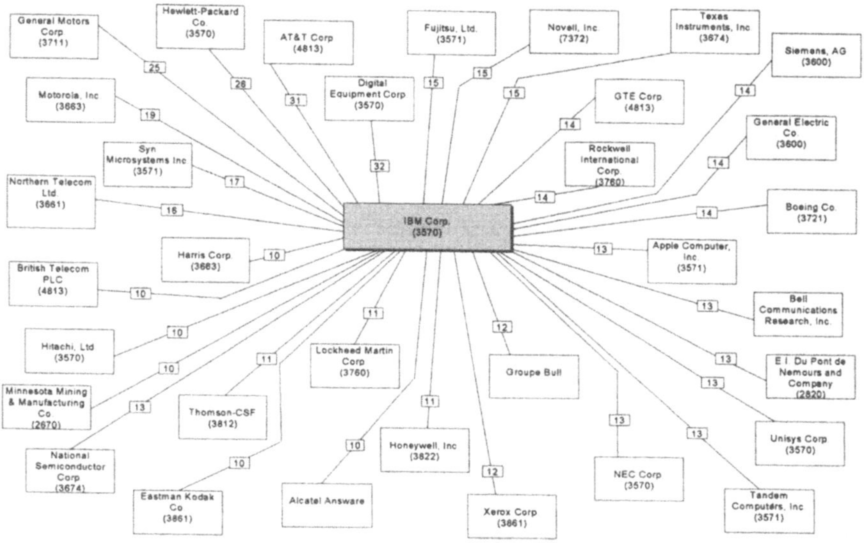

Fig. A2. Multiproject contact in NCRA RJVs: International Business Machines Corporation. Numbers in squares indicate the number of linkages between IBM Corp. and the companies in the outer boxes. Numbers in parentheses indicate the primary line of business of the respective company

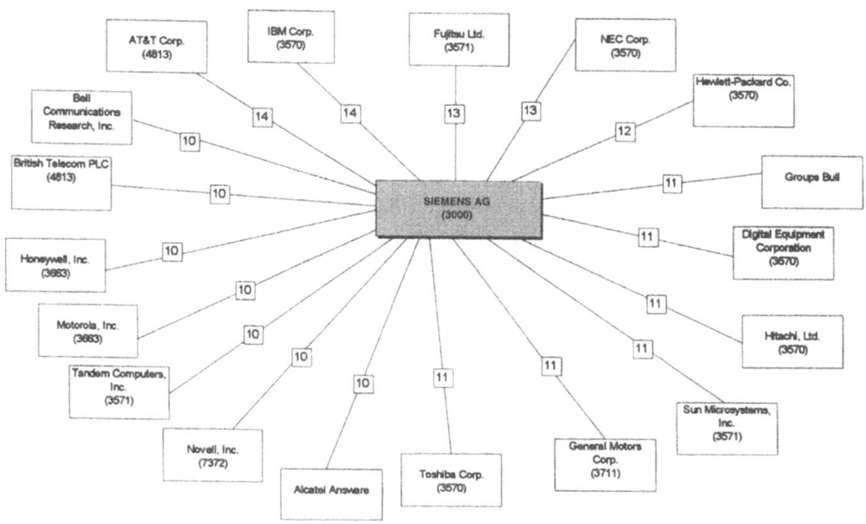

Fig. A3. Multiple contact in NCRA RJVs: Siemens AG. Numbers in squares indicate the number of linkage between Siemens AG and the companies in the outer boxes. Numbers in parentheses indicate the primary line of business of the respective company

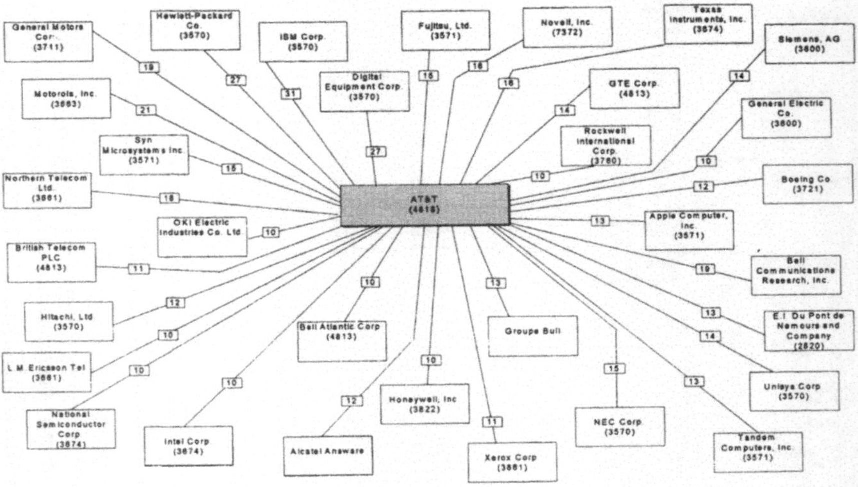

Fig. A4. Mulitproject contact in NCRA RJVs: American Telephone & Telegraph. Numbers in squares indicate the number of linkages between AT&T and the companies in the outer boxes. Numbers in parentheses indicate the primary line of business of the repsective company

References

Alexander DL (1985) An empirical test of the mutual forebearance hypothesis: The case for bank holding companies. Southern Economic Journal 52: 122–140

Bernheim BD, Whinston MD (1990) Multimarket contact and collusive behavior. Rand Journal of Economics 21: 1–26

Clarke RN (1984) Collusion and the incentives for information sharing. Bell Journal of Economics 14(2): 383–394

Contractor FJ, Lorange P (1988) Cooperative strategies in international business. Lexington Books, Lexington, MA.

Coombs R, Richards A, Savioti PP, Walsh V (eds) (1996) Technological collaboration. Edward Elgar, Cheltenham, Brookfield

D'Aspremont, Jacquemin (1988) Cooperative and noncooperative R&D in duopoly with spillovers. The American Economic Review 78: 1133–1137

De Bondt R, Slaets P, Cassiman B (1992) The degree of spillovers and the number of rivals for maximum effective R&D. International Journal of Industrial Organization 10(1): 35–54

Dodgson M (1993) Technological collaboration in industry. Routledge, London

Dosi G (1988) Sources, procedures and microeconomic effects of innovation. Journal of Economic Literature 26: 1120–1171

Edwards CD (1955) Conglomerate bigness as a source of power. In: Stigler GJ (ed) Business concentration and price policy. Princeton University Press, New York

Feinberg RM (1985) Sales at risk: A test of the mutual forebearance theory of conglomerate behavior. Journal of Business 58: 225–241

Fusfeld HI (1994) Industry's future: Changing patterns of industrial research. American Chemical Society, Washington, DC

Gerlach ML (1992) Alliance capitalism. University of California Press, Los Angeles, CA

Gomes-Casseres B (1996) The alliance revolution: the new shape of business rivalry. Harvard University Press, Cambridge, MA

Hagedoorn J, Schakenraad J (1990) Inter-firm partnerships and co-operative strategies in core technologies. In: Freeman C, Soete L (eds) New explorations in the economics of technical change. Pinter, London

Harrington JE Jr (1987) Collusion and multiproduct oligopoly games under a finite horizon. International Economic Review 28: 1–14

Kamien MI, Muller E, Zang I (1992) Research joint ventures and R&D cartels. The American Economic Review 82(5): 1293–1306

Katz ML (1986) An analysis of cooperative research and development. Rand Journal of Economics 17(4): 527–543

Kodama F (1995) Emerging patterns of innovation. Harvard Business School Press, Boston, MA

Link AN, Bauer LL (1989) Cooperative research in U.S. manufacturing: Assessing policy initiatives and corporate strategies. Lexington Books, Lexington, MA

Martin (1994) Private and social incentives to form R&D joint ventures. Review of Industrial Organization 9: 157–171

Mytelka LK (1995) Dancing with wolves: Global oligopolies and strategic partnerships. In: Hagedoorn J (ed) Technical change and the world economy. Edward Elgar, Aldershot Brookfield

Nelson RR (1961) Uncertainty, learning, and the economics of parallel research and development efforts. Review of Economics and Statistics XXXXIII: 351–364

Nelson RR (1994) Why do firms differ, and how does it matter?. In: Rumelt RP, Schendel DE, Teece DJ (eds) Fundamental issues in strategy. Harvard Business School Press, Boston, MA

Penrose ET (1959) The theory of the growth of the firm. Wiley, New York

Scott JT (1982) Multimarket contact and economic performance. The Review of Economics and Statistics 64: 368–375

Scott JT (1993) Purposive diversification and economic performance. Cambridge University Press, New York

Simpson RD, Vonortas NS (1994) Cournot equilibrium with imperfectly appropriable R&D. The Journal of Industrial Economics XLII(1): 79–92

Suzumura K (1992) Cooperative and noncooperative R&D in an oligopoly with spillovers. The American Economic Review 82(5): 1307–1320

Teece DJ (1987) Capturing value from technological innovation: integration, strategic partnering, and licensing decisions. In: Guile BR, Brooks H (eds) Technology and global industry: companies and nations in the world economy. National Academy Press, Washington, DC

Teece DJ (1992) Competition, cooperation, and innovation: Organizational arrangements for regimes of rapid technological progress. Journal of Economic Behavior and Organization 18: 1–25

Van Wegberg M, Van Witteloostuijn A (1995) Multicontact collusion in product markets and joint R&D ventures: the case of the information technology industry in an integrating Europe. In: Hagedoorn J (ed) Technical change and the world economy. Edward Elgar, Aldershot Brookfield

Vonortas NS (1994) Inter-firm cooperation with imperfectly appropriable research. International Journal of Industrial Organization 12(3): 413–435

Vonortas NS (1997a) Cooperation in research and development. Kluwer, Norwell, MA Dordrecht

Vonortas NS (1997b) Research joint ventures in the United States. Research Policy 26(4–5): 577–595

Vonortas NS (1998) Business diversification through research joint ventures: advanced technology program. Report, National Institute of Standards and Technology, Gaithersburg, MD

Vonortas NS (forthcoming) How do participants in research joint ventures diversify? Review of Industrial Organization

Political entrepreneurship and bidding for political monopoly

Michael Wohlgemuth*

Max-Planck-Institut zur Erforschung von Wirtschaftssystemen, Kahlaische Strasse 10, D-07745 Jena, Germany (e-mail: wohlgemuth@mpiew-jena.mpg.de)

Abstract. An analytical framework for dealing with political entrepreneurship and reform is proposed which is based on some new combinations of Schumpeterian political economy, an extended version of Tullock's model of democracy as franchise-bidding for natural monopoly and some basic elements of New Institutional Economics. It is shown that problems of insufficient award criteria and incomplete contracts which may arise in economic bidding schemes, also – and even more so – characterise political competition. At the same time, these conditions create leeway for Schumpeterian political entrepreneurship. The same is true for various barriers to entry in politics. These barriers affect a trade-off between political stability and political contestability which will be discussed with special emphasis on incentives and opportunities for political entrepreneurship in the sense of risking long-term investments in basic political reforms.

Key words: Schumpeter and public choice – Political entrepreneurs – Entry barriers – Policy reform – Political competition

JEL-classification: D72, D78, L10

1 Introduction: unexploited ideas and combinations

In 1942, Joseph Schumpeter published the famous book "Capitalism, Socialism and Democracy". Among various provocative ideas it contains

---

Paper presented at the 1998 World Conference of the International Joseph A. Schumpeter Society, Vienna, June 13–16, 1998.

* I gratefully acknowledge comments and suggestions by Ivan Baron Adamovich, Harold Demsetz, Thráinn Eggertsson, Uwe and Annette Mummert, Dennis C. Mueller, Werner Mussler, Thomas Ulen and Stefan Voigt. The usual disclaimer applies.

"another theory of democracy" based on the definition of democracy as "competition for leadership" (1942/87, p. 271). Although Schumpeter is often called precursor of modern Public Choice, demand-driven models of political competition in the Hotelling-Downs tradition and modern Chicago variants have since become dominant which neglect Schumpeterian ideas of political leadership. In 1965, Gordon Tullock published "Entry Barriers in Politics" which provides still another theory of democracy based on the analogy of an auction mechanism which allocates rights to a "natural monopoly". Tullock's short article not only anticipates the famous proposal for auctioning temporary rights to natural monopolies made by Harold Demsetz (1968), but also sketches a model for analysing democracy along Schumpeterian lines. Within modern Public Choice Tullock's paper has also remained largely neglected.

Reasons for neglecting these ideas are easier to understand in Schumpeter's case. For Dennis Mueller "the public choice approach to non-market decision making has been ... to ask the same questions as traditional price theory (Do equilibria exist? Are they stable? Pareto efficient? How are they obtained?)" (1989, p. 3f). Schumpeter gives no answers to these questions. Meanwhile, most models of party competition have reduced politicians to "retailers of existing or but marginally different policies among voters with fixed policy preferences" (Mitchell 1984. p. 166). With voters' preferences nicely distributed over a given issue-space to which politicians only adjust – knowing in advance what positions to take in order to reap given shares of votes – one can argue in Schumpeter's (1912/34, p. 76) words that the entrepreneur "has no function of a special kind there, he simply does not exist".[1] The neglect of Tullock's contribution is more difficult to explain.[2] One reason may be that he left the key-aspects of the analogy insufficiently explained. In addition, as we will see, Tullock's model helps to discover and specify not only similarities but also crucial differences between franchise-bidding and political elections – both of which tend to be ignored in simplistic policy models.

It is the main intention of this paper to show that parts of Schumpeter's view of political entrepreneurship and parts of Tullock's view of political competition can be usefully applied and combined for analysing elementary aspects of democratic systems. In Part 2, we summarise some elements of Schumpeter's political economy which will be used in the ensuing parts. In Part 3, we present and enlarge Tullock's basic model of democracy. Part 4 gives a systematic overview of entry barriers in politics, followed by a discussion of political information and agency problems. The effects of entry barriers in politics on incentives and opportunities for political

---

[1] To be sure, active roles for politicians have been added to the rich arsenal of Public Choice. These contributions include different approaches like, e.g., Buchanan and Wagner (1977), Frohlich and Oppenheimer (1978, ch. 4), Dunleavy and Ward (1981), Riker (1986); Buchanan/Vanberg (1989); Dunleavy (1991, ch. 5), Schneider and Teske (1992); Williamson and Haggard (1994), Bartolini (1995).

[2] Some elements of Tullock's idea are implicitly taken into account in Brennan and Buchanan (1980), North (1981), Moe (1990), Palmer (1995), Bartolini (1995).

entrepreneurship in the sense of engaging in long-term, positive-sum reforms are discussed in Part 5. We conclude with a short summary.

2 Schumpeter on political and economic entrepreneurship

For Schumpeter (1942/87, p. 132) the foremost function of the entrepreneur is innovation – the carrying out of "new combinations". His entrepreneur is the promoting "leader" who recombines factors of production, and not necessarily the capitalist who owns them. His motivation is not dull maximisation of net-revenues but rather "the will to conquer: the impulse to fight, to prove oneself superior to others, to succeed for the sake, not of the fruits of success, but of success itself ... the joy of creating, of getting things done, or simply of exercising one's energy and ingenuity." (1912/34, p. 93). As already his choice of words indicates, Schumpeter – on the motivational level – makes no distinction between a business entrepreneur and a political leader.

Schumpeter's work on the relation of entry, market structure and business size on the one hand and entrepreneurial incentives and opportunities on the other provoked intensive debates (see Scherer, 1992). It has often been noted that there seem to be two quite contradicting "Schumpeter hypotheses" in this context. In his "Theory of Economic Development" (1912/34) the central idea is that free market entry of outsiders, of innovative small enterprises is the crucial factor fostering innovative entrepreneurship, because "new combinations are, as a rule, embodied, as it were, in new firms which generally do not arise out of the old ones but start producing beside them ... in general it is not the owner of stage-coaches who builds railways." (p. 66).

The more famous "Schumpeter hypothesis" plays a prominent part in his "Capitalism, Socialism and Democracy" (1942/87). It reads as follows (p. 102f): "The main value to a concern of a single seller position that is secured by patent or monopolistic strategy does not consist so much in the opportunity to behave temporarily to the monopolist schema, as in the protection it affords against temporary disorganization of the market and the space it secures for long-range planning". The advantages Schumpeter attributes to large enterprises that enjoy some amount of monopoly power are those of innovation *capability*. He hastens to add that "mere size is neither necessary nor sufficient for it" (p. 101). However, what later were called barriers to entry – such as patents or long-period contracts – are acknowledged by Schumpeter as at least necessary conditions for propelling "[l]ong-range investing under rapidly changing conditions" (p. 88).

In the same book, we find Schumpeter's theory of democracy. His basic assertion is that politicians cannot be led by any preconceived notion of "the will of the people" as the classical doctrine of democracy suggests. Politicians must and should act as leaders who dominate public policies and even manufacture public opinion. This view is based on a description of citizens as ignorant and unable to act for themselves in political affairs: "the private citizen musing over national affairs ... is a member of an unworkable committee, the committee of the whole nation, and this is why he expends less disciplined effort on mastering a political problem than he expends on a game of bridge ... At the bridge table ... success and failure are clearly defined; and we are prevented from behaving irresponsibly because every mistake we make will not only immediately tell but also be immediately allocated to us. These conditions, by their failure to be fulfilled for the political behavior of the ordinary citizen, show why it is that in politics he lacks all the alertness and the judgement he may display in his profession" (p. 261).

Here Schumpeter anticipates arguments used later to explain "rational abstention" and "rational ignorance" of voters.[3] However, Schumpeter would not call his citizen-voters *rationally* ignorant. He insists that they are as irrational as ignorant, hence: "the question about the definiteness and independence of the voter's will, his powers of observation and interpretation of facts, and his ability to draw, clearly and promptly, rational inferences from both ... belongs to a chapter of social psychology that might be entitled Human Nature in Politics" (p. 256). Experimental findings have provided several chapters of evidence supporting much of what Schumpeter took for granted: Due to the inconsequential nature of the individual act of voting "the typical citizen drops to a lower level of mental performance as soon as he enters the political field" (ibid.).[4]

The same, of course, does not follow for politicians. They cannot afford to yield to irrationality or pure impulse in choosing their actions if they seek success in the competitive struggle for office and power. Politicians face "high-powered" incentives and opportunities knowingly and rationally to exploit or even expand voters' ignorance and irrationality (Frey and Eichenberger, 1994). This is exactly what Schumpeter (1942/87, p. 263) ascribes to political leadership, arguing that politicians "are able to fashion and, within very wide limits, even to create the will of the people". His redefinition of democracy also embraces political entrepreneurship in the sense of carrying out political innovations with the result that "[p]recisely in the best instances, the people are presented with results they never thought of and would not have approved of in advance." (p. 278). Note that this political leader not only contrasts sharply with the provider of the common good in the classical doctrine but also with the median-vote-seeker in the Hotelling-Downs world. Introducing innovative political leadership may have consequences as far-reaching as the substitution of the entrepreneur for the price-taker in the original market model. Unfortunately, the lead of Schumpeter's ideas stops here. Let us now see what we can gain from using Tullock's model of politics and then go on to attempt some new combinations of both.

3 Tullocks's idea: democracy as bidding for political monopoly

Political competition among political parties and candidates as well as the interaction between voters and politicians bear almost no resemblance to

[3] See already Downs (1957, part III), see Aranson (1990) for a survey of the ensuing literature.

[4] See, e.g. Quattrone and Tversky (1988) or Wahlke (1991).

ongoing market *processes*. Rather, in their basic structure, democratic elections are much more similar to periodical auctions of a licence to exclusive monopoly rights. This is the core idea of Tullock (1965): (1) There is a "natural" monopoly of government, because also in a democracy "we can have only one cabinet, governor, mayor, president or majority in a legislature. The scale advantage which acts as a barrier to entry is the majority voting rule which provides that the 'entrepreneurial group' which obtains half the customers can drive the other entrepreneurial group out of the market" (p. 464). (2) Periodical auctions of the right to use the monopoly rights of government may prevent some abuses of the monopoly of government. (3) The workability of this pre-stage competition depends, inter alia, on barriers to entry in politics.

Thus, Tullock identified for the political realm what has later become a hotly debated issue in Industrial Organisation: franchise bidding for natural monopolies. Its basic idea is that a "franchise system that awards the franchise to that company which seems to offer the best price-quality package would be one that allows market competition between bidding rivals to determine that package. The restraint of the market is then substituted for that of the regulatory commission" (Demsetz 1968/89, p. 82). In other words: while natural monopoly precludes competition of simultaneously producing firms ("competition within the field"), the right to operate the monopoly can be competitively determined ("competition for the field"), thus – it is hoped – precluding monopolistic behaviour of those who won the bidding contest and who have to defend their position in coming bidding rounds.

The basic rationale of democratic elections is similar: There cannot be in one jurisdiction various producers enforcing alternative laws and policies at the same time. There is a monopoly of force. However, the right to operate this monopoly is competitively allocated among various contenders who bid for votes of their citizen-"customers". This – it is hoped – would reduce incentives to behave opportunistically after winning a bidding since incumbents would have to withstand ensuing "bidding rounds" (elections) in order to keep enjoying political power and office.

Compared to median-voter analysis Tullock's model more readily discloses the central peculiarity of political "market structures", which is that political competition does *not* entail "competition within the field", since there are no rival political *producers* simultaneously competing for the favours of citizen-consumers of political goods. What it does entail is that *potential* suppliers compete "for the field" of exclusive provision of laws and policies. Democracy is indeed analogous to Demsetz's notion of (1989, p. 89) "rivalry for incumbency" in the following structural aspects:

- based on declarations and *promises*
- made by *potential* producers
- *one* (group of) candidate(s) is given the
- *exclusive* right to provide certain goods and services
- for a specified *period of time* and a specified *area*.

These are the basic *structural* similarities between a Demsetz-mechanism and democracy as a method for allocating political property rights to political entrepreneurs. A closer look, however, shows that (a) already the workability of Demsetz's proposal must be qualified and (b) these *material* objections and complications apply *a fortiori* to political "competition for leadership". We now briefly turn to these differences.

Demsetz's (1968/89) contention that monopoly rents could rather easily and completely be reduced through price-cutting auctions without affording further regulation of the use of the franchise has provoked important criticisms by Oliver Williamson (1976) and Victor Goldberg (1976). They point at complications and "severe contractual disabilities" (Williamson, 1976, p. 73) that arise as soon as one allows for "conditions of uncertainty" (p. 79). These real-life conditions create problems of (1) assessing the quality and efficiency of the contenders "for the field", (2) ensuring good performance of the winning party that has become sole producer "within the field", and (3) making "competition for the field" sufficiently contestable.

The first two kinds of problems basically involve principal-agent problems and problems of incomplete contracts between those who give the licence and those who get the licence to produce for a given time as sole providers of utilities. In the political analogy of "competition for leadership", these problems can be easily translated into a host of principal-agent problems between voters and politicians. In this paper (section 4) we will concentrate on the third kind of complications: Contestability and entry barriers. Some comparative observations concerning the first two kinds, however, are also due in order to depict some peculiarities of political entrepreneurship.

(1) Award criteria. Williamson (p. 81) made the point that "although franchise awards can be reduced to a lowest price criterion, this is apt to be artificial if the future is uncertain and the service in question is at all complex". Obviously, the winning bidder's promise to supply most cheaply is "scarcely a well-defined commitment unless the quality of service is well specified..." (p. 80).

Problems of complex and insufficiently defined "price-quality packages" as criteria for selection of the "fittest" competitor apply also – but with much greater force – to political elections. While political entrepreneurs may also compete on a "lowest tax criterion" for comparable qualities of political services, the voters' task to compare packages of promised levels and structures of taxes and of political goods seems more demanding than that of a franchise-giving agency. This is even more so because, while Demsetz bidding schemes are about a fixed and small number of utilities (and specified services) to be provided, political parties and candidates offer far more complex packages of (not necessarily consistent) promises on an open field of issues. It is right here that political entrepreneurship in "competition for the field" enters the stage. There is no pre-defined political "issue space"; there are no readily fixed political services to be rendered. Only if these conditions existed, politicians could indeed be reduced to "retailers of existing or but marginally different policies". If not, they will find Schumpeterian roles in differentiating their offers, proposing new problem solutions, shaping public opinion and the like.

From a principal-agent point of view, of course, such entrepreneurial leeway is exactly the heart of the problem, because in this Schumpeterian world no longer do citizens or voters act as agenda-setters who determine what political services are to be rendered and then simply select the political agents who would do it most "cheaply". In the real world of active political entrepreneurs, political parties set the agendas and voters can only voice their preferences on a limited set of obscure promises. Finally, electoral promises are much less operational and binding than contractual provisions agreed upon in a Demsetz franchise bidding scheme. This leads to many severe "contractual disabilities" at the political execution level to be discussed now.

(2) Incomplete contracts. As a second qualification to Demsetz' proposal, Williamson and Goldberg claim that after "competition for the field" has produced its winner much remains for further regulation. The licence is an "incomplete" contract. Uncertainties about future contingencies, complex attributes of the goods to be supplied, and bounded rationality of the acting individuals prevent the conclusion of fully-contingent licence-contracts. At the same time it could even be in the interest of principals (customers) to have some built-in flexibility in the contract to allow the agents to react to new circumstances due to unforeseen changes in technologies, preferences, relative scarcities etc. The control of the use of such entrepreneurial leeway, however, once again makes some kind of regulating agency necessary.

Such contractual disabilities again increase on the level of *political* monopoly. The "contract" between voters and politicians is not just "incomplete"; it is at best implicit, but in actuality non-existent. Elections only assign power (seats) to parties and candidates, thereby (pre-) determining who should govern. They do not give binding instructions on how to govern. The political principal receives no claim on any particular political service as a result of her voting. The winning political party is under no legal obligation to perform any particular act as a consequence of its electoral promises. Indeed, the party in power can, if it likes, do just the opposite. And again, this lack of a binding contract is the very basis for the political entrepreneur to act as Schumpeter wants her to act. It enables the pushing through of political innovations which the principals never thought of and would not have approved of in advance.

At the same time, these severe contractual disabilities create enormous leeway for post-election opportunism of elected agents to pursue policies which a minority or even a (badly informed or weakly interested) majority of principals would never have approved at all. From this perspective, there certainly is need for a political equivalent of the "licence agency" that Williamson and Goldberg demanded in order to heal shortcomings of incomplete licence contracts. At this stage, Tullock's basic analogy leads us right into the centre of the perennial question "*quis custodiet ipsos custodes*?" Democratic nations that subscribe to the rule of law have found a more or less satisfying solution to this problem: In the execution of particular policies politicians are controlled by general rules of public and constitutional law. Thus the rule of law can regulate at least some of the countless contingencies that are not covered by electoral "franchise-contracts". However, one fundamental peculiarity of the regulation of politics appears in this context: the rules of the game – including constitutional rules – are produced and can be changed by the group of "players" which ought to be controlled; political competition is a fundamentally self-regulated process.

One might expect that political "self-regulation" would not lead to excessive opportunism of incumbents since the licence to govern is temporary and has to be gained again in new rounds of open "competition for the field". Thus, in a very Demsetzian way, incumbents would be induced to act just as well as the most benevolent and well-informed supervisory agency could ever induce them to act. Such an argument would rely on the benefits of *potential* competition equal to those expected by Schumpeter (1942/87, p. 85) who argues that "competition of the kind we now have in mind ... disciplines before it attacks. The businessman feels himself to be in a competitive situation even if he is alone in his field". The same argument may be applied to the incumbent government which after the elections finds itself alone in the field of national policy-making: the threat of losing the next election would "discipline before it attacks". This is the rationale of the "principle of anticipated reactions" (Sartori, 1987, p. 152ff) according to which incumbents are continuously influenced by the anticipation of voters' reactions thus being led by some "invisible hand" in politics. Such optimism, however, rests on a number of dubious assumptions and analogies. An important subset of such assumptions relates to the "contestability" of political competition and hence to entry barriers in politics.

4 Entry barriers in politics

Williamson's (1976, p. 83) third major qualification of Demsetz' model relates to entry barriers. He argues: "Lest meaningful competition at the contract renewal interval be upset, participation in contract execution should not place winners of the original competition at a substantial advantage over nonwinners." Once again, very similar problems will arise with respect to bidding for political monopoly as we discuss conditions of political rivalry for incumbency and political analogues to a number of "barriers to entry for the bidding" (v. Weizsäcker, 1980, p. 32). We now discuss three categories of such barriers: (1) legal (2) "innocent" and (3) "strategic".[5]

(1) Legal barriers to entry in politics mainly relate to the "rules of the game" of the electoral contest. A fundamental and characteristic legal barrier to entry for the political bidding is erected by the periodicity of elections, i.e. the frequency with which new parties or candidates are allowed to enter new electoral contests. Parties in opposition and even more so

[5] We use an analogy to the distinction of "innocent" and "strategic" barriers to entry in economics made by Salop (1979, p. 335): "An innocent entry barrier is unintentionally erected as a side effect of innocent profit maximization. In contrast, a strategic entry barrier is purposely erected to reduce the possibility of entry". The legal barriers presented here are not necessarily of a third kind. As long as these rules of the political game are acknowledged by the players and not opportunistically changed by the winners, they remain quite "innocent". If they are manipulated by those in power in order to reduce contestability, however, they turn into instruments of "strategic" entry barring (see below).

parties that have not yet entered parliament are excluded from the monopolised use of legitimate rights to produce political goods until they get a new chance with the next election. The basic rationale of incumbency periods is the same in Demsetz' bidding and in Tullock's democracy: to produce stability of expectations and thus encourage agents and principals alike to engage in long-term investments. On the other hand, one wants to oust incompetent holders of licences as quickly as possible in new rounds of "competition for the field" which may also facilitate taking in new opinions of citizens. Thus, as a rule, one would expect that the more frequently bidding for political monopoly is repeated, the higher will be the responsiveness and "contestability" of monopolistic government and the lower will be the degree of political stability and "governability" of the polity. Effects of bidding frequency on political entrepreneurship will be discussed in Part 5.

Other rules of the game act as legal barriers to entry and affect trade-offs between "contestability" of political "competition for the field" and political stability "within the field". Whereas incumbency periods influence the *frequency of contests*, the following rules mainly influence the *number of contestants*: (a) The admission of parties and candidates to political elections is often subject to legal "barriers to entry for the bidding" like the requirement of a minimum number of members and supporters or of loyalty to the country's constitution. (b) The entry of small parties to representative assemblies is often blocked by requiring minimum shares of votes (like the German 5% threshold). (c) The number of parties is typically very small in plurality voting systems like the British "first-past-the post-" rule which acts as an almost insurmountable barrier to entry for small or new parties (especially if minority-interests are distributed quite equally throughout voting districts).[6]

These rules of the game tend to reduce the number of contestants in an election and/or the number of parties in parliament. Share thresholds reduce the number of possible coalitions and thus the costs of searching and bargaining a multi-party government. Thresholds can also help increase political stability and sustainability of governments. On the other hand, they may act as frustratingly high barriers to entry for new parties, to the representation of political minorities and to the introduction of new political ideas, styles etc. These arguments apply even more strongly for plurality vote systems which tend to greatly increase political stability or "governability" as compared to complex and fragile political coalitions which sometimes have to yield to radical parties and bridge large ideological gaps. However, plurality rules also increase the likelihood of large disproportionalities between votes and seats and the frustration of new parties and political movements.[7]

---

[6] See also Riker (1982) or Myerson (1995, p. 82): "plurality voting tends to create barriers to entry against third parties (because votes for those third parties could be 'wasted')".

[7] In the UK, a party with an absolute majority of total votes did not reap a majority of seats in 1951 and 1971 (Roberts, 1987, p. 294). In 1983, the Liberal Party received only 3.5% of the seats with 25.4% of total votes; the Labour Party in the same election transformed only few more votes (28%) into nine times as many seats, the Conservative Party reduced its share of votes by 1.5%-points but gained 58 additional seats!

(2) "Innocent" barriers to entry in politics relate to the simple fact that "we can have only one cabinet, governor, mayor, president or majority in a legislature" (Tullock, 1965, p. 464). Only winners of the political franchise are entitled to actually provide political goods and services, whereas members of the opposition can hardly do more than offering dissenting opinions, critique and proposals. Three kinds of "innocent" barries can result:

(a) Incumbents may enjoy a goodwill-advantage because the quality of new bidders' offers can be even less easily and reliantly assessed (Tullock, 1965, p. 463). Winners of exclusive long-term rights to produce also acquire the exclusive possibility to build up a reputation as a consequence of "the investment in an honourable long history" (Demsetz, 1982/89a, p. 38). For voters, candidates and programmes have essential attributes of experience goods (Telser, 1976, p. 337f): the quality of the offer can only be poorly evaluated by inspection prior to "purchase" (election). It will be revealed *ex post* by experiencing the actual performance. The usual reaction of consumers (voters) is then to rely on past experience. In this case, outsider-competitors have a systematic disadvantage as long as consumers (voters) are risk-averse.[8]

(b) Williamson (1976, p. 81f) claimed that "idiosyncratic" relations between award giving agencies and incumbents can also act as barriers for outsiders. He expects that "publicly accountable decision makers acquire political and psychological stakes in their own decisions and develop a justificatory rather than critical attitude towards them." Such bias should at first sight not be expected from voters as political "franchise award givers". Voters are not in the same sense "publicly accountable decision makers". The individual voter is anonymous and has no decisive influence on the result – so why should she feel responsible for her "choice" and be biased in her assessment of it? In fact, however, studies of "human nature in politics" have shown that voters do feel committed to their political choices and that they do take "justificatory attitudes" towards their choices. In politics, as in other areas, individuals try to avoid being exposed to "cognitive dissonance".[9] Their selective search for, interpretation and storing of information and opinions aims at confirming personal political views. For the voting citizen, unreflected voter-loyalty and even the holding of erroneous views is "cheap" since "wrong" voting remains inconsequential. In addition, political parties, interest groups and mass-media deliver (for free)

---

[8] The empirical findings are ambigous, however. Some studies of voting behaviour support a systematic "incumbency advantage" (e.g. Reed/Schansberg, 1992; King, 1991; Bernhardt/Ingberman 1985). Other studies yield indications for a "cost of ruling", i.e. the depreciation of voter support during one election period (see Nannestad/Paldam, 1994, p. 235f).

[9] Akerlof/Dickens (1982, p. 307) summarise the consequences of cognitive dissonance theory (Festinger 1957): "First, persons not only have preferences over states of the world, but also over their beliefs about the state of the world. Second, persons have some control over their beliefs ... they can also manipulate their own beliefs by selecting sources of information likely to confirm 'desired' beliefs. Third, ... beliefs once chosen persist over time." Political applications can be found in Brady et al. (1995).

ideologically pre-selected information, argumentation and other aids for cognitive self-confirmation.[10]

(c) More or less "innocent" barriers to effective and radical change can be the result of specific investments. If (economic) incumbents have invested in specific, long-term capital (including human-capital investments of workers) which can not easily be transferred to alternative uses, changing the staff in charge becomes a costly and risky affair (Williamson, 1976, p. 84ff). Similarly, political incumbents' investments in projects that are hard to reverse and skills that are hard to transfer can erect (more or less "innocent") barriers against the opposition's entering government *and* changing its policies. Inexperienced newcomers face problems of achieving the knowledge and skills – including non-transferable "tacit knowledge" in the sense of Polanyi (1967) – needed for handling bureaucracy, diplomacy and other political affairs. This complication may not only add to an incumbency advantage as far as it influences voters' assessments of competing candidates. It also helps to explain why new entrants in political power do not radically change the personnel of political agencies – at least in the lower and middle ranks. Such conservatism is needed for new ministers and political leaders to make use of the political know-how and routines established by their forebearers.

(3) Barriers to change can also be deliberately erected to protect investments in particular laws, regulations and programmes. The emergence of such devices has been analysed by Terry Moe (1990, p. 227 ff.) arguing that incumbents create structures for their conduct including "self-binding" commitments. At a closer look, such acts of self-binding are basically intended to bind political rivals and especially to keep them from destroying political creations and investments after a change in power. Incumbents try to protect their political legacy including privileges of their political clients by using strategies which are not just unavoidable by-products of incumbency. Hence, they turn into "strategic" entry barriers' in the sense of Salop (1979):

(a) Incumbents can try to induce the executing bureaucracy to rely on complex, almost irreversible idiosyncrasies and routines. This strategy involves, among other things, "for today's authorities to specify, in excruciating detail, precisely what the agency is to do and how to do it, leaving as little as possible to the discretionary judgement of bureaucrats – and thus as little as possible for future authorities to exercise control over, short of passing new legislation" (Moe, 1990, p. 228).[11]

(b) Alternatively, the present government can erect legal barriers to change, most of all by way of giving a policy the status of constitutional law. Such amendment-barriers, of course, require that the present

[10] Voters also find reinforcement of their own views because they tend to associate disproportionately with like-minded individuals (Huckfield and Sprague, 1995, p. 46ff).

[11] An "outsourcing" of policies can have a similar effect of removing political tasks from public debate and electoral change. The delegation of tasks to widely independent bodies like central banks, regulation agencies, or supra-national organisations works in this direction when competence is a key resource and the prestige for sticking to credible commitments a key incentive.

majority be large enough to amend the constitution – or that (parts of) the opposition can be convinced (e.g. using log-rolling) to support lasting changes.

(c) To include (parts of) the opposition by way of various forms of co-optation in order to create lasting political compromises can in many cases be a rational device to protect given policies from being overwhelmed by future authorities. Again, log-rolling at the expense of unrepresented, "latent" groups can be used to secure particular projects and privileges a life after the next elections (Shepsle and Weingast 1981).

(d) Programmatic continuity can also be achieved through the inclusion of vested interest groups in political decisions and in the administration of policies. This not only lends political programmes an allure of additional legitimacy (due to the so-called "consent" of all concerned). In addition, the power base against which political reform would have to struggle is hereby enlarged.

(e) Further examples of strategic barriers to entry involve above all manipulative changes of the rules of the game initiated by those in power in order to bar outsiders and to increase the rents of insiders. The group of insiders may now well include all or most established political competitors within the "political class" engaged in cartelised attempts to reap their rents while the general public and unorganised or non-opportunistic political activists stay outside (Frey, 1994, p. 340). In this context, we once more encounter the above-mentioned self-regulating character of politics. The incumbent majority – if necessary in collusion with (parts of) the opposition – is enabled to "make laws about elections, ... set rules governing voter qualifications, campaign contributions, the form of the ballot, the role of political parties, and virtually anything they want to regulate about how the public can legitimately 'control' them" (Moe, 1990). Given that the political freedom to compete is thus guaranteed by no external power but the competitors themselves, then the rules of the game cannot be expected to be very open for outsiders and newcomers.[12]

5 Effects of entry barriers in politics on political entrepreneurship

Having discussed basic elements of political entrepreneurship à la Schumpeter and the political "market structure" à la Tullock, we now want to inquire more deeply into possible combinations of both. The essential link has already been shown: The Schumpeterian political entrepreneur needs room for manoeuvre. But just as models of perfect competition leave no room for entrepreneurship, models of political competition based on similar assumptions (given issue-space, given preferences, given knowledge) cannot account for political leadership. If, however, one starts with Tullock's basic model of political competition, the very foundations of political entrepreneurship do become visible: To begin with, during "competition for the field" the political issue space is not given; political entrepreneurs set

[12] Many more examples of "institutional manipulation" are presented in Dunleavy and Ward (1981).

agendas, shape preferences and create complex differentiated offers for citizens who cannot politically act for themselves. And "within the field", politicians are not bound to election promises. The "contractual disabilities" of the electoral licence provide room for independent action within a wide open field which is only partly fenced by fundamental constitutional prohibitions. To ignore past promises may not provoke sanctions at the next elections as long as incumbents can rely on voters' deficient memories or the vagueness of their own promises.[13] By contrast to this backward-looking principal-agent perspective, political leadership becomes more pronounced in view of the forward-looking "principle of anticipated reactions". A political leader can be re-elected if she presents voters with results they never thought of before but which they want to keep as soon as they can see the benefits. This, however, would require that political entrepreneurs find favourable conditions for creating and pushing through new problem solutions.

5.1 The problem of sustainable investments in political reform

We have to qualify our following discussion with an important clarification: Political entrepreneurship and innovation as such is not a normative concept. Again, we have to confront fundamental differences to the respective economic counterparts: In the economic sphere, the entrepreneurial pushing through of innovative production processes and the creation of innovative goods and services is, in almost every case, beneficial to the economy as a whole. Not so in politics. The reason is simply that in a market economy, innovation means additional variations that can be selected by market participants; it enlarges the choice set; people are free to choose from a greater supply of alternatives. In a polity, new political goods tend to simply replace old ones and their "consumption" by citizens usually remains just as unavoidable as before; hence: new policies do not increase the number of choices. New policies create winners and losers and they are not as such related to any notion of political "progress".

With this caveat in mind, we will now concentrate on *one* possible expression of political entrepreneurship: The pushing through of fundamental political reforms assumed to be of a positive-sum kind. Arguably, reforms that try to transform post-socialist societies and developing countries into systems that adhere to market co-ordination and the rule of law, but also reforms of welfare states that try to overcome protectionist and redistributionist policies belong to this category. Positive-sum reforms would aim at establishing or strengthening non-discriminatory general rules

---

[13] To be sure, to put much emphasis on an unambiguous promise of the kind "read my lips: no new taxes!" can come back to haunt reelection. George Busch is quoted on this subject as follows: "The biggest mistake of my presidency was that I damaged my credibility by agreeing to a tax increase ... I worked out a compromise and it cost me plenty" (see Boudreaux and Lee, 1997, p. 367).

of market co-ordination and open entry to economic competition while abandoning or weakening special privileges, subsidies or other exemptions from the general rules of market competition. As Williamson and Haggard (1994, p. 531) observed, such reforms "are like an investment that should ultimately benefit the majority by enough to make them happy they made it, but that in the short run will – like all investments – involve sacrifices." What makes these reforms politically risky is a combination of the following unfavourable conditions:

- the benefits may be substantial, but they are not as visible as the costs;
- the benefits may be long-term, but they also appear only in the long-run while costs (sacrifices) become visible much earlier;
- the beneficiaries may be in a large majority, but they are also diffuse or even unknown in advance while the costs are readily evident and concentrated on a special group;
- the potential beneficiaries would thus often belong to an unorganised (latent) group while the potential losers would usually be parts of a powerful group which for attaining its favours has already formed a powerful rent-seeking organisation.

Hence, for a political entrepreneur to become re-elected by a majority of voters, it is not sufficient to invest in policies that would benefit a majority of voters. If they should expect re-election on the basis of investments in positive-sum reforms, politicians must find additional incentives and/or opportunities. Many of these incentives and opportunities depend on the specific properties of entry barriers in politics. This issue can be discussed in close analogy to the general tenets of the two Schumpeter-hypotheses referred to in Part 2. We now translate both hypotheses into rather straightforward theses and anti-theses concerning possible effects of various entry barriers and then proceed to a more balanced synthesis.

5.2 Political "Schumpeter"-hypotheses

(a) entry barriers frustrate political innovators. As an analogy to the older Schumpeter hypothesis (1912/34, p. 66) that "new combinations are, as a rule, embodied ... in new firms which generally do not arise out of the old ones but start producing beside them" one could state that political competition for leadership would, as a rule, hardly ever allow new political combinations to see the light of day. And indeed, the contestability of the political "market" is extremely low when compared to typical economic markets. Within the field of party politics new "firms" rarely arise and even among the few established parties one party can cling to power for a considerable time, as e.g. Demsetz (1982/89b, p. 291f) has observed: "In the twenty year period from 1932 to 1952, with the exception of one Congress, the Democrats in the US firmly controlled both the administration and Congress, and, even after losing the presidency to Eisenhower in 1952, again with the exception of one Congress, they continued to control

Congress until 1980. In no major unregulated US industry has one firm been dominant so long."[14]

One obvious reason for this is that in unregulated industries, firms and entrepreneurs face essentially different award criteria. With usual market competition, if a firm gains, say, 20% or as a newcomer some 4% market share, this can often be called a success. By contrast, entry barriers in politics make it that only with a "market" share of over 50% of the seats can a group of political entrepreneurs (say, a coalition of parties) have innovative policies "produced" at all. Innovative newcomers or risk-taking reformers cannot just come and start to bring out legislation beside the elected insiders. In this respect problems of entry of political innovators are very similar to those of admitting innovative producers in socialism where the "man with the new idea will have no possibility of establishing himself by undercutting, the new idea cannot be proved until he has convinced [the central board, MW] that his way of producing is cheaper." (Hayek 1940/94, p. 247). Similarly, the political "man with the new idea" cannot start producing new politics until he has convinced a majority of voters to elect him to office.[15]

In addition, capitalist markets hold out the prospect of considerable material rewards for entrepreneurs as a premium for personal risk-taking. Political entrepreneurs, by contrast, do not become very rich as a consequence of taking risks. And indeed, political agencies seem to reward and thus create and/or attract people with a higher amount of risk-aversion. To be sure, our discussion so far is not a critique of democracy. This is just the way politics works under the rule of monopolised coercion – and how it ought to work if we take into account that the risks of failed political innovations are not private but have to be shared by the citizens as a whole.

However, as we have seen, various other circumstances or entry barriers in politics are the result of institutional design. While this does not make their lowering very probable in view of self-interested incumbents, it does allow useful comparative assessments of different political systems. Translating the first Schumpeter-hypothesis into the terms of our Tullock-model one can state that lower entry barriers would stimulate "competition for the field" thus inducing incumbents "within the field" to be more active, creative and innovative. In this line already Tullock (1965, p. 464) wanted to make sure "that the entry barrier is low enough so that this potential competition is a real restriction on the activities of the present occupant of

---

[14] More extreme cases can be found in European countries with high degrees of "concordance". In the first decades of post war Austria, both major parties built pacts to share the power and frame all parliamentary decisions beforehand in joint "coalition committees". After some years of mainly socialist rule, Austria has since 1987 returned to great coalitions. Even more encompassing arrangements of party participation in government are typical for the Swiss system – combined, however, with low barriers to citizens' entry in politics as a consequence of direct democracy.

[15] Viewed as a multi-stage process it is more realistic to argue that the "woman with the new idea" would first have to convince her party and fraction to adopt the new ideas in a new programme or parliamentary initiative and then convince voters to elect or (re-)elect her party. Thus, intra-organisational barriers to the introduction of novelty also have to be taken into account.

the monopoly." Increasing rivalry for incumbency might not only be a real restriction, but also a real impulse to come up with political innovation and reform. It could be attempted in many forms:

(1) The most obvious way would be to shorten the incumbency period, thus increasing the bidding frequency and the actualisation of potential competition. If the cards are reshuffled more frequently, one could argue, opposition parties would have a better chance to enter the electoral contest with new ideas and conquer the political apparatus with new policies. But also incumbents might be more urgently challenged to enter the bidding with new ideas.

(2) A less obvious way to increase potential political competition is suggested by Tullock (1965, p. 464) who proposes "to raise the rewards of office to a level where they would be worth more than the organizational costs of an opposition group properly discounted by the risks involved". As an alternative, Tullock proposes to directly "pay a potential opposition group" (p. 465). How (and by whom) such calculations and payments can be properly performed in reality, is not explained.

(3) A more indirect but arguably more promising way to increase the competitive challenge for incumbents would be to open jurisdictions for the exit and entry of mobile factors of production. Lowering exit barriers for citizen-demanders of politics is an excellent alternative to lowering entry barriers for potential suppliers of politics. Possibly, it is also the more effective tool, since it exposes incumbents to competition *within* the field of rival jurisdictions where they find their equals.[16] Politicians would now face incentives to engage in comparative institutional economics trying to discover and introduce new political combinations that might attract foreign resources. In addition, federalism, i.e., competition between decentral states within one nation also lowers the incumbency advantage barrier to national elections. It yields opportunities for voters to observe the opposition at the federal level engaged in producing political goods at the state level and hence to assess the political capability of the opposition (and often the top-contenders for presidency) in action.

(4) Finally, barriers due to the self-regulation of the *classe politique* can be lowered by introducing direct democracy. Especially popular initiatives break the agenda-setting and self-protecting cartel of politicians while giving *private* institutional entrepreneurs opportunities to enter the political field with ideas of their own – some of which incumbent politicians may not even have thought of before.[17]

---

[16] We now find that different jurisdictions compete *simultaneously* and as producers of basically the *same* category of goods: legitimate political decisions. To the extent that such a "choice of rules" is open to citizens, the natural monopoly of incumbent governments is seriously qualified. While national policy making is still subject to a consecutive bidding for exclusive licence ("choice of rulers"), citizens are no longer strictly confined to a "forced consumption" of political goods. Their exit provokes incumbent political entrepreneurs of different jurisdictions to engage in a parallel bidding for mobile resources (for a more detailed analysis, see Wohlgemuth, 1995).

[17] Frey (1994, p. 341) reports that "among the 250 referenda held in Switzerland between 1848 and 1990, the majority's will deviated from the stated will of parliament in 39 percent of the cases."

(b) entry barriers encourage political investors. Analogously to the second Schumpeter hypothesis that firms which enjoy at least temporary monopoly protection will find innovation attractive, one may argue that some of the entry barriers in politics are necessary to increase the capability and hence the likelihood of wide-scale political innovations and far-sighted reforms. The thrust of this argument aims especially at the political risks of market-oriented reforms sketched above. Risky long-term investments (economic or political) may be more likely if entrepreneurs can deploy some restrictive practices to protect their investment.

For economic innovators, one way of protecting returns on investment and hence encouraging innovation is patent protection. This way is not open to political innovators. Politicians cannot even be sure to get any return – there might be another government at the time when positive effects of the reform start to show, thus successors would reap the electoral rewards. In short: in politics there is no "entitlement to the fruits of past investment" (Demsetz, 1982/89a, p. 38). Exactly for such a case, Schumpeter (1942/87, p. 88) provides a substitute: "if a patent cannot be secured ... other means may have to be used in order to justify the investment" and he goes on to propose exactly that class of means which is used in the political context: "long-period contracts secured in advance ... in order to tie prospective customers to the investing firm". The four or five year licence to govern that politicians win at democratic elections can be interpreted as a long-period relationship that ties citizens to the winning government and gives the government time to invest, to stand through the hard times following the introduction of reforms and hope still to be there when the reform is expected to prove a success.

However, this period of protection from direct contestability has not been able to prevent an often lamented short-sightedness of democratic politics. This argument can also be found in Schumpeter who anticipates parts of what were later to become theories of the "political business cycle" (e.g. Nordhaus, 1975; Frey, 1978). He argues that "the democratic principle of the government's dependence upon the voting of parliament and of the electorate ... forces upon the men at or near the helm a short-run view and makes it extremely difficult for them to serve such long-run interests of the nation as may require consistent work for far-off ends" (1942/87, p. 287). The politician who is exposed to excessive struggle for power and office would "be likened to a horseman who is so fully engrossed in trying to keep in the saddle that he cannot plan his ride" (ibid.). The longer the protected incumbency, one can argue, the longer will the horseman have time to master his horse and the more wide-reaching will be his ride.

Our political innovator or reformer not only needs time but also resources. The most critical resource in the early times of comprehensive reform is citizens' loyalty and goodwill. The combination of political stability and loyalty can be an asset for both, citizens and politicians, but for different reasons. For citizens the continuance of government combined with a confirmed belief in the general trustworthiness of incumbents helps reduce uncertainty (Kuran, 1988, p. 144). Since private investors and partners in long-term contracts appreciate secure political "data" and political stability, some barriers to entry in politics may increase the prospects of economic growth.[18] For incumbent politicians, trust, loyalty and goodwill yield political credit which helps them through wide-reaching reforms during an initial period of "blood, sweat and tears". There is a clear analogy to what v.Weizsäcker (1980, p. 85) describes as a virtue of the "seemingly conservative extrapolation principle" of consumers in highly innovative industries: "If his experience ... was good with the products of a supplier in the past, he will have trust in the new products of the same supplier. This then greatly accelerates acceptance of new products and hence greatly increases the incentive to develop new products in the industry".

Again, we have so far discussed general, "innocent" implications of democratic policy making as such. We now turn to those barriers to entry which differ across democratic systems and are thus potential objects of policy reform. Following our translation of the second Schumpeter hypothesis into conditions of political entrepreneurship, one could think of raising the following barriers to entry in order to strengthen political reformers' staying power:

(1) Obviously, one could prolong incumbency in the attempt to find a better match with the time needed to gain political "amortisation" of investments in reforms. The longer the period until re-election, the longer (c.p.) the "honeymoon" of a new government. During that period initial problems and sacrifices can be more easily sustained if they are forgotten at the next election or if they can be claimed to be burdens of the past.[19]

(2) Other rules of the game can help to prevent erosion of political entrepreneurs' power base during the difficult times. Certainly effective in this respect would be the introduction of plurality vote systems. If one wants to stick to proportional representation and multi-party systems, the building of grand coalitions, the requirement of a constructive vote of non-confidence before parliament can dismiss a cabinet, or the introduction of barriers for representation could make the survival of incumbents more probable and give reforms a better life-expectancy (see Kavanagh, 1980, p. 223ff).

(3) Alternatively to protecting incumbents, one can directly aim at protecting particular reform projects. As we have seen above, this can be done by giving the reform a higher legal status (e.g. constitutional law), by "outsourcing" policies to independent agencies, by including (parts of) the opposition in the decision making or by binding bureaucracy to the execution of detailed reform projects.

(4) The incumbents' capability to survive initial hard times can also be supported with outside help. The importance of foreign financial aid for

---

[18] Effects of political (un)certainty on private investments are discussed by Dixit and Pindyck (1994). Comparative country studies also show positive relations between political stability and investment. Even the single variable "frequency of changes in government" produces good correlations (Cuckierman et al., 1992). Using multidimensional indicators for "credibility of laws, regulations and policies" Brunetti et al. (1997) also show positive relations to private investment and growth.

[19] See Williamson and Haggard (1994, p. 571) for empirical cases supporting the "honeymoon hypothesis".

helping reformers to survive is stressed, e.g., by Jeffrey Sachs (1994) – refering to the transformation of former socialist countries and reforms in post-war Germany and Japan. Besides the money, conditionality can be a support. Conditional aid not only increases the rewards of market-based reforms but also lowers their political costs if outside organisations can be used as scape-goats.

(5) Finally, one can once again propose institutional competition and referenda as means to support political innovations and long-term political investments. First, the ominous foreign threat of outside competition might in some cases be used for scape-goating by pointing at forces outside the incumbents' reach which necessitate radical strategic change. Similarly, if backed by referenda, positive-sum and long-term political reforms can gain more binding force and lasting support than the usual parliamentary decisions. The ability to refer to an explicit and focused consent of a majority of the governed is perhaps the most effective protection a political entrepreneur can command to ensure the viability of risky political investments.

(c) a tentative synopsis. It is extremely difficult to give a conclusive general judgement on our two political "Schumpeter"-hypotheses. To be sure, the same has always been true for the original discussion in the economics area concerning potential costs and benefits of barriers to entry. Demsetz (1982/89a, p. 38) concludes that the final valuation "must necessarily be one that is rich in intuition and faith, and poor in discernible measurements... There exist neither cost-benefit analyses nor market-given prices by which to weigh benefits and costs in most of these trade-offs." This is even more true in our case. In addition, we expect that another result of the intensive empirical and theoretical debate on the two original Schumpeter-hypotheses would be paralleled after investigating deeper into our proposed political Schumpeter-hypotheses: "... both competitive pressures and market opportunity seem relevant. Further work is required. ... the sought after relationships are quite likely non-linear. Intermediate values of the market structure elements may be most conductive to research efforts and its success, with extreme values providing less incentive" (Kamien and Schwartz, 1975, p. 24). Quite likely, further work on entry barriers and innovation in politics would also find that the sought after relationships are non-linear, with at least satisfying general effects to be expected from *combinations* of arguments from both hypotheses.

In terms of "competitive pressures", lower barriers to entry would increase the contestability of the political "market" or openness of the electoral race to challengers and thus tend to

- enhance incumbents' incentives to adapt to changing preferences of voters;
- increase the chances to get rid of agents who are unable to fulfil past promises;
- encourage political entrepreneurs outside government to enter the arena of political discourse or the field of political action with new "combinations".

On the other side, and mainly in terms of political "market opportunity", higher barriers to entry would increase the stability of political expectations, and thus tend to

- enhance the incumbents' capability to engage in long-term planning and
- to risk reforms which potentially benefit a large unorganised majority in the long run while directly and immediately hurting a small but organised minority;
- increase the citizens' (and foreigners') stability of expectations which contributes to their willingness to invest in long-term economic ventures.

In order to show once more how both political "Schumpeter hypotheses" find their exact counterparts in the debates on "bidding for franchise monopoly", let us briefly go back to Williamson's discussion of Demsetz' proposal. Basically with the intention to strengthen principal-agent relations and cure contractual disabilities of the licence, Williamson (1976, p. 83f) advocates the use of "recurrent short-term contracts": "short-term contracts facilitate adaptive, sequential decisionmaking ... bridges are crossed one (or a few) at a time, as specific events occur ... Opportunism is thereby curbed as well." The very same argument can be easily translated into a demand for shorter election "renewal intervals" if adaptive, sequential decisionmaking or the curbing of opportunism is given priority on a political agenda. Things look very different, however, if political stability and the capability to engage in long-term reforms are regarded as more urgent. Now, the time to invest in the building of long and lasting "bridges" may afford long-term horizons. Exactly this argument has been acknowledged by Williamson (p. 81) who argues that "a leading reason to make the contract long term is to provide the supplier with the requisite incentives to install long-lived assets." This argument exactly corresponds to our translation of the second Schumpeter-hypothesis into the realm of political competition.

As usual with trade-offs of this kind, specific optima cannot be specified once and for all since this would afford knowledge of quite complex relations and, above all, it would force one to weigh the importance of competing values (like: adaptability and stability). Just like optimal patent lifetimes cannot generally be identified ex ante, so in the political realm optimal election frequencies or optimum heights of other barriers are impossible to determine generally and ex ante. Still, the identification of such trade-offs may not be in vain. At least the classification of extreme cases as unlikely but also as not recommendable is possible. Thus, we find a rationale for the very existence of barriers to entry in politics which corresponds to Schumpeter's (later) view that "[t]he introduction of new methods of production and new commodities is hardly conceivable with perfect – and perfectly prompt – competition from the start." (1942/87, p. 105).

As a final preliminary conclusion we can offer the following: If conditions for political entrepreneurship are to be analysed, created or changed, it would not suffice to have recourse to the barriers to entry in representative domestic politics. There are additional institutional arrangements that create incentives for politicians to act as entrepreneurs and reformers while still enjoying the incumbency protection which yields the capability to act with a long-term perspective. We optimistically suggest institutional competition to have such an effect: it encourages piecemeal reforms and at the same time allows the making use of the particular learning and discovery opportunities inherent in a parallel competition within the field of competing jurisdictions. Similar benefits might be achieved with the introduction of referenda: this could impel incumbents to either actively propose or *nolens volens* accept institutional innovations – once again on a piecemeal basis and with opportunities to make use of revealed preferences and skills focused on a particular policy. And finally, referenda help to lower entry barriers of new ideas and new groups to the field of political action at least occasionally.[20]

6 Summary: new combinations in political economy?

This paper proposes an analytical framework for dealing with political entrepreneurship and reform based on "new combinations" of Schumpeterian political economy, an extended version of Tullock's model of democracy and some basic assessments of the New Institutional Economics. These proposals are also expressions of the same combination of insistence regarding the importance of entrepreneurship in reality and modesty regarding the possibilities of its conceptualisations in theories that Schumpeter (1949/51, p. 257f) has expressed as follows:

"What we observe is rather a behavior pattern, possibly supplemented by a schema of motivation; a typical way of giving effect to the possibilities inherent in a given legal and social system both of which change in the process ... All these things may be conceptualized in a more or less complicated schema, every item of which has to be nourished with facts and corrected and amplified under their influence. And this is all."

References

Akerlof GA, Dickens WT (1982) The economic consequences of cognitive dissonance. American Economic Review 72: 307–319

Aranson PH (1990) Rational ignorance in politics, economics and law. Journal des Economistes et des Etudes Humaines 1: 25–42

Bartolini Stefano (1995) Electoral competition: Analytical and empirical problems. European University Institute Working Paper SPS No. 95/6

Bernhardt MD, Ingberman DE (1985): Candidate reputations and the incumbency effect. Journal of Public Economics 27: 47–67

Borner S, Brunetti A, Straubhaar Th (1994) Die Schweiz im Alleingang. NZZ, Zürich

[20] The paradigm case of Switzerland is, however, not very encouraging in this respect. As Borner et al. (1994) argue, one of the greatest problems of Swiss politics is its inability to risk substantial necessary reforms. As a consequence of conservative interest groups' ability to finance and organise vetoing referenda, they argue, Switzerland has developed an all-embracing consensual and corporatistic system which produces much more inertia and sclerosis than a more competitive democracy would have done.

Boudreaux DJ, Lee DR (1997) Politics as the art of confined compromise. Cato Journal 16: 365–381
Brady GL, Clark JR, Davis WL (1995) The political economy of dissonance. Public Choice 82: 37–51
Brennan G, Buchanan JM (1980) The power to tax. Cambridge University Press, Cambridge
Brunetti A, Kisunko G, Weber G (1997) Economic growth with 'incredible' rules – Evidence from a world wide private sector survey. Mimeo
Buchanan JM, Wagner RE (1977) Democracy in deficit. Academic Press, New York
Buchanan JM, Vanberg V (1989) A theory of leadership and deference in constitutional construction. Public Choice 61: 15–27
Cuckierman A, Edwards S, Tabellini G (1992) Seignorage and political instability. American Economic Review 82: 537–555
Demsetz H (1968/89) Why regulate utilities. In: Efficiency, competition, and policy – The organization of economic activity, Vol II. Blackwell, Cambridge Oxford
Demsetz H (1982/89a) Barriers to entry. In: Efficiency, competition, and policy – The organization of economic activity, Vol II. Blackwell, Cambridge Oxford
Demsetz H (1982/89b) Competition in the public sector. In: Efficiency, competition, and policy – The organization of economic activity, Vol II. Blackwell, Cambridge Oxford
Demsetz H (1989) Postscript to Chapter 6: Contestability and competition for the field. In: Efficiency, competition, and policy – The organization of economic activity, Vol II. Blackwell, Cambridge Oxford
Dixit A, Pindyck R (1994) Investment under uncertainty. Princeton University Press, Princeton
Downs A (1957) An economic theory of democracy. Harper, New York
Dunleavy P (1991) Democracy, bureaucracy and public choice. Harvester Wheatsheaf, Hemel Hempstead
Dunleavy P, Ward H (1981) Exogenous voter preferences and parties with state power: some internal problems of economic models of party competition. British Journal of Political Science 11: 351–180
Festinger L (1957) A theory of cognitive dissonance. Stanford University Press, Palo Alto
Frey BS (1978) Politico-economic models and cycles. Journal of Public Economics 9: 203–220
Frey BS (1994) Direct democracy: Politico-economic lessons from Swiss experience. American Economic Review 84: 338–342
Frey BS, Eichenberger R (1994) Economic incentives transform psychological anomalities. Journal of Economic Behavior and Organization 23: 215–234
Frohlich N, Oppenheimer JA (1978) Modern political economy. Prentice-Hall, Englewood Cliffs
Goldberg VP (1976) Regulation and administered contracts. The Bell Journal of Economics 7: 426–448
Hayek FA (1940/94): Socialist calculation III: The competitive 'solution'. In: Kirzner IM (ed) Classics in Austrian economics – A sampling in the history of tradition, Vol III. The age of Mises and Hayek. William Pickering, London
Huckfeldt R, Sprague J (1995) Citizens, politics, and social communication: Information and influence in an election campaign. Cambridge University Press, Cambridge
Kamien MI, Schwartz NL (1975) Market structure and innovation: a survey. Journal of Economic Literature 13: 1–37
Kavanagh D (1980) Political leadership: the labours of sisyphus. In: Rose R (ed) Challenge to governance – Studies in overloaded polities. Sage, Beverly Hills London
King G (1991) Constituency service and incumbency advantage. British Journal of Political Science 21: 119–128
Kuran T (1988) The tenacious past: Theories of personal and collective conservatism. Journal of Economic Behavior and Organization 10: 143–171

Mitchell WC (1984) Schumpeter and public choice, Part II – Democracy and the demise of capitalism: The missing chapter in Schumpeter. Public Choice 42: 161–174
Moe TM (1990) Political institutions – The neglected side of the story. Journal of Law, Economics, and Organization 6: 213–253
Mueller DC (1989) Public choice II – A revised edition of Public Choice. Cambridge University Press, Cambridge
Myerson RB (1995) Analysis of democratic institutions: Structure, conduct and performance. Journal of Economic Perspectives 9: 77–89
Nannestad P, Paldam M (1994) The VP-function: A survey of the literature on vote and popularity functions after 25 years. Public Choice 79: 213–245
Nordhaus WD (1975) The political business cycle. Review of Economic Studies 42: 169–190
North DC (1981) Structure and change in economic history. Norton, New York
Palmer MSR (1995) Toward an economics of comparative organization: Examining ministerial responsibility. The Journal of Law, Economics, & Organization 11: 164–188
Polanyi M (1967) The tacit dimension. Doubleday & Company, New York
Quattrone GA, Tversky A (1988) Contrasting rational and psychological analysis of political choice. American Political Science Review 82: 719–736
Reed WR, Schansberg DE (1992) The behaviour of congressional tenure over time: 1953–1991. Public Choice 73: 183–203
Riker W (1982) The two-party system and Duverger's law. American Political Science Review 76: 753–766
Riker W (1986) The art of political manipulation. Yale University Press, New Haven
Roberts GK (1987) Representation of the people. In: Holler MJ (ed) The logic of multiparty systems. Nijhoff, Dordrecht
Sachs J (1994) Life in the economic emergency room. In: Williamson J (ed) The political economy of policy reform. Institute for International Economics, Washington
Salop SC (1979) Strategic entry deterrence. American Economic Review 69: 335–338
Sartori G (1987) The theory of democracy revisited, Part one. The contemporary debate. Chatham House, Chatham
Scherer FM (1992) Schumpeter and plausible capitalism. Journal of Economic Literature 30: 1416–1433
Schneider M, Teske P (1992) Toward a theory of the political entrepreneur: Evidence from local government. American Political Science Review 86: 737–747
Schumpeter JA (1912/34) The theory of economic development – An inquiry into profits, capital, credit, interest, and the business cycle. Harvard University Press, Cambridge
Schumpeter JA (1942/87) Capitalism, socialism and democracy. Unwin, London
Schumpeter JA (1949/51) Economic theory and entrepreneurial history. In: Clemence RV (ed) Essays of J.A. Schumpeter. Addison-Wesley Press, Cambridge
Shepsle KA, Weingast BR (1981) Political preference for the pork barrel: a generalization. American Journal of Political Science 25: 96–111
Telser LG (1976) Comment on 'Political Information' by Phillip Nelson. The Journal of Law and Economics 19: 337–340
Tullock G (1965) Entry barriers in politics. American Economic Review 55: 458–466
Wahlke JC (1991) Rational-choice theory, voting behavior, and democracy. In: Somit A, Wildenmann R (eds) Hierarchy and democracy. Nomos, Baden-Baden
Weizsäcker CC von (1980) Barriers to entry – a theoretical treatment. Springer, Berlin Heidelberg New York
Williamson J, Haggard St (1994) The political conditions for economic reform. In: Williamson J (ed) The political economy of policy reform. Institute for International Economics, Washington
Williamson OE (1976) Franchise bidding for natural monopolies – in general and with respect to CATV. Bell Journal of Economics VII: 73–104
Wohlgemuth M (1995) Institutional competition – Notes on an unfinished agenda. Journal des Economistes et des Etudes Humaines 6: 277–299

Market institutions and economic evolution

Brian J. Loasby

Department of Economics, University of Stirling, Stirling FK9 4LA, UK
(e-mail: b.j.loasby@stir.ac.uk)

Abstract. Our cognitive limitations cause us to rely on institutions to guide reasonable behaviour; market institutions reduce the costs of search, negotiation, and monitoring entailed in making single transactions. The making of markets requires an investment of immaterial capital, the major share of which typically is provided by those who expect to be very active on one side of the market. This 'external organisation' provides producers with information for the development of new products; by simplifying transactions it also allows consumers greater scope for developing consumption capabilities. Thus the evolution of institutions guides the evolution of goods and services.

Key words: Institutions – Markets – Producers – Consumers – Evolution

JEL-classification: D1, D2, L1, L2, O1

A *market* is a specific institutional arrangement consisting of rules and conventions that make possible a large number of voluntary transfers of property rights on a regular basis.

Ménard 1995, p. 170.

1 Introduction

Readers of this Journal may be willing to accept without further justification, as a premise of this paper, that institutions develop through evolutionary processes, where such processes are characterised by trial and error rather than ex-ante optimization. In economic systems these trials are often

---

Paper presented at the 1998 World Conference of the International Joseph A. Schumpeter Society, Vienna, June 13–16, 1998.

the result of purposeful, though fallible, behavior, and therefore the ways in which particular options are formulated should not be modelled in accordance with any a priori assumption, but are proper subjects for investigation. The first major theme of this paper is the formation of the 'specific institutional arrangements' which define markets. As Lachmann (1986) suggested, we shall be interested in markets rather than 'the market', for markets differ in their institutional arrangements.

It may also be sufficient for this readership to state that institutions provide a framework within which other evolutionary processes operate, on a time-scale within which it can usually – though not always – be assumed that this framework does not change. The second major theme of this paper is an examination of the processes which are influenced by the institutions of a market, and this includes not only market processes but also non-market processes which these market processes make possible. Within the constraints of space, this examination will be no more than indicative.

2 The evolution of markets

2.1 Cognition and institutions

Evolutionary processes generate development 'from within', in Schumpeter's (1934, p. 63) phrase. Rational choice theory, even when extended to include contingencies and information costs, ties outcomes firmly to premises, and these premises are supplied exogenously, in principle by events, but in practice often by the analyst. Any change in behavior is therefore a consequence of a change which is not itself capable of explanation within the analysis; all innovation originates outside the system. If we wish, as in this paper, to develop a basis for internal explanation, it is necessary to avoid rational choice theory.

That does not mean avoiding the concept of acting for a reason; what it means is that the actor cannot know whether the reasons for action are sufficient. That follows directly from a further premise which should be clearly stated, and which may not be quite as readily accepted as the previous two. Because our cognitive capacities cannot match the complexities of our situation, we must act on the basis of representations which are often of dubious adequacy and procedures which are of uncertain value. Moreover we do not have the time or ability to formulate more than a very small proportion of these representations and procedures for ourselves, and therefore often rely on those which appear to be used by other people. Thus the rules and conventions that we call 'institutions' are first of all aids in solving individual problems; they make these problems manageable by allowing us to close our models and thus deduce what we should do (Choi, 1993). Tightly drawn rules and conventions we may call routines; but we should note that even routine behavior is not possible unless we are willing to act as if our classification system were complete. Parts of these classification systems, likewise, are often adapted from other people; and often gratefully so.

In addition to supplementing our cognitive capabilities, institutions give us confidence. Our readiness to act, whether based on explicit reason or implicit routine, is frequently supported by a belief that other, successful, people rely on similar representations and similar procedures; sometimes, indeed, such a belief may be crucial, as has been noted in rather different contexts by Adam Smith (1976a) and Keynes (1937). The personal value of rules and conventions is an important factor in explaining how they come to be accepted as aids to the solution of co-ordination problems, and thus forms part of the explanation of the development of institutional arrangements in particular markets. But this sequence can also be reversed; and in the latter part of this paper I shall suggest how the institutions of a market, which are indeed aids to the solution of co-ordination problems, may also help us, sometimes indirectly, to manage our lives.

Institutions are frictions which, like frictions in mechanical systems, by restricting movement may make controlled movement possible. 'Thanks to friction, innovation is preserved, organization kept up, and permanence maintained' (Lesourne, 1992, p. 9). It is by preventing the exploration of many possibilities that institutions economise each individual's scarce resource of cognition and focus the attention of that individual on a particular range of options. The institutions of an academic discipline or a commercial organization encourage similar representations, similar possibilities, and similar procedures among its members, and thus reduce the costs of transacting ideas. (The first two paragraphs of this paper should illustrate this reduction in transaction costs; there are groups of economists for which this means of reduction would not be effective.) What people, individually or collectively, decide is substantially influenced by how they decide; and thus the institutional framework of decision-making is an important factor in the explanation of endogenous change.

Institutions are necessarily a mixed blessing. Cognitive maps, decision premises, procedural rules, and the like are necessarily retrospective; they anchor the definition of problems and the repertoire of responses to past environments, and inhibit the range of experimentation. In some circumstances they may be actively misleading: who needs a telephone when the telegraph system provides a ready-made record of all messages; who needs a photocopier when carbon copies are produced by the typing process? (Garud et al., 1997). But in applying the logic of appropriateness they relinquish some claims on the imagination, and release it for other uses; they allow people to apply the logic of consequence that is required for reasoned decisions, or alternatively to make bold conjectures which go beyond either logic. A significant innovation may be produced by opening up one segment of the institutional framework, or by seeking intelligently to apply rules and conventions outside the familiar limits. As G.K. Chesterton once remarked 'A man must be orthodox on most things, or he will never have the time to practice his own particular heresy'.

2.2 Why markets?

In much of economics, markets appear as a natural given; if there is a good, then there is a market; and the classification of goods is part of the analyst's natural endowment. Indeed, in the analysis of those economic problems in which markets are missing, such as public goods and unpriced externalities, the first task is to explain why markets fail to appear. But markets are themselves goods (of what Austrians would call a higher order, being indirect means to human satisfaction) and we can enquire into their costs and benefits. We should begin with the latter, and we immediately notice that in an economy which is operating within an Arrow-Debreu equilibrium no markets are open. In that analysis markets are required only for arriving at a set of contracts which supports an equilibrium; once a consistent set of contracts has been agreed for every date and every contingency no-one has any further need of them. A market that has cleared is a market that has closed. The Arrow-Debreu model thus shows us what the world would have to be like for continuous markets not to be necessary – as, not coincidentally, it shows us what the world would have to be like if it were to be free from Keynesian problems (Hahn, 1984, p. 65). Markets facilitate the making of new contracts; the first requirement therefore is that at least some people either have not already settled everything or now wish to change some of the agreements which they have previously made. Markets are goods only in circumstances of uncertainty and change; in those circumstances, we might say, they substitute for rational expectations.

However, the wish to make new agreements does not automatically entail a wish to use a market – not, that is, if we are thinking of a market as an institutional arrangement rather than a convenient analytical fiction, which is the way that it is treated (as is the firm) in most economic analysis. Many such agreements are concluded by private negotiation. But negotiating a long series of private agreements to handle a large number of voluntary transfers of property rights may entail a good deal of time and trouble. Coase (1937) drew attention to the costs of finding potential trading partners and negotiating with them as costs of using markets; but because his purpose was to identify some costs within markets which might be compared with the costs of managing a firm he did not pause to note how much higher the costs of finding and negotiating with trading partners might be without the support of market institutions. What makes a market a good is its potential for enabling large numbers of transactions to be arranged and carried out at lower costs than would be incurred if that market did not exist. A market is not a source of transaction costs, but a means of reducing transaction costs below the levels experienced in the absence of markets. (The analytical costs of general equilibrium theory which are saved by the market institution of the supposedly-Walrasian auctioneer provide an appropriate parable for theorists.) Because standard microeconomics does not explicitly consider the costs and benefits of the exchange process it has no theory of exchange; what would be the content of an economic theory in which production was costless?

'Large numbers' are important because the institutions of a market provide an oriented set of complementary immaterial capital goods which reduces the direct cost of individual transactions, just as an oriented configuration of complementary physical capital goods reduces the direct cost of manufacturing a single product; how much it is worth investing in capital goods for either purpose depends upon the potential investor's expectations of volume. But since the creation of a market reduces the costs of transacting for many transactors, these institutions appear to have the characteristics of public goods; and so in accounting for the evolution of markets we have to explain how this stock of complementary capital comes to be accumulated.

Sometimes the necessary investment is made by those who expect to benefit by charging the users – originally, for example, by kings, town governors, or merchant guilds, and later by private individuals or companies, who constructed buildings such as Corn Exchanges in which potential transactors could meet and trade according to specified procedures, or inaugurated newsheets in which people paid to specify which transactions they wished to arrange. Exchanges which are organized for profit are still important for some transactions, and classified advertisements in newspapers, many of which are distributed free, constitute an important class of market institutions which reduce the costs of the transactors sufficiently to allow the providers of these institutions to charge users enough to cover their costs. However, such identifiable markets, organized for direct profit from the supply of transaction services, are not the subject of this paper.

2.3 Making markets

It is natural to think of most modern markets as having no single physical manifestation (though often they have many well-advertised locations and regular times of opening), and it might seem equally natural to think that, in contrast to the designed organizations called firms, they have evolved as unintended consequences of individual human action. That they are the product of evolutionary processes, the outcomes of which were designed by no-one, is correct; but that there were no deliberate commitments of resources in order to create institutional arrangements that would reduce the direct costs of single transactions is not – just as it is not true that the present position of any firm which has been in existence for some time is exactly what its founders intended. Most of the investment in making a particular market is provided by those who expect to be large-scale transactors on one or both sides of that market, and who therefore expect to gain a large enough share of the benefits to justify bearing an even greater share of the costs. Their incentive to create this particular higher-order good lies in the additional gains from trade that they expect to secure for themselves.

Casson (1982, p. 164) provides a convenient summary of the initial obstacles to trade: no contact between buyer and seller, no knowledge of reciprocal wants, no agreement over price, the need to exchange custody of goods, no confidence that goods correspond to specification, and no confidence about restitution in case of default. The combined effect of all these obstacles interposes substantial transaction costs between the potential benefits to the purchaser and the direct costs of production; and the creation of a market within which these transaction costs will be greatly reduced is identified by Casson as a crucial entrepreneurial function. Casson emphasises that the most effective way of overcoming the obstacles to trade is not to proceed transaction by transaction but to make substantial investments in the creation of a system of conventions and rules; he therefore associates market-making with the creation of a new business which is based on a new product. When, as is often the case, the entrepreneur's valuation of a specific productive opportunity is higher than that of any prospective purchaser of the rights to this opportunity, the costs of developing the opportunity can be recovered only by setting up a business, which entails further investment. What is produced must then be sold, and that requires yet more investment in creating a market in order to recover the previous investments.

Firms seek to create a market for their own products by making it easier for people to deal with them; and an initial commitment by the supplier is necessary in order to help the potential purchasers to close their decision-making model in favour of a purchase. What may be necessary to achieve this closure is apparent from Rogers' (1983) analysis of the factors affecting the diffusion of innovations. In addition to the relative advantage of the new product, which itself may be multidimensional and of varying relevance among potential customers, Rogers notes potential problems with the complexity of the product, its compatibility with the customers' current lifestyles and ways of thinking, the means of communication and persuasion, and the degree of commitment demanded of the consumer in order to sample the product. Early business computers illustrate all these difficulties, and it is easy (in hindsight) to see why the capabilities and established relationships of IBM gave that company substantial advantages in making that market. That customers should often be receptive to help from suppliers is very important; that is why the widespread reliance on representations and procedures adopted from others was emphasised early in this paper.

The link between cognition and institutions is crucial to the explanation of market-making. In developing its own organization and its particular market, each business draws on the institutions of the society within which it operates, and then develops, through a mixture of deliberate decisions and the consequences of day-to-day interactions, rules and conventions which serve to co-ordinate its activities and to align them with the activities of its suppliers and customers. Of course, not all businesses manage to create an appropriate set of institutions; they disappear. Other businesses are so obviously successful that rival businesses seek to copy or adapt their methods, both of internal management and of making markets. Of particular interest for this paper is the adoption of successful new market routines by others. Once it is clear that a significant number of people find the new institutional arrangements helpful, other firms look for similar ways of facilitating their own transactions. Thus the innovator's successful investment generates externalities, which are an important feature of institutional evolution; customers who have adapted to the new arrangements find it easy to transact with alternative suppliers in a similar way, and alternative suppliers can use the experiments of the pioneer in devising their own ways of encouraging transactions.

This widening of the scope of market transactions may benefit the original market-maker; indeed the innovator may encourage others to join in the creation of a new market, hoping not only to share the costs but also enjoying increasing returns from this enlargement of the market. Each present pattern of institutional arrangements originated in an idea for creating a market for a particular good or service, an idea for reducing transaction costs or creating transaction benefits, typically associated with a new kind of product (such as mass-produced cars or personal computers) or a new category of customer (such as American farmers far from any shopping centre or working families who wanted, and could afford, quickly-prepared meals). The eventual outcome is unlikely to be foreseen by anyone; it results from the interaction of many plans, in part conflicting but also in part complementary. But though prediction is hazardous, in explaining outcomes we should pay attention not only to the unintended consequences but to the plans which precipitated them.

Drucker (1964, p. 64) once defined the purpose of a business as the creation of a customer, that is, someone who will continue to buy from the same supplier. Such a continuing relationship, as is well known, reduces the costs to the supplier of subsequent transactions, and thus helps to recover the cost of the investment; but it is also a significant benefit to the customer, for it allows the management of future transactions of the same kind to be reduced to routine, and thus reduces their cost – in particular, as we shall note later, the opportunity cost of cognition. Marshall (1919, p. 182) noted that 'nearly everyone has . . some "*particular*" markets; that is, some people or groups of people with whom he is in somewhat close touch: mutual knowledge and trust lead him to approach them, and them to approach him, in preference to strangers. . . He does not generally expect to get better prices from his clients than from others. But he expects to sell easily to them because they know and trust him'. The costs of transacting within this special relationship are reduced for both parties. As a consequence both will have some disinclination to break it.

3 Evolutionary consequences of markets

3.1 Producers

The enormous volume of transactions in a modern economy is a consequence, not of the variation in original endowments, but of the division of labour; and those who have the greatest dependence on transactional efficiency for a particular commodity are those who specialise in that commodity, either as merchants or as producers. As Marshall (1919, pp. 271–274) pointed out, these are the people who have the greatest incentive to invest in the development of a particular market. One of Adam Smith's best-known principles is that 'the division of labour is limited by the extent of the market' (Smith, 1976b, p. 31); by reducing the cost, in money, time or trouble, which is borne by the customer in making a transaction the supplier can expect to extend that market, thus creating new possibilities for the division of labour. Making it easier for the customer to buy is therefore an important contribution to economic progress through increasing returns; and because this progress entails qualitative change and departures from equilibrium (Young, 1928, p. 528) there is a continual need to find ways of organizing new classes of transactions. '[T]he finding of markets is one of the tasks of modern industry' (Young, 1928, p. 536); it has been suggested that Chamberlin's (1933) *Theory of Monopolistic Competition* is a theory of the search for customers (Robinson, 1970), and Chandler (1977, 1990) has emphasised the importance of investments in marketing, as well as manufacturing and management, in the development of large-scale enterprise.

Marshall (1920, p. 500) observed that every business needs to create both an internal and an external organization, which together provide frameworks for managing and developing the business. The external organization is not only a means of reducing transaction costs for products and services that are already well defined; it provides, as Marshall pointed out, two major contributions to the qualitative change which Young emphasised. It creates a selection environment within which each firm can carry out its own experiments with new products or new means of marketing; but it also gives access to knowledge on which to base these experiments. Prices are not sufficient statistics for those contemplating qualitative change. It is no accident that microeconomic theories of atomistic markets, which lack institutional features, provide an inadequate basis for analysing product innovation.

Marshall's recognition that most producers operate in both a general market and their own special market indicates the ambiguity of market definitions. This ambiguity has found no support among modern analytical representations of markets; yet it is a useful, as well as accurate, recognition for evolutionary economists. There are two linked causes of this ambiguity: the products on offer and the market institutions. However similar may be the products of rival producers, they will hardly ever be identical in the judgement of all potential customers, and neither will be the conventions and rules which govern the transactions between different producers and their customers. Yet this does not justify modelling this situation as a monopolistically competitive equilibrium. As Marshall noted, this kind of distinctiveness does not support a higher price; it provides an identity which supports transactions, and provides the friction which makes investment in new goods and services possible. Moreover, though there are incentives to differentiate in order to create and retain customers, there are also strong incentives to follow successful ideas for both products and market institutions – for cognitive as well as financial reasons. As with all innovation, the balance between novelty and continuity is crucial to success; but what balance will be successful differs from circumstance to circumstance in ways which, as we can see, are not easy to anticipate. It seems a good working principle to assume that any successful new entry changes, in some way, the definition of either the product or the institutions of a market – or both, since they are often interdependent.

An entrepreneur who cannot find a way of reducing the obstacles to trade may be unable to introduce the new product which she has created, in Schumpeter's (1934, p. 85) words, as 'a figment of the imagination'. Menger ([1871] 1976) noted that the choice of goods for commodity production was influenced by their marketability, to which he devoted a whole chapter, but instead of following that analysis with an account of market-making he concentrated on the very important special case of money as a means of reducing transaction costs. We shall comment on the importance of money from the consumer's point of view in the final section of this paper.

Marketability is not simply an inherent characteristic of a particular class of goods. It is subject to human action. Marshall (1919, p. 181) recognised that the division between production and marketing costs was somewhat arbitrary: product design and the manufacturing process are not irrelevant to both the supplier's and the customer's costs of investigating and deciding on a particular transaction, and the organization of the transaction is not irrelevant to the design criteria. The marketability of the product depends on the alignment of product, customer, and the institutions of the market, and that alignment can be influenced from each direction. This is even more obviously true of service industries. If one looks, for example, at the changes in the market institutions for financial services, it is clear that the products as well as the institutions have changed, and the primary enabling factor for these changes has been the development of novel transaction technology. This is nothing new: Marshall (1920, pp. 674–675) observed that the principal factors in British economic progress had been developments in transport and communications, which, by reducing the costs of arranging and executing exchanges, had increased the scope for both specialisation and integration within the economy.

That there has been room for substantial innovation by suppliers in the organization of transactions is demonstrated by such developments as self-service retailing, supermarkets, and telephone selling of insurance; there is currently much speculation about the potential of the internet for reducing the costs of individual transactions. Such innovations usually involve the substitution of capital costs for current costs, often taking the form of investment in knowledge which can then be cheaply reused. Each of these developments has entailed a substantial change in rules and conventions, which required a substantial investment by the initiating sellers, and the evolution of new market institutions was marked by the adoption and modification by each participating firm of arrangements that had been successfully introduced by rivals, as was suggested earlier.

3.2 Consumers

In the introduction to this paper I noted the cognitive limitations of human beings and the importance both of internal representations and external institutions in allowing us to economise this scarce resource. This complex structure of patterns and procedures, partly developed for ourselves and partly adapted from others, provides our cognitive capital. In a highly interdependent society, market institutions, by providing us with readily-usable knowledge about how to make particular classes of transactions, are substantial contributors to that capital; they constitute what we might call, borrowing from Marshall, our personal 'external organization'. What is particularly valuable to consumers is the producers' major share in developing these institutions, stimulated by the producers' incentives to make it easy for us to buy what they have to offer. Frequent transactions in particular markets lead to well-tried rules for action, and by helping us to discover who will serve us well (Hayek, 1948, p. 97) competition helps to simplify our decision making. Transaction costs are likely to be higher in less frequented markets, where there is consequently more scope for suppliers to benefit by offering to bear some of them, for example by free demonstrations, home trials, and money-back guarantees. The producers' initiative obviously carries risks of manipulation, which is occasionally spectacular; but we should recognise that the establishment of market institutions creates the possibility of developing skills in choosing – not for all products but for more than would be possible if we had to spend much more time in arranging transactions.

At this point we should return to Menger's explanation of money as a device for reducing the cost of transacting by eliminating the need for barter. This clearly releases time and cognitive resources; but it also leads to the formation of an elaborate system of money prices, and this is an institution which not only simplifies the process of exchange but also provides a numerical scale against which we can assess the value of any particular product, as Marshall duly noted. It thus helps us to develop a more coherent pattern of consumption without any need to make direct comparisons between goods which serve very different needs. The role of prices as conventions is much underrated in microeconomics. It is underrated in macroeconomics too; since changes in the price level occur through a succession of changes in individual prices, such changes undermine the usefulness of this convention, and people therefore have to devote their cognitive powers to the interpretation of particular prices, instead of interpreting them according to familiar routines, and so are unable to give much attention to improving their skills in consumption. Since price stability is an aid to skilful choosing, inflation reduces the rationality of choices.

In the present context, two functions of market organization are important. The first, and direct, function is to give us confidence in our transaction capabilities, allowing us to plan our consumption activities on the assumption that the transactions which may be necessary in order to carry them out will pose no particular difficulty. The importance of this confidence at once becomes apparent if, exceptionally, our plan requires us to transact in a market of which we have no experience and which we have no good reason to believe is like any market with which we are familiar; by contrast, a familiar and efficient set of market institutions gives us ready access to those who can supply us with what we may need. The second function is indirect; by allowing us to cope easily with transactions it frees our cognitive powers for other uses. Because we don't need to think carefully about how to transact, we can think much more carefully about what to transact, and what uses we can make of whatever it is that we choose to buy.

Individuals and households may be regarded as producers of consumption activities. However, instead of seeking to analyse these activities with the aid of a household production function, with the analytical baggage (or 'institutions') implied by that term, it will be more helpful to follow Penrose (1959) and Richardson (1972) by linking activities to capabilities, or skills and knowhow (for a more extensive treatment, see Loasby, 1998). Consumption activities require consumption capabilities. Capabilities, in Austrian terminology, are goods of higher order, which make certain first order goods attainable; they are also capital goods, which require investment, and thus the allocation of scarce resources. Stable institutions, among which market institutions are important, reduce other demands on these resources, and thus make possible the development of additional consumption capabilities.

People do not consume goods, or characteristics; they attempt to satisfy needs or solve problems, and in the process they may create new goods for themselves. Drucker (1964, p. 87) long ago observed that 'the customer rarely buys what the business thinks it sells' because customers and suppliers are thinking in different ways about different problems. We may add that different customers who are apparently engaged in identical transactions are often buying different goods, in Menger's sense. This is a major reason why the definition of goods, and of the markets in which they are traded, is ambiguous. To impose a list of goods at the outset of analysis is to exclude an important feature of economic evolution. Making more effective consumption choices and using products and services more effectively both require more than the acquisition of information to which a correct value can be assigned in advance; they entail an increase in knowledge, which cannot be known before it has been discovered, and in increase in the skills of certain kinds of decision making. Consumption capital is built up by forming connections and creating patterns, some of which allow particular groups of commodities to be treated for some purposes as homogeneous, while others become closely complementary. Like physical capital, consumption capital (and indeed all forms of human capital) is not well suited to aggregation; what matters is its structure and its orientation. The development of such capital is particularly likely to exhibit the features which Marshall (1920, p. 318) specified in his 'law of increasing return: an increase of labour and capital leads generally to improved organization, which increases the efficiency of the work of labour and capital'. (Consumer initiatives are explored in Bianchi, 1998.)

However, this improved organization imposes a framework which is not capable of rapid and substantial change; close complementarity which enhances efficiency is likely to reduce adaptability, except in favoured directions. The value of consumption capital may be destroyed by some kinds of change; indeed it may even be rendered negative. As in Schumpeter's (1934, pp. 79–80) account of the producer's plight when faced with the disruption of major innovation, '[w]hat was formerly a help becomes a hindrance'. The frictional value of institutions helps to avoid such destruction, though if the friction is very great it may, by preventing timely adjustment, allow pressures to accumulate which eventually precipitate a landslide of competence-destroying change. The continuing development of relevant capabilities requires variation within a stable ambience. Without variation there is no experience to act as a basis for learning; without a stable framework there is no assurance that any valid connections can be made between actions and outcomes that will have any future relevance. The appropriateness of institutions, including the institutions of many markets, to the maintenance of this balance is a major determinant of evolutionary pathways.

In an evolving economy we should not assume an unchanging set of preferences. Cognitive limitations imply that individual preference orderings are never complete and are quite likely to be unformed for goods or services that have never been considered for purchase. When products which are considered for the first time, either because they are new or because we now think that we can afford them, it is often the case that the process of choice defines preference, rather than preference defining choice (Woo, 1992). But it may also be true that a change in income may lead to a reconsideration of substantial parts of our lifestyle, and even to new ways of thinking about preferences (Maslow, 1970, p. 37). These new ways of thinking may well be partially adapted from other people, as, we began by suggesting, are many of the rules and conventions that we follow; they may very well be influenced by the institutions of the markets in which we are contemplating new kinds of transactions.

4 Conclusion

The evolution of economic systems depends on the tendency to variation, between individuals, between organizations, and between institutional arrangements. The institutions of each market provide a framework within which variations among suppliers can be introduced and tested by the responses of consumers, which may include direct comment as well as the potential information contained in their buying decisions; and the results of this testing, supplemented by other direct contacts between buyers and sellers – notably in industrial markets, which have been consciously neglected in this paper – provide the basis for informed conjecture by suppliers (though never rational choice) about new products or new services. The availability of markets, and therefore of transactions which make only limited claims on cognition, also encourages consumers to give attention to finding better ways of meeting their needs, sometimes through more roundabout means, and even of recognising needs that have hitherto been ignored, thus creating new goods. In turn these consumer innovations, and the enhancement of consumption capabilities, provide opportunities for innovations by suppliers. Thus a market is not an arena for the co-ordination of predefined supply and demand functions, but an institutional setting for the cognitive processes by which supply and demand are continually reshaped (Dubuisson, 1998, p. 86). Suppliers and consumers differ in their circumstances and in their interpretations; and these differences are reflected both in the options that they create and in the selections which they make among these options. Some innovations may require the creation of new market institutions, thus modifying the framework within which further innovation takes place. Economic evolution includes both evolution within institutional constraints and the evolution of institutions.

References

Bianchi M (ed) (1998) The active consumer. Routledge, London
Casson M (1982) The entrepreneur: an economic theory. Martin Robertson, Oxford
Chamberlin EH (1933) The theory of monopolistic competition. Harvard University Press, Cambridge, MA

Chandler AD (1977) The visible hand. Belknap Press, Cambridge, MA
Chandler AD (1990) Scale and scope. Belknap Press, Cambridge, MA
Choi YB (1993) Paradigms and conventions: uncertainty, decision-making, and entrepreneurship. University of Michigan Press, Ann Arbor
Coase RH (1937) The nature of the firm. Economica N S 4: 386–405
Drucker PF (1964) Managing for results. Heinemann, London
Dubuisson S (1998) Codification et ajustement: deux moyens pour l'élaboration d'une mémoire de l'organisation. le cas d'une activité de service. Revue Internationale de Systémique 12: 83–98
Garud R, Nayyar PR, Shapira ZB (1997) Technological innovation: oversights and foresights. Cambridge University Press, Cambridge
Hahn FH (1984) Equilibrium and macroeconomics. Basil Blackwell, Oxford
Hayek FA (1948) The meaning of competition. In: Individualism and economic order, pp 92–106. University of Chicago Press, Chicago
Keynes JM (1937) The general theory of unemployment. Quarterly Journal of Economics 51: 209–223
Lachmann LM (1986) The market as an economic process. Basil Blackwell, Oxford
Lesourne J (1992) The economics of order and disorder. Clarendon Press, Oxford
Loasby BJ (1998) The organisation of capabilities. Journal of Economic Behavior and Organization 35: 139–160
Marshall A (1919) Industry and trade. Macmillan, London
Marshall A (1920) Principles of economics, 8th edn. Macmillan, London
Maslow A (1970) Motivation and personality, 2nd edn. Harper and Row, New York London
Ménard C (1995) Markets as institutions versus organizations as markets? Disentangling some fundamental concepts. Journal of Economic Behavior and Organization 28: 161–182
Menger C ([1871] 1976) Principles of economics, translated by J. Dingwall and B.F. Hoselitz. New York University Press, New York
Penrose ET (1959) The theory of the growth of the firm. Basil Blackwell, Oxford
Richardson GB (1972) The organisation of industry. Economic Journal 82: 883–896
Robinson R (1970) Edward H. Chamberlin. Columbia University Press, New York
Rogers EM (1983) The diffusion of innovations, 3rd edn. Free Press, New York
Schumpeter JA (1934) The theory of economic development. Harvard University Press, Cambridge, MA
Smith A (1976a) The theory of moral sentiments, edited by Raphael DD, Macfie AL. Oxford University Press, Oxford
Smith A (1976b) An inquiry into the nature and causes of the wealth of nations, edited by Campbell RH, Skinner AS, Todd WB. 2 vol. Oxford University Press, Oxford
Woo HKH (1992) Cognition, value and price. University of Michigan Press, Ann Arbor
Young A (1928) Increasing returns and economic progress. Economic Journal 38: 527–542

Competitive selection, self-organisation and Joseph A. Schumpeter

John Foster*

Department of Economics, University of Queensland, Brisbane, QLD 4072, Australia
(e-mail: foster@commerce.uq.edu.au)

Abstract. Post-Schumpeterians have tended to use biological analogies to understand economic evolution, in contrast to Schumpeter himself. In this paper it is argued that the biological analogies used tend to be outdated and that Schumpeter espoused an intuitive understanding of the evolutionary economic process that is closely related to modern conceptions of self-organisation, suitably adapted for application in socioeconomic systems. Using a self-organisation approach, competition can be understood without recourse to biological analogy, in terms of general systemic principles that operate in the presence of variety. Viewing economic evolution in terms of complex adaptation in self-organising systems yields nonequilibrium and nonlinear perspectives that parallel Schumpeter's own intuitions, reinvigorating them as the basis of evolutionary economic thinking in the new Millennium.

Key words: Joseph A. Schumpeter – Self-organisation – Competition – Selection – Evolutionary economics – Biological analogy – Nonequilibrium process – Nonlinear discontinuity

JEL-classification: B25, B4, L2, O3

Paper presented at the 1998 World Conference of the International Joseph A. Schumpeter Society, Vienna, June 13–16, 1998.

* I have received many helpful comments on earlier drafts of this article. I would particularly like to offer thanks to: Guido Bunstorf, Burkhard Flieth, Antonio Calafati, Karen Knottenbauer, Jan Kregel, Brian Loasby, Stan Metcalfe, Bart Nooteboom, Pavel Pelikan, Paulo Ramazzotti, Christian Sartorius and Ulrich Witt. The usual *caveat* applies.

1 Introduction

It is well known that Joseph Schumpeter did not believe that biological analogies were of much use in understanding economic evolution. Yet, following the lead of Nelson and Winter (1982), many post-Schumpeterian evolutionary economists have tended to rely upon the biological analogy of natural selection, either of a Darwinian or Lamarkian type. In this paper, this contradictory aspect of post-Schumpeterian evolutionary economics will be examined and Schumpeter's evolutionary thinking will then be re-assessed within an alternative self-organisational perspective provided in Foster (1997). It is argued that such a perspective clarifies and revitalises Schumpeter's insights, ensuring that they will continue to provide the main inspiration for evolutionary economics in the new Millennium.

Already, some post-Schumpeterians have begun to disengage themselves from biological analogies. For example, Metcalfe (1998) carefully considers Nelson and Winter's (1982) suggestion that the approach to natural selection offered by the biologist, Ronald A. Fisher, can provide a formal basis for dealing with evolutionary processes in economic systems. Metcalfe (1998) agrees with them but then argues that the statistical mechanics employed by Fisher are, in fact, quite general in their application to any kind of evolving system. Thus, what can be viewed as a 'principle of competitive selection' in the presence of variety does not involve a biological analogy at all. Rather, it is a general principle that operates in both the economic and biological domains in different ways. For example, Metcalfe stresses the greater importance of the storage and dissemination of knowledge in the economic case. Having abandoned biological analogy in favour of what is, in essence, a general systems approach, he argues that there is a correspondence between his competitive selection model of economic evolution, and the intuitions of Joseph Schumpeter.

Metcalfe (1998) builds upon the neglected insights of Steindl (1952) and Downie (1958) and makes a highly significant contribution not only to evolutionary economics, but also to economics in general. His formal and clear redefinition of the concept of equilibrium and his vivid depiction of competition as a process that eliminates variety offers one of the most coherent challenges to mainstream competitive thinking in recent years (see Foster, 1998). However, in this paper, it is argued that, although he has provided an essential building block, he does not offer a complete theory of economic evolution – what is lacking is Schumpeter's emphasis upon novelty and the generation of new variety. It is suggested here that processes of competitive selection must be set within in a more general self-organisation approach to economic evolution, as discussed in Foster (1997) and Foster and Wild (1998, 1999), before it can be integrated with Schumpeter's fundamental insights concerning economic evolution.

It is not the intention here to re-iterate in any detail what is meant by 'economic' self-organisation but, instead, to make two main points. First, it is argued that evolutionary biology, the source of selectionist analogies in evolutionary economics, is itself embracing self-organisation as an important part of the evolutionary process. Thus, those engaging in analogous thinking must consider the implications of this for their own evolutionary economic theorising. Second, it is argued that Schumpeter's vision of economic evolution offered intuitions and insights, which are highly compatible with a specifically 'economic' self-organisation approach. In particular, his juxtaposition of equilibrium and nonequilibrium depictions of processes, which has puzzled some economists for decades, is found to be consistent with a modern self-organisational perspective on the behaviour of evolving systems. Thus, it is concluded that Schumpeter offered a much better analytical foundation for understanding economic evolution than biological analogies concerning natural selection.

In Section 2, contemporary thinking in evolutionary biology will be briefly reviewed to evaluate the relevance and usefulness of biological analogies favoured by many evolutionary economists. In Section 3, Schumpeter's writings are examined to compare and contrast his vision of economic evolution with that of contemporary evolutionary biologists. Parallels are drawn between his non-biological representation of economic evolution and recent attempts to understand such evolution using a self-organisation approach. Section 4 contains some concluding remarks concerning the integration of the principle of competitive selection within a self-organisation approach to economic evolution.

2 Contemporary thinking in evolutionary economics

It is a daunting task for an economist to unravel the debates in evolutionary biology and the extent to which they should is questionable. However, economic and biological ideas have been inextricably linked for at least two centuries and it is clear that an understanding of contemporary currents in biological thinking can enlighten us as to what evolutionary economics might come to mean in the future. A good place to start is the work of Ronald A. Fisher, who revitalised a flagging Darwinian research program in the early twentieth century. Building upon Mendel's genetic insights, Fisher (1930) argued that Darwin's conclusions could be deduced from statistical mechanics by choosing the gene, rather than the individual, as the unit of selection. In so doing, the analogy used was Boltzmann's statistical mechanics representation of thermodynamic processes. Given time, any gene variety would be resolved to the most probable state of gene homogeneity. Thus, he saw fitness as maximised in the same way that entropy is maximised in Boltzmann's thermodynamic model. Crucially, Fisher redefined equilibrium from a Newtonian balance of forces to a Boltzmannian state where all structural change ceases. By focussing upon the statistical outcome of genetic interactions, the human analogies used by Darwin became unnecessary. In particular, Malthus' 'balance of moral forces' in the face of universal scarcity and associated survival struggles between individuals were exorcised from Darwinism. In their stead was a consistent treatment of two opposing universal tendencies, evolution and entropy, drawing upon the same type of statistical mechanics and the same, non-Newtonian conception of equilibrium.

This new 'Hardy-Weinberg' equilibrium was offered to biologists at the same time as the physical analogy of a Newtonian balance of competing forces equilibrium was just beginning to hold sway in economics. So, just as economics shifted towards deterministic theorising about stable Newtonian equilibrium outcomes, evolutionary biology became a matter of statistical mechanics. Variety, yielded by random mutation, is resolved by natural selection in a relative and probabilistic manner: 'appropriate' genetic mutations grow faster in numbers than 'inappropriate' ones, leading to the ascendancy of the former. Natural selection, envisaged as a product of small changes in a vast number of genes, ceased to be seen as a product of conditions of scarcity but rather something going on at all times. Genes do not compete in any direct sense but rather form new localised combinations that grow at differential rates. The relative growth of genomes through the relative reproductive success of individuals, rather than the Malthusian struggle for survival, became the heart of evolutionary biology.

So, while Joseph Schumpeter studiously avoided analogies with dangerous Darwinian ideas, Darwinism was re-inventing itself. However, evolutionary biology did not become a branch of statistical mechanics as, to a large degree, thermodynamics had done, nor did it become part of genetics. To the contrary, Darwinists were reluctant to abandon their traditional type of theorising and soon discovered that they had to retain the Newtonian conception of equilibrium to continue to engage reductionist forms of deduction, now at the level of the gene, rather than the individual organism. Despite the fact that Fisher's statistical theory is concerned with averages and probable macrostates, deductions concerning microstates were favoured and human behaviour analogies remained popular.

By the 1970s, Dawkins (1976) offered the most extreme example in his 'selfish' gene conception and, in parallel, game theorists, such as Maynard Smith (1983), modelled individual behaviour at the level of the gene as more rationally 'human' than the humans that they inhabit and constitute. Of course, no one believed that genes actually exhibited sophisticated behaviour – the "watchmaker" is always blind – the outcome of Fisher's statistical process was viewed 'as if' strategic, optimising behaviour had occurred. Of course, 'as if' assumptions are analogies. Two are involved: first, random statistical behaviour yields an outcome as if a human being had been engaged in solving an optimisation problem and, second, a thermodynamical type of equilibrium state is treated as if it is a Newtonian equilibrium, i.e., a balance of forces.

For an economist, the invocation of such 'as if' assumptions has a familiar ring and, by the 1980s, we began to observe strong parallels between the analytics used by neoclassical economists and neo-Darwinian evolutionary biologists. Both dealt with equilibrium outcomes rather than processes; both used a characterisation of equilibrium that is not of the thermodynamic type; both applied game theoretics to examine the existence and stability of equilibrium states. The neoclassical economist saw optimisation models as justified by the presumed existence of competitive selection processes, following Alchian (1950) and Friedman (1953), rather than anything akin to the genetic evidence available in biology. By the end of the 1980s, the Nash equilibrium and the associated 'evolutionary stable strategy' had become shared conceptualisations in both neoclassical economics and neo-Darwinian biology. Neo-Darwinians had shown great reluctance to abandon human analogies and, ultimately, they developed a body of theory using analogies, not related to actual human behaviour but to human *idealisations* concerning optimisation and ultra-rationality.

To what extent does neo-Darwinism of this type conform to Fisher's depiction of natural selection? The answer is 'not much' because evolutionary game theorists refer to analytical states of equilibrium whereas Fisher's equilibrium is a steady state with historical meaning, just as thermodynamic equilibrium is a definite outcome of a historical process. Neo-Darwinians, with some notable exceptions (see Depew and Weber, 1995), were, unlike Fisher, uninterested in thermodynamic processes or statistical mechanics. Fisher had been intent upon providing an approach that he regarded as true to Darwin's fundamental insights, but his Mendellian focus upon genes was, initially, rejected by many Darwinists. Acceptance that competitive struggle between individual organisms in conditions of scarcity is not the sole source of evolutionary change and that gene combinations create the variety upon which natural selection works, threatened to move evolutionary biology away from botanists and zoologists to geneticists in a different scientific tradition.

The notion that the outcome of a Fisherian genetic selection process is analogous to an equilibrium solution of an optimisation problem did not fit well with the genetic evidence. Dobzansky (1951) argued that organisms store large amounts of variation and, thus, it is difficult to argue that natural selection is responsible for maintaining it. Thus, accumulations of genetic combinations occur that are not the outcome of natural selection, breaking the tenuous link from natural selection to variation. Roughly a decade later, the revolution in molecular genetics, initiated by Crick and Watson, struck another body blow to neo-Darwinism, since DNA variations were found to arise from mutation and recombination. Another decade on, Jacob and Monod (1961) demonstrated that much of the order that emerges in the genome is the result of the self-organising properties of large genetic arrays. By the 1990s, the genetic evidence against neo-Darwinian explanations had cumulated to such an extent that strong objections by respected biologists became common (see, for example, Swenson, 1991; Fontana et al., 1994).

Depew and Weber (1995) argue that the emergence of serious objections to exclusively natural selection views of evolution through the 1980s, in effect, allowed developmentalist thinking to make a comeback in evolutionary biology. It bore little relation to earlier developmentalist traditions, since it was based upon the self-organisation approach to the emergence of organised complexity in systems. This approach, in turn, had its roots in non-equilibrium thermodynamical thinking and, thus, is consistent, in an ontological sense, with the original Fisherian approach – both apply similar statistical mechanics to processes of structural change. However, the self-organisational approach to biological evolution was not new (see, for example, Prigogine and Waime, 1946) but generally ignored in the neo-Darwinian surge to capture and defend the theoretical high ground in evolutionary biology. When Brooks and Wiley (1986) built upon Prigogine's self-organisation approach to provide a different vision of biological self-organisation, dealing with information, as well as energy stocks and flows, neo-Darwinian opposition was strong, as it had always been against all forms of 'developmentalism'.

However, by the early 1990s, neo-Darwinists became more accustomed to the idea that some kind of self-organisation operates in biological evolution, in addition to the selective force of natural selection. Thus, when Salthe (1993) and Kauffmann (1993), in their different ways, made strong and controversial cases that evolution has to be thought of in terms of both self-organisation and natural selection, they were no longer dismissed out of hand. Salthe (1993) argued that the traditional distinction between development and evolution becomes blurred once we set both in the context of self-organisation. Kauffmann (1993) is less radical, seeing natural selection as still pivotal, maintaining complex, self-organised genetic systems within a range between freedom and fixity, making it possible for evolution to take place. However, in so doing, he demotes competitive selection to the status of a boundary phenomenon "that is constantly pushing emergent, self-organising systems towards the edge of chaos" (Kauffman, 1993). By the mid-1990s, self-organisation had become an accepted part of the ongoing debates concerning evolutionary biology, with neo-Darwinians exploring ways in which it could be incorporated into their theoretical representations of natural selection. Depew and Weber (1995) review the various approaches now being explored to combine self-organisation and natural selection in evolutionary biology.

For two centuries, the scientific authority of Newtonian thinking about systems has come from its analogous association with the observable functioning of physical systems. In the same way, the scientific credibility of the self-organisation approach, like the competitive selection approach of Fisher, comes from the fact that it is built up from observable thermodynamic principles. In turn, thermodynamics came from inquiries into the properties of machines engineered using Newtonian scientific principles. Thus, Fisher sought to strengthen Darwinism by basing it upon a thermodynamical analogy concerning change and equilibrium in closed systems. Over a decade later, the self-organisation approach was born when thermodynamicists began to deal with *open* systems maintaining themselves far from thermodynamic equilibrium through the ingestion of free energy. Biologists have come to understand that self-organisation is more than just an energetic process in the biological domain, it involves the acquisition and processing of information that yields the novelty and variety upon which competitive selection operates.

Increasingly, the process of self-organisation in biology is being viewed through the lens of nonlinear dynamics which, in one sense, confirms Salthe's claim that development and evolution are overlapping *historical* processes but, in another sense, suggests that they are *analytically* separable as distinct phases of self-organisation:

Functionality in general (and hence development) derives from the property of equifinality, or many-to-one mapping, possessed by all nonlinear oscillators, while adaptability in general (and hence evolution) arises from the dynamical property of one-to-many mapping, or bifurcation. Functionality and adaptability are the two faces of all living things, and nonlinear dynamics captures this dual property of organisms in a simple and natural way... Thus, both functionality and adaptability can be encompassed by one and the same mathematical model. One could not ask for a more elegant unification of the two complementary facets of the evolutionary process. (Barham, 1995, pp. 290–291)

Thus, a formal, mathematical representation of the growth and oscillatory characteristics, associated with the process self-organisation, has begun to spread into evolutionary biology, merging with, and reinforcing, an established non-linear mathematical tradition in population ecology. By relaxing the concept of an equilibrium from a point to a curve or a region, mathematics ceases to be used to deduce point equilibrium outcomes but, instead, it is used to represent the non-linear dynamics of processes. There is an on-going debate in evolutionary biology concerning the adequacy of mathematics to represent evolutionary processes that will not be discussed here, except to say that similar questions will be discussed below in the context of economic evolution.

An alternative approach to biological self-organisation that has come to prominence is to see species as keeping themselves away from the point of Fisherian equilibrium by engaging in the cultural transmission of beneficial practices, acquired through individual organisms interacting with their environment. Restrictions on energetic and material intake, of the type that are viewed as leading to genetic selection, can be neutralised. Thus, cultural groupings can slow the resolution of genetic variety by introducing and consolidating behavioural novelty – the kind of biological self-organisation that Brooks and Wiley (1986) speculated upon a decade earlier. Such cultural groupings remain 'far from Fisherian equilibrium' through the acquisition of new information and the exploitation of attendant new energy sources, leading to genetic inertia and non-linear phases of genetic selection between distinctive groups, if and when exploitable information runs out. It follows that the expansion of organised complexity of culture in a highly developed species, such as our own, diminishes the impact of natural selection on its genetic make-up and increases its ability to pressure other species at a lower level of cultural development. Again, it is inappropriate here to pursue this new theme in evolutionary biology. However, Heyes and Galef (1996) provide a good starting point, Alexander (1987) made the contribution that got the ball rolling and Novak and Sigmund (1998) provide a very recent example of the kind of analytic support now being offered, using conventional simulations of strategic behaviour.

Enough has now been said here to establish that many biologists have come to accept that self-organisation is an important aspect of biological evolution and the debate is now concerned with ways of best representing such processes, both theoretically and empirically. Turning our attention back to economics, it is clear that Darwinian and Lamarkian natural selection analogies, so often favoured by neo-Schumpeterian evolutionary economists, are founded upon ideas that are fast becoming obsolete. Bearing in mind the emergence of the view amongst many biologists that cultural self-organisation is important, there is little doubt that economic evolution should also contain powerful self-organisational tendencies.

Depew and Weber (1995) conclude their book with a strong warning to all social scientists that ignore contemporary currents in evolutionary biology and persist in relying only upon natural selection analogies:

These reflections suggest that it should be at least a mild constraint on any evolutionary theory that claims to explain human phenomena that it should throw light on, rather than eliminate or reduce away, the interactional, relational, intentional, and symbolic features that interpretative social scientists have already discovered about social reality. Perhaps it is not too much to say that what we need is an evolutionary theory worthy of the best social theory, not a social theory trimmed to fit a rapidly receding, overly simplistic evolutionary theory. (Depew and Weber, 1995, p. 495)

What is striking about this quote is that one could imagine that it came from the writings of Joseph Schumpeter half a century ago. Could it also be the case that, in some intuitive way, he had come to understand the self-organisational character of evolutionary processes, in an economic setting, even before processes of self-organisation had become recognised in physics, chemistry and biology?

3 Schumpeter revisited

Did Schumpeter espouse Darwinian biological analogy concerning natural selection? Hodgson (1993) argues that he did not and, further, that his use of general equilibrium ideas, combined with the absence of an explicit biological analogy concerning natural selection, implies that he was not really dealing with economic evolution but, rather, economic development. In effect, Hodgson (1993) suggests that Schumpeter dealt only with the functional/developmental process, which Barham (1995) alludes to, in his discussions of biological evolution. However, it will be argued below that it is incorrect to characterise Schumpeter's representation of economic evolution as an equilibrating developmental process. Hodgson (1993) misunderstands Schumpeter's use of equilibrium/disequilibrium terminology and confuses it with later post-Schumpeterian and neo-Austrian characterisations of economic evolution. Consider, for example, Kirzner's (1973) discussion of the entrepreneur:

For Schumpeter the entrepreneur is the disruptive, disequilibrating force that dislodges the market from the somnolence of equilibrium; for us the entrepreneur is the equilibrating force whose activity responds to the existing tensions and provides those corrections for which the unexploited opportunities have been crying out. (Kirzner, 1973, p. 127)

Schumpeter, like other innovative economic thinkers in his time, such as F. von Hayek and J.M. Keynes, felt obliged to start his analysis in familiar economic theory, to show the radical nature of his insights. General equilibrium is, therefore, only a pedagogic starting point, not an analytical end point, in his depiction of economic evolution. Furthermore, Hodgson (1993) conveys the impression that Schumpeter dealt mainly with the role of technological innovation in the business cycle and, thus, had a narrower view of economic evolution than American institutionalists, such as Veblen (1898). In point of fact Schumpeter stressed that economic development is due to *organisational*, not simply technical, change or, in his words, "new combinations":

Development in our sense is... carrying out of new combinations, (Schumpeter, 1934, p. 66)

This type of development was viewed as endogenous to the economic system and, thus, could not be described by general disequilibrium:

By "development" therefore, we shall understand only such changes in economic life as are not forced upon it from without but arise by its own initiative from within. (Schumpeter, 1934, p. 63)

He was also very careful not to confuse development with conventional notions of economic growth:

... development consists primarily in employing existing resources in a different ways, in doing new things with them, irrespective of whether those resources increase or not. (Schumpeter, 1934, p. 68)

It is clear that the developmental processes that he discusses are concerned with organisational change at several levels and these are orchestrated by entrepreneurship, which is a behavioural attribute that only has meaning in organisational contexts:

Everyone is an entrepreneur only when he actually "carries our new combinations" and loses that character as soon as he has built up his business, when he settles down to running it as other people run their businesses. (Schumpeter, 1934, p. 78)

The entrepreneurial desire to discover new and profitable organisational combinations provides what we can now label as a self-organisational impetus within the economic system, creating organised complexity. "Combination" implies, not competition, but the deliberate formation and re-formation of cooperating groups engaged in production. The result is expanding variety in products and processes. Thus, although, Hodgson (1993) is correct in questioning the widespread belief that Schumpeter used a biological analogy concerning natural selection, he misses Schumpeter's unique contribution to evolutionary economics: a preoccupation with organisational change and an associated abandonment of the conventional Newtonian conception of the equilibrium/disequilibrium dichotomy.

Just as the Newtonian equilibrium analogy was taking over in economics, Schumpeter, like Fisher in biology, rejected it as an analytical device for dealing with evolutionary processes. However, Mendel and Boltzmann did not inspire Schumpeter. Instead, his self-organisational intuitions were derived from his extensive and detailed study of economic history. Furthermore, his representation of the process of evolution in the economic system was more complex and adaptive than that of Fisher. As we have seen, half a century had to elapse before biologists began to accept that the kind of complex adaptation, proposed by Schumpeter in economic settings, has a role to play in biological evolution. However, given the strength of Hodgson's (1993) attack upon the logical consistency of Schumpeter's analysis, it is necessary to return to the debate concerning Schumpeter and his use of biological analogy, to see just how misunderstood his writings have been in this regard.

Kelm (1997) versus Hodgson (1997) represents a recent instalment in this debate and it provides a useful vehicle for establishing Schumpeter's self-organisational credentials. Both miss the point that Schumpeter's discussion of concepts of equilibrium outcomes and non-equilibrium processes are fundamental in his discussion of economic evolution. Where Hodgson (1993) sees confusion, there, instead, lies remarkable self-organisational insight concerning economic evolution. Contrary to the neo-Walrasian interpretation of Hodgson (1993) echoed in Hodgson (1997), for Schumpeter, the key feature of an evolutionary economic process is, undoubtedly, the *absence* of equilibrium. He saw both economic development and economic evolution as historical processes and, as such, *nonequilibrium* in nature:

... we will not postulate the existence of states of equilibrium where none exist, but only where the system is moving towards one. When, for instance, existing states are in the act of being disturbed, say, by.... a mania of railroad building, there is very little sense in speaking of an ideal equilibrium coexisting with all that disequilibrium. It seems much more natural to say that while such a factor acts there *is no equilibrium at all*. (Schumpeter, 1939, p. 70) [Italics added]

Hodgson (1997) is generally correct in dismissing Kelm's attempt to interpret Schumpeter in Darwinian terms. However, because he does not fully appreciate the radical nature of Schumpeter's rejection of the Newtonian equilibrium construct, he does not spot a fundamental mistake, committed early in Kelm's discussion:

Since Darwinian theory is arguably the most powerful scientific theory of endogenous change, it would not be too surprising of Schumpeter's theory of economic evolution had more elements in common with it.... (Kelm, 1997, p. 107)

Despite Darwin's extensive discussion of the adapted qualities of the flora and fauna that he observed and how they might have come about because of natural selection, Darwinian theory is *not* concerned with endogenous change. It is concerned with equilibrium *outcomes* of unspecified competitive selection processes that are akin to disequilibrium dynamics, given some exogenous environmental shock that disturbs some ecological equilibrium (see Maynard Smith, 1970; Ruse, 1982). Kelm (1997) then goes on the confuse *dis*equilibrium and *non*equilibrium:

But even if such an equilibrating tendency can be assumed to exist, it is in reality constantly upset by disequilibrating forces, some which *originate from within the economic system*. (Kelm, 1997, p. 105)[Italics added]

Disequilibrium implies equilibrium and therefore, disequilibrating forces must come from without – should one come from within, then there can be no equilibrium – a nonequilibrium state must prevail. Schumpeter understood this and that is why a Darwinan analogy was not useful for his purpose.

In offering an alternative representation with features that we can now label 'self-organisational', Schumpeter had to be careful with his terminology. He chose to refer to an evolutionary process as in a disequilibrium state when discussing it from the perspective of the initial pedagogic starting point of Walrasian static equilibrium. When discussing the evolutionary process in its own right he discussed it as a nonequilibrium process. From the perspective of the analytical general equilibrium starting point, the entrepreneur constitutes an exogenous shock but from the perspective of the nonequilibrium evolutionary process, entrepreneurship is endogenous.

Schumpeter turned methodological convention, derived from physics, on its head: in the domain of economics, nonequilibrium processes of evolutionary change are the norm. Around the nonlinear historical paths, generated by such processes, there are oscillations. These are precipitated by exogenous shocks that are dissipated by homoeostatic mechanisms, resulting in equilibrating tendencies in circular flows. Schumpeter argued that economists could usefully understand these short-term equilibrating tendencies using Marshallian and Walrasian analytical tools. Thus, static economic logic can be brought to bear at any point in historical time, but is wholly unable to assist in gaining an understanding of evolutionary developments:

> ... "static" analysis is not only unable to predict the consequences of discontinuous changes in the traditional ways of doing things; it can neither explain the occurrence of such productive revolutions nor the phenomena, which accompany them. (Schumpeter, 1934, p. 62)

Thus, Schumpeter brought endogeneity to the centre of evolutionary analysis, not by mimicking Darwin, as Kelm (1997) suggests, but by departing, fundamentally, from Darwin's Newtonian analogy. Schumpeter stressed that the Newtonian conceptualisation of equilibrium could only be used in an analytical sense to understand systemic interconnections and the operation of homeostasis in conditions where growth is approximately linear. Thus, stationary states to which historical growth processes often tend are not equilibria in this analytical sense, but rather, states where linear equilibrium thinking begins to lose its usefulness in understanding the short-term behaviour of a system:

> ... we will ... recognise existence of equilibria *only at discrete points on the time scale at which the system approaches states which would, if reached, fulfil equilibrium conditions.* And since the system in practice never reaches such a state, we shall consider, instead of equilibrium points, ranges in which the system as a whole is more nearly in equilibrium than it is outside of them. (Schumpeter, 1939, p. 71)

Like Alfred Marshall before him, he saw the mechanical concept of equilibrium as a rough approximation to be used with great caution in connecting the principles of economic logic with historical facts (see Foster, 1993). Indeed, Schumpeter's view of evolutionary processes as non-linear and discontinuous *necessitates* that historical stationary states, attained after phases of economic development, are structurally unstable and, thus, lack stable equilibrating tendencies. In identifying economic evolution as a nonequilibrium process, Schumpeter summarised his conceptualisation in the following terms:

... hence, our position may be characterised by three corresponding pairs of opposites. First, by the opposition of two real processes: the circular flow or the tendency towards equilibrium on the one hand, a change in the channels of economic routine or a spontaneous change in the economic data arising from within the system on the other. Secondly, by the opposition of two theoretical *apparatuses*; statics and dynamics. Thirdly, by the opposition of two types of conduct, which, following reality, we can picture as two types of individuals; mere managers and entrepreneurs. (Schumpeter, 1934, p. 82)

Two connecting threads run through his three pairs of opposites. First, *circular flow – statics – managers*, deals with the repair, maintenance and incremental improvement of economic organisational structures and their products – this is the marginalist and gradualist world that preoccupied Alfred Marshall. Second, *spontaneous change – dynamics – entrepreneurs* deals with nonequilibrium processes that yield increases in organisational complexity, where "dynamics" refer to evolutionary, not simply 'developmental' processes:

... that kind of change arising from within the system *which displaces its equilibrium point that the new one cannot be reached form the old one by infinitesimal steps*. Add successively as many mail coaches as you please, you will never get a railway thereby. (Schumpeter, 1934, p. 64)

Entrepreneurship contributes both to the developmental process of organisational innovation and to discontinuous change when historical stationary is approached or attained.

Thus, we have a correspondence between Schumpeter's conception of evolution and that contained in the self-organisation approach. However, in dealing with economic evolution, Schumpeter clearly did not subscribe to Barham's (1995) neat and tidy nonlinear dynamic distinction between functional development and adaptive evolution. For Schumpeter, the processes of development and evolution overlap so much that they are almost interchangeable terms. Thus, if he thought, intuitively, in self-organisational terms, it is unlikely that he would have concurred with nonlinear discrete dynamic representations of the growth profiles of self-organising systems, since they do not dispense with analytical equilibrium but, rather, generalise it into points, curves and regions.

Attempting to capture nonequilibrium processes in terms of weakened concepts of equilibrium preserves the determinism of mathematics but removes its analytical power. A complex equilibrium region is of little or no help to the economist attempting to bring to bear the power of economic logic upon unfolding historical events. Predictive power is lost and the myth that logical equilibrium and historical stationary states can be connected is perpetuated. Through simulation and calibration, a nonlinear dynamic model can be made to follow a growth trajectory that looks realistic, but the mathematical mechanism employed bears no relation to the self-organisational processes executed by irreversible and dissipative structures. Employing a deterministic nonlinear dynamic mathematical model deductively is to use, in effect, a *mathematical analogy*, to attempt to understand economic evolution.

Schumpeter was clearly opposed, as Richard Goodwin often recounted, to the use of discrete, nonlinear dynamic logic to capture the growth dimension of economic evolution. Furthermore, he did not use cumulative causation, path dependence or 'lock-in' arguments to provide a rationale for dynamic mathematical representations of evolutionary processes. Despite this, some post-Schumpeterians, such as Richard Day in his many distinguished contributions, have been attracted to mathematical analogy. This has been due, in part, to the repeated empirical observation of nonlinear logistic diffusion curves in the presence of innovation. Thus, the use of discrete versions of this curve has been attractive to deduce bifurcation points that mimic observed nonlinear discontinuities. Schumpeter did recognise that there exist tendencies in historical data that can be captured in mathematical form and given an empirical dimension through econometric estimation but his commitment to a nonequilibrium view of the associated evolutionary process precluded the deductive use of such discovered mathematical structure.

In Foster and Wild (1998, 1999) it is argued that an approach which is truer to Schumpeter's vision is to view logistic diffusion curves, not as deductive devices but as abstractions of historical tendencies present when economic self-organisation is occurring. The presence of a logistic growth trajectory can be confirmed or falsified using suitably transformed historical growth data, provided that short term equilibrating tendencies are allowed for by employing conventional economic logic to suggest variables for inclusion in an augmented logistic diffusion model. The likelihood of structural discontinuity is then addressed by examining the properties of the unexplained residuals as a historical stationary state is approached. Thus, Schumpeter's view that equilibrium thinking is only useful in acceptable ranges of historical experience can be given operational meaning.

Of course, econometric estimation of logistic diffusion curves is not novel and has been employed widely in studies of innovation since the seminal study of Griliches (1957). However, studies of innovation do not always appear to have been undertaken in line with Schumpeter's nonequilibrium depiction of organisational change. First, as has been pointed out, his stress on organisational change has tended to be reduced to a narrower preoccupation with technical change. Second, we see many innovation diffusion studies which, either explicitly or implicitly, associate historical stationarity at the top of a logistic curve with a state of analytical equilibrium. Development is, thus, depicted as disequilibrium, not as an emergent process with an unknown outcome. It is remarkable that such studies are often labelled as 'neo-Schumpeterian', despite the clear contradiction with Schumpeter's 'self-organisational' thinking.

4 Concluding remarks

In this paper, recent developments in evolutionary biology have been briefly reviewed and it has been concluded that the self-organisation approach is in the process of being integrated with natural selection to define a 'new' evolutionary biology. In evolutionary economics there are only limited signs of such a parallel development: old-fashioned biological analogies are still widely favoured and very little attention is given to self-organisation or the 'systems thinking' from which it is derived. It is worth noting, in this regard, that biological analogies of competitive selection have now come to be challenged strongly in the field of management science where 'ecosystem thinking' has stimulated an emerging self-organisation perspective upon business strategy (see Brandenberger and Nalebuff, 1995; Moore, 1996; Hagel and Armstrong, 1997). It is also concluded that Joseph Schumpeter's insights concerning economic evolution are highly compatible with recent attempts to develop a specifically economic variant of self-organisation. Correspondingly, much confusion is identified both amongst those who see Schumpeter as a closet Darwinian and also amongst those who seek to try to formalise economic evolution in terms of discrete dynamic nonlinear mathematics. We can expand upon these two conclusions.

First, many evolutionary economists do not appear to appreciate that the competitive biological analogies which they apply have become heavily circumscribed in evolutionary biology due to a growing acceptance that self-organisation plays a key role in evolution. The self-organisation approach has been shown to be more compatible with the findings of geneticists than the reductionist and mechanical approach of neo-Darwinists, with their reliance upon 'storytelling' by human analogy. Furthermore, the self-organisation approach and the Fisherian perspective upon competitive selection are compatible in an ontological sense, given their common roots in thinking concerning thermodynamical systems. As Metcalfe (1998) stresses, the statistical mechanics that Fisher borrowed from thermodynamics does not constitute an analogy but, rather, represents a process of resolution that must operate in the presence of variety in any kind of dissipative system. Similarly, self-organisation is not an analogy either but, rather, an enduring property of dissipative systems which manifests itself in different ways in different contexts (see Foster, 1997).

Second, it is argued that the debate as to whether Joseph Schumpeter espoused biological analogy is sterile because it is clear that he, like Alfred Marshall before him (see Foster, 1993), had an intuitive understanding of what self-organisation constitutes in the economic domain. Schumpeter, was, however, more expansive in his evolutionary economic thinking, making explicit the nonlinear character of what we would now see as a self-organisational process in the economy. Schumpeter did not accept Marshall's view that the economic system was always capable of evolving through incremental adaptation. In Schumpeter's schema, Marshall's view relates to the managerial drive to engineer efficiency-enhancing new combinations, rather than the entrepreneurial drive to discover novel combinations. Furthermore, Schumpeter's more expansive depiction of the circular flow led him to prefer a more general analytical conception of equilibrium in Walrasian terms to understand the complex interconnections involved at any point in time. It is argued that Schumpeter offered an intuitive understanding of "economic self-organisation" (see Foster, 1997) that differs in important respects from what is now understood as biological self-organisation. In particular, development and evolution are not viewed as distinct processes in the economic domain.

The idea that competitive selection and self-organisation should both feature in a neo-Schumpeterian model is not new. It was suggested in the late 1980s by, among others, Silverberg, Dosi and Orsenigo (1988). These authors combined a Fisherian model of competitive selection with a mixture of adoption, learning and imitation. Although the latter mixture is inspired by the analogy of physio-chemical self-organisation, in the respective traditions of Ilya Prigogine and Hermann Haken, organisational development is held constant in their simulations. Thus, in the end, they do not employ an economic self-organisation approach, in the sense of Schumpeter, but, rather, a more complex form of competitive selection. In choosing to represent innovation in logistic diffusion curves emerging from learning, adoption and imitation, they followed a well-tried tradition in studies of innovation. Wisely, they did not attempt to use the analogy of physio-chemical self-organisation in any direct sense. However, in so doing, they tend to understate the importance of self-organisation in economic evolution.

Just as Metcalfe (1998) has pointed out that competitive selection is a general principle with different characteristics in the domains of economics and biology, so it is true with self-organisation. Self-organisation is not a physio-chemical analogy but a general principle in systems that process energy, matter and information. Economic self-organisation is not the same as biological self-organisation, despite the fact that they share common properties. Thus, a unified neo-Schumpeterian model must deal with *economic* self-organisation and *economic* competitive selection. Such a unified approach has the potential to solve the problem that Fisherian modellers of competitive selection face in the economic domain: if variety is always changing, often because firms access new niches as they innovate, and the unit of selection changes as more organisation parallels increasing complexity, how can it be applied in real world settings? Typically, the fear of competition is itself a stimulus to innovation, thus the tendency towards a stationary state affects the stationary state itself and we have a non-equilibrium process.

What we have to accept is that, in economic systems, variety is never fixed, as Schumpeter stressed, repeatedly. Variety at the individual level leads to further new variety as individuals form into cooperative organisations. Thus, we have a process of economic self-organisation and the cumulative formation of organised complexity. For Schumpeter, those with entrepreneurial skills are instrumental in generating such variety by bringing together new techniques and/or new organisational arrangements. They, in turn, draw upon the mass of variety in knowledge and productive skills that pre-exists. The methodological difficulty that arises with Metcalfe's Fisherian model is that it is only analytically tractable if we view new variety as being exogenous, constantly revising the equilibrium outcome. If we follow Schumpeter and think of variety as being endogenously created, as a response to problems and opportunities in the system in question, then we cannot sustain an analytical equilibrium set-up. A non-equilibrium process cannot have an evolutionary equilibrium outcome that can be *deduced*.

However, the 'absence of change' definition of equilibrium used in Metcalfe (1998) is not analytical, but involves attainable historical stationary states. Difficulty arises only if we choose to proceed 'as if' such an equilibrium is analytical, in the neo-Darwinian manner. Otherwise, the Metcalfe model continues to have explanatory content – differential growth will always change market share, even though the units of selection never stay still – it is predictive content that is missing. However, if, for whatever reason, variety generation becomes insignificant, then the model will have both explanatory and predictive content, not in the sense of a tendency towards a stable *analytical* stationary state but towards a *historical* stationary state. As we learn from Schumpeter, the temporary stemming of the flow of new variety in such circumstances is precisely the reason why such stationary states are punctuated by structural discontinuities. Given the historical nature of such discontinuities, it is not to the dynamic mathematics of bifurcation that we should turn, but, instead, to a post-Schumpeterian analysis of the historical processes involved. Mueller (1997) provides a pioneering contribution in this regard.

The Schumpeterian notion that there is a continual, spontaneous generation of novelty in the socioeconomic system breaks the Darwinian causal link between selection and variety generation. When this link is cut, the competitive selection model becomes secondary in economic evolution – the primary engine of evolution is variety generation. Even in cases where organisational failure is high, such as the restaurant business (see Hannan and Freeman, 1989), novelty creation is decisive. Consumers select those restaurants with the best organisation, products and services provided by the most creative and most entrepreneurial in the business. However, the market process does not generate new variety, only opportunities to test out new novelty. It is the combination of creative skill and entrepreneurial desire to take such opportunities, often against very unfavourable odds, which creates a self-organised and vastly complex population of restaurants. Restaurants do not usually compete with each other directly simply because their products and services are heterogeneous. What they attempt to do is establish repeat trading arrangements, or even a contract, with targeted consumers. What we think of a competition in this sector is, in fact, novelty entering at a high rate. Should novelty stop entering, then the Metcalfe model tells us that competition would be eliminated in favour of the strongest and/or most efficient. Economic evolution, at least temporarily, would cease.

Before we can use a competitive selection model predictively, we need to be able to establish that conditions exist where variety is relatively constant and that other factors influencing the expansion and survival of techniques and the firms in which they are used are relatively unimportant. First of all, the competitive selection model will predict nothing when the elements of the population dealt with are entering a niche that is still open. When the niche is open, individuals will cooperate to their mutual advantage and, in so doing, may develop novel organisational links and, thus, continually alter the unit of selection. Secondly, it is when a niche limit is approached, that variety is most likely to tend towards the type of homogeneity predicted by a competitive selection model. However, even in these conditions, a process of selective competition and attendant homogenisation need not occur, simply because awareness of the possibility of competitive elimination, in itself, is a spur towards the generation of new variety and structural adaptation. It is here that we have a key feedback loop – the internalisation of selection and adaptation – that is unimportant in the biological case but one which Schumpeter came to believe was of central importance in the case of the evolution of large economic organisations.

The Metcalfe (1998) model is a considerable achievement because it offers an explanation of a crucial aspect of economic evolution and relies upon an alternative definition of equilibrium to the 'balance of forces' one preferred by most economists. However, in the natural sciences, the Boltzmann/Fisher representation of statistical mechanics has been superseded. Long ago, thermodynamics moved on from its classical to its non-equilibrium phase, to understand the self-organisational qualities of chemical and physical structural change, and biology has, more recently, begun to open up its Fisherian genetic fundamentals to provide its own distinctive conceptualisation of biological self-organisation. Thus, we should look upon the Metcalfe (1998) model as only a beginning in the quest to discover a general characterisation of economic self-organisation within which creative, cooperative and competitive processes can be analysed. To begin this quest, we need look no further than the remarkable insights of Joseph Schumpeter.

References

Alchian AA (1950) Uncertainty, evolution and economic theory. Journal of Political Economy 58: 211–222

Alexander RD (1987) The biology of moral systems. de Gruyter, New York

Barham J (1995) Ni Darwin ni Derrida. Journal of Social and Evolutionary Systems 18: 277–308

Brandenberger A, Nalebuff B (1995) Co-opetition. Doubleday, New York

Brooks DR, Wiley EO (1986) Evolution and entropy: toward a unified theory of biology. Chicago University Press, Chicago

Dobzhansky T (1951) Genetics and the origin of the species, 3rd edn. Columbia University Press, New York

Dawkins R (1976). The selfish gene. Oxford University Press, Oxford

Depew DJ, Weber BH (1995) Darwinism evolving: system dynamics and the geneology of natural selection, MIT Press, Cambridge, MA

Downie J (1958) The competitive process. Duckworth, London

Fisher RA (1930) The genetical theory of natural selection. Oxford University Press, Oxford

Fontana W, Wagner G, Buss LW (1994) Beyond digital naturalism. In: Langton CG (ed) Artificial life I, pp 211–227. MIT Press, Cambridge, MA

Foster J (1993) Economics and the self-organisation approach: Alfred Marshall revisited? The Economic Journal 103: 975–991

Foster J (1997) The analytical foundations of evolutionary economics: from biological analogy to economic self-organisation. Structural Change and Economic Dynamics 8: 427–451

Foster J (1998) Competition, competitive selection and economic evolution. Papers on Economics and Evolution No. 9801. Max Planck Institute for Research into Economic Systems, Jena

Foster J, Wild P (1998) Econometric modelling in the presence of evolutionary change. Cambridge Journal of Economics (forthcoming)
Foster J, Wild P (1999) Detecting self-organisational change in economic processes exhibiting logistic growth. Journal of Evolutionary Economics 9: 109–133
Friedman M (1953) The methodology of positive economics. In: Essays in positive economics. Chicago University Press, Chicago
Griliches Z (1957) Hybrid corn and the economics of innovation. Econometrica 25: 501–522
Hagel J, Armstrong J (1997) Net gain. Harvard Business School Press, Boston
Hannan MT, Freeman J (1989) Organisational ecology. Harvard University Press, Cambridge, MA
Heyes CM, Galef BG (1996) Social learning in animals: the roots of culture. Academic Press, New York
Hodgson G (1993) Economics and evolution: bringing life back to economics. Polity Press, Cambridge
Hodgson G (1997) The evolutionary and non-Darwinian economics of Joseph Schumpeter. Journal of Evolutionary Economics 7: 131–146
Jacob F, Monod J (1961) Genetic regularity mechanisms in the synthesis of proteins. Journal of Molecular Biology 3: 318–356
Kelm M (1997) Schumpeter's theory of economic evolution: a Darwinian interpretation. Journal of Evolutionary Economics 7: 97–130
Kauffman S (1993) The origins of order: self-organisation and selection in evolution. Oxford University Press, New York
Kirzner IM (1973) Competition and entrepreneurship. University of Chicago Press, Chicago
Maynard Smith JM (1970) Time in the evolutionary process. Studium Generale 23: 266–272
Maynard Smith J (1983) Evolution and the theory of games. Cambridge University Press, Cambridge
Metcalfe JS (1998) Evolutionary economics and creative destruction. Routledge, London
Moore J (1996) The death of competition. Harper Business, New York
Mueller DC (1997) First mover advantages and path dependence. International Journal of Industrial Organisation 15: 827–850
Nelson R, Winter S (1982) An evolutionary theory of economic change. Harvard University Press, Boston
Novak MA, Sigmund K (1998) Evolution of indirect reciprocity by image scoring. Nature 393: 573–577
Prigogine I, Waime JM (1946) Biologie et thermodynamique des phenomenones irreversibles. Experientia 12: 451–463
Ruse M (1982) Darwinism defended: a guide to evolutionary controversies. Addison-Wesley, Reading, MA
Salthe S (1993) Development and evolution: complexity and change in biology. MIT Press, Cambridge, MA
Schumpeter JA (1939) Business cycles, Vol I. McGraw Hill, New York
Schumpeter JA (1934) The theory of economic development. McGraw Hill, New York
Silverberg G, Dosi G, Orsenigo L (1988) Innovation, diversity and diffusion: a self organisation model. The Economic Journal 98: 1032–1054
Steindl J (1952) Maturity and stagnation in American capitalism. Monthly Review Press, New York
Swenson R (1991) End-directed physics and evolutionary ordering: obviating the problem of the population of one. In: Geyer F (ed) The cybernetics of complex systems. InterSystems Publications, Salinas, CA
Veblen TB (1898) Why is economics not an evolutionary science? Quarterly Journal of Economics 12: 373–426

Convergences with Schumpeter: An essay Hirschman has yet to write

Peter Wynarczyk

Division of Economics, University of Northumbria at Newcastle,
Newcastle upon Tyne, NE1 8ST, UK (e-mail: peter.wynarczyk@unn.ac.uk)

Abstract. The paper explores the contributions of Joseph Schumpeter and Albert Hirschman to our understanding of the dynamics of modern democratic capitalist economies and suggests that much of their respective work displays intellectual overlap and complementarity. It is primarily focused upon the role of economic and political processes as forces of change and adjustment and the necessary degree of built-in inertia required to permit orderly rather than chaotic responses.

Key words: Schumpeterian themes and commonalities – Production – Consumption – Endogenous dynamics – Inertia – Capitalism, socialism and democracy

JEL-classification: A11-A14, B3, D72, P1-P3

1 Introduction: Intellectual convergence

A.O. Hirschman has recently written about the possible types of intellectual convergence that can occur between one thinker and another and highlighted those intellectual encounters which display elective affinity or

---

Paper presented at the 1998 World Conference of the International Joseph A. Schumpeter Society, Vienna, June 13–16, 1998.

This paper is part of a larger project, a book currently being written, concerned with both Schumpeter and Hirschman's ideas on the dynamics of modern democratic capitalist economies and the position and significance of economics within the social sciences.

Wahlverwandtschaft and the coming together of minds.[1] The discovery of such intellectual kinship can often result in cross-fertilization for the parties actively engaged in drawing together disparate strands. In what follows it will be argued that whilst J.A. Schumpeter and Hirschman both offer distinct contributions to our understanding of the dynamics of modern democratic economies they also share complementary concerns which warrant treatment together. Indeed, it will be suggested presently that some fusion of their ideas would enhance both their respective positions since not only do they share much common ground (intellectual overlap) with the potential for mutually advantageous interchange but, in addition, and more importantly, a synthesis would help overcome particular weaknesses, shortcomings and blindspots identified in their separate approaches hence being self-reinforcing rather than self-defeating. Rather uncannily, Schumpeter and Hirschman even come together on this matter of intellectual congruity. Whilst Schumpeter was aware of the potential benefits of any attempted synthesis of distinct approaches he was also keen to express reservations related to the inherent dangers and difficulties of such fusion. The key danger was that 'cross-fertilization might easily result in cross-sterilization' (Schumpeter, 1954a, p. 27), this point is echoed almost verbatim by Hirschman (1995, p. 133), Schumpeter was keen to emphasise here the potential threat posed by any endeavour to hastily marry elements of economics and sociology and elsewhere highlighted the actuality of synthesis along Marxian lines which issued in 'both worse economics and worse sociology' (1952, p. 57). He also displayed, on the same page, anxiety with the fact that synthesis in general was extremely difficult to achieve, requiring great competency. Whilst one should remain wary of such real dangers one should not allow oneself to be immediately forced off the intellectual road of overlap and potential improvement. Schumpeter also unearingly anticipated Hirschman in pointing to the fact that men's minds were 'apt to converge in similar views' and he went further in arguing that they and their epigoni 'see secondary differences between one another more clearly than the essential similarities' (1952, p. 251). Cognizant of this fact, the paper will go on and attend to those fundamental commonalities which tend to remain dormant and detached within Schumpeter and Hirschman and their respective contributions to the dynamics of capitalism.

2 Intellectual geography: Mapping the shared terrain

Schumpeter has continued to cast an enduring, if somewhat variable, shadow over economics throughout the twentieth century and Hirschman in the second half. The recent revival of interest in Schumpeter bears

[1] See his 'Convergences with Michel Crozier', reprinted in Hirschman (1995, pp. 132–136). As stated in the title of my paper much of the discussion that follows is in anticipation of 'Convergences with Joseph Schumpeter' that Hirschman may one day write.

testimony to the continued vitality and longevity of his ideas as well as their greatness[2] although Giersch (1984) went too far in the mid nineteen eighties suggesting that the last quarter of this century may be characterised as 'The Age of Schumpeter'. Indeed, in his early historical sketch *Epochen der Dogmen- und Methodengeschichte* [1914] (1954b) Schumpeter's quip that 'in science as in hunting it is possible to progress further by remaining behind, at least apparently' (1954b, p. 74n1) served to capture, with the benefit of hindsight, an important aspect of his contribution of increased standing today – its detachment from all things Keynesian and its compatibility with much modern revivalist neoclassicalism. However, much of value in Schumpeter remains to be fully embraced by orthodoxy, especially that which poses a fair degree of epistemic threat to the mainstream. Likewise, given Hirschman's critique of the underpinnings and over-simplicism of the dominant rational choice framework within economics and its imperialistic failure to trade with other social science disciplines, we also find a large amount of his contribution either neglected or marginalised by core economics. Both Schumpeter and Hirschman continue to hold our attention because they remain relevant not only to our grasp of the dynamic and persistent forces underpinning economic, political and social change but also to the redefining of boundaries currently taking place within social science.[3]

A large part of the Schumpeterian system is concerned with what may be termed production dynamics. His *Theory of Economic Development* [1911] (1934), *Business Cycles* (1939), and *Capitalism, Socialism and Democracy* [1942] (1987), highlighted the significance and role of production in economic evolution. As Schumpeter stated 'the capitalist engine is first and last an engine of mass production' (1987, p. 67). In contrast, Hirschman concentrates upon consumption dynamics as the driving force, especially in his *Exit, Voice and Loyalty* (1970) and *Shifting Involvements: Private Interest and Public Action* (1982). Taken together they serve to emphasise two of the essential motors of capitalist development over time. It is interesting to note that within both approaches it is success whether on the supply side (Schumpeter) or the demand side (Hirschman) which serves to undermine the prevailing situation. For Schumpeter, capitalism's economic success would result in its political failure. For Hirschman, consumer-citizens strive and search for happiness but are doomed to the disappointment of

---

[2] Schumpeter wrote (1952, p. 3) that 'Most of the creations of the intellect or fancy pass away for good after a time that varies between an after-dinner hour and a generation. Some, however, do not. They suffer eclipses but they come back again, and they come back not as unrecognizable elements of a cultural inheritance, but in their individual garb and with their personal scars which people may see and touch. These we may well call the great ones – it is no disadvantage of this definition that it links greatness to vitality... But there is an additional advantage to defining greatness by revivals: it thereby becomes independent of our love or hate.'

[3] See the excellent book edited by Swedberg (1990). In addition, Swedberg's biography of Schumpeter (1991a), and his presentation of some of Schumpeter's key papers in economics and sociology, in the edited volume (1991b), provide readible and accessible material on the continuing relevance of Schumpeter today.

attainment. Within both approaches much change is brought about via swarm-like behaviour, whether of entrepreneurs (Schumpeter) or consumers cum citizens (Hirschman).

In both frameworks there is an emphasis upon the systemic or endogeneous nature of change. Schumpeter argued that Marx's 'truly great achievement' resided in his vision of the economic process 'under its own steam, in historic time, producing at every instant that state which *will of itself determine the next* one' (1987, p. 43, emphasis added).[4] Schumpeter's emphasis upon the internal dynamics of change is well known. The hallmark of economic development or evolution was change that arose from within the system 'from its own initiative' (Schumpeter, 1934, pp. 63–64). The entrepreneur was the key agent responsible for innovation, introduced in periods of tranquility or equilibrium, resulting in a disturbance to the circular flow and the onset of discontinuity. Such innovation breakouts had a concrete time dimension located within free or trust capitalism and the march into socialism. However, his presentation of the circular flow appears to be outside of historical time – being an economy in full Walrasian stationary equilibrium undergoing constant reproduction. Tradition, custom and routine are the key features accounting for the direction of production in the circular flow and the degree of inertia and lock-in responsible for constraining the system. As Schumpeter noted, with regard to the circular flow, 'all actions and reactions are performed within the bounds of familiar practice that has evolved from long experience and frequent repetition' (1939, p. 47). Entrepreneurs carry innovations into effect by leading the means of production into new channels. They are reliant upon the banking system to finance their break-out since factors of production have to be diverted from present (and past) use into the new (combination) and guided by faith in potential anticipated profit (based upon the belief that the innovation is superior to past practice). Innovation needs resources to be carried out and generates novelty, surprise and qualitative change. Such disturbances to tranquility do face resistance but will, in turn, if successful, eventually lead to imitation and the creative destruction of outmoded ways so that the system will eventually generate a new improved circular flow. Schumpeter presented capitalist reality as 'first and last a process of change' brought about by revolution from within and the incessant force of creative destruction (1987, p. 77n5).[5]

[4] Whilst Schumpeter found much at fault with Marx's analysis this was more than offset by the latter's elaboration of the inherent logic of production as 'a propeller the action of which does not itself require any impetus external to it', so that the economic process 'will eventually break its own institutional framework', and 'will of itself determine the next one' by revolution 'from within', with capitalist evolution eventually destroying the very foundations of capitalist society (see 1987, p. 12, p. 20, p. 31 and pp. 42–43).

[5] As Schumpeter (1987, p. 83) stated 'Those revolutions are not strictly incessant; they occur in discrete rushes which are separated from each other by spans of comparative quiet. The process as a whole works incessantly however, in the sense that there always is either revolution or absorption of the results of revolution, both together forming what are known as business cycles'.

This importance attached to internal processes is seen by Hirschman as a particularly Schumpeterian characteristic[6] alongside his focus upon the discontents engendered by the economic, social and political order. His classic *The Passions and the Interests* (1977) explored the 'complex and roundabout' rise and acceptance of self-interest alongside the fall of the heroic ideal and self-sacrifice as an endogenous tale whereby 'the new arose out of the old'.[7] Likewise, in his *Shifting Involvements* (1982) Hirschman examined the internal forces at work within modern democratic capitalism to generate cycles between a preoccupation with either private interest or public action. He believed that such oscillations were strictly endogenous, being independent of outside events. He even suggested that World War One had an internal explanation: a long period of peace and prosperity in Europe before conflict had led to widespread revulsion against the bourgeois order and its values by the middle and upper classes and the restoration of the heroic ideal and self-sacrifice. The war allowed escape from the boredom of capitalist rational calculation and the return of feudalistic notions placing *Helden* (heroes) before *Händler* (traders). Much of this argument echoes Schumpeterian themes. For example, Schumpeter in his famous essay 'The Sociology of Imperialisms' (1918–19) drew attention to the atavistic character of imperialism and the fact that the development of capitalism would result in pacifism and the gradual disappearance of hostile impulses. He argued that 'According to the "pure" capitalist mode of life, the bourgeois is unwarlike' and presented a rich and complicated picture of the movement from feudalism to capitalism as marked by a shift towards the democratization, individualization, and rationalization of everyday life (Schumpeter in Swedberg, 1991b, pp. 212 and 190). Similar arguments are advanced in *Capitalism, Socialism and Democracy* when Schumpeter stated that 'capitalist civilization is rationalistic "and anti-heroic"' and further that 'The stock exchange is a poor substitute for the Holy Grail' (1987, pp. 127 and 137).[8] Interestingly enough then, both Schumpeter and Hirschman recognised the continuation of certain feudalistic elements in capitalism. In addition, when Schumpeter focused upon imperialism as

[6] Both mainstream and non-mainstream economics appears to be increasingly following this endogenous line whether applied to such phenomena as growth theory, choice and preference change, general endogenous forces, or financial fragility. Rizzo has rather interestingly argued, in the new introduction to his co-authored work with O'Driscoll (1996, p. xxiv) that 'the essence of the contemporary Austrian research program... is the idea of endogenously-produced change'.

[7] He conceded that his story displays 'endogenous bias' and that 'To portray a lengthy ideological change or transition as an endogenous process is of course more complex than to depict it as the rise of an independently conceived, insurgent ideology concurrent with the decline of a hitherto dominant ethic' (see Hirschman, 1977, pp. 4 and 12).

[8] He clearly anticipates Hirschman's thesis when he commented (Schumpeter, 1987, p. 128) that 'Success in industry and commerce requires a lot of stamina, yet industrial and commercial activity is essentially unheroic in the knight's sense – no flourishing of swords about it, not much physical prowess, no chance to gallop the armored horse into the enemy, preferably a heretic or heathen – and the ideology that glorifies the idea of fighting for fighting's sake and of victory for victory's sake understandably withers in the office among all the columns of figures'.

atavistic militarism underpinning conflict and the power of capitalist free markets to reduce such conflict he appeared to be embracing aspects of what Hirschman has termed[9] the 'feudal-shackles thesis' and the 'doux-commerce thesis' respectively. Likewise, Schumpeter's presentation of the gradual demise of capitalism in *Capitalism, Socialism and Democracy* betrays elements of the other two theses highlighted by Hirschman namely 'feudal-blessings' and 'self-destruction'.

Both Schumpeter and Hirschman are grand system theorists of capitalism. They explore dynamics and change at a high, rather than a reduced, level and deal with major problems and solutions. They endeavour to provide a broad and conceptually rich picture of the capitalist tradition which attempts to integrate social science theory (including economics) with history. Both display the rare talent to mix complex theory with a rich patina of history. Schumpeter believed that Marx and the German Historical School knew how to 'rationalize history' and he aimed to do likewise. As he stated in a letter 'I have arrived at the conclusion that theoretical equipment, if uncomplemented by a thorough grounding in the history of the economic process, is worse than no theory at all' (reprinted in Swedberg, 1991a, p. 230). They were both engaged, albeit at different times, with the need to complicate the nature of economic discourse by moving away from simple explanations and models in order to provide more elaborate and realistic structures. Much of Schumpeter's contribution was directed at: i) extending the Walrasian framework from a closed and static to an open and dynamic plane; ii) embracing Marx's vision of the capitalist process, whilst correcting his flawed analysis, alongside a commitment to systematically transform economic theory into historical analysis and the historical narrative into *histoire raisonnée* (1987, p. 44); and iii) increasing the real-world correspondence of economics by widening its compass to embrace dialogue and exchange within social science.[10] Likewise, Hirschman questions the new conventional wisdom of rational choice theory, particularly the appropriateness and applicability of its limited presentation of human motivations (as strictly economic) and neglect of social structures, by highlighting the behavioural and institutional deficiencies inherent in such an approach and offering an alternative perspective which is concerned with capturing the complexity of interests and passions that underpin action in a given situational context.[11] They both provide some variant of institutional individualism where human action is partly embedded and partly free. Hirschman would accept Schumpeter's criticism of orthodox economics as 'a schema which looks upon society as if it were an amorphous assemblage of individuals or families' (1987, p. 14).

A central element of Schumpeter's and Hirschman's respective research agendas was the need to embrace a wide idea of social science which included

---

[9] See his article 'Rival Views of Market Society', reprinted in Hirschman (1992).

[10] The recent notable contribution by Shionoya (1997), strongly highlights these three features in Schumpeter alongside an investigation of his metamethodology and methods.

[11] See, for example, his essay 'Against Parsimony: Three Easy Ways of Complicating Some Categories of Economic Discourse', reprinted in Hirschman (1992).

economics as a distinct but related discipline. There is the recognition of a mutually linked relationship between economics, politics and society (culture) such that economics cannot completely reduce the other elements to itself nor be completely reduced or contained by them. This leads *to the rejection of*: i) a total differentiation of economics from politics and sociology; ii) its total inclusion under the rubric of either politics or sociology; and finally, iii) the total displacement of politics and/or sociology by economics. The result, for both Schumpeter and Hirschman, is a general model of interdisciplinary exchange which allows for a certain but varying degree of integration and shared intellectual gains from trade between economics and the other social sciences. Of course, both practised what they preached by making notable contributions at the interface between economics and the other social sciences.[12] Schumpeter is well-known for having made important contributions to sociology proper, for example his study of social classes, fiscal sociology, and imperialism. In addition, much of his work in politics, such as his presentation of an early economic rationalisation of the democratic process – presenting the political arena as a market where politicians/bureaucrats compete to supply the demands of voters, was seminal. Schumpeter followed Max Weber in supporting a 'Sozialökonomik' approach to economics which was necessarily social (what we would now term economic sociology) and provided social science with the key concept of 'methodological individualism'. Much of Hirschman's contribution has been directed at forging an important bridge between economics and politics – his exit (economic) and voice (political) mechanisms demonstrate the symbiotic association between these two disciplines and the benefits from 'trespass'. His *Essays in Trespassing: Economics to Politics and Beyond* (1981) perfectly demonstrates the links that continue to kindle his interest.

The two perspectives endorse the need to take institutional individualism[13] seriously – they both reject an artificial and forced separation between individuals and institutions which often leads to extreme, caricatured, and unbridgeable divides between naive variants of individualism and holism. They embrace a sophisticated middle-ground position where individual action is neither completely independent nor completely determined but rather, undeniably human, since it is located within a given social context, and meaningful, because decisions matter. Individuals do not exist in a vacuum and institutions (in a broad sense including rules and conventions) serve to both constrain and enable purposeful behaviour.[14] Both Schumpeter

[12] As stated earlier, Schumpeter endorsed greater integration between economics and the other social sciences believing that it would be likely to result in greater mutual benefit and 'richer meaning' but he was also not unaware of the dangers of any sloppy synthesis. Likewise, Hirschman dreams of 'a social science for our grandchildren' which liberates cross-boundary analysis from the chains of an imperialist core.

[13] See Agassi (1975) for a discussion of this term.

[14] As Hirschman has so correctly remarked (1982, p. 72) 'To explain important turns in our lives and societies exclusively in terms of precipitating events would downgrade us to mere playthings of chance; to attribute such turns only to autonomously occurring changes in volitions would on the contrary make us appear as more noble and capable of self-determination than we really are'.

and Hirschman provide rich models of human agency, whether at the particular level of the entrepreneur (Schumpeter) or the more general consumer cum voter (Hirschman), which are located within the Smithian rather than the neoclassical tradition of economic man.[15] As such, behaviour is guided by biography, background and situational context. A key feature of this tradition is the emphasis placed upon inertia as a force inhibiting change. Schumpeter's model of entrepreneurial innovation highlighted the resistance imposed by inertia and lock-in. He was always at great pains to emphasise the fact that 'all knowledge and habit once acquired becomes as firmly rooted in ourselves as a railway embankment in the earth' (Schumpeter, 1934, p. 84), to point to tradition as 'always [out] surviving its usefulness' alongside the ancient truth that 'the dead always rule the living' (Schumpeter in Swedberg, 1991b, p. 183 and p. 214), and finally, to maintain that 'Social structures, types and attitudes are coins that do not readily melt' (Schumpeter, 1987, p. 12). Schumpeter had no clinical break between feudalism and capitalism, no complete emancipation of free markets from a fully embedded system. He recognised that the capitalist order rested 'on props made of extra-capitalist material' and 'extra-capitalist patterns of behaviour' which it would gradually destroy (Schumpeter, 1987, p. 162). In his essay 'The March into Socialism' Schumpeter suggested that the forces of inertia and resistance to institutional change served an important function to glue or hold an economic order together by keeping 'the speed of this change within the limits of safety' (1987, p. 427). Any tendencies to institutional change may find themselves 'battling with resistances' and stuck in a rut (Schumpeter, 1987, p. 422). This all serves to highlight the importance of a path-dependency framework within Schumpeter's general schema; and is clearly illustrated by his distinction between immature and mature socialism and the implausibility of the former. Likewise, the Hirschman framework depends upon a certain degree of inertia and lock-in to provide some stability by curtailing the impact of the exit and voice mechanisms. His concept of loyalty, by holding exit at bay and activating voice, serves just such a function. There has to be a balance of alert and inert consumers/voters/members for recuperative mechanisms to function effectively so that Hirschman relies upon limited response elasticities as a central feature of his framework. He has followed Schumpeter in embracing a path-dependency framework where there is a need to understand 'the dynamic of *sequences* in economic and social change' and the fact that systems can get stuck with inertia and resistance forestalling further advance.[16] Hirschman's *The Rhetoric of Reaction* (1991) drew attention to the perversity, futility and jeopardy theses which serve to constrain change and reform by underpinning the status quo.

Schumpeter and Hirschman share, from early on in their respective careers, an interest in the nature of economic development, especially the

[15] For a sophisticated examination of the Smithian (cum Millian) tradition see the recent insightful contribution by Oakley (1994).

[16] See the two essays 'The Rhetoric of Reaction-Two Years Later' and 'The Case against "One Thing at a Time"' reprinted in Hirschman (1995).

cyclical nature of capitalism alongside its long-period evolution. For Schumpeter there are innovation breakouts from the circular flow leading to business cycles and finally the march into socialism where a once predominantly private economic process becomes inherently public by socialising itself. Hirschman is much more circumspect about the destination of capitalism (and its alternatives), whether in some stationary state, socialism, or the end of history and the triumph of liberalism. He is primarily concerned with the predisposition of modern democratic capitalist economies to private interest-public action *cycles*. Although he follows Schumpeter in emphasising the duration of such cycles as about a generation in length (with each generation failing to learn from the previous) he does not suggest that there will be any conclusion in terms of a complete and final victory of private over public or vice versa. Alongside their interest in economic development was an eternal enthusiasm to explore the development and impact of intellectual ideas in general and economic ideas in particular. Schumpeter is especially known for his magisterial *History of Economic Analysis* (1954a), published after his death and marking the close of his contribution, and his *Economic Doctrine and Method: An Historical Sketch* [1914] (1954b) which marked the beginning. More directly, Hirschman has traced out the evolution, legitimation and triumph of the self-interest behaviour postulate in his widely acclaimed *The Passions and the Interests* (1977).

Finally, neither Schumpeter nor Hirschman developed a school *specifically concerned* with safeguarding and advancing their respective research agendas. Whilst economists (and other social scientists) adopt, adapt, and apply aspects of their frameworks they do not embrace the totality. This lack of disciples is, perhaps, less surprising in terms of Hirschman's impact, given his position at the periphery of economics and eclectic stance, but rather more surprising in the case of Schumpeter, since he remained tied to the core and was often seen as the main rival to Keynes. Part of an explanation would appear to reside in the fact that Schumpeter was never a complete revolutionary but remained wedded to developing his Walrasian (and part Marxian) intellectual heritage. In addition, he found such schools to be overly divisive. Sweezy has stated that Schumpeter 'made no attempt whatever to form a group of disciples around him'.[17] In his essay on Irving Fisher in *Ten Great Economists* (1952) Schumpeter, rather revealingly, appears to be writing about himself when he stated that Fisher formed no school, having 'many pupils but no disciples', in consequence lacking 'all the benefits that schools, protecting, interpreting, developing their masters every word, confer upon their chosen protagonist' (1952, p. 238).

3 (Some) intellectual divergence

Schumpeter believed that capitalism would gradually erode itself from within: a crumbling of its walls would be brought about by internal changes which worked against its economic order. The entrepreneurial function

[17] See Sweezy's Editor's Introduction to Schumpeter (1951, pp. xxii–xxiii).

which drove capitalism would become routinized and largely redundant, there would be the destruction of its non-bourgeois protecting strata which had helped to buttress capitalism, alongside a largely self-inflicted attack upon its own institutional privately-based value framework and, finally, an increased hostility and resentment by intellectuals engaged in social unrest (see Schumpeter, 1987, pp. 131–163 and pp. 425–426). An alternative order was destined to arise out of capitalism namely socialism. On objective grounds, based upon the above tendencies, Schumpeter argued that socialism was both highly likely and feasible. Unlike the oscillations in Hirschman, Schumpeter advanced the view that the movement was uni-directional and irreversible marked by the 'migration of people's economic affairs from the private into the public sphere' (1987, p. 421).

In an age quite unlike our own (ie. without the revealed and acknowledged tragedies of central planning),[18] and doubtless partly under the influence of his Walrasian inheritance, Schumpeter was led to conclude that 'There is nothing wrong with the pure logic of socialism' (1987, p. 172). He largely endorsed the competitive socialist solution to the economic calculation problem (without accepting the naivety of their perfectly competitive framework which underpinned it). He refers to the work of Barone, Lange and Taylor, amongst others, as a 'rich crop' which served to demonstrate that 'the fundamental logic of economic behaviour is the same in both commercial and socialist society from which the solution follows' (Schumpeter, 1987, p. 173n2). Schumpeter pays scant regard to the profound criticisms made by Mises and Hayek: with the benefit of hindsight we can state that he conceded too much to the socialist case and too little to the Austrian one.[19] He appears to skirt around the information, knowledge and incentive problems confronting socialism; particularly underestimating the demand side weaknesses inherent in socialism.[20] Schumpeter remains classical in generally neglecting the demand side in the economic arena (particularly Keynes's contribution here) whilst at the same time expecting the electorate to be rather *undemanding* in the political sphere. The latter point is particularly brought out in his discussion of socialism and democracy. Whilst correctly arguing that 'modern democracy is a product of the capitalist process' he fails to take seriously the intensity of feeling for active and meaningful political participation, whether in capitalism or socialism, apart from agreement to play by 'the rules of the democratic game' (Schumpeter, 1987, pp. 297 and 301) which may serve to increasingly encroach upon the economic sphere. Schumpeter appears to be far more concerned with the talents and skills of politicians and bureaucrats rather than the needs and motivations of the electorate. Whilst it was earlier conceded that Hirschman tends to take the supply side for granted, he takes demand whether in the

[18] As Irving Kristol rightly commented 'The major political event of the twentieth century is the death of socialism' (quoted by Graham and Clarke, 1986, p. 1).

[19] For a recent contribution to the reinterpretation of this debate in favour of the Austrians see Caldwell (1997).

[20] There were, of course, notorious supply side weaknesses in socialism. See Rosser and Rosser (1997) for a sympathetic appreciation of the heuristic power of the Schumpeterian framework on the supply side.

economic or political sphere seriously (quite the reverse of Schumpeter). His *cycles* of private interest and public action presume changing preferences and possibilities between both activities. Hirschman is generally sceptical of traditional socialism's ability to attend to consumer-citizen demands and the twin elements of exit and voice.[21]

Part of the problem, paradoxically for Schumpeter given the seminal nature of his contribution, may reside in his drawing of an analogy between the economic and political marketplace.[22] He presented a theory of democracy which emphasised the 'competitive struggle for the people's vote' (Schumpeter, 1987, p. 269) in order to gain power and office which was not dissimilar to the competitive struggle for the people's dollars in order to gain profit. In highlighting the existence of the self-interest postulate in politics as well as economics Schumpeter quotes an anonymous successful politician who is alleged to have commented "What businessmen do not understand is that exactly as they are dealing in oil so I am dealing in votes" (1987, p. 285). In drawing this analogy between economic and political spheres he may have been premature and over-hasty in his conclusions. Reducing democracy (and politics) to the economic marketplace hides fundamental differences between them. Whilst Hirschman has drawn attention to the fact that 'the traditional concept of the consumer with exogenously given, firm, and *non-est-disputandum* tastes bears a considerable resemblance to that of the citizen with a full array of strong and fully formed opinions' there are also important differences.[23] Likewise in his discussion of private interest and public action in *Shifting Involvements* he is keen to contrast economic and political processes (as he did previously in *Exit, Voice and Loyalty*). A conventional comparison of economic (dollar) votes and political votes tends to emphasise the superiority of the latter in terms of an equal registering of one person one vote alongside the shortcomings of the inequities in the former. Hirschman suggests this has made us blind to the strengths of the economic vote vis a vis the political vote: the dollar vote allows us to frequently register the intensity of our feeling whilst the political vote does not. The periodic political vote may provide a defence against repression but it also serves to restrict an excessively expressive citizenry from expressing its intensity of support or disagreement. The rise of the single-issue group is used by Hirschman as an indication that there is a demand for greater political participation than under offer in a democracy. If Schumpeter had been more sensitive to such demand side features he may have held out more hope for the continued survival of a more vibrant capitalism over a weakened socialism.[24]

---

[21] See Hirschman's essay 'Exit, Voice, and the Fate of the German Democratic Republic', reprinted in his (1995) for an informative discussion of the role of exit and voice under traditional socialism.

[22] See Wohlgemuth (1995) for an interesting critique of simplistic and overdrawn analogies between the economic and political marketplace.

[23] See his essay 'Opinionated Opinions and Democracy', reprinted in Hirschman (1995).

[24] In his survey of 'the impact of economics on contemporary political science', Miller (1997), rather surprisingly, understates the importance of Schumpeter and neglects Hirschman.

4 Concluding remarks

The paper has argued that there are important and unexplored intellectual affinities between the contributions of Schumpeter and Hirschman. They both allude to the forces of change and inertia which help account for the orderly rather than chaotic dynamics of modern democratic economies. In addition, it has been suggested that they serve to complement each other: Schumpeter on the supply side and Hirschman on the demand side. Such a synthesis may result in a more optimistic appreciation of the vitality of capitalism as we rapidly approach the new millenium.

References

Agassi J (1975) Institutional individualism. British Journal of Sociology 26: 144–155
Caldwell B (1997) Hayek and socialism. Journal of Economic Literature XXXV: 1856–1890
Giersch H (1984) The age of Schumpeter. American Economic Review 74: 103–109
Graham D, Clarke P (1986) The new enlightenment: the rebirth of liberalism. Macmillan, London
Hirschman AO (1970) Exit, voice and loyalty. Harvard University Press, Cambridge, MA
Hirschman AO (1977) The passions and the interests: political arguments for capitalism before its triumph. Princeton University Press, Princeton, NJ
Hirschman AO (1981) Essays in trespassing: economics to politics and beyond. Cambridge University Press, Cambridge
Hirschman AO (1982) Shifting involvements: private interest and public action. Princeton University Press, Princeton, NJ
Hirschman AO (1991) The rhetoric of reaction: perversity, futility, jeopardy. Harvard University Press, Cambridge, MA
Hirschman AO (1992) Rival views of market society and other recent essays. Harvard University Press, Cambridge, MA
Hirschman AO (1995) A propensity to self-subversion. Harvard University Press, Cambridge, MA
Miller GJ (1997) The impact of economics on contemporary political science. Journal of Economic Literature XXXV: 1173–1204
Oakley O (1994) Classical economic man: human agency and methodology in the political economy of Adam Smith and J S Mill. Edward Elgar, Aldershot
Rizzo MJ, O'Driscoll GP (1996) The economics of time and ignorance. Routledge, London
Rosser JB, Rosser MV (1997) Schumpeterian evolutionary dynamics and the collapse of soviet-bloc socialism. Review of Political Economy 9: 211–223
Schumpeter JA (1918–19) The sociology of imperialisms. Reprinted in Swedberg (1991b)
Schumpeter JA [1911] (1934) The theory of economic development. Harvard University Press, Cambridge, MA
Schumpeter JA (1939) Business cycles: a theoretical, historical and statistical analysis of the capitalist process. McGraw-Hill, New York
Schumpeter JA (1951) Imperialism and social classes. Augustus M Kelley, New York
Schumpeter JA (1952) Ten great economists: from Marx to Keynes. Allen and Unwin, London
Schumpeter JA (1954a) History of economic analysis. Allen and Unwin, London
Schumpeter JA [1914] (1954b) Economic doctrine and method. Allen and Unwin, London
Schumpeter JA [1942] (1987) Capitalism, socialism and democracy. Unwin Paperbacks, London (6 and *counterpoint* edn)

Shionoya S (1997) Schumpeter and the idea of social science. Cambridge University Press, Cambridge
Swedberg R (ed) (1990) Economics and sociology: redefining their boundaries. Princeton University Press, Princeton, NJ
Swedberg R (1991a) JA Schumpeter: his life and work. Polity Press, Cambridge
Swedberg R (ed) (1991b) JA Schumpeter: the economics and sociology of capitalism. Princeton University Press, Princeton, NJ
Wohlgemuth M (1995) Economic and political competition in neoclassical and evolutionary perspective. Constitutional Political Economy 6: 71–96

Schumpeter and Steindl on the dynamics of competition*

Harry Bloch**

School of Economics and Finance, Curtin University of Technology,
GPO Box U 1987, Perth 6845, Australia (e-mail: blochh@cbs.curtin.edu.au)

Abstract. This paper compares and contrasts the contributions of Joseph Alois Schumpeter and Josef Steindl to the competitive paradigm. Both reject the static nature of traditional profit maximizing analysis and the analytical device of a representative firm. Instead they both opt for a dynamic framework in which there is a key role for innovation. Differences emerge in terms of the characteristics of individual firms that nurture the competitive struggle and are responsible for technical change.

The maturation process of a capitalist economy, whereby a natural progression will involve an increase in concentration, as prescribed by Schumpeter and Steindl is also explored, as is criticism of their analyses. Finally the holistic approach to competitive modelling, a legacy of these two economists, is expounded and challenges for the future identified.

Key words: Schumpeter – Steindl – Technological change – Innovation – Competitive process

JEL-classification: B21, L11, O31

'Despite valiant attempts to dynamize microeconomics, large parts of modern economics remain trapped in a static framework. Worse than that is the fact that modern economics lacks any true theory of the competitive

---

* Paper presented at the 1998 World Conference of the International Joseph A. Schumpeter Society, Vienna, June 13–16, 1998.

** The author is grateful for the invaluable research assistance of Paula Haslehurst in the preparation of this paper and for comments from participants at the seventh conference of the International Joseph A. Schumpeter Society in Vienna and at a seminar at the Österreichisches Institut für Wirtschaftsforschung. The usual disclaimer applies.

process; what it actually possesses is the theory of the outcome of that process in an equilibrium *state*.' (Blaug, 1986, p. 171) (italics in the original)

1 Introduction

Two economists who clearly try to alter theorizing about competition are Joseph Alois Schumpeter and Josef Steindl. Each places the analysis of the dynamic process of competition at the centre of his approach to the development of capitalist economies. Their respective contributions are the subject matter of this paper.

Schumpeter and Steindl each analyze the competitive process against a background of continuous technological change. This distinguishes their analyses from the mainstream in economics. Schumpeter and Steindl also share an abhorrence of the imposition of profit-maximizing equilibrium in the analysis of dynamic competition. Each also rejects the use of the analytical device of a representative firm, insisting that differences between firms, particularly in terms of the adoption of new technology, drive the competitive struggle. The common ground to their analyses is reviewed in Section 2.

There are also substantial differences, at least in their early writings, between Schumpeter and Steindl in their characterization of the competitive process. In particular, their analyses differ in terms of the type of firms that undertake innovation and the source of financing for this activity. Steindl focuses particularly on the role of large, established firms, while Schumpeter initially locates innovative activity as coming from outsiders. Also, Steindl's analysis relies on internally generated funds acting as a constraint on overall investment activity, while Schumpeter argues that bank credit is the fundamental source of finance for innovation. These differences and others are examined in detail in Section 3.

Both Schumpeter and Steindl argue that capitalism is an evolving system. For each author, this evolution leads to difficulties in a mature capitalist system. Although the nature of the expected difficulties is different, increasing industrial concentration plays a role in each author's analysis. The roles attributed by Schumpeter and Steindl to increasing concentration in the evolution of capitalism to a stage of maturity are discussed in Section 4.

The expectations of both Schumpeter and Steindl concerning the evolution of capitalism have been subjected to substantial criticism on grounds of both logic and predictive accuracy. Criticisms that relate specifically to the dynamics of competition are discussed in Section 5. The final section of the paper then discusses how the separate analyses of Schumpeter and Steindl might be integrated to help meet some of the criticisms and, thereby, improve our understanding of the dynamics of competition.

2 Common ground

The concern of Schumpeter and Steindl with the dynamics of competition distinguished them from their mainstream contemporaries, whose focus was generally on static market equilibrium. There is little doubt that each was clearly aware of his heresy, for each provides a forceful critique of aspects of the prevailing orthodoxy in the analysis of market competition.[1]

Both Schumpeter and Steindl emphasize the role of technological change in the dynamics of competition. While technological change can be incorporated into mainstream analysis, it certainly has not been a primary concern of mainstream economists until recent decades. More importantly, when technical change is introduced into mainstream analysis, there is generally a movement to a new equilibrium without any impact on the character of competition. Technical change in the analyses of both Schumpeter and Steindl is associated with fundamental changes in market structure, altering the nature of competition.

A key to understanding the analyses of either Schumpeter or Steindl is the recognition that each bases his analysis on the existence of differences among firms operating in a single market. Each author attributes the differences, at least in part, to the influence of technical change, such that a key aspect of the difference between firms is in their cost of production or in the quality and/or marketing of their products. To Schumpeter ([1942] 1950, p. 83), these differences arise from, 'the fundamental impulse that keeps the capitalist engine in motion ... the new consumer goods, the new methods of production or transportation, the new markets, the new forms of industrial organization', where each such innovation is introduced by a specific capitalist enterprise. Steindl ([1952] 1976, p. 45) makes a corresponding distinction in setting the stage for his analysis of the dynamics of competition, noting 'we shall refer to these firms which initiate new methods as "progressive firms". They need not necessarily be the largest firms, and it is possible that their methods may be imitated by some of the other firms later; but it is essential that not all firms be capable of adopting these methods.'

The competitive process in both Schumpeter and Steindl involves the working out of the impact of innovating or progressive firms on the other firms operating in the same market. In working out the nature of the competitive process, they share an aversion to the imposition of assumptions of either perfect competition or profit maximization, arguing that these assumptions are inconsistent with the circumstances of firms operating under conditions of changing technology. Instead, they each deal with market structures characterized by imperfect competition among firms.[2] Furthermore, the behavior patterns of these firms deviate in at least some respects from those of profit-maximizing firms.

---

[1] See, for example, Schumpeter's ([1942] 1950, p. 1060) stinging criticism of the prevailing use of perfect competition as a "model of ideal efficiency". Also, see Steindl's (1945, Ch.1) attack on the use of the representative firm as an analytical device.

[2] Schumpeter ([1942] 1950, p. 105) notes that, 'perfect competition is and always has been temporarily suspended whenever anything new is being introduced'. Steindl ([1952] 1976) begins his analysis with a critique of the then prevailing theory of imperfect competition, neglecting to even mention the possibility of perfect competition.

3 Different paths

The common features of the analyses of Schumpeter and Steindl stand out most clearly when contrasted with their mainstream contemporaries. When their analyses are compared directly, important differences emerge. At least in part, these differences arise from contrasting treatments of the agents of economic change, with the contrast in treatment being the greatest when comparing the early works of both authors.

Entrepreneurs, generally acting through a new firm, are the agents of change in Schumpeter's ([1934] 1961) earliest analysis of economic development. Schumpeter ([1934], 1961, p. 66) notes, 'new combinations are, as a rule, embodied, as it were, in new firms which generally do not arise out of the old ones but start producing beside them; to keep to the example already chosen, in general it is not the owner of stage-coaches who builds railways.' The location of entrepreneurs in new firms helps the entrepreneurs to overcome resistance to change in an environment in which they have great influence if not total control.

The major constraint on the entrepreneur is the need to secure finance from the banking system.

'Entrepreneurs demand resources to produce a new product, process or form of organization; the banker responds by supplying, even creating, the financial support needed to acquire these resources after careful evaluation of the proposal's merit. There is both cooperation and opposition between the two – the commonplace societal conflict. Bankers form a class of *achrons* in the economy making judgments about the future of development, while entrepreneurs are the carriers of the development. In this give-and-take relationship, the banker often refuses to enter so risky a contractual arrangement because every important innovational vision entails a formidable risk.' Waters (1994, p. 263)

In his first monograph, Steindl (1945) addresses the differential advantage of big business over small business. He gives particular emphasis to economies of scale and the limits to expansion imposed by the cost of borrowing, drawing inspiration for the analysis of the latter from Kalecki's principle of increasing risk. In this analysis, it is private wealth, rather than bank credit, that is the primary source of finance for all business activity.

Steindl ([1952] 1976) further develops his analysis of the competitive process, writing against the background of the relative price stability characterising the US economy up to the Second World War. He argues that oligopolistic industries exhibit nominal price rigidity. A "progressive firm" that initiates cost-reducing technical change originally experiences a rise in its gross and net profit margins. This allows it to increase its rate of expansion, which, according to Steindl, is generally limited by internal accumulation through retained profits. When this expansion exceeds that necessary to meet market growth, the "progressive firm" resorts to aggressive price or sales competition to drive marginal firms from the market. This competitive process, originating in technical change, leads eventually to the absolute concentration of the industry. As Steindl ([1952] 1976, p. 45) notes, 'an increased profit margin in an industry will lead to an increased rate of internal accumulation; and that this in turn will lead to an increase in output capacity, which, if it is greater than the expansion of the industry's sales, must lead to "absolute concentration".'

In Steindl, it is the expansion of output through internal accumulation, the reinvestment of retained profits, which drives the competitive process. Also, while large firms need not be the initiators of change, once a "progressive firm" initiates change, a cumulative process begins with the initial advantage generally reinforced by economies of scale. This focus on the expansion of established firms as the driving force of competition contrasts to Schumpeter, who locates the driving force of competition in new firms acting with the support of banks.

Heertje (1988, p. 80) argues that there is a distinct shift in Schumpeter's views on the role of new firms between his early writings and *Capitalism, Socialism and Democracy*, 'It is of the utmost importance to note that Schumpeter no longer refers to the establishment of new firms or the entry of new entrepreneurs; innovative activity, if it exists at all, is concentrated in large monopolistic firms that block potential competition.' Presumably, the conduct of innovative activity by large monopolistic enterprises no longer requires access to external finance. There is certainly no discussion of the role of credit in the introduction of new combinations in *Capitalism, Socialism and Democracy* to parallel that in *The Theory of Economic Development*.

Steindl also modifies his views on the role, if not the locus, of technical change. In Steindl (1966), he departs from his earlier treatment and allows that technological change may be an important influence on firm investment decisions. He also acknowledges that investment may even be a response to technical change (see, for example Steindl ([1980], 1990) and ([1982] 1990)). In particular, he introduces a potential role for technical change in explaining why the internal accumulation of capital can proceed without leading to stagnation and a decline in the rate of profit. However, this does not alter his fundamental view on the dynamics of competition:

'My analysis in *Maturity and Stagnation* (1952) – which was carried out on the naive assumption that an endogenous trend (analogous to that of Harrod) exists and technical progress does not affect the investment process – has not been essentially changed by my conversion to the "semi-autonomous" trend. On the basis of that I can still maintain, as I did, that the emergence of an oligopolistic structure in the American economy near the turn of the century, *via* its effect on the "profit function" has reduced utilisation and created fear of excess capacity, and through the adverse effect on investment has led to a gradual reduction of the growth rate.' (Steindl ([1981] 1990, p. 137))

We can see that Schumpeter's later view on the agents of change approaches that espoused by Steindl and that Steindl's later view of the importance of technical change in the evolution of capitalism approaches that of Schumpeter. However, there are still important differences. In particular, at no stage does Schumpeter adopt a view that incorporates cumulative causation in the competitive process. Perhaps, this is because as Heertje and Perlman (1990, p. 5) note, 'Schumpeter had a theory of entrepreneurship without a theory of the firm.'

4 Mature capitalism

Both Schumpeter and Steindl argue that capitalism is a system in a process of change. Each posits an ultimate stage to this process, during which the capitalist system is expected to encounter difficulties. We follow Steindl's practice and refer to this stage as maturity. In this section, we examine the notion of maturity as it applies to each author, particularly in terms of the dynamics of competition.

Schumpeter's analysis of the dynamics of competition emphasizes the evolutionary concept of "creative destruction". There is no end to "creative destruction" with the growth of big business, only a "perennial gale" from which no firm is immune. In contrast, "progressive firms" in Steindl's analysis gain a cumulative advantage from technological change. This leads eventually to "absolute concentration" in the sense of the gradual elimination of the bulk of their competitors. This transforms an industry into a mature oligopoly, which he argues generally provides an enduring market structure.

Chaloupek (1994) distinguishes Steindl's analysis of maturity from that of Schumpeter, among others. Chaloupek argues that while maturity in Steindl's analysis is endogenous, the other authors, including Schumpeter, see capitalism reaching maturity through the action of exogenous forces. Steindl's analysis of dynamic competition is clearly endogenous, as it is directly rooted in his theory of the firm. However, it is also clear that Schumpeter considers that socialization of capitalism is part of the endogenous holistic evolution of the system of capitalism. Without economic development, including the increase in industrial concentration, the basis for the socialization of capitalism would disappear. Thus, Schumpeter ([1942], 1950, p. 219) argues

'Most of the argument of Part II may be summed up in the Marxian proposition that the economic process tends to socialize *itself* – and also the human soul. By this we mean that the technological, organizational, commercial, administrative and psychological prerequisites of socialism tend to be fulfilled more and more. Let us again visualize the state of things which looms in the future if that trend be projected. Business, excepting the agrarian sector, is controlled by a small number of bureaucratized corporations. Progress has slackened and become mechanized and planned. The rate of interest converges toward zero, not temporarily or only under the pressure of governmental policy, but permanently owing to the dwindling of investment opportunity. Industrial property and management have become depersonalized – ownership having degenerated to stock and bond holding, the executives having acquired habits of mind similar to those of civil servants. Capitalist motivation and standards have all but wilted away. The inference as to the transition to a socialist regime in such fullness of time is obvious.' [italics in the original]

While both Steindl and Schumpeter consider increased industrial concentration to be part of the maturation of capitalism, the difference between maturity under "creative destruction" and under "absolute concentration" is of some considerable importance to the prospects for continued economic growth. The perennial gale of creative destruction encourages continual investment in new products, new production techniques and development of new markets. This provides the antidote to the vanishing investment opportunities suggested by neoclassical analysis. Steindl also rejects the notion of vanishing investment opportunities. However, he argues that firms in mature oligopolies restrain their investment in new equipment to avoid the accumulation of unutilized capacity, even when such investments would bring savings in operating costs. This imports a stagnation bias to economies dominated by mature oligopolies.[3]

5 Criticisms

Critics within the Schumpeterian camp argue that Schumpeter failed to recognize the true vitality of innovation through new (small) firms. For example, Heertje (1988, p. 88) states, 'Finally, I can only express regret that Schumpeter did not stick to his original idea of considering the setting up of new firms as an important vehicle for innovations. The revival of Schumpeterian economics in the eighties seems to go hand in hand with the establishment of many new firms in the formal and informal sectors of the economy. Most of them are reacting to the commercial potential of both process and product innovations and are driven by a Schumpeterian spirit.' This argument is supported in empirical studies of the entry of new firms (see, for example, Audretsch and Acs, 1994) and of the distribution of innovative activity across firm size classes (see, for example, Acs and Audretsch, 1988).

The difficulty identified in this criticism above can be attributed to the lack of any theory of industry concentration in Schumpeter's analysis. Schumpeter's shift from his original emphasis on new firms as the primary innovators accompanies his general recognition of the increasing importance of big business, as suggested by his use of "trustified capitalism" to describe twentieth century industrialization. However, no theoretical basis is provided for any change in market structure with the evolution of capitalism towards maturity, other than the generic argument that capitalism is always changing. If capitalism changes to a more concentrated market structure in one epoch due to some innovation in business organization, there is nothing to prevent another innovation leading to a less concentrated structure in the next epoch. Indeed, this type of reversion to innovation coming from new firms seems consistent with the observations above of the Schumpeterian critics.

In analyzing the process of industry concentration, Steindl (1965) makes an important distinction between two factors affecting the firm size distribution. This distinction is between the effect of diffusion associated with random effects on firm growth and the effect of factors that alter the steady state distribution (or factors that prevent a steady state from being ob-

[3] The moderation of this argument in Steindl's later work is noted Section 3.

tained). He notes, 'Since Gibrat was rediscovered, the opinion is sometimes expressed that the process of diffusion implicit in his model offers in itself an explanation of concentration, which is an alternative or substitute for an *economic* theory of concentration, such as given by Marx and others. This is a rather unfortunate idea which can only discredit the stochastic view of most economists, who instinctively feel this cannot be true.' (Steindl, 1965, p. 69) [italics in the original]

Bloch (1993) reviews Steindl's various attempts at constructing a theory of industry concentration and concludes that none of them adequately meets Steindl's own requirements of an *economic* theory. The analysis in Steindl ([1952] 1976) comes close, in that mature oligopoly is given as the steady state that emerges from the process by which an industry adjusts to the shock of a cost-reducing innovation. Maturity occurs when the share of marginal firms falls below a critical level that makes further elimination through aggressive price competition unattractive. Investment expenditures are then set with regard to the level of excess capacity rather than the availability of internal finance. However, as Bloch (1993) notes, continued operation of the random process associated with technical progress can disturb the steady state associated with maturity, particularly by upsetting the distribution of costs across firms. If a sufficient portion of industry sales thereby come to be produced by marginal firms, the process of absolute concentration resumes.[4]

Shapiro (1988) argues that Steindl's analysis of the dynamics of competition is flawed because it focuses only on intra-industry competition. She points out that new product development is implicit in the process innovations carried out by "progressive firms" in Steindl's analysis. These process innovations presuppose the development of new producer goods. Further, because it is a growth objective that drives firm actions in Steindl's analysis, 'product development is as much a part of the firm's expansionary dynamic as the process innovation that increases the firm's "internal accumulation".' (Shapiro, 1988, p. 79) Allowing for product development leads to inter-industry competition and undermines the concept of industry maturity because, 'The products of oligopolistic industries can be displaced ("creatively destroyed") by new goods, and large firms can lose out to small ones when competition is technological.' (Shapiro, 1988, p. 79) Thus, Shapiro uses Schumpeterian concepts to criticise Steindl.

6 The way ahead

The interest of both Schumpeter and Steindl in the dynamics of competition distinguished them from the bulk of their contemporaries. There is now a growing interest in this issue. What can we learn from examining

[4] Steindl recognises the possibility of innovation by a new entrant upsetting the steady state of a mature industry in Steindl ([1987] 1990, p. 313). However, he does not modify his earlier analysis of the process of dynamic competition to accommodate this possibility.

the works of the masters, especially through the integration of their separate analyses?

Schumpeter teaches us that, 'Capitalism, then, is by nature a form or method of economic change and not never is but never can be stationary.' (Schumpeter, [1942] 1950, p. 82) Change is endemic to capitalism. Indeed, the receptiveness of the system to innovation is the key to its success. The manifestation of change that initiates the dynamics of competition is the "perennial gale of creative destruction", in which whole new industries are born.

Schumpeter also teaches us that change alters the nature of capitalism. Part of this evolution is the growth of "trustified capitalism" and a corresponding shift in the locus of innovation, from new firms to the internal concern of big business. This shift need not slow the rate of technological progress, but does tend to change its character, 'economic progress tends to become depersonalized and automatized. Bureau and committee work tends to replace individual action.' (Schumpeter, [1942] 1950, p. 133)

Change in the nature of competition is central to Steindl's analysis of the dynamics of competition. In Steindl's analysis, competition is self limiting. "Progressive firms" build on their advantage by expanding their capacity, which leads to lower unit cost through economies of scale or embodiment of labor-saving technology. However, once absolute concentration has proceeded to a stage where small inefficient firms account for a negligible portion of industry output, the attraction of aggressive price cutting or sales promotion disappears. Thus, competition leads inexorably to mature oligopoly, with its attendant lack of competitive behavior.

Many economists have explicitly or implicitly taken the lessons of Schumpeter and Steindl to heart. For example, Mueller (1997, p. 827) notes, as a 'good Schumpeterian', that industries generally 'come into existence following an important innovation.' He then observes that usually 'the one or two firms that eventually emerge as the industry leaders tend to be among the first to enter the industry.' (Mueller (1997, p. 828) Mueller uses the concepts of "the first-mover's advantage" and path dependence to explain this regularity. The language and specifics are different than in Steindl's analysis of the cumulative advantages of "progressive firms", but the spirit is the same. As with Steindl, the firm's initial advantage is the foundation for achieving market dominance. However, in Schumpeterian spirit, a subsequent innovation can undermine the first-mover's advantage and install a new market leader. Mueller considers in some detail the factors that make such a loss of leadership position more or less likely.

The work of modern Schumpeterians, such as Mueller, has helped to reawaken interest in dynamics, even in the mainstream analysis of competition.[5] However, there is a sense in which the flow of new research fails to capture the full spirit of the holistic approach of either Schumpeter or

---

[5] The work of Nelson and Winter (1982) has undoubtedly been seminal in encouraging economists to analyze the dynamics of competition in a Schumpeterian spirit, but with the techniques of modern economic analysis.

Steindl. In particular, a holistic approach to the dynamics of competition needs to pursue Steindl's aim of providing an *economic* theory of concentration.

A starting point for such a theory is a full statement of the characteristics of the dynamic process, such as that provided by Mueller (1997). Further, the implications of the dynamic process for whether there is a steady state and, if so, what distribution of firm size occurs in this state need to be developed. In doing this, it is important to consider the behavior of firms and the conditions of entry, both of which might be altered by the ongoing dynamic process. Steindl's analysis of the change in investment behavior associated with the transition to mature oligopoly is an example, although his analysis is naive by modern standards.[6] The work of behavioral economists dealing with the adaptation of internal firm structure to a changing environment is likely to be helpful in this regard. Finally, the possibility of induced changes in supporting political and social institutions needs to be incorporated into the analysis.

The last point would be particularly important to Schumpeter and Steindl. As Lazonick (1990, p. 78) notes in his review of the Schumpeterian agenda,

'The relation between economic institutions and economic outcomes is a dynamic, evolutionary process. The specification of a "model of ideal efficiency" – market coordinated or otherwise – is problematic because the "ideal" is continually changing as new structures of economic organization bring new firms, industries, and economies to international dominance. Institutional arrangements that previously yielded "ideal" economic outcomes become the victim of creative destruction.'

Without contemplating the dynamics of competition at the level of the capitalist system as a whole, the implications of a maturation of competition for the future effective operation of the system can not be properly evaluated.

The criticisms identified in the previous section call into question the visions of maturity proposed by both Schumpeter and Steindl. Failure of such predictions would probably not have surprised either Schumpeter or Steindl, given their holistic approach to the strongly evolutionary nature of a complex and highly interdependent system. The failure of predictions about the evolution of the capitalist system over a period some fifty years into the future does not negate the validity of the approach. If capitalism is a dynamic system, we can only properly understand any of its fundamental elements such as competition, by identifying the inherent forces driving the system and fully working out their implications. This is the great challenge that Schumpeter and Steindl have left us.

---

6 An interesting early contribution to making Steindl's analysis of firm behavior more sophisticated is that of Jack Downie (1958). Nightingale (1997) argues that Downie's work anticipated the later development of the evolutionary analysis of the competitive process in Nelson and Winter (1982).

References

Acs ZJ, Audretsch DB (1988) Testing the Schumpeterian hypothesis. Eastern Economic Journal 14: 129–140

Audretsch DB, Acs ZJ (1994) Entrepreneurial activity, innovation and macroeconomic fluctuations. In: Shionaya Y, Perlman M (eds) Innovation in technology, industries and institutions, pp 173–183. Ann Arbor, University of Michigan Press

Blaug M (1986) The entrepreneur in Marx and Schumpeter. In: Helburn SW, Bramhall DF (eds) Marx, Schumpeter and Keynes, pp 167–178. Sharpe, Armonk, NY

Bloch H (1993) Steindl's analysis of firm growth and the tendency toward industry concentration. Discussion Paper 1993–05, Department of Economics, University of Tasmania

Chaloupek G (1994) The concept of maturity and the transformation of economic systems. Review of Political Economy 6: 430–440

Downie J (1958) The competitive process. London, Duckworth

Heertje A (1988) Schumpeter and technical change. In: Hanusch H (ed) Applications of Schumpeter's ideas, pp 71–89. Cambridge University Press, New York

Heertje A, Perlman M (1990) Introduction. In: Heertje A, Perlman M (eds) Evolving technology and market structure, pp 1–13. University of Michigan Press, Ann Arbor

Lazonick W (1990) Organizational integration in three industrial revolutions. In: Heertje A, Perlman M (eds) Evolving technology and market structure, pp 77–97. University of Michigan Press, Ann Arbor

Mueller DC (1997) First-mover advantages and path dependence. International Journal of Industrial Organization 15: 827–850

Nelson R, Winter S (1982) An evolutionary theory of economic change. Harvard University Press, Cambridge, MA

Nightingale J (1997) Anticipating Nelson and Winter: Jack Downie's theory of evolutionary change. Journal of Evolutionary Economics 7: 147–167

Schumpeter JA [1934] (1961) The theory of economic development (translation of 2nd German edn by Redvers Opie). Oxford University Press, London

Schumpeter JA [1942] (1950) Capitalism, socialism and democracy. Harper and Row, New York

Shapiro N (1988) Market structure and economic growth: Steindl's contribution. Social Concept 4: 72–83

Steindl J (1945) Small and big business: Economic problems of the size of firms. Blackwell, Oxford

Steindl J [1952] (1976) Maturity and stagnation in American capitalism. Monthly Review Press, New York

Steindl J (1965) Random processes and the growth of firms. Griffin, London

Steindl J (1966) On maturity in capitalist economies. In: Problems of economic dynamics and planning. pp 423–432. Pergamon Press, Oxford

Steindl J [1980] (1990) Technical progress and evolution. In: Sahal D (ed) Research, development and technical innovation. Lexington Books, Lexington. Reprinted as Chapter 7 in: J Steindl (1990) Economic Papers 1941–1988. Macmillan, London

Steindl J [1981] (1990) Ideas and concepts of long run growth. Banca Nazionale del Lavoro 136. Reprinted as Chapter 10 in: J Steindl (1990) Economic Papers 1941–1988. Macmillan, London

Steindl J [1982] (1990) Technology and the economy: the case of falling productivity growth in the 1970s. In: Sahal D (ed) The transfer and utilisation of technical knowledge. Lexington Books, Lexington. Reprinted as Chapter 8 in: J Steindl (1990) Economic Papers, 1941–1988. Macmillan, London

Steindl, J [1987] (1990) Kalecki's theory of pricing: notes on the margin. In: Finl G, Poll G, Riese M (eds) Economic theory, political power and social justice. Reprinted as Chapter 21 in: J Steindl (1990) Economic Papers, 1941–1988. Macmillan, London

Waters WA (1994) Joseph A. Schumpeter: an introduction. Review of Social Economy 52: 256–265

Schumpeter and the 'Schmollerprogramm': integrating theory and history in the analysis of economic development

Alexander Ebner

Fachbereich Wirtschaftswissenschaften, Johann Wolfgang Goethe-Universität, Postfach 11 19 32, Fach 62, D-60054 Frankfurt a.M., Germany
(e-mail: alex.ebner@wiwi.uni-frankfurt.de)

Abstract. This essay addresses the historical and institutional aspects of Schumpeter's thought. It suggests that Schumpeter prepared a pluralist research agenda, formulated in accordance with the conceptual perspective of the German Historical School, as presented by major scholars such as Schmoller, Sombart, Spiethoff and Max Weber. Schumpeter's notion of development, with its emphasis on the correspondence of economic and socio-cultural evolution, is therefore to be viewed in the context of the comprehensive Schmollerian approach. Moreover the ethical-evolutionary components of Schmoller's ideas point at the vital role of the German Historical School in the elaboration of a modern evolutionary economics in Schumpeterian terms. The essay concludes that the *Schmollerprogramm* is going to inspire further developments in Schumpeterian economics, as the integration of theory and history continuously marks the research agenda of evolutionary approaches to economic development.

Key words: History of economic thought – German Historical School – Schmoller program – Schumpeter – Schumpeterian economics – Methodology – Historical theory – Economic evolution – Development

JEL-classification: A12, B15, B25, B31, O10

1 Introduction

This essay examines the conceptual relationships between Schumpeter's theory of economic development and those approaches of the 'Youngest' German Historical School, which have been based upon Gustav Schmol-

---

Paper presented at the 1998 World Conference of the International Joseph A. Schumpeter Society, Vienna, June 13–16, 1998.

ler's works and the corresponding historist research program. The comparative analysis of these visions and concepts is framed by the major problem of integrating theory and history to grasp the complexity of economic and socio-cultural development. As critical acclamations of the German Historical School and its comprehensive *Schmollerprogramm* can be traced throughout Schumpeter's works, accordingly, a 'Schmoller-Weber-Schumpeter nexus' has been identified quite recently by authors such as Shionoya (1997), Swedberg (1989) and others. While this strand of research reflects the renewed interest in a genuinely Schumpeterian, that is, a historical-evolutionary approach to economic sociology, still the decisive influence of the post-Schmollerian 'Youngest' Historical School on Schumpeter's ideas has this far been neglected.

Schumpeter's advocacy of formal analytical methods, on the one hand, and historical institutional perspectives, on the other hand, has been described as a 'paradox' due to a so-called 'tool problem' concerning the analysis of economic dynamics (Andersen, 1994, p. 5). In contrast to that position I shall argue that both the formal-analytical as well as the historical-institutional aspects of analytical procedure represent an integrated conceptual vision within Schumpeter's thought. They are to be differentiated with regard to the specific research objects of economic growth, development and evolution. Thus the so-called paradox may be resolved by recognizing that Schumpeter formulated a pluralist research agenda in accordance with the *Schmollerprogramm*. It follows that his notion of economic development, with its emphasis on the correspondence between economic and socio-cultural evolution, is best viewed in the context of the Schmollerian as well as the post-Schmollerian approaches.

The essay is organized in four sections. First, Schmoller's approach to economic development is discussed regarding the most critical methodological as well as conceptual dimensions. Second, the post-Schmollerian approaches of the 'Youngest' Historical School are presented, as they have been put forward by Sombart, Spiethoff, and Max Weber. These approaches represent the major conceptual link among the Schmollerian approach and the related Schumpeterian ideas, which are accordingly put forward in the third and fourth sections, relating the topic of economic sociology to the notion of economic evolution. It is concluded that the *Schmollerprogramm* of the German Historical School may inspire further efforts at establishing an institutional and evolutionary economics in the Schumpeterian tradition, based upon an integration of theory and history.

2 The *Schmollerprogramm* established: Gustav Schmoller's ethical-evolutionary economics

Contemporary economics has largely ignored the ideas and concepts of the German Historical School's major scholar, Gustav Schmoller, for at least the past five decades. Even worse, a kind of folk wisdom propagates an allegedly anti-theoretical Schmollerian position in the context of the *Methodenstreit* against the Austrian Carl Menger. All of this has concealed the original concerns of the German Historical School, for Schmoller not only aimed at an historical-institutional complement to the reductionist abstractions of formal economic theories, but even more, he longed for an integration of historical and theoretical perspectives into a multidisciplinary approach (Shionoya, 1997, p. 201n).[1] Consequently, it is not a lack of theoretical orientation, but rather the rejection of *ceteris-paribus* perspectives in favor of comprehensive multi-factor analyses, which characterize the Schmollerian agenda (Schefold, 1989). This conceptual agenda has been labeled the *Schmollerprogramm* by Schumpeter himself, and it has exerted an important influence on his own attempts to integrate historical and theoretical concerns.

Regarding an interpretation of the essence of the Schmoller program, elements of the historical, empirical, ethical, and political dimensions have been distinguished (Backhaus, 1993), all of this accompanied by the recognition of evolutionary, culturalist and etatist modes of theorizing (Prisching, 1993). Consequently, the Schmoller program, deriving many aspects of its genuine perspective from preceding elaborations of historically-minded German economists such as Roscher and Knies, represents the intellectual climax of historism, not to mention the high tide of its academic influence (Priddat, 1995). Concerning the methodological concerns of the historist tradition, a major postulate demands that economic phenomena need to be viewed as time-conditioned, that is, as research objects which are to be interpreted in their particular historical-cultural context. This is paralleled by the organicist idea that historical phenomena have to be treated individually, as coherent developing entities of various interdependent elements (Betz, 1988).

The historical method according to Schmoller, then, denotes an attempt to survey the general cultural development of peoples, nations, and thus at last the whole of humankind (Schmoller, 1893, p. 261). A most important analytical unit of Schmoller's approach is constituted by the notion of *Volkswirtschaft*, denoting the type of national economy which has evolved as a specific developmental stage in the historical process of economic and socio-cultural evolution. It represents a particular type of economic formation, a specific whole, which is grounded on certain 'psychological', that is, intellectual and instinctive motive patterns, as well as on a material structure which consists of a distinct system of institutions and organizations, including the modern state, certain socio-economic structures and natural as well as technological specificities. This perspective corresponds with Schmoller's notion of the evolution of developmental stages according to a schema of increasing complexity. Economic phenomena thus represent integral parts of the general social life of a particular society, and are to be analyzed as such (Schmoller, 1893, p. 220n).

Institutions and organizations, denoted as 'organs', constitute the core of Schmoller's quite original blend of institutionalism, as becomes manifest in his notion of political economy as a *Volkswirtschaftslehre*, which shall explicitly integrate institutional and technological aspects (Schmoller, 1893,

---

[1] Schmoller, for instance, sympathized with Austrian concepts of value theory and, elaborated on bilateral monopoly (Peukert, 1998, ch. 3). Moreover his contributions to a theory of social insurance may be mentioned (Priddat, 1995, ch. 5).

p. 223). Schmoller goes on to define institutions and organizations as follows:

'By a political, legal, economic institution we mean a particular order of community life, which acts as the solid vessel for the agency of generations for centuries and millennia, serving certain purposes, having reached an autonomous development. Every institution represents the sum of conventions and the rules of morals, custom and law, which have a common center or purpose, interdependent among each other, building a system... By the formation of organs we mean the personal side of the institution; marriage is the institution, family is the organ.' (Schmoller, 1901, p. 61, my translation)[2]

The suggested analytical procedure then encompasses appropriate empirical observations, the formulation of definitions and classifications, and finally the reconstruction of patterns as well as the elaboration of causal explanations (Schmoller, 1901, p. 100). In this context, a gradual shift in Schmoller's methodological considerations has been outlined, ranging from an inductive empiricism to a more hermeneutical point of view which allows for an appreciation of the notion of *Verstehen*, that is, the interpretation of actions and their meaning (Peukert, 1998, p. 72n). Schmoller still did not fully embrace the quite influential neo-Kantian distinction between natural and cultural-historical sciences, which had been grounded on the assumption that exact scientific laws are to be reduced to the sphere of nature. In fact, he never abandoned the idea that comparative research might uncover a sufficient amount of empirical regularities and thus lead to the formulation of the historical laws of socio-economic development. Confronted with that characterization, one might ask for the actual relationship between the historical and the evolutionary aspects of Schmoller's approach, for it has been suggested that an appropriate treatment of the historical character of economic dynamics needs to be based upon concepts such as time-asymmetry, denoting irreversible and indeterminate processes (Dopfer, 1988). While this suggestion might contradict Schmoller's methodological positions on economic laws, it is still very much in accordance with his vision of the essential aspects of economic life, and thus with a characterization of his approach as ethical-evolutionary.

This corresponds with instructive comments by Veblen, who himself is regarded as the major pioneer of an evolutionary approach to institutional economics (Hodgson, 1993). Veblen was critical of some methodological and conceptual aspects of Schmoller's ideas, especially regarding their normative implications, but he clearly pointed at the indispensable importance of Schmoller's works on the dynamics of socio-economic evolution:

'the distinguishing characteristic of Professor Schmoller's work, .., is that it aims at a Darwinistic account of the origin, growth, persistence, and variation of institutions, in so far as these institutions have to do with the

[2] This distinction between institutions and organizations resembles current debates on the same topic. For a related comparison of Schmoller's ideas and Douglass North's approach to institutional economics, see Richter (1996).

economic aspect of life either as cause or effect... In this line of theoretical inquiry Professor Schmoller is not alone, ... ; but the seniority belongs to him, and he is also in the lead as regards the comprehensiveness of his work.' (Veblen, 1901, p. 264n).[3]

It may be concluded that the project of an evolutionary and institutional economics transcends the Veblenian influences, for it is also rooted in the traditions of the Schmoller program of the German Historical School, although quite obvious differences between these strands of thought are to be observed. Schmoller repeatedly expressed his reservations concerning the intense use of metaphors and analogies from the natural sciences, including, of course, evolutionary biology. Nonetheless, some Lamarckian, as well as extensive organicist and social-Darwinist arguments prevailed in his notion of socio-cultural development (Hutter, 1993). But all these evolutionary biological analogies and metaphors, built upon notions like the 'struggle for existence' or the 'survival of the fittest' and applied to areas such as competitive market selection, were conceptually combined with the at least likewise influential sphere of intellectual and cultural aspects, such as customs, conventions and social learning capabilities (Schmoller, 1901, p. 66). This mirrors Schmoller's differentiation between so-called mechanical-materialistic and idealistic approaches to development. Schmoller's vision of the evolutionary process underlines the non-mechanistic position, for the seemingly natural process of socio-economic evolution is accordingly regulated by the impact of a parallel cultural development which substitutes intellectual insights for pure instincts. The core of Schmoller's approach is hence subdivided into an ethical and an evolutionary segment, both pointing at specific sources of the process of change. The ethical aspect points at a historical orientation regarding the notion of custom and the idea of ethical progress in history. Moreover, concerning the normative political dimension, Schmoller emphasizes the feasibility of a policy that reconciles economic market dynamics and social justice. That position is also reflected by Schmoller's related ideas on the embeddedness of profit motives in the ethical spheres of trust and fairness (Schmoller, 1901, p. 37n). This interplay of instinct and intellect allows for labeling the Schmollerian ideas, which he himself of course tended to present as 'ethical-historical', as a genuinely ethical-evolutionary perspective within the broad paradigm of historism.

Institutional aspects, such as customs and habits, do also account for the generation of developmental dynamics, as Schmoller identifies the vital function of the leading personalities as energetic sources of economic and cultural change. By doing so, he primarily hints at the heroic individuals of traditional political historiography, exhibiting a quite Hegelian flavor, but he additionally mentions the type of entrepreneurial business leaders (Schmoller, 1901, p. 413–415). These topics contribute to Schmoller's

---

[3] Veblen proceeds with the verdict that Schmoller still lacks a complete evolutionary research program as well as a corresponding theoretical schema. This apparently controversial statement underlines the fact that historism and institutionalism argue on different meta-theoretical levels.

'psychological' interpretation of modern capitalism, which accounts for the fact that he was skeptical regarding the term 'capitalism' as it had been used before by Marx and Sombart:

'Capital plays certainly a great role in the economy as well as in the modern firms of today, but this is going to be explained only psychologically, by the men of a particular time, race, group of nations, and their spiritual powers, furthermore by the psychic results of these powers, the ideas and moral systems of the time, customs and law, institutions of the time...' (Schmoller, 1903, p. 144, my translation)

That argumentation is continued in the general exposition of the economic development of national economies. Schmoller introduces the cyclical character of the development process as a specific feature of increasingly complex and therefore potentially unstable modern societies, which are subject to internal social class struggles as well as to external policy conflicts in the sphere of foreign trade and international market competition (Schmoller, 1904, p. 465n). What crystallizes as the most common pattern of economic development is the repeated rise and decline of nations and civilizations, illustrated by a development cycle, which is essentially caused by the actual condition of the moral powers of a particular society (Schmoller, 1904, p. 673n). Consequently, Schmoller's attempts of integrating theory and history result in the formulation of an ethical-evolutionary approach to economic development, interpreted as a process of cyclical socio-cultural change.

3 The *Schmollerprogramm* modified: the 'Youngest' Historical School

Modifications of the Schmoller program were pursued by those historically-minded German economists and sociologists such as Max Weber, Werner Sombart and Arthur Spiethoff, who were labeled the 'Youngest Historical School' by Schumpeter (1954, p. 815). The post-Schmollerian approach postulated an integration of theory and history by stressing the historical specificity of economic theories. Sombart, for instance, introduced his 'Modern Capitalism' with the remark that, in the context of a 'renaissance of the theoretical interest', the contrast between historical and abstract political economy should have lost all of its meaning and relevance (Sombart, 1916, p. XIV). Beyond these methodological concerns, which were reflected by the Weber-Sombart axis against the Schmollerian tradition of value judgements during the *Werturteilsstreit*, the post-Schmollerian perspective basically focused on modern capitalism as an epochal phenomenon. While earlier theories of development stages, including Schmoller's approach, had been marked by a developmental optimism which characterized socio-economic evolution as progress in material wealth and political-ethical standards, the post-Schmollerian 'Youngest' Historical School emphasized the individual 'Gestalt' of the various historical economic formations, and by doing so pointed at the possible bureaucratic degeneration of capitalism (Schefold, 1995).

A point of departure for the critique of Schmollerian ideas on capitalist perfection was provided by the debate on the historical evolution of modern capitalism. Sombart presented the notion of 'economic system' as a conceptual framework to grasp the essential institutional and technological features of actually existing economic formations (Sombart, 1916 p. 14n). These economic systems should encompass three dimensions: first, an 'economic spirit', representing dominant economic attitudes, principles and norms; second, an 'economic order' which denotes constitutional regulations as well as typical socio-economic relations; third, a specific mode of using technology and accumulating technological knowledge. Sombart thus characterized capitalism as a coherent configuration of economic institutions, organizations, and technology, which was divided into early, high, and late developmental stages. While the systemic endogenization of technological and organizational change was a major theme of Sombart's approach, with both spheres subject to a bureaucratic mechanization in the course of late capitalism (Krabbe, 1996), he identified the economic spirit as the major characteristic and driving force of capitalist evolution. The *Gestaltidee* of economic systems then served as the key concept of his increasingly hermeneutical approach, for he suggested that an 'objective spirit' corresponds with the historical meaning of an economic formation (Sombart, 1930, p. 184n). Influenced by Schmoller and Marx, Sombart concentrated on the elaboration of his theory as an approach that strives for an interpretative understanding of the essence of economic formations, resulting in a hermeneutical modification of the Schmoller program in Sombart's late works (Betz, 1993). Actually, he excluded Schmoller from the ancestry of his interpretative concept of an 'understanding economics' (Sombart, 1930).[4]

Sombart's earlier approach of combining abstract theory with historical-institutional perspectives was also pursued by Arthur Spiethoff, who used Schumpeter's and Sombart's names when he differentiated between 'pure theories' which may abstractly grasp those elements that are common to all historical economic formations, and an 'economic Gestalt' theory, which should serve the analysis of time-conditioned economic life (Spiethoff, 1932). It is that appreciation of pure theory as a nomothetic core, applicable to all historical formations, among others, which brings Spiethoff's approach in line with Schmoller's intentions (Dopfer, 1988, p. 560n). Spiethoff then distinguished three systems of economic knowledge. There is, first, a 'timeless', non-institutional and therefore non-historical theory, that is, a pure theory which abstracts from the historical specificities of economic life. Second, under the banner of historical theory, pure theory, with an ideal typical character and economic Gestalt theory, that is *anschauliche Theorie*, with a real typical character are distinguished. Third, there is the sphere of economic history as such (Spiethoff, 1952, p. 134).

---

[4] Max Weber who labelled his own approach an 'interpretative sociology', while modifying the hermeneutical methodology in favour of his ideal types. Regarding these issues, his position comes quite close to Schumpeter's, though there are differences to be observed, as outlined by Shionoya (1991, 1997).

The core of Spiethoff's approach to historical theories is constituted by the notion of economic styles, which had emerged from earlier discussions within the German Historical School, basically reflecting an influential definition of economics as a cultural science (Schefold, 1994). In contrast to Sombart's late works, Spiethoff emphasized the role of empirical observations, since his economic styles were derived from Sombart's economic systems concept but striving for its empirical perfection (Spiethoff, 1932). The style notion was thus redirected to Schmollerian positions, and indeed also resembled major elements of Schmoller's *Volkswirtschaft*, while the basic idea of that perspective aimed at the elaboration of a historical theory of the dynamics of capitalist evolution, based upon methodological considerations as well as intense business cycle research (Gioia, 1997). With additional references to scholars such as List, Knies and Dilthey, Spiethoff defined an outline of his style approach as follows:

'Most economic phenomena are time-conditioned and are rooted in specific geographical areas. They are subject to change over time and cannot be treated, therefore, with the help of concepts and theorems purporting to be of universal applicability. Economic theory can deal with those phenomena only by differentiating patterns of economic life, patterns which have come into being in the course of the historical process. As a matter of fact, as many patterns must be delimited as there are essential and typical differences in the basic economic institutions. Patterns of this kind are here called economic styles. Every one of them demands its own economic theory, which, though being genuine theory, is applicable only for the domain of that style.' (Spiethoff, 1952, p. 132)

Regarding the historical character of economic theories it follows that these are to be viewed in the context of certain economic styles: 'Under these circumstances economic theory is a "historical" category to the extent to which its applicability depends on the existence and dominance of a certain economic style, elements of which are embodied in the theoretical structure' (Spiethoff, 1952, p. 132). Spiethoff's economic styles reflect a coherent system of interdependent elements, which are rooted in specific institutional configurations: 'the concept of economic style ...reflects the properties which make out of an institutional setup a unique case of economic life...The concept of economic style is the tool with the help of which uniformities in time are made available for theoretical research' (Spiethoff, 1952, p. 137). Elements of Spiethoff's economic styles have been outlined as follows (Spiethoff, 1932, p. 76n):

(1) Economic spirit, denoting attitudes and motives of economic action;
(2) Natural and technological foundations, such as population dynamics, division of labor, technological regime;
(3) Constitution of society, regarding social cohesion and structuration;
(4) Economic constitution, concerning property rights as well as modes of production, distribution, and labor;
(5) Economic dynamics.

This catalogue reflects the range of the 'Youngest' Historical School, built upon the modified Schmoller program. The rationàle behind the factor of economic spirit is derived from the assumption that capitalist economic attitudes tend to deconstruct non-capitalist motives, such as religious beliefs, and therefore support a hedonistic consumerism. Furthermore, the way of grasping the institutional conditions of technological change is noteworthy, for Spiethoff refers to the dominant attitudes toward technological change within a range of habitual or innovating attitudes. Moreover, the natural and technological foundations as well as the social and economic constitution are mentioned as style elements. The aspect of economic dynamics is seen as an endogenous element of economic styles, business cycles are therefore classified as phenomena with a specific capitalist character. This gives evidence of Spiethoff's pioneering contributions to theoretical and statistical research on long waves:

'It must be clearly understood that business cycles are time-conditioned and belong to the capitalistic style within which they represent a specific and typical phenomenon. Should capitalism change its characteristics or entirely disappear, business cycles would change their characteristics or disappear also.' (Spiethoff, 1952, p. 139)

Schmoller presented cyclical fluctuations as the typical mode of the socio-cultural development of modern societies, rooted in institutional factors. Spiethoff modifies that aspect of cyclical movements and, by making use of Juglar's concept of crises and cycles, designs the notion of *Wechsellagen*, that is, major economic fluctuations which are induced by an endogenous mechanism of over-production. His economic styles represent the material and institutional characteristics of an epochal economic formation such as modern capitalism. It might be suggested that Schumpeter's theory of economic development accounts for both the socio-cultural and economic aspects, at least regarding the visionary character of the underlying ideas (Schumpeter, 1912, p. 492). In this sense, Schumpeter followed the Schmollerian agenda.

4 The *Schmollerprogramm* executed, part 1: the Schumpeterian synthesis of economic sociology

The idea of a historical and institutional approach to economic dynamics can be seen throughout Schumpeter's works. In fact, Schumpeter executes the Schmoller program as he proceeds with a combined theoretical, statistical and historical analysis of capitalist economic evolution, as for instance in his 'Business Cycles.' Moreover he presents the concept of an economic sociology that keeps most of the useful ideas of Schmoller's. Schumpeter summarizes his assessment of the Schmollerian approach within the German Historical School in six topics: first, the historical relativity of theoretical insights; second, the unity and 'Gestalt' character of social life, where all constitutive elements are interdependent and not to be isolated; third, the variety of economic motives encompassing rational as well as non-rational aspects; fourth, the evolutionary and developmental perspective; fifth, the interest in a detailed analysis of individual research objects; sixth, the anti-mechanistic, organicist point of view (Schumpeter, 1924, pp. 110–113). The

Schmoller program is presented as an approach that strives for grasping the essence of history itself, as it aims for the integration of a general sociology with a universal history (Schumpeter, 1926b). In the 'History of Economic Analysis', Schumpeter's comments on that program, though apparently more distanced, remain quite friendly: 'Nothing in the social cosmos or chaos is really outside of Schmollerian economics. In principle, if not quite in practice, the Schmollerian economist was in fact a historically minded sociologist in the latter term's widest meaning' (Schumpeter, 1954, p. 812). He adds that the Schmollerian approach supports an understanding interpretation of socio-economic processes which may establish an unique historical perspective on the coherence of the particular research objects (Schumpeter, 1954, p. 813). The late Schumpeter thus tended to label the Schmollerian approach as historical sociology, not as genuine economic theory.

Favorable remarks on the representatives of the 'Youngest Historical School', basically Spiethoff and Sombart, but also Max Weber, are quite common. Spiethoff's theory of business cycles, for instance, is portrayed as a most indispensable influence on Schumpeter's own theorizing on that subject (Schumpeter, 1926a, p. 320n, 1954, p. 816). Moreover, Spiethoff is characterized as a major scholar of economic sociology in the Schmollerian tradition (Schumpeter, 1926a, p. 377). While Schumpeter criticizes the idea of an objective 'meaning' of historical epochs and hence points at the dangers of hermeneutical distortions of the economic style perspective (Schumpeter, 1926b, p. 50), he suggests that the analysis of economic motives is of utmost importance for 'the sociological theory of economic styles, economic epochs and "economic spirits", but not for static economic theory' (Schumpeter, 1926a, p. 132). Most of these statements reflect the intellectual debt Schumpeter owed to the German Historical School.[5] Even his more ambiguous treatment of Sombart exhibits some critical acclamation in the mid-1920s (Schumpeter, 1927), until it is dominated by an almost complete rejection later on, possibly echoing Sombart's hermeneutical turn which seemed to have 'out-Schmollered Schmoller' (Schumpeter, 1954, p. 874n).

An examination of Schumpeter's works reveals the major impact of the Schmollerian ideas. In his first book *Wesen und Hauptinhalt der theoretischen Nationalökonomie*, Schumpeter (1908) presents a manifesto which should mark his future research regarding the matter of theory, history and historical theories. Although a historical theory such as Sombart's seems to be too much concerned with individual historical moments and thus lacks rigidity and exact results, it still offers useful procedures for the analysis of economic development. Consequently, while pure theory is essentially static, historical theories might be more appropriate for the exploration of

[5] In contrast to Schumpeter's appreciative assessments, Stolper (1988, p. 16) comments on Spiethoff that he was 'static in proposing to construct...any number of possible economic systems by combining 20 variables in all possible ways.' He goes on to remark that 'Schumpeter could not have been more different'. These remarks rather apply to personalities than to analytical contents. In fact, Spiethoff himself directed a similar criticism against Sombart and postulated that the various criteria of an economic style were necessarily open to extensions (Spiethoff, 1948, p. 577n).

economic dynamics (Schumpeter, 1908, p. 18). Schumpeter then differentiates between certain economic phenomena such as commodity exchange, which are relevant for static theory, and dynamic problems such as technological change, which should be analyzed by a combination of theoretical and historical research. In this context, he notes that the most valuable contributions to this matter have been delivered by the German Historical School (Schumpeter, 1908, p. 617).

In the 'Theory of Economic Development' this point of view is continuously underlined (Schumpeter, 1926a, p. 90n). Therefore, Schumpeter not only keeps a mediating position regarding the *Methodenstreit* among Menger and Schmoller, but even proposes that Schmoller's research agenda should act as a conceptual source for further attempts concerning the integration of theory and history (Schumpeter, 1926b). That mode of argumentation is kept in the 'Business Cycles', where he stresses that economic and technical change evolves in historical time and thus enforces a historical-institutional view on economic dynamics which may be supported by economic theory and statistics. Schumpeter goes on to postulate a major role for historical analyses:

'General history (social, political, and cultural), economic history, and more particularly industrial history are not only indispensable but really the most important contributors to the understanding of our problem. All other materials and methods, statistical and theoretical, are only subservient to them and worse than useless without them.' (Schumpeter, 1939, p. 13)[6]

In the 'History of Economic Analysis' Schumpeter identifies as techniques of economic analysis the particular fields of economic history, statistics, theory, and economic sociology. Due to the proposition that 'the matter of economics is essentially a unique process in historic time', which enforces an analytical command of institutional facts as well as historical experience, economic history is appreciated as the most important of these techniques (Schumpeter, 1954, p. 12n). Economic sociology then denotes a typified, stylized or reasoned economic history, for it transcends the usual theoretical question of how people behave and what effects their behavior produces, and asks instead why they actually behave the way they do. All of this is discussed with reference to Max Weber's notion of *Sozialökonomie* as a specific 'German practice' (Schumpeter, 1954, p. 21). Analyzing the variety of motives and economic attitudes is a major contribution of economic sociology: 'Economic sociology covers, first, the facts of economic behavior from which economists forge certain assumptions and, second, the institutions that characterize the economic organization of the societies to be studied' (Schumpeter, 1954, p.544). The impact of that perspective on methodological issues leads to the matter of actions, meanings and their appropriate interpretation: 'Economics lacks the benefits that physics derives from laboratory experiments...but enjoys instead...man's extensive

6 Schumpeter's 'Business Cycles' have been classified as one of the most important monographs of the German Historical School (Streissler, 1994, p. 37). This statement is supported by the fact that business cycle approaches have been a prominent topic among scholars of the Historical School since Roscher's early contributions.

knowledge of the meanings of economic actions' (Schumpeter, 1954, p. 16). Thus the method of *Verstehen*, which had risen to prominence with various elaborations of Sombart and Weber as an attempt 'to try to understand what things meant to people concerned', constitutes an indispensable part of Schumpeter's economic sociology (Schumpeter, 1954, p. 34).[7]

From these intentions, a 'Schmoller-Weber-Schumpeter nexus' has been identified, based upon their shared vision of economic life (Shionoya, 1991, 1997). Schmoller, Weber and Schumpeter argue on common ground, which is constituted, despite some methodological differences, by an institutional analysis of modern capitalism as a unique historical formation.[8] While the research agenda of Schumpeter may be divided into several phases of intellectual struggles with the matter of economic evolution, the continuous influence of the Schmoller program is never to be denied. It follows: 'The model of economic sociology, in Schumpeter's view, was that of the German Historical School, and he determined that his work in economic sociology would belong to this line of thought' (Shionoya, 1997, p. 278).

5 The *Schmollerprogramm* executed, part 2: the Schumpeterian vision of economic evolution

Beyond the notion of economic sociology as an analytical technique, a well-defined sociological perspective marks some of Schumpeter's most elaborate works on imperialism and social classes. Furthermore, it contributes to the very core of the Schumpeterian theory of economic development, due to his vision of the capitalist process and the notion of entrepreneurship. Schumpeter's definition of capitalism does not refer to a particular spirit, as the late Sombart might have argued, but to a private property economy where innovations are carried out by means of borrowed purchasing power. This amounts to saying that modern capitalism exhibits a certain economic style, which is, according to Schumpeter, primarily related to the unique role of the monetary sphere and the impact of credit-creation (Schumpeter, 1926a, p. 107).[9] The capitalist economy is additionally characterized by

---

[7] In an additional comment on Dilthey, the neo-Kantian dichotomy of natural and historical-cultural sciences is rejected due to the actual complexity of the social sciences. Nonetheless, the specific difference between the explanation of nature and the understanding interpretation of cultural phenomena is acknowledged as a useful device. (Schumpeter, 1954, p. 777). With regard to Weber, the basic intention of that perspective is summarized as follows: 'There is no sense in asking what the falling stone is about beyond stating the law of its fall. But there is sense in asking what a consuming household is about' (Schumpeter, 1954, p. 818n).

[8] For a comprehensive discussion of methodological and conceptual differences among Schmoller, Weber and Schumpeter, see Shionoya (1991). Schumpeter, for instance, remained skeptical concerning some of Weber's methodological instruments, such as the notion of ideal types.

[9] The term *Wirtschaftsstil* has been translated simply as 'type' in the 1934 English edition of the 'Theory' by Redvers Opie. This is inadequate, for the more appropriate term 'economic style' is of course rooted in the area of humanities and the arts and thus reflects the metaphorical orientations towards the cultural sciences.

specific social and institutional patterns. On the one hand, these are constituted by a certain civilization which represents essential institutional characteristics such as the rationality that is related to the use of money as a unit of account or the intellectual attitude of modern science. That common drive for quantification and rationalization gives capitalism its historically unprecedented appearance. On the other hand, the typical features of capitalism are necessarily supported by pre-capitalist institutions and social strata. While innovations repeatedly dissolve industrial structures in the successive 'gales of creative destruction', a decomposition of the pre-capitalist and finally even capitalist institutional and social spheres is taking place, resulting in the indeterminate tendency of capitalist decline (Schumpeter, 1942). Schumpeter therefore uses Weberian as well as Sombartian visions of capitalist degeneration toward a state-socialist bureaucratization, as he adopts decisive elements of the latter's notion of late capitalism as the final stage of capitalist economic evolution.[10]

Hence institutions do simultaneously constrain and support the capitalist process. This ingredient of the Schmollerian agenda was also constitutive for Schumpeter's attempt to grasp the 'motive power' of economic behavior by focusing on the notion of entrepreneurship (Rothschild, 1986). His entrepreneurial type views profits not as ends in themselves, but as means to achieve further ends, for instance, a dynasty-building effort with regard to the family. Actually, the latter was portrayed as a social organization which is subject to decomposition in the course of capitalist development (Schumpeter, 1942, pp. 156–163). The entrepreneur is thus driven by motivations which resemble, next to a creative segment, also a Nietzschean 'will to power' (Schumpeter, 1908, p. 618). Consequently, entrepreneurs remain strangers in the value sphere of pure capitalist rationality until they lose their evolutionary functions and are absorbed by the mass of adaptive economic agents.

Regarding these institutional aspects of his theory, it should not come as a surprise that Schumpeter opted for a comparative multi-factor approach to economic growth and development with further implications concerning the necessity of a comprehensive and holistic view:

'economic growth is not autonomous, being dependent upon factors outside of itself, and since these factors are many, no one-factor theory can ever be satisfactory. That is to say, such theories as that economic growth is a function, chiefly, of the objective opportunities of the environment, of increase in population, of the 'spirit' of a nation's civilization, of technological progress (increasing 'control over nature') can never be adequate ... But if we tried to use mathematics, we would immediately run up against the difficulty that some of the most important of these interdependent factors cannot be quantified...' (Schumpeter, 1947, p. 4n)

---

[10] For a discussion of Sombart's impact on Schumpeter's ideas concerning capitalist stagnation and degeneration, see Chaloupek (1995). The corresponding similarities in Weberian and Schumpeterian views on the bureaucratization of the firm are consistently emphasized in Langlois (1998).

As a result, Schumpeter's approach to economic dynamics should allow for the specific 'Gestalt' of the object under examination. This perspective had been influenced by the ideas of 'Gestalt psychology', for Schumpeter claimed that these were highly useful for establishing a non-metaphysical concept of society, as they contained that 'individual elements of any set of elements are not perceived or appraised individually but as part of the definite set in which they occur' (Schumpeter, 1954, p. 798).[11] Relating the matter of institutional variety to an interpretative method, the Schumpeterian credo then implies that individual actions are embedded in social relations that are open to multiple possibilities of change, while individual phenomena are to be viewed within the context of an unitary 'Gestalt' configuration (De Vecchi, 1995, p. 8n). This corresponds with the basic intentions of Spiethoff's approach to an economic Gestalt theory, which encompasses the phenomenological concepts of the economic style perspective, while a decisive common aspect is provided by the rejection of mechanistic notions of economic change (Schefold, 1996, p. 313).[12]

Regarding the course of the historical process, Schumpeter argues against metaphysically prejudiced ideas of an unitary meaning of history and the related assumption of an uniform development path of nations or civilizations. His own approach stresses that social conditions become historical individuals in historical time (Schumpeter, 1926a p. 88n). The process of evolution is accordingly defined as follows: 'Social phenomena constitute a unique process in historic time, and incessant and irreversible change is their most obvious characteristic. If by Evolutionism we mean no more than recognition of this fact, then all reasoning about social phenomena must be either evolutionary in itself or else bear upon evolution.' (Schumpeter, 1954, p. 435) In this context he criticizes the allegedly vulgar approaches of a biological economics as well as behaviorist analyses of economic action, for they would reduce complex motive structures to a simple social reflex. According to Schumpeter, this mode of reductionist determinism denotes an attitude which had discredited the most promising evolutionary perspectives in economics. (Schumpeter, 1926a, p. 88n). In contrast to that, Schumpeter presents a vision of economic evolution where the economic action of energetic agents acts as the decisive endogenous evolutionary force.

This leads to the important observation that Schumpeter's notion of economic evolution is conceptually nested in the broader framework of a

---

[11] A corresponding note of Schumpeter's on Spann's universalist school of economics provides further insights on that topic: 'If universalists were content to preach a 'holist' meta-economic or philosophical interpretation of both economic reality and economic theory, there would be no objection; in fact I should actually sympathize with their meta-economics, though I might interpret it to myself in terms of *Gestalt* psychology' (Schumpeter, 1954, p. 413).

[12] The term 'economic Gestalt theory' has been introduced by Fritz Redlich, who translated Spiethoff's 1952 article on the historical validity of economic theories, with explicit reference to phenomenology and Gestalt psychology (Spiethoff, 1952, p. 135, Translator's note). Gioia's (1997) translation of the term in question, that is *anschauliche Theorie*, as 'historical-concrete theory' may serve as an appropriate complement.

'philosophy of history', which denotes the guiding principles of socio-cultural development, as outlined in the seventh chapter of the first edition of the *Theorie der wirtschaftlichen Entwicklung* (Schumpeter 1912, ch. 7). In that particular chapter, the core of Schumpeterian economics, that is, the notion of entrepreneurship with its dynamic character, is discussed in the context of the long-run perspective of cultural change. This procedure resembles, not surprisingly, much of the Schmollerian vision of development, basically due to its analytical comprehensiveness.[13] Moreover, the matter of the rise and decline of nations is discussed with explicit reference to Schmoller's ideas on institutional development cycles, although these are clearly separated from the more focused theoretical outline of the business cycle approach (Schumpeter, 1912, p. 492). In effect, Schumpeter maintains 'that every area of social life has its mode of development, based upon similar mechanisms, such as the factor of social leadership' (Schumpeter, 1912, pp. 545–548). It is this institutional argumentation which constitutes the conceptual core of Schumpeter's thought and thus simultaneously underlines his close relationship with the German Historical School.[14] Summing up, we even find that Schumpeter's evolutionary vision continues with most of the Schmollerian, Sombartian and Weberian questions, while it provides answers the conceptual elaboration of which would have been unthinkable without Schumpeter's further modification and execution of the *Schmollerprogramm* of the German Historical School.

6 Conclusion

In this essay, I have put forward the argument that both the formal-analytical as well as the historical-institutional procedures represent an indispensable dimension of Schumpeter's theory of economic development. In accordance with the conceptual perspective of the German Historical School, they constitute a pluralist research agenda. Schumpeter's notion of economic development which emphasizes the correspondence of economic and socio-cultural evolution, is therefore to be viewed in the context of the comprehensive Schmollerian and post-Schmollerian approaches to an integration of theoretical and historical concerns. This suggestion has been accompanied by the thesis that the German Historical School played an implicit but vital role for the elaboration of a modern evolutionary economics in Schumpeterian terms.

---

[13] The meaning of that 'seventh chapter', which had been omitted from the second edition primarily due to didactical reasons, has been discussed by Shionoya as the constitutive corner-stone of the whole Schumpeterian research agenda (Shionoya, 1997, ch. 3).

[14] This statement does not imply an underestimation of other theoretical influences. In addition to Walras and Marx, the Austrian School of economics, of course, had a major impact on Schumpeter, not only with regard to the theory of interest, but also concerning the concepts of entrepreneurship and social leadership. To acknowledge that fact means to point at the intellectual proximity of the respective German and Austrian schools which is well reflected by Schumpeter's works.

Further attempts of integrating theory and history in the analysis of economic development have resulted in the current formation of a genuine Schumpeterian paradigm. Regarding the formulation of a combined evolutionary and historical perspective, it has been emphasized that both segments are indispensable for the analysis of innovation processes (Lazonick, 1994). Furthermore, Edquist (1997), who discusses the neo-Schumpeterian systems of innovation approach, points at the matter of historical time and path-dependency as he finds that a historical perspective refers to dynamic, indeterminate and irreversible socio-economic processes. The appreciation of historical perspectives has thus inspired extensive ventures to develop a sound theoretical framework for a 'reasoned history' in the Schumpeterian tradition. Freeman (1995), for instance, has presented a comprehensive research program to grasp the historically rooted relationships between the processes of economic growth and development with the spheres of science, technology, politics and culture.

I conclude with the impression that the *Schmollerprogramm* of the German Historical School, primarily in its actual Schumpeterian interpretation, promises further inspirations for research on the historical character of economic evolution.

References

Andersen ES (1994) Evolutionary economics: post-Schumpeterian contributions. Pinter, London New York

Backhaus J (1993) Gustav Schmoller and the problems of today. History of Economic Ideas 1: 3–25

Betz HK (1988) How does the German Historical School fit? History of Political Economy 20: 409–430

Betz HK (1993) From Schmoller to Sombart. History of Economic Ideas 1: 331–356

Chaloupek G (1995) Long-term economic perspectives compared: Joseph Schumpeter and Werner Sombart. The European Journal of the History of Economic Thought 2: 127–149

De Vecchi N (1995) Entrepreneurs, institutions and economic change: the economic thought of J.A. Schumpeter (1905–1925). Elgar, Aldershot

Dopfer K (1988) How historical is Schmoller's theory? Journal of Institutional and Theoretical Economics 144: 552–569

Edquist C (1997) Systems of innovation approaches: their emergence and characteristics. In: Edquist C (ed) Systems of innovation: technologies, organizations and institutions. Pinter, London

Freeman C (1995) History, co-evolution and economic growth. IIASA Working Paper WP-95-76

Gioia V (1997) Historical changes and economics in Arthur Spiethoff's Theory of Wirtschaftsstil (Style of an Economic System). In: Koslowski P (ed) Methodology of the social sciences, ethics, and economics in the Newer Historical School. Springer, Berlin Heidelberg New York

Hodgson GM (1993) Economics and evolution: bringing life back into economics. Polity, Oxford

Hutter M (1993) Historicist biologism and contemporary evolutionism: where is the difference? History of Economic Ideas 1: 179–196

Krabbe JJ (1996) Nature and technology as economic categories: Sombart in the mainstream. In: Backhaus J (ed) Werner Sombart (1863–1941) – social scientist. His theoretical approach Reconsidered. Metropolis, Marburg

Langlois RN (1998) Personal capitalism as charismatic authority: the organizational economics of a Weberian concept. Industrial and Corporate Change 7: 195–213
Lazonick W (1994) The integration of theory and history. Methodology and ideology in Schumpeter's economics. In: Magnusson L (ed) Evolutionary and neo-Schumpeterian approaches to economics. Kluwer, Boston
Peukert H (1998) Das Handlungsparadigma in der Nationalökonomie. Metropolis, Marburg
Priddat BP (1995) Die andere Ökonomie. Eine neue Einschätzung von Gustav Schmoller's Versuuch einer 'ethisch-historischen' Nationalökonomie im 19.Jahrhundert. Metropolis, Marburg
Prisching M (1993) Schmoller's theory of society. History of Economic Ideas 1: 117–142
Richter R (1996) Bridging old and new institutional economics: Gustav Schmoller, the leader of the Younger German Historical School, seen with neoinstitutionalists' eyes. Journal of Institutional and Theoretical Economics 152: 569–592
Rothschild KW (1986) Capitalists and entrepreneurs: prototypes and roles. In: Wagner H-J, Drucker JW (eds) The economic law of motion of modern society: a Marx-Keynes-Schumpeter centennial. Cambridge University Press, Cambridge
Schefold B (1989) Schmoller als Theoretiker. In: Backhaus J, Shionoya Y, Schefold B (Hrsg) Kommentarband zum Facsimile der Erstausgabe von Gustav Schmoller's 'Grundriß' in der Reihe Klassiker der Nationalökonomie. Wirtschaft und Finanzen, Düsseldorf
Schefold B (1994) Nationalökonomie und Kulturwissenschaften: Das Konzept des Wirtschaftsstils. In: Schefold B, Nörr KW, Tenbruck F (Hrsg) Deutsche Geisteswissenschaften zwischen Kaiserreich und Republik. Zur Entwicklung von Nationalökonomie, Rechtswissenschaft und Sozialwissenschaft im 20. Jahrhundert. Steiner, Stuttgart
Schefold B (1995) Theoretical approaches to a comparison of economic systems from a historical perspective. In: Koslowski P (ed) The theory of ethical economy in the Historical School. Springer, Berlin Heidelberg New York
Schefold B (1996) Are economic theories historically specific? In: Marcuzzo MC, Pasinetti LL, Roncaglia A (eds) The economics of Joan Robinson. Routledge, London
Schmoller G (1893) Die Volkswirtschaft, die Volkswirtschaftslehre und ihre Methode. In: Schmoller G (Hrsg) Über einige Grundfragen der Socialpolitik und der Volkswirtschaftslehre. Duncker und Humblot, Leipzig
Schmoller G (1901) Grundriß der Allgemeinen Volkswirtschaftslehre, Bd 1. Duncker und Humblot, Leipzig
Schmoller G (1903) Werner Sombart, Der moderne Kapitalismus. Schmollers Jahrbuch für Gesetzgebung, Verwaltung und Volkswirtschaft im Deutschen Reiche 51: 349–369
Schmoller G (1904) Grundriß der Allgemeinen Volkswirtschaftslehre, Bd 2. Duncker und Humblot, Leipzig
Schumpeter J (1908) Das Wesen und der Hauptinhalt der theoretischen Nationalökonomie. Duncker und Humblot, Berlin
Schumpeter J (1912) Theorie der wirtschaftlichen Entwicklung. Eine Untersuchung über Unternehmergewinn, Kapital, Kredit, Zins und den Konjunkturzyklus, 1. Aufl. Duncker und Humblot, Berlin
Schumpeter J (1924) Epochen der Dogmen- und Methodengeschichte. In: Grundriss der Sozialökonomik, Bd 1, 2. Aufl. Mohr, Tübingen
Schumpeter J (1926a) Theorie der wirtschaftlichen Entwicklung. Eine Untersuchung über Unternehmergewinn, Kapital, Kredit, Zins und den Konjunkturzyklus, 2. Aufl. Duncker und Humblot, Berlin
Schumpeter J (1926b) Gustav v. Schmoller und die Probleme von heute. Schmollers Jahrbuch für Gesetzgebung, Verwaltung und Volkswirtschaft im Deutschen Reiche 50: 1–52
Schumpeter J (1927) Sombarts Dritter Band. Schmollers Jahrbuch für Gesetzgebung, Verwaltung und Volkswirtschaft im Deutschen Reiche 51: 349–369

Schumpeter J (1939) Business cycles: a theoretical, historical and statistical analysis of the capitalist process, Vol I. McGraw-Hill, New York
Schumpeter J (1942) Capitalism, socialism and democracy. Allen and Unwin, London
Schumpeter J (1947) Theoretical problems of economic growth. The Journal of Economic History (Suppl) VII: 1–9
Schumpeter J (1954) History of economic analysis. Oxford University Press, New York
Shionoya Y (1991) Schumpeter on Schmoller and Weber: a methodology of economic sociology. History of Political Economy 23: 193–219
Shionoya Y (1997) Schumpeter and the idea of social science: a metatheoretical study. Cambridge University Press, Cambridge
Sombart W (1916/1987) Der moderne Kapitalismus. Historisch-systematische Darstellung des gesamteuropäischen Wirtschaftslebens von seinen Anfängen bis zur Gegenwart, Bd 1.1. dtv, München
Sombart W (1930) Die drei Nationalökonomien. Geschichte und System der Lehre von der Wirtschaft. Duncker und Humblot, Berlin
Spiethoff A (1932) Die Allgemeine Volkswirtschaftslehre als geschichtliche Theorie. Die Wirtschaftsstile, Schmollers Jahrbuch für Gesetzgebung, Verwaltung und Volkswirtschaft im Deutschen Reich 56: 51–84
Spiethoff A (1948) Anschauliche und reine volkswirtschaftliche Theorie und ihr Verhältnis zueinander. In: Salin E (Hrsg) Synopsis: Festgabe für Alfred Weber. Schneider, Heidelberg
Spiethoff A (1952) The "historical" character of economic theories. The Journal of Economic History 12: 131–139
Stolper WF (1988) Development: theory and empirical evidence. In: Hanusch H (ed) Evolutionary economics: applications of Schumpeter's ideas. Cambridge University Press, Cambridge
Streissler EW (1994) The influence of German and Austrian economics on Joseph A. Schumpeter. In: Shionoya Y, Perlman M. (eds) Schumpeter in the history of ideas. University of Michigan Press, Ann Arbor
Swedberg R (1989) Joseph A. Schumpeter and the tradition of economic sociology. Journal of Institutional and Theoretical Economics 145: 508–524
Veblen T (1901/1994) Gustav Schmoller's economics. In: Veblen T (ed) The place of science in modern civilisation and other essays. The collected works of Thorstein Veblen, Vol 8. Routledge, London

The manufacturer's authorised representative in the EU is Springer Nature Customer Service Centre GmbH, Europaplatz 3, 69115 Heidelberg, Germany. If you have any concerns regarding our products, please contact ProductSafety@springernature.com

Printed and bound by CPI Group (UK) Ltd, Croydon, CR0 4YY
22/09/2026
02220988-0002